Community Psychology

Community Psychology

Theoretical and Empirical Approaches

Edited by
Margaret S. Gibbs, Ph.D.
Juliana Rasic Lachenmeyer, Ph.D.
Janet Sigal, Ph.D.

Fairleigh Dickinson University

GARDNER PRESS, INC. NEW YORK
Distributed by Halsted Press
Division of John Wiley & Sons, Inc.
New York · London · Sydney · Toronto

GARDNER PRESS, INC.
19 Union Square West
New York 10003

Distributed solely by the Halsted Press Division of
John Wiley & Sons, Inc., New York

Library of Congress Cataloging in Publication Data

Main entry under title:
Community psychology.

"A Halsted Press book."
1. Community psychology. 2. Community mental health services. I. Gibbs, Margaret S.
II. Lachenmeyer, Juliana Rasic. III. Sigal, Janet.
RA790.5.C64 362.2jpr1 79-13755
ISBN 0-470-26787-9

Printed in the United States of America

For our families

Contributors

GEORGE ALBEE, PH.D.
Department of Psychology
University of Vermont
Burlington, Vermont

HARRY APONTE, M.S.W.
Philadelphia Child Guidance Clinic
Philadelphia, Pennsylvania

CATHERINE P. CLEARY
Department of Psychology
University of Illinois
Urbana-Champaign, Illinois

EMORY COWEN, Ph.D.
Department of Psychology
University of Rochester
Rochester, New York

RICHARD G. ERICKSON, Ph.D.
Portland Veterans Administration Medical Center
Portland, Oregon

ELLIS L. GESTEN, Ph.D.
Department of Psychology
University of Rochester
Rochester, New York

MARGARET S. GIBBS, Ph.D.
Department of Psychology
Fairleigh Dickinson University
Teaneck, New Jersey

BOBBIE HYERSTAY, Ph.D.
Veteran's Administration Hospital
Seattle, Washington

RONNIE JANOFF-BULMAN, Ph.D.
Department of Psychology
University of Massachusetts
Amherst, Massachusetts

JANE KNITZER, Ed.D.
Children's Defense Fund
Washington, D.C.

CHARLES LACHENMEYER, Ph.D.
Department of Management
Hofstra University
Uniondale, New York

JULIANA RASIC LACHENMEYER, Ph.D.
Department of Psychology
Fairleigh Dickinson University
Teaneck, New Jersey

THOMAS F. McGEE, Ph.D.
Mercy Hospital
San Diego, California

JULIAN RAPPAPORT, Ph.D.
Department of Psychology
University of Illinois
Urbana-Champaign, Illinois

JANET SIGAL, Ph.D.
Department of Psychology
Fairleigh Dickinson University
Teaneck, New Jersey

BONNIE STRICKLAND, Ph.D.
Department of Psychology
University of Massachusetts
Amherst, Massachusetts

STANLEY SUE, Ph.D.
Department of Psychology
University of Washington
Seattle, Washington

NOLAN ZANE
Department of Psychology
University of Washington
Seattle, Washington

MELVIN ZAX, Ph.D.
Department of Psychology
University of Rochester
Rochester, New York

Preface

The idea for this book arose out of a course in community psychology taught by the three editors. The course served as an impetus in several ways. First, each editor came to community psychology from a different orientation and background: an eclectic clinical training, a social learning orientation to clinical issues, and a classical academic background in social psychology. We saw community psychology from these perspectives, and as such saw it embedded in the tradition of academic clinical and social psychology. The overall perspective of the book evolved out of this orientation. That is, it seemed to the editors that in trying to increase the impact of community psychology, its proponents had overemphasized its revolutionary aspects, its differences from the rest of psychology. The community mental health movement is now firmly enough established that it can be said to have moved out of the phase of establishing an identification through differentiation, and into a more adult maturity. At this point the field can only be strengthened by examination of the past and potential contributions from academic psychology. Thus, what this volume offers that is different from other texts on community psychology is the attempt to explore in detail what we can learn from other fields within psychology. Specific chapters explore the contributions to community psychology from attribution theory, learned helplessness, labeling theory, epidemiology and environmental stress. In addition, our introductory chapters and our evaluation chapters provide a framework for community psychology that shows the continuities as well as the discontinuities with the past and future of mental health services.

We have, as well, tried throughout to keep the focus on practical applications. Our students, with their continual clamor, "But tell us how to do it," have helped us in this respect. The theoretical chapters mentioned above are concrete in their application. The several chapters on strategies of intervention—consultation, family therapy, advocacy, crisis intervention and prevention— are detailed and specific enough that we think they will be useful to the practitioner in the field as well as to the student.

Another impetus to preparing this volume was our difficulty in developing a reading list for our course that did not demand undue student time in the reserve reading rooms in the library. The community literature is expanding rapidly and there are now good basic texts as well as books for specialized interests. For the advanced student, however, both graduate and undergraduate, there seemed no one source that gave the reader a truly intensive look at an extensive range of topics relevant to the field. This book is our attempt to meet this need for ourselves, and we hope it will meet a need for other instructors as well.

The final motive for organizing this book was simply the fun we had in teaching together, which we wanted to continue by writing and editing together. Contrary to the predictions of many fellow editors, we have indeed enjoyed the putting together of the book; the laughs have far outweighed the headaches. We would like to thank our contributors most heartily for this absence of difficulties; everyone has been prompt, efficient, and has more than fulfilled our expectations as to the content of their chapters. In addition, we would like to thank our departmental secretaries, Mrs. Gloria Gruber, who gave our work priority when she was overloaded, and Mrs. Peggy Anders, for her excellent and uncomplaining typing. Only she knows how many times the chapter outline had to be retyped. We would also like to thank our graduate assistants, including Nancy Roberts, who helped in the preparation of our own manuscripts, and particular thanks go to Patricia Davis for her skill in handwriting analysis as well as in typing.

CONTENTS

Part I

HISTORICAL PERSPECTIVE

CHAPTER 1

History and Background of the Community Mental Health Movement

Melvin Zax, Ph.D.

Freud's revolutionary thought concerning human behavior, its development, how problems arise, and what must be done to alleviate these problems, set the tone and direction of the mental health field for many years. For students of thirty or forty years ago, it was enough to steep oneself in a few psychology "bibles" to feel on top of the field. Moreover, students in former years had the sense that the material in these great reference works was unchallengeable. These books contained the absolute truth about a God-given psychological order that was revealed by especially prescient and sensitive people.

Ah, those were the good old days! What those early notions may have lacked in validity, they made up for in the comfort, security and sense of order that they conveyed. The past twenty years or more have been marked by a wave of idol-shattering. None of the old heroes has gone unchallenged. There seems to be no limit to the new types of psychotherapy that are being proposed, the new types of theories advanced to explain behavior and its vicissitudes. Perhaps the greatest change involves the challenge that has arisen to established ways of rendering service to troubled human beings. The various community movements are responsible for this latest assault on tradition.

The effect of this wave of new ideas has been to raise myriads of new questions, to suggest numerous new directions, and to demand of all practitioners and researchers a reexamination of their approach to service. To many, the community movement may seem to involve an altogether new set of concepts that have burst on the contemporary scene like a bombshell. This is probably because many of these ideas represent such a radical departure from established notions. Stepping back, therefore, and examining the origins and development of these ideas provides a perspective that can help to assimilate them more readily. It is to this end that this chapter has been written.

WHAT CHARACTERIZES COMMUNITY APPROACHES?

The essence of all community mental health approaches is that they emphasize the contribution of external forces to the development of emotional disorder. This is, of course, counter to the general view which characterizes many traditional approaches, best exemplified by psychoanalysis. The traditional stance holds that when a person is troubled emotionally it is because something internal is wrong and needs correction. At one time virtually all of what was recognized as emotional disorder was thought to be organically based. In these psychologically sophisticated times, internal psychological forces seen to have been set in motion in the early years of life are generally regarded as the major contributor to emotional problems. Hence one-on-one psychotherapy was for many years regarded as the potentially most effective treatment mode. But it wasn't always this way.

EARLY ROOTS OF COMMUNITY APPROACHES

We often find that what seems entirely novel in our own time turns out to have had roots that go way back in man's history. It is that way with the seemingly new-fangled notion that the setting within which a person lives contributes greatly to how he or she feels and behaves. We could trace such roots back as far as the utopian communities created by religious zealots in biblical times, such as that of the Essenes along the Dead Sea (Zax & Specter, 1974). To remain in closer touch with problems of our own time, however, it would be best to sacrifice scholarship and begin with more recent history.

The Mental Hospital

One of the outstanding historical examples of the recognition of the significance of external forces on the lives of the mentally disturbed occurred within mental institutions. In fact, the importance of this movement associated with early hospital reforms is underlined by the fact that it has been commonly referred to as the first "mental health revolution."

The form and function of the mental hospital has evolved over a period of literally hundreds of years. The mental hospital originated in the Middle Ages. One historian (Foucault, 1965) has pointed out that the manner with which leprosy was dealt in Europe during the Middle Ages provided the model for treating the mentally disturbed. Lepers were isolated from their communities and sent far outside of cities and towns to live out their lives in leprosaria with others who were similarly afflicted. This treatment for leprosy eventually eliminated that dread disease from Europe because in effect it controlled the sources of infection. Converting leprosaria to institutions for public nuisances, most of whom were mentally deranged, was a simple step.

The records of conditions of life in early mental institutions substantiate the claim that they were dumping grounds for a troubled and troublesome humanity. The conditions found in the early mental hospitals can only be understood as reflections of the general attitude that the deranged were less than human. Furthermore these conditions bespoke a conviction that these poor unfortunates were hopeless, that nothing could be expected in the way of a cure, or even of improvement.

Those responsible for the hospital reforms of the early nineteenth century, Pinel in France, Tuke in England, Chiarugi and Pisani in Italy, were not great theoreticians who could see that the way people had to live had a good deal to do with how they felt and behaved. Rather they were humanitarians who as administrators of mental institutions, simply abhorred the way patients were treated in such hospitals. They opposed unreasonable restraints and inhumane living conditions, and they proposed greater freedom for patients in the face of considerable opposition from a public that regarded the deranged only as potentially destructive wild beasts. Thus "the first mental health revolution" consisted essentially of an early form of hospital community psychology in which living conditions were improved. Unnecessary restraints were removed. Patients were given responsibilities aimed at improving their own environment. The kinds of environmental improvements instituted in a few European hospitals were carried even further in the newly founded United States in the first half of the nineteenth century (Bockoven, 1956, 1957).

Growing Interest in Brain Physiology

The nineteenth century was a time in which much was being learned about the physiology of the human body. Important discoveries were being made about the functioning of the human brain. The growth of knowledge seemed to promise an eventual breakthrough which would allow us to understand aberrant behavior on the basis of neurological defect. For the self-conscious psychiatrists of the time, whose work was generally regarded as a cross between religion and magic, these developments promised to establish their field on a sound scientific basis. In effect, of course, the hope that all behavior could come to be understood on a strictly physical basis denied the role played by external forces in shaping man's behavior. It reemphasized looking inside man to discover the causes of his behavioral and emotional problems with the expectation that correction of these problems would come about by manipulating internal forces.

In such an intellectual climate, there was no need for environmental approaches. All that seemed necessary was to wait for the important scientific discoveries that seemed sure to come. And, while the mental health field waited, it seemed unnecessary to treat patients in warm, familylike but relatively expensive settings. It was far more efficient and inexpensive to warehouse them in large institutions.

The Aftercare Movement

The next notable impetus for community approaches within the mental health field came only after a certain amount of disenchantment had set in concerning the prospect for an early and complete solution to the problems posed by mental illness. In the meantime, of course, unsophisticated lay groups were establishing programs, such as the Salvation Army, which stressed environmental change as the way to treat various kinds of behavioral maladjustment. But within the mental health field the work of Adolph Meyer (1948) in the early 1900s was impelled by a rekindling of the idea that the circumstances under which people live contribute to their mental functioning. Meyer started his career as a pathologist working in several state institutions in Illinois and New York. He shifted to psychiatry and rose to prominence as one of America's most influential teachers and thinkers in that specialty.

Meyer's work in mental hospitals made him sensitive to the need for the maintenance of a close tie between the larger community and the hospital. He became convinced of the need to educate the public about mental illness and the way mental hospitals operated. To achieve this, he advocated breaching the barriers between the general public and the mental hospital. This called for the hospital to extend its efforts beyond the bounds of the institution. Meyer felt the best way to bring this about would be through service called aftercare, which was then common in Europe. This practice involved preparing both the patient and the community for the patient's reentry into society. In his thinking, Meyer looked beyond the welfare of the individual patient and foresaw how aftercare could eventually lead to the prevention of mental disorder:

> . . . I have always felt that the term "after-care" in the name of a committee of this character is one that limits the field of interest below that which is actually the result. It is not only "aftercare" as it was established in England, that is to say, one or two months' care for people

> who are discharged and need a boarding place or something of that nature, but it consists of finding occupation for patients who are leaving the institution and trying to live again in the community, and helping to make their reentrance into the community easy and safe against relapses. There we have the after-care movement turned into the prophylaxis movement; and anyone who once gets interested in the prophylaxis of recurrences cannot help but get interested in the prevention of the first attacks, and there you are in a center of what we must hope from this movement (Meyer, 1948, p. 300).

The Rise of Psychoanalysis

Despite the fact that Meyer's ideas about aftercare and prevention expressed more than sixty years ago would be widely applauded today, they provoked little enthusiasm in his own time. Again, the problem seemed to be that preventive notions and concern about the effect of external forces on emotions and behavioral adjustment were pushed into the background by what appeared at the time to be a promising new approach to mental disorder: a focus on internal forces. Meyer's work with aftercare was taking place at the same time that Freud's writings were being disseminated widely among those interested in emotional disorders. These writings were beginning to be popular, particularly in the United States.

Freud's approach, while ground breaking in many ways, was quite traditional in his emphasis on internal forces as the source of mental disorder and on a treatment approach devoted to altering internal forces. Freud's innovative contribution was that instead of stressing constitutional causes of mental aberration, he tried to demonstrate the importance of psychological dynamics which had been set in motion through early life experiences. Psychoanalytic treatment attempted to manipulate or alter the troublesome psychological forces. External or social forces were often referred to by Freud as "accidental factors" which implied that they were so irregular that they couldn't be studied scientifically. Only what occurred internally was suitable for the scientific study of human behavior.

Meyer's time was simply not ready for an enthusiastic approach to prevention and community mental health. The closest the mental health field came to an emphasis on community and preventive measures in the early twentieth century was through the mental hygiene movement. In this movement, in which Meyer played a prominent role, many child guidance clinics were established to treat disorders early in patients' lives, and public information programs were mounted to improve attitudes toward the mentally disturbed (Zax & Specter, 1974). By and large, though, the mental health fields became immersed in a new quest to understand and treat emotional problems on the basis of internal psychological forces. Even the profession of psychiatric social work, which grew out of Meyer's aftercare movment and worked with the families and the environments of troubled individuals, gradually turned away from the community and toward the one-to-one treatment of patients in out-patient clinics and hospitals.

RECENT IMPETUS FOR COMMUNITY APPROACHES

The relatively recent thrust toward community mental health approaches had several different sources which, like a number of small streams, combined to create a large, energetic river. Some of these sources derived from new theoretical contributions, some from a revival of preventive efforts, some from dissatisfaction with the inadequacies of traditional approaches, and some from sheer dread of the magnitude of the mental health problems of our country.

Theoretical Supports for Prevention

Up until the mid-1930s, most well-known theories of personality in humans tended to grow out of a concern about behavioral dysfunction, and the content of theories reflected the need to understand how problems develop and what must be done to clear them up. In the mid-1930s, the writings of the so-called "ego psychologists" began to appear. These writers were psychoanalysts who took issue with Freud's conception of the ego. In classical psychoanalytic theory the ego was seen as an aspect of personality that emerged to mediate first between the demands of the id and the limitations placed on the satisfaction of id needs by reality. In essence, the ego was seen as a servant of the id. The ego's job was to learn about the workings of the world around the person and find ways to get the greatest satisfaction for the id, which was seen as the repository of all of the organism's basic drives.

The id was seen to demand immediate and complete satisfaction of any impulse that arose: in effect to seek only gratification. The ego was seen to manipulate the real world in order to provide as much of the demanded gratification as possible while avoiding the conflict that might result in future pain if id drives were quenched injudiciously. To do its job well the ego needed to be well acquainted with the reality that had to be dealt with, to think logically, and to adhere as closely as possible to the limitations that the real external world places on people. At its command the successful ego has a variety of important cognitive processes such as imagination and memory, as well as the sensory, perceptual and motor processes, all of which are, in effect, the essential tools for learning about and manipulating the environment.

From this classic psychoanalytic view, everything that a person does involving ego functions is for the purpose of smoothing over potential conflicts between the id and the environment and later in development, between the id and the super ego, which consists of the person's conscience and ideals. Thus in the classical view, the person who develops unusual cognitive and/or motor skills, even though they seem unnecessary for immediate need gratification, is doing so because they may be useful at some time in the future to satisfy basic urges. One becomes a cook, therefore, to increase the likelihood that future oral needs will be met.

The ego psychologists took issue with this concept of the ego. They felt that many human functions were pleasurable and worthwhile in and of themselves, without necessarily resulting in id gratification. In effect, they proposed that people use some of their psychic energy merely to pursue talents and interests that are fun. Thus not all ego functions were seen as contending with conflict. Furthermore the ego psychologists asserted that too much attention had been devoted to the ways in which the ego handled conflict and far too little to the way it achieved a good adjustment to life's demands. Rather than studying people with psychological problems as the sole avenue for understanding human behavior, the ego psychologists urged that studies be done of people who were particularly successful at coping.

A number of thinkers during the late thirties and early forties tried to apply the approach advocated by the ego psychologists (Turner & Cumming, 1967). Among these theorists, Erikson has become one of the best known. He has conceived that people constantly encounter problems in the environment in the process of developing (Erikson, 1950). The process of mastering these problems leaves the individual with new skills that go into his or her general bag of tools for use in dealing with future problems. And, of course, the more skills acquired through successful mastery, the better equipped one is likely to be to contend successfully with future crises. In effect, "competence begets competence."

Erikson classified crises into two groups: normative ones, which could be predicted; and nonnormative or unpredictable traumas. Both types of crisis were seen to present problems and opportunities for further growth. Therefore it followed from this view that assistance in crisis resolution was a way to help people who were not yet clinically disturbed to acquire or master coping skills that would insulate them against becoming disturbed later in life. This theoretical approach became a basis for the *prevention* of emotional or behavioral disorder.

Practical Applications of Prevention through Crises

In the early 1940s Erich Lindemann (1944), a psychiatrist and psychoanalyst interested in the way people dealt with bereavement, had the opportunity to observe and treat a number of people who were suddenly bereaved. A tragic fire took place in a Boston nightclub in which approximately 500 people were killed. Most of the victims were local people who had families and friends nearby, and many survivors of the fire had lost friends and relatives in it. Lindemann identified acute grief as involving a set of reasonably consistent somatic and psychological manifestations. These included guilt feelings, anger, depression and various acute somatic upsets. Further, Lindemann noted that many people who had the most difficulty in overcoming their grief tried to avoid the distress of the normal grieving process by being "strong" and not "breaking down."

It was resistance to grieving that seemed, in Lindemann's view, to lead the victim to remain preoccupied with the dead person for an extended period of time. He recommended, therefore, that to prevent prolonged psychological impairment resulting from the loss of a loved one, the bereaved needed to be helped to engage in the normal mourning process. In addition, he felt this process could be furthered by a variety of people who were not necessarily highly trained mental health workers. Clergymen, for example, are almost always in a good position to assist a bereaved family during the mourning period.

Moving beyond his interest in bereavement, in 1948 Lindemann with private foundation support, established a community mental health laboratory in Wellesley, Massachusetts. There he applied broad preventive techniques. Lindemann's center served all who face "crises and predicaments." These included individuals faced with the loss of important relationships as well as groups who were about to become involved with stressful experiences, such as children entering kindergarten and young girls embarking on nurse's training.

One of Lindemenn's coworkers at Wellesley, Gerald Caplan, reported in 1961 (Caplan, 1961) on 16 studies in which measures were taken to prevent emotional disturbance in children. Later (Caplan, 1964) Caplan produced a textbook to guide mental health professionals in establishing preventive programs. In this text Caplan described three types of prevention. The first, primary prevention, involves programs that have an impact on the entire population of a community for the purpose of reducing the overall incidence of mental disorder. The second, secondary prevention, is targeted at identifying already manifest disorders as soon as possible and limiting their duration. The third, tertiary prevention, is directed at those who have already manifested mental disorder. Its purpose is to reduce impairment suffered as a result of their upset.

While the efforts of Lindemann and Caplan were respected in their time, it was not these attempts alone that served to orient a large segment of the mental health establishment toward preventive and community mental health. The time was also ripe for a reorientation because of a number of other factors.

Questions about the Effectiveness of Psychotherapy

Earlier in this chapter it was pointed out that Adolph Meyer's fledgling attempt to institute preventive procedures in the mental health field around the turn of the twentieth century was largely ignored in the wave of enthusiasm over the new psychoanalytic techniques. This enthusiasm for psychoanalysis and psychoanalytic psychotherapy persisted for the entire first half of the century (Shakow & Rapaport, 1964). Most mental health professionals were eager to learn these techniques, which soon became basic in their armamentarium for dealing with psychological problems. To be sure, some new therapeutic approaches based on principles other than the psychoanalytic were introduced between 1900 and 1950. These, though, like psychoanalysis, assumed that the royal road to curing society's emotional ills was through psychotherapy of some sort.

In 1952, the rather blind faith of the preceding 50 years was shaken by a challenge from Eysenck (1952), who asserted that the effectiveness of psychotherapy had never really been established. He surveyed a large number of studies that reported improvement rates resulting from various types of psychotherapy and concluded that roughly two-thirds of the patients improve. However, Eysenck reasoned that we couldn't claim that psychotherapy was truly effective until these improvement rates were compared to those resulting merely from the passage of time in untreated people suffering problems similar to those treated in psychotherapy. Two studies were found in the literature that seemed to involve such subjects. One reported a 72 percent improvement rate among severe neurotics hospitalized in the New York State system between 1917 and 1934. The other involved 500 individuals who filed disability claims for psychoneuroses with an insurance company. These were consecutive cases taken from the files of a single company and as such came from all parts of the country and displayed all types of neuroses. All subjects in the study had been totally disabled for at least three months and each was seeing his or her own physician and being treated with various drugs, reassurance, suggestion or whatever other techniques the ordinary general practitioner had available, *but not with traditional psychotherapy*. All 500 cases were followed up for at least five years after the disability period began. With the criteria for improvement being ability to return to work and to make an adequate economic adjustment, 45 percent were found to recover in one year and another 27 percent within two years, or a total of 72 percent.

Eysenck's conclusion from these results was that psychotherapy was not proven to be any more effective than hospital care or the care a general practitioner could provide. Further, comparing studies reporting on the effects of long-term psychotherapy such as psychoanalysis, with studies of more superficial approaches, produced surprising results. Eysenck found that an average of about 44 percent of those in long-term psychotherapy improved, whereas 64 percent of those treated by more superficial, less intensive approaches improved. This suggested that the relationship between recovery and psychotherapy is inverse: the more intensive the psychotherapy, the lower the improvement rate.

Eysenck's paper aroused considerable criticism from other professionals (DeCharms, Levy, & Wertheimer, 1954; Rosenzweig, 1954; Cartwright, 1955, 1956; Bindra, 1956). Some attacked Eysenck's assumption that the outcome criteria in the experimental and control groups were equivalent; others asserted that the control groups did receive some form of psychotherapy and weren't entirely "untreated"; still others attacked Eysenck's logic in concluding that psychotherapy is ineffective and possibly harmful. None, however, could refute Eysenck's most basic conclusion: that the effectiveness of psychotherapy had yet to be proven. In fact, Levitt (1957) did a survey similar to Eysenck's involving the treatment of children and arrived at conclusions similar to Eysenck's. In 1961 Eysenck (1961) himself extended his original study and reasserted his original conclusions. By the mid-1960s, what had seemed like heresy in Eysenck's early paper had become a well accepted fact. Schofield (1964), for example, wrote, ". . . we are still awaiting definitive research—we still do not have acceptable evidence that psychotherapy accomplishes significant reduction of neurotic symptomatology, let alone evidence that the several different forms of psychotherapy have different levels of efficacy" (p. 99).

Questions about Psychotherapy as a Solution to Mental Health Problems. Eysenck's challenge concerning the efficacy of psychotherapy was not the only kind of concern raised about that treatment procedure. Many in the 1950s and 1960s who did not dispute the worth of psychotherapy, at least with some types of problems, simply did not see the one-on-one approach as practiced by highly trained professionals as a *practical* way of coping with the mass of mental health problems in modern society. Eisenberg (1962), for example, has put it this way:

> The limitations of present therapeutic methods doom us to training caretakers at a rate that ever lags behind the growing legions of the ill, unless we strike out successfully in new directions in the search for cause

> and treatment . . . Society can ill afford today's precious overspecialization in which trainees may learn one method even superbly well but a method that ever lags behind the demands placed upon it, while they remain abysmally unaware of the problems besetting the bulk of the mentally ill (p.825).

Those who take Eisenberg's position do not deny the value of psychotherapy. They just see society's need as so overwhelming that they cannot possibly be met by the pitifully small cadre of skilled professionals who are in a position to do the time-consuming work of psychotherapy. For such thinkers only community-wide preventive efforts offer any long-range hope.

Related to Eisenberg's critique was that of the distinguished commission set up by President Eisenhower to study the nation's mental health needs. This group, the Joint Commission on Mental Illness and Health (1961), hereafter referred to as the Joint Commission, expressed many concerns about traditional approaches. The Commission's report opened with the following statement:

> We are tempted simply to take the position that there is a crying public demand and needs are easily observable in the difficulty many persons experience in seeking a psychiatrist when they feel the need of one, in the long waiting lists of mental health clinics, the small amount of treatment many clinic patients receive, the total absence of mental health workers and clinics in many communities, the overcrowding of public mental hospitals, and their professional staff shortages (p. 3).

Inequities in the Distribution of Available Services

In addition to the fact that we simply haven't had enough professionals to handle society's mental health problems in traditional ways, many were concerned that the services that were available were distributed inequitably. The Joint Commission, for example, found that those with the most disabling mental problems had least access to the limited pool of trained professionals. The Commission's report (1961) put it this way:

> When we confront the total problem of care of the mentally ill, we find that, despite much talk and some progress, the greatest shortage still occurs in the area where patients with major mental illness are concentrated—in state hospitals. . . The inevitable result is that those States with the least available money have the fewest psychiatrists, and the average State hospital continues to occupy its historic position in the forgotten corner of medicine (p. 146).

Conclusions similar to those of the Joint Commission were also arrived at in several other surveys of the way services are distributed in our society. Hollingshead and Redlich (1958) did a survey in New Haven, Connecticut to determine whether mental illness was related to social class and whether social class was related to the kind of treatment received for mental illness. They found in the case of neurosis an inverse relationship between the number treated in public agencies and social class. That is, the lower the social class, the more likely was a neurotic to be treated in a public agency. This is easily understood when we consider that the lower classes cannot afford private fees. However, the type of treatment received was also class linked. While overall, neurotics were treated primarily with psychotherapy, the lower social classes were more likely than members of higher social classes to receive directive psychotherapy, shock treatment, or drugs. Furthermore, these differences are found even within agencies. Private practitioners were found to engage in the most intensive approaches, such as psychoanalysis, with the higher classes and briefer, more directive approaches with lower classes. This means that private practioners see members of the upper social classes more frequently than those of the lower classes, but distressingly, the same was found to be true in public agencies as well. Among psychotic patients, Hollingshead and Redlich found a similar relationship between social class and treatment. Upper-class schizophrenics, for example, were likely to receive psychotherapy, while those of the lower classes were most likely to be placed in custodial care.

Results similar to those of Hollingshead and Redlich were reported in a survey of Midtown Manhattan (Srole, Langner, Michael, Opler, & Rennie, 1962). The Midtown Manhattan study was done to assess the prevalence of mental illness within one area of New York City. The study involved intensive interviews of approximately 1,600 residents of the area and assessment of their mental condition. Interviewees who were receiving treatment in a mental health facility were identified. Subjects in high socioeconomic classes were found more likely to be in treatment than those in lower classes, despite the fact that mental impairment was highest in the lowest socioeconomic class and lowest in high-income subjects.

Sanua (1966) reviewed many studies of the relationship between sociocultural class and treatment. His conclusions concerning the lower classes were: they were less likely than the upper classes to enter psychotherapy, and if they did, they were more likely to quit treatment after a few sessions. The lower classes were also more likely than the upper classes to receive symptomatic treatment. Sanua's findings indicate that traditional treatment approaches are probably inappropriate for the lower classes.

One explanation for the types of inequities revealed in Sanua's work might simply be that in a society where mental health services are scarce, the upper classes will be taken care of before the lower classes. The solution to such a problem would seem to be simply to provide more mental health services so there could be enough to go around. Unfortunately the problem is apparently more complex than this. Lorion's review (1973) of studies of traditional treatment approaches with low socioeconomic classes suggests that rather than needing more of the traditional services, we need *different* approaches for the poor. Traditional practitioners whose techniques were developed through work with middle-class patients are simply not attuned to the problems of the poor or to their ways of relating. As a result, these therapists "turn off" the poor and undereducated or chalk them off as not suited for psychotherapy. Those patients from lower social classes who do stick with psychotherapy seem to benefit as much or more than upper-class patients. Lorion feels that to be effective with lower-class patients, practitioners need to be more sensitive to their problems and careful to adapt therapeutic techniques to the patient's style.

Estimates of Latent Need for Mental Health Services. With existing traditional services strained by the large demand for them, suggestions that the potential demand is even higher than is presently manifested further destroy confidence in traditional approaches. During the 1950s, such disquieting suggestions were clearly made in several studies.

One report of an epidemiological study done in Canada (Stirling County, Nova Scotia) indicated that among people who were *not* being treated for emotional disorders in that area, a frighteningly high percentage needed help. Fully 37 percent were found to have symptoms that virtually certainly indicated mental disorder; these people suffered more than 10 percent of their ability to function effectively. Another 7 percent were judged to show definite symptoms of mental disorder but had less than ten percent impairment. In summary, the overall findings of the Stirling County study were that mental disorder was present in roughly eight times the number of people who were being treated (Leighton, 1956).

Another study aimed at assessing latent mental health needs was undertaken at the behest of the Joint Commission (Gurin, Veroff, & Feld, 1960). The University of Michigan Survey Research Center was engaged to determine what kinds of emotional problems Americans have, what they do about them, and who they turn to for help. The large sample surveyed was representative in terms of age, sex, education, income, occupation and place of residence of a cross-section of normal, stable American adults. Of this group, one-fourth said they had had problems for which they could have used professional help. Of these, about 14 percent actually sought help. Among the help seekers, however, only 18 percent went to mental health professionals such as psychiatrists, psychologists and social workers. The biggest percentage (42 percent) turned to clergymen and 19 percent saw physicians. The enormous latent need for mental health services is reflected in this study's finding of both the large numbers who felt they had needed help and in the more than 60 percent who actually sought help from other than mental health agencies or professionals.

The previously mentioned Midtown Manhattan study (Srole et al., 1962) conducted in New York City provided still further evidence of a frighteningly large latent need for mental health services. In this study, only 18.5 percent of the 1,600 subjects surveyed were classified as free of emotionally related symptoms. At the other end of the continuum, 13 percent showed marked symptomatology, 7.5 percent had severe symptoms, and almost 3 percent were totally incapacitated. The roughly 23 percent in these three categories reflect, as did the earlier-mentioned studies, an enormous latent need for mental health services.

As was the case when inequities in service delivery were discussed, the solution suggested most immediately by these findings would seem to be an increase in the supply of traditional mental health manpower. Without this, the success of programs to encourage people to seek professional help for emotional disorders might well swamp an already taxed mental health system.

Mental Health Manpower Projections

If one solution to the nation's mental health needs is to increase the professional manpower supply, what are the prospects for achieving this successfully? To answer this question, the Joint Commission sponsored a study by Albee (1959) to assess the supply and demand for traditional mental health workers (psychologists, psychiatrists, psychiatric nurses and psychiatric social workers).

Demand was reflected in the difficulty public agencies had been having for years in finding people to fill the jobs that were available. The years immediately prior to Albee's study saw an aggravation of this situation because of the fact that many agencies, such as the schools and courts, which had never before used psychological services, were beginning to do so in increasing numbers. As a result, in the late 1950s, fully 75 percent of the budgeted jobs for psychologists and psychiatrists in public hospitals were unfilled. Similarly, one out of every five available jobs for psychiatric nurses were unfilled. Furthermore, these grim statistics could be expected to worsen since the country's population was steadily expanding.

On the supply side, the numbers of psychiatrists being trained were found to be increasing. Unfortunately, though, a very high percentage of fully trained psychiatrists enter private practice. Thus their increase in numbers nationally does little to meet the desperate needs of public institutions. Albee also found that psychologists were being produced in increasing numbers. Again, however, that fact seemed to offer little hope that the necessary supply would be available to man public hospitals properly. Only about one-third of the psychologists being trained were specializing in clinical psychology, the specialty that contributes most to caring for the mentally ill. Furthermore, the largest number of clinicians being turned out by psychology departments were gravitating to academic jobs.

In the social work profession, the outlook for producing a sufficient supply was even grimmer than in the psychology field. Albee pointed out that because the social worker's role is ill-defined for the lay public as well as in the profession itself, social work schools were attracting far fewer students than they could train. Albee estimated that while an additional 50,000 social workers would be needed by 1960, social work schools were graduating only about 2,000 per year.

Nursing, unlike social work, enjoys a clear public image and does attract increasing numbers of trainees. Despite that fact, however, the supply of nurses regularly fails to keep up with demand. This occurs because 50 percent of the trained nurses drop out of the profession, primarily to marry. Furthermore, only about 5 percent of those training as nurses enter psychiatric nursing even though nearly half of all hospitalized patients need psychiatric care. Thus, rather than being a bright spot in the supply picture, it appeared to Albee that psychiatric nursing needed to attract a much larger percentage of the available pool of nurses or the profession would face increasing shortages.

From an overall view, too, it needs to be recognized that manpower problems in the mental health field interact with the manpower situation in all other professions that require college-trained people. If any one profession succeeds in attracting talent, it does so at some cost to other profession which need the same kind of talented people. Albee was concerned, too, that in the 1950s there was a generalized depreciation of intellectual achievement which would shrink to some degree the talented manpower pool from which all professions must draw. Overall, Albee's conclusions were pessimistic indeed. Rather than expecting traditional mental health manpower supplies to catch up with demand, he foresaw a widening gap. Population expansion and the increasing competition of other professions would increase mental health shortages. When he reexamined the manpower problem eight years after his original study, Albee (1967) found little reason to change this original pessimistic forecast.

THE AWAKENING OF THE COMMUNITY MENTAL HEALTH MOVEMENT

The Establishment of Community Mental Health Centers

The facts, the concerns, the fears, and dissatisfactions described here led inevitably, in the late 1950s and early 1960s, to a vigorous community mental health movement. Unlike the instances in earlier years when a few lonely, energetic, farseeing figures tried to promote community preventive approaches, the recent movement has been powerful. The arguments for it seemed undeniable! The limitations of traditional approaches seemed all too obvious! Community mental health's time had come!

A major phase of the recent movement has been devoted to dealing with already manifest mental disorder in many of the same old ways, but in some new ways as well, utilizing community resources. The manner of treating mental disorder was promulgated largely by the federal government. The earlier-mentioned Joint Commission on Mental Illness and Health (1961) made a strong case in its final report to President Kennedy for the federal support of an increase in research, training and new services for the mentally disturbed. The Commission set forth a number of specific recommendations. It argued for the establishment of community mental health centers to serve population units of 50,000, in which the acutely disturbed could receive immediate care. It recommended that all general hospitals of moderate size have inpatient psychiatric units. It asserted that psychiatric hospitals should be limited in size to 1,000 beds. It called for the establishment in mental health centers of rehabilitation and a variety of other services such as aftercare and partial hospitalization. Finally, it urged that education programs be launched to change the public's tendency to reject the mental patient.

President Kennedy was very receptive to the recommendations of the Joint Commission. In February 1963 he proposed to Congress that a new national mental health program be established, and indicated that he would be preparing legislation to implement it (Kennedy, 1963). He asserted that the country needed "a bold new approach" with three major objectives. The first of these focused on prevention:

> We must seek out the causes of mental illness and of mental retardation and eradicate them. . . . for prevention is far more desirable for all concerned. It is far more economical and it is far more likely to be successful. Prevention will require both selected specific programs directed especially at known causes, and the general strengthening of our fundamental community, social welfare, and educational programs which can

> do much to eliminate or correct the harsh environmental conditions which often are associated with mental retardation and mental illness (p. 2).

The second objective involved expanding training and research to "strengthen the underlying resources of knowledge and, above all, of skilled manpower which are necessary to mount and sustain our attack on mental disability for many years to come" (pp. 2–3). Finally, President Kennedy affirmed the need to bolster existing services for treating the mentally ill.

The sincere interest of the President in furthering the aims of the mental health movement was enormously important. And this interest and commitment was followed by congressional action with the passage of a Community Mental Health Centers Act that President Kennedy signed in October 1963. The act provided federal funding for the construction of mental health centers as well as for the cost of staffing the centers. All of the states in the country were divided up into geographical units called catchment areas, with populations from 75,000 to 200,000. Funds were made available by the federal government to build and staff the new centers. The federal contribution to setting up the new centers ranged from 33 percent to 67 percent of the total cost, depending upon what could be afforded by the particular state involved. The government share of staff costs began at 75 percent and decreased gradually until these costs were eventually taken over entirely by local communities. The mandate of the centers that were to be created was fivefold. Centers were expected to provide emergency services, outpatient treatment, partial hospitalization, inpatient care, and consultation and education.

The Community Mental Health Centers Act of 1963 provided funds for a three-year period. By the time this original authorization expired, nearly 300 centers had been supported and the federal investment in the program remained strong. Therefore, in 1967, the act was extended for three more years, and still other extensions have followed though not without some struggle as a result of fiscal strain. In addition, since passage of the original mental health center act, federal money has been appropriated to create special programs to treat addicts and to provide services for children (Bloom, 1977).

Programs to Prevent Mental Disorders

In great measure, although the community mental health centers have been expected to have a preventive function, their role is largely to treat already manifest disorder as promptly and as effectively as possible without removing the sufferer from the community arena. Such centers usually provide a crisis service aimed at helping people cope successfully with acutely disturbing situations so that any long-range problems may be averted. The consultative and educative roles played by mental health centers also contribute to prevention. Clearly, though, the bulk of most center efforts goes into direct service to clients who already have problems. Most of the new preventive approaches have developed in a far less organized way than has the community mental health center movement. Preventive programs have emerged as the pet idea of particular individuals or groups of individuals who sought the support of existing fund-granting agencies to help them. Thus such programs address a variety of problems and are found in a variety of settings.

Since this is but one chapter in a book, we can only hope to provide the most superficial overview of the kinds of preventive programs that have emerged in recent years. Much will be left out, and the few examples we can mention cannot be covered in the detail they truly merit. One way of classifying these programs is by the population groups on which they focus. However, mental health consultation is a preventive *technique* that is used so widely and in so many different kinds of programs that it deserves special mention.

Mental health consultation. As Bloom (1977) points out, consultation is an "indirect service." It does not deal directly with a client or patient. Instead, it deals with a person or persons who provide direct services to clients or patients. As such, it is a process that can upgrade the skills of those who do have primary, frontline contact with those needing service. Furthermore, consultation extends the reach of the highly trained professional, since through less-well-trained consultees who are on the front lines, the professional can have a beneficial effect on far more people than he could ever hope to see directly. In this way, mental health consultation is often an important solution to the problem of manpower shortages in the mental health field.

Mental health consultation is used in a variety of areas. At times it is the basis of an entire program, as was the case in Spielberger's work in a small rural community having limited professional mental health resources (Spielberger, 1967). In a school program in Texas (Iscoe, Pierce-Jones, Friedman, & McGehearty, 1967) consultation was also the primary service provided. Morse (1967) also based an entire program with school teachers on consultation.

In many other cases, consultation is part of a program that has a variety of other elements. Therefore, as we briefly describe programs focusing on various problems and population groups, the pervasiveness of the mental health consultation technique will become clear.

Programs in schools. The schools have been a major focus for preventive programs of both a primary and early secondary nature. This has been true for a number of reasons. First of all, in thinking about preventing the development of mental disorder, it is natural to seek to do that as early as possible in the lifetime of those about whom you are concerned. The schools, and primarily the very early grades, gather together virtually the entire young population of a community. Furthermore, the task of managing the requirements of school is the child's major life business. Helping to make school adjustment as effective as possible and using the school experience to build strengths that can insulate one against later life stresses seems very worthwhile. Finally, since parents often have a great investment in their children's success in school, they tend to coöperate with school-based preventive programs. So the schools have been a primary locus for such programs.

Some school programs have focused on primary prevention. One approach of such programs is to consciously vary school atmospheres to find that which seems to promote optimal psychological development. That route was followed in a program developed at the Bank Street College of Education (Zimiles, 1967). The Bank Street project was concerned with comparing the effects of a school program based on traditional school ideology with one based on modern school ideology. Traditional ideology was seen to stress intellectual achievement based on some fixed curriculum. Modern ideology was seen to emphasize individuality and "the *processes* of thinking and learning" as opposed to content mastery.

Other primary preventive efforts in schools have been less global. Roen (1967), for example, carried out a program based on the introduction of a course in the behavioral sciences for fourth graders. The rationale was that learning about the effects on behavior of heredity, the environment, intelligence, emotions, self-concept, birth order and the like would provide useful tools for dealing with the human problems children might be expected to face.

Another good example of a school's primary preventive approach is found in the work of Ojemann (Ojemann, Levitt, Lyle, & Whiteside, 1955). Ojemann distinguishes between *causal* thinking, in which the behavior of others is seen to have antecedents that need to be considered before responding, and noncausal thinking, which disregards such antecedents and results often in punitive reactions and unsatisfying human relationships. He felt further that the typical school taught noncausal thinking. Thus, operationally Ojemann works with teachers and encourages them to instill causality into their teaching approach regardless of the particular subject content.

School programs oriented toward secondary prevention are concerned with recognizing the earliest signs of behavioral disorder and working to correct them in order to ameliorate the child's school adjustment. One notable example of such a program that focuses on children with fairly serious emotional problems is Project Re-ED (Hobbs, 1966, 1967, 1969).

It is an educationally oriented program that stresses a 24-hour therapeutic milieu. The child is separated from family and environment for a time-limited period during which he or she lives in a residential school with "teacher-counselors" who are concerned with providing both academic training and emotional support. Though the child is removed from his family and normal environment, the tie to the environment is carefully maintained. Upon entry into the program, plans are formulated for the child's release, weekend visits at home are encouraged, and project staff maintain regular contacts with the child's family, school and the referring agency.

Another school secondary prevention program that has enjoyed considerable recognition and success is the Rochester Primary Mental Health Project (Cowen, Trost, Izzo, Lorion, Dorr, & Isaacson, 1975). This project, in contrast to Re-ED, is concerned with the very early identification of potential for maladjustment in primary-grade children. The project has undergone a steady evolution in form but basically it involves the introduction of trained and closely supervised help agents known as child-aides, into the school. The aides work with teachers by accepting referrals from them of children who show signs of faltering academically or socially. The aides' job is to provide whatever help the child needs in order to work him back into the mainstream of school functioning.

College programs. College students are seen to be subject to a great many stresses that strain their psychological resources (Zax and Specter, 1974). They often experience considerable anxiety over separation from home and the community, sexual adjustment, and, ultimately, occupational choice. In addition, the academic demands of college are often more stringent than what had been experienced in high school. Finally, college students are at that awkward stage between adolescence and adulthood when neither their parents, the college, nor they themselves, for that matter, are clear on who they are.

Many programs within the college community have been directed toward entering freshmen. Wolff (1969), for example, worked at the University of Rochester with resident dormitory advisers, themselves college juniors or seniors, who set up discussion groups focusing on interpersonal relations. Freshmen under the advisers' supervision were invited to volunteer to participate.

Spielberger and Weitz (1964) also concerned themselves with entering college freshmen. They limited their focus, however, to what they regarded as a high-risk group consisting of students who, though having high aptitudes, were also found to have high anxiety on a personality inventory.

A program at Kansas State University (Sinnett, Weisner, & Freiser,

1967) was designed to serve students displaying chronic adjustment problems. In this program, a halfway house was created on the campus to provide services to students to satisfy needs that were far in excess of what could be met in a traditional student health service. The disturbed students in this program seemed unlikely to complete college and not unlikely to need hospitalization. They resided in the halfway house along with a large number of "normal" students. While all disturbed students were in individual treatment, all house residents in the program participated in group sessions to encourage the communication of feelings. In effect, this effort attempted to create a therapeutic community within the college.

Perhaps the most ambitious effort to create a communal, preventive approach took place at the University of Florida (Barger, 1963; Barger, Larson & Hall, 1965). Primary, secondary, and tertiary preventive goals were set up in this program. By way of primary prevention, studies were carried out to identify the environmental stress students had to contend with. Secondary prevention was implemented by identifying incoming students with disturbed personality profiles and offering them treatment. In addition, faculty members and residence hall personnel who could spot early evidences of emotional disturbance were contacted by mental health workers. The tertiary preventive aspect of the Florida program was based on the establishment of a variety of treatment modes such as group and individual psychotherapy, psychodrama, chemotherapy and hospitalization.

Another popular innovation having preventive potential involves the establishment of campus crisis programs. In one such program at Southern Colorado State College (Tucker, Magenity, and Vigil, 1970) a telephone hotline was set up manned primarily by undergraduate volunteers, although faculty and staff were invited to volunteer as well. A 24-hour training program preceded actual hotline experience for each volunteer. The program included lectures, listening to actual taped phone conversations, and role playing.

The community at large. Programs in the community at large suffer in comparison to school programs in that they have a hard time finding a focus in terms of who will be served and where programs will be located. As a result, most programs that have emerged have been directed at particular social problems. For example, the New Careers program (Pearl & Riessman, 1965) was developed to serve the unskilled, undereducated poor who found it hard to establish a foothold on our society's economic ladder. The avenue recommended in this program was training in human service work as well as establishing jobs through which such trainees could develop careers.

The Lincoln Hospital Neighborhood Service Center Program (Peck

& Kaplan, 1969) was directed toward the multitude of coping and psychological problems encountered by ghetto dwellers who are badly educated, impoverished, have poor housing, live in crime-ridden areas, and generally experience chaotic life conditions. These centers were neighborhood storefronts staffed by trained nonprofessionals indigenous to the neighborhoods served. The goal of these centers was to promote mental health in people who came to them by providing prompt service, as well as to encourage social cohesion within the neighborhood and influence community agencies to improve their services. It was also the hope of the program's founders that the center staff would serve as models for their clients of how to cope successfully with "the establishment."

A number of community programs have been directed toward the problem of delinquency. Schwitzgebel (1964) set up a storefront in which delinquents were hired and paid to be "subjects" in an experiment on the causes of delinquent behavior. The subject's job in the study was simply to talk into a tape recorder, explaining how and why he got into trouble with the police. The process of communicating about their delinquent careers and the causes thereof is seen to be potentially therapeutic for the subjects.

Sarason & Ganzer (1969) developed a program for delinquents based on modeling procedures. These researchers assumed that, as people who have been rejected by the culture, delinquents lack a variety of socially adaptive skills. Thus many common experiences such as a job interview, or a situation where one is pressured by peers to break the law, or having to approach an authority for help with a problem, are modeled for the delinquent by people who role-play a good way of dealing with each situation.

Still another approach used to prevent further malajustment in inner-city youth, many of whom have police records, was used by Goldenberg (1971). He set up a residential youth center which provided a short-term, living-in setting for its residents. The goal of the setting was to promote personal growth. The staff consisted largely of indigenous nonprofessionals. The responsibility for setting the institution's goals and choosing values was placed on the staff as a whole. Center residents were expected to take jobs outside the center and to pay rent for their housing in the center. Center staff helped residents find jobs and attempted to help them work out conflicts with their families in such a way as to permit their return to family living as soon as possible. Weekend and evening programs were arranged at the center for residents' families.

Still other community programs have focused on consultation with "caregivers," people in the community whose regular work, though not in the mental health field, bring them in contact with individuals troubled by emotional problems. Bard's program (Bard & Berkowitz, 1967) with the New York City police is a good example. Bard taught mental health principles to a group of patrolmen whose work involved dealing primarily with family crises.

CONCLUSION

This chapter has been able to cover only a few of the many preventive programs that have emerged since the swing away from the long-established psychotherapy tradition. The community mental health center movement is solid and represents an improvement over the types of public services that were available before its inception. Still, its preventive impact has been negligible. Prevention programs of lasting impact have not become institutionalized. Many approaches have appeared briefly and died out. In part this is because to win a solid foothold, such programs must be tested in the crucible of experience over many years. Continuing financial support has been a problem that stands in the way of accruing that long-range experience.

A recent development offering the hope that the problem of continuing support for the establishment, testing and refinement of primary preventive programs is the recent report of the task panel on prevention (President's Commission on Mental Health, 1978) that was set up by the federal government. This group has recommended the creation of a Center for Primary Prevention within the National Institute of Mental Health with the support needed to promote education in primary prevention as well as to support research in this area. It is hoped that such a center could guide and promote the development of programs that will become institutionalized on the mental health scene. If so, some not-too-distant future history to be written on the community mental health movement will be able to report on a much more substantial preventive thrust.

References

Albee, G. W. *Mental health manpower trends.* New York: Basic Books, 1959

Albee, G. W. The relation of conceptual models to manpower needs. In E. L. Cowen, E. A. Gardner, & M. Zax (Eds.), *Emergent approaches to mental health problems.* New York: Appleton-Century-Crofts, 1967.

Bard, M., & Berkowitz, B. Training police as specialists in family crisis intervention: a community psychology action program. *Community Mental Health Journal*, 1967, *3*, 315–317.

Barger, B. The University of Florida mental health program. In B. Barger and E. Hall (Eds.), *Higher education and mental health.* Gainesville: University of Florida, 1963.

Barger, B., Larson, E. A., & Hall, E. Preventive action in college mental health. *Journal of the American College Health Association*, 1965, *15*, 80–93.

Bindra, D. Psychotherapy and recovery from neuroses. *Journal of Abnormal and Social Psychology*, 1956, *53*, 251–254.

Bloom, B. L. *Community mental health: a general introduction.* Monterey, Calif.: Brooks/Cole, 1977.

Bockoven, J. S. Moral treatment in American psychiatry. *Journal of Nervous and Mental Disease*, 1956, *124*, 167–194, 292–321.

Bockoven, J. S. Some relationships between cultural attitudes toward individuality and care of the mentally ill: A historical study. In M. Greenblatt, D. J. Levinson, and R. H. Williams (Eds.), *The patient and the mental hospital.* Glencoe, Ill.: The Free Press, 1957.

Caplan, G. *Prevention of mental disorders in children: initial explorations*, New York: Basic Books, 1961.

Caplan, G. *Principles of preventive psychiatry.* New York: Basic Books, 1964.

Cartwright, D. S. Effectiveness of psychotherapy: A critique of the spontaneous remission argument. *Journal of Counseling Psychology*, 1955, *2*, 290–296

Cartwright, D. S. Note on "changes in psychoneurotic patients with and without psychotherapy." *Journal of Consulting Psychology*, 1956, *20*, 403–404.

Cowen, E. L., Trost, M. A., Izzo, L. D., Lorion, R. P., Dorr, D., & Isaacson, R. V. *New ways in school mental health: Early detection and prevention of school maladaptation.* New York: Human Sciences Press, 1975.

DeCharms, R., Levy, J., & Wertheimer, M. A note on attempted evaluations of psychotherapy. *Journal of Clinical Psychology*, 1954, *10*, 233–235.

Eisenberg, L. Possibilities for a preventive psychiatry. *Pediatrics*, 1962, *30*, 815–828.

Erikson, E. H. *Childhood and society.* New York: Norton, 1950.

Eysenck, H. J. The effects of psychotherapy: An evaluation. *Journal of Consulting Psychology*, 1952, *16*, 319–324.

Eysenck, H. J. The effects of psychotherapy. In H. J. Eysenck (Ed.), *Handbook of abnormal psychology.* New York: Basic Books, 1961.

Foucault, M. *Madness and civilization.* New York: Random House, 1965.

Goldenberg, I. *Build me a mountain: Youth, poverty, and the creation of new settings.* Cambridge, Mass.: MIT Press, 1971.

Gurin, G., Veroff, J., & Feld, S. *Americans view their mental health: A nationwide interview survey.* New York: Basic Books, 1960.

Hobbs, N. Helping disturbed children: Psychological and ecological strategies. *American Psychologist*, 1966, *21*, 1105–1115.

Hobbs, N. The reeducation of emotionally disturbed children. In E. M. Bower & W. G. Hollister (Eds.), *Behavior science frontiers in education.* New York: Wiley, 1967.

Hobbs, N. Re-education, reality and community responsibility. In J. W. Carter (Ed.), *Research contributions from psychology to community mental health.* New York: Behavioral Publications, 1969.

Hollingshead, A. G., & Redlich, F. C. *Social class and mental illness: a community study.* New York: John Wiley, 1958.

Iscoe, I., Pierce-Jones, J., Friedman, S. T., & McGehearty, L. Some strategies in mental health consultation. In E. L. Cowen, E. A. Gardner, & M. Zax (Eds.), *Emergent approaches to mental health problems.* New York: Appleton-Century-Crofts, 1967.

Joint Commission on Mental Illness and Health. *Action for mental health.* New York: Basic Books, 1961.

Kennedy, J. F. *Message from the President of the United States relative to mental illness and mental retardation.* Washington, D.C.: U.S. Government Printing Office, 1963.

Leighton, Dorothea C. Distribution of psychiatric symptoms in a small town. *American Journal of Psychiatry*, 1956, *112*, 716–723.

Levitt, E. E. The results of psychotherapy with children: an evaluation. *Journal of Consulting Psychology*, 1957, *21*, 189–196.

Lindemann, E. Symptomatology and management of acute grief. *American Journal of Psychiatry*, 1944, *101*, 141–148.

Lorion, R. P. Socio-economic status and traditional treatment approaches reconsidered. *Psychological Bulletin*, 1973, *79*, 263–270.

Meyer, A. After-care and prophylaxis. In A. Lief (Ed.), *The commonsense psychiatry of Dr. Adolph Meyer*. New York: McGraw-Hill, 1948.

Morse, W. C. Enhancing the classroom teacher's mental health function. In E. L. Cowen, E. A. Gardner, & M. Zax (Eds.), *Emergent approaches to mental health problems*. New York: Appleton-Century-Crofts, 1967.

Ojemann, R. H., Levitt, E. E., Lyle, W. H., & Whiteside, M. F. The effects of a "causal" teacher-training program and certain curricular changes on grade school children. *Journal of Experimental Education*, 1955, *24*, 95–114.

Pearl, A., & Riessman, F. *New careers for the poor*. New York: Free Press, 1965.

Peck, H. B., & Kaplan, S. R. A mental health program for the urban multiservice center, In M. F. Shore & F. V. Mannino (Eds.), *Mental health and the community: problems, programs and strategies*. New York: Behavioral Publications, 1969.

President's Commission on Mental Health. *Task panel reports*. Washington, D.C.: U.S. Government Printing Office, 1978.

Roen, S. R. Primary prevention in the classroom through a teaching program in the behavioral sciences. In E. L. Cowen, E. A. Gardner, & M. Zax (Eds.), *Emergent approaches to mental health problems*. New York: Appleton-Century-Crofts, 1967.

Rosenzweig, S. The effects of psychotherapy: A reply to Hans Eysenck. *Journal of Abnormal and Social Psychology*, 1954, *49*, 278-304.

Sarason, I. G., & Ganzer, V. J. Social influence techniques in clinical and community psychology. In C. D. Spielberger (Ed.), *Current topics in clinical and community psychology*. New York: Academic Press, 1969.

Sanua, V. D. Sociocultural aspects of psychotherapy and treatment: A review of the literature. In L. W. Abt & L. Bellak (Eds.), *Progress in clinical psychology* (Vol. III). New York: Grune and Stratton, 1966.

Schofield, W. *Psychotherapy: The purchase of friendship*. Englewood Cliffs, N.J.: Prentice-Hall, 1964.

Schwitzgebel, R. L. *Streetcorner research*. Cambridge, Mass.: Harvard University Press, 1964.

Shakow, D., & Rapaport, D. The influence of Freud on American psychology. *Psychological Issues* (Vol. IV, No. 1). New York: International Universities Press, 1964.

Sinnett, E. R., Weisner, E. G., & Frieser, W. S. Dormitory half-way house. *Rehabilitation Record*, 1967, *8*, 34–37.

Spielberger, C. D. A mental health consultation program in a small community with limited professional mental health resources. In E. L. Cowen, E. A. Gardner, & M. Zax (Eds.), *Emergent approaches to mental health problems*. New York: Appleton-Century-Crofts, 1967.

Spielberger, C. D., & Weitz, H. Improving the academic performance of anxious college freshman: A group counseling approach to prevention of underachievement. *Psychological Bulletin Monographs* (No. 590), 1964, *78*, 20 pp.

Srole, L., Langner, T. S., Michael, S. T., Opler, M. K., & Rennie, T. A. C. *Mental health in the metropolis* (Vol. I). New York: McGraw-Hill, 1962.

Tucker, B. H., Magenity, D., & Vigil, L. Anatomy of a campus crisis center. *Personnel and Guidance Journal*, 1970, *48*, 343–348.

Turner, R. J., & Cumming, J. Theoretical malaise and community mental health. In E. L. Cowen, E. A. Gardner, and M. Zax (Eds.), *Emergent approaches to mental health problems*. New York: Appleton-Century-Crofts, 1967.

Wolff, T. Community mental health on campus: Evaluating group discussions led by dormitory advisors and graduate students. Doctoral dissertation, University of Rochester, 1969.

Zax, M., & Specter, G. A. *An introduction to community psychology*. New York: John Wiley, 1974.

Zilboorg, G., and Henry, G. W. *A history of medical psychology*. New York: Norton, 1941.

Zimiles, H. Preventive aspects of school experience. In E. L. Cowen, E. A. Gardner, & M. Zax (Eds.), *Emergent approaches to mental health problems*. New York: Appleton-Century-Crofts, 1967.

CHAPTER 2

Historical Perspectives on the Treatment of the Mentally Ill

Richard C. Erickson, Ph.D.
and
Bobbie J. Hyerstay, Ph.D.

In this chapter we will address the question of how well informed and effective are our efforts to treat seriously disturbed persons: those who are and have been in mental hospitals. This question cannot be answered by simply reviewing outcome studies. Larger issues of public and professional attitudes and policies make more of an impact on what happens to a patient than any of our specific, controllable interventions. While we cannot exercise control over these larger issues, we can, as individuals and groups of professionals and citizens, influence the shape they will take in the future.

In the interest of informing the reader about these larger issues as well as specific issues relative to our efforts to treat seriously disturbed persons, we will sample materials from three areas: the history of the treatment of the mentally ill, the effectiveness of our treatments, and current attitudes and policies toward those persons ordinarily accorded institutional care.

HISTORY OF THE TREATMENT OF THE MENTALLY ILL

Humans characteristically produce chauvinistic histories. Evidence is selected and the story edited in such a way as to suggest that the author's position (and that of his compatriots) constitutes a kind of end point, resolving the misunderstandings and correcting the shortcomings of the past. While certain questions remain unanswered, the author's point of view is seen as "being on the right track": It is only a matter of time before these remaining problems are resolved.

Histories of special-interest groups often refer to persons and ideas from the distant past which embody or prefigure the group's ideals and values. Such persons and ideas are contrasted with others which differed, and history is written in such a way as to suggest protracted warfare between the forces of right and the forces of wrong. The briefer the historical survey, the more the story suffers from distortion and oversimplification.

A survey of introductory texts in abnormal psychology and psychiatry documents these observations relative to the history of psychiatry. In broad outline they present a common sequence of events: the primitive period, the Greek and Roman advances over primitivism, the medieval regression, the emergence of the modern view during the Renaissance, and the slow and uneven but inevitable progress of the modern ideal. In terms of dramatic effect, the reader witnesses emerging forces of enlightenment being suppressed prematurely by the forces of superstition and brutality, but reemerging to gain the final victory. The victorious group includes those who have the right view of mental illness, who deal humanely and effectively with the problem; and the vanquished group contains the superstitious, who deal cruelly and ineffectively with the problem. Classically the antagonistic groups have been depicted as science and religion (White, 1896).

The dangers in such a historical oversimplification are legion. Santayana has said, "Those who cannot remember the past are condemned to repeat it." It can also be said that those who oversimplify or distort history are doomed to repeat its errors. A moralistic warfare motif, while dramatic, is poorly chosen if we wish to learn lessons from history. We risk replacing a supernaturalistic dogmatic tradition with a naturalistic dogmatic tradition and risk complacently assuming that adherence to the right (read "scientific") view will guarantee humaneness and effectiveness.

In point of fact, writing the history of psychiatry in terms of warfare between science and religion is out of date, a practice continued out of habit rather than need or conviction. It is time to propose another outline or set of outlines if we are to draw pertinent lessons. We would like to suggest that the history of human efforts to relate to the mentally ill is composed of not one, but three, histories. The first history has to do with the emergence of a naturalistic and empirical way of conceptualizing the problem. The second has to do with how humanely the mentally ill were treated. The third concerns how effectively their problems were addressed. If we measure progress along these three time lines, we soon discover that advances and declines in one history do not coincide with advances and declines in the others. We discover that names prominent in one history are not necessarily prominent in the others. To combine the histories is to confound the issues.

We will outline these three time lines and mention some prominent names and examples. We cannot hope to be comprehensive. Fortunately, readers can easily find further examples and documentation in Alexander and Selesnick (1966), Bromberg (1954, 1975) and Zilboorg and Henry (1941) if they read these excellent histories keeping in mind the several outlines we will present.

The Emergence of Naturalistic and Empirical Conceptualizations

This time line supports the usual way of looking at psychiatric history. It traces human efforts to interpret mental illness in naturalistic terms, noting historical figures who took a "rational" approach to the problem, who made perceptive clinical observations and attempted to establish meaningful ways of classifying the phenomena before them. From this perspective, Hippocrates (460–337 B.C.) is rightly called the father of medicine, and Hellenistic and Roman thinkers such as Celsus (first century A.D.), Soranus (second century A.D.), Caelius Aurelianus (fifth century A.D.), Asclepiades (ca. 100 B.C.), and Galen (A.D. 130–200) are rightly honored. Before their time, the problem of mental illness had been cast in terms of supernaturalistic categories, and it was not until the sixteenth century that such thinkers as Vives (A.D. 1492–1540), Paracelsus (A.D. 1493–1541), Cornelius Agrippa (A.D. 1486–1545), and Weyer (A.D. 1515–1588) stemmed the tide of medieval supernaturalistic thinking and reintroduced naturalistic ways of thinking.

Even so, it is naive to construe the history of ideas as a warfare between science and religion. If we can overcome our bias against supernaturalistic ways of expressing ideas, it becomes clear that we owe intellectual debts to the ancient Babylonians, Egyptians, Hebrews, Persians, and East Asians as well as to the Greeks and Romans (Alexander & Selesnick, 1966, Chapter 3). The history of a thoughtful reflection on how best to deal with troubled souls is a rich and unbroken one (McNeill, 1951). No less a supernaturalist than St. Augustine has been proclaimed the "greatest introspective psychologist before Freud" (Alexander & Selesnick, 1966, p. 33). Other medieval figures (e.g., Bartholomew Anglicus, ca. A.D. 1275) were also incisive thinkers, perceptive observers, and rational in their approach to the mentally ill. The more we know about the Dark Ages, the less dark they seem. Even after that, during the height of witch hunts in the sixteenth and seventeenth centuries, the names of devout clergy and laity such as Vives, Weyer, Father Spee (ca. A.D. 1623), and St. Vincent de Paul (A.D. 1576–1660) represent humanistic and rational responses to the prevailing madness.

Even more to the point is the observation that the history of psychiatric ideas is not a history of common practice. The thinkers we revere from our vantage point were not necessarily reflecting a widely accepted point of view. Their words were often those of a few unique and brilliant individuals who had little impact on their societies. The

Greek and Roman thinkers produced grand formulations, but it was the priests at the Aesculapean temples who managed the health care delivery system.

Nor should we assume that modern ideas and practices would have evolved all the sooner if it had not been for the untimely demise of Greek and Roman naturalism. It must be recognized that the congenial ideas and practices we take pleasure in citing were embedded in other ways of looking at the world. These thinkers were not modern men misplaced in time. Galen may not represent the last light before the repressive darkness, but the last calcification of a misconceived approach. The thoroughgoing empiricism at the core of our present practices is the product of more recent ways of thinking. The noting of historical coincidences is gratifying but should not be confused with historical causation or influence.

It must also be noted that naturalistic thinkers have themselves given birth to tenacious dogmatisms that have blocked progress. The centuries-long ascendancy of Galenistic orthodoxy and the nineteenth-century point of view that assumed that insanity was to be understood as the result of incurable physical diseases are cases in point. Even psychoanalysis established itself as an obstructive dogma in short order (Ullman & Krasner, 1965). So it is that naturalistic ways of thinking have done their share in slowing intellectual progress. Not only that, but they have also given rise to their share of strange, ineffective and even brutal treatment practices.

If we are to draw valid lessons from history, then we must understand ourselves as participants in history in the making. Events will keep overtaking us. Yesterday's heroes will become tomorrow's villains (see Szasz, 1974; Ullman & Krasner, 1965, 1969). It is entirely likely that our ways of thinking will be superseded by ways of thinking that are as foreign to us as our "scientific" theories are to theories of demon possession. The story of the theatrical Mesmer, his rejection and eventual place of honor in the history of psychotherapy, is a lesson of history we ignore at our peril. Elegant scientific theories and orthodoxies are the most perishable of historical commodities: what will remain for the future is our record of humanistic treatment and careful systematic clinical observation.

Humane Treatment of the Mentally Ill

The history of how humane has been our treatment of the mentally ill is quite other than the history of ideas. Our reading of history suggests that the mentally ill have been accorded humane (if not well-informed) treatment for most of human history. In making this judgment, of course, we recognize that we are assuming a relative standard. More often than not, humane treatment was not readily available to the indigent, and they were left to wander the countryside. Even so, it is unfair to fault a society for not expending resources it does not have. The lot of the mentally ill must be compared with the common lot of humankind in that time and place. Our judgment will be based, then, on the treatment accorded to those who were fortunate (or unfortunate) enough to receive treatment in keeping with the prevailing professional and public attitudes of the time. On this basis, we note that there are two periods in history during which inhumane treatment prevailed. For different reasons, the sixteenth to the eighteenth centuries, which saw the rise of modern civilization, and the latter half of the nineteenth and first half of the twentieth centuries are to be judged unfavorably.

Our understanding of the distant past is obscured for lack of records. It appears, however, that mentally disturbed persons were sometimes treated with honor on the assumption that their madness was a gift of the gods. At other times, they were treated sympathetically by priests and shamans on the assumption that they were unfortunate victims of malignant spirits. This humane approach appears to be characteristic among primitive tribes and ancient civilizations. Incubation sleep and benign activities were as much a mark of healing temples in Egypt and Greece as were the dramatic exorcisms. Greek and Roman physicians were known to prescribe benign activities along with their blood lettings, purgatives, and strange concoctions. Among ancient humanists must be included the names of Asclepiades and Soranus (A.D. 93–138) whose benign methods can be contrasted with the brutal methods of Celsus (28 B.C.–A.D. 50).

The collapse of the Roman system led to a return to supernaturalistic ways of thinking, but not to barbarism. It is recognized that Christian faith and ethics were responsible for the humane treatment of the mentally ill for hundreds of years, an observation all the more remarkable given the economic and political chaos of the times. Churches and monasteries became santuaries for sufferers, and leaders such as St. Benedict of Nursia (A.D. 480–543) and Cassiodoras (A.D. 490–585) laid the groundwork for medieval medicine. The famous center at Gheel, Belgium, is only one example of a number of places that sprang up throughout Europe and the Arab world during this period and the one that followed. Alexander and Selesnick (1966, p. 80) have observed that the physical care of the institutionalized insane during the early Middle Ages was superior to that accorded the insane during the seventeenth and eighteenth centuries. While the thinking and therapeutic practices of this period are certainly alien to us, it is important to note that their sensitivity toward suffering is not.

Theories of demon possession and the labeling of certain persons as witches were common during the Middle Ages (Williams, 1941). However, the lurid witch hunts and brutal practices that figure so prominently in psychiatric history did not become a significant reality until the latter half of the fifteenth century. For the sake of convenience, we may date the declaration of war with the publication of *The Witches' Hammer* in 1487 and the effective end of hostilities with the Salem Retraction in 1693. The horror reached its peak during the second of the two centuries.

The timing of the horror is informative. Seldom has human history had so much to deal with at one time. Established religious, economic and political systems were being threatened and overturned. Human thought was being revolutionized. Plagues and warfare were devastating Europe. It was a paradoxical time that gave rise to the best and the worst of human behaviors.

The horrible state of affairs uncovered by Pinel (A.D. 1745–1826) and Tuke (A.D. 1732–1822) should not be linked to this time of religious persecution. By their time, much of the care or abuse of the mentally ill had fallen into the hands of secular authorities and what ensued was the product of public attitudes and medical aloofness and ignorance.

With Pinel the physician and Tuke the Quaker, the moral treatment movement was set in motion. They were joined by others in Europe and America, including Benjamin Rush, the first American psychiatrist. That they erected models rather than effecting widespread reforms and that they often employed archaic, ill-informed and occasionally inhumane treatment procedures seems forgivable given the magnitude of their contribution to the eventual welfare of the mentally ill. Their example did finally prevail so that the mentally ill were treated as unfortunate human beings rather than subhuman animals fit only to be restrained and beaten. The most humane of modern services do well to emulate what these hospitals and retreats accomplished in their own hospitals and retreats (Bockoven, 1956).

History records that the hope represented by these reformers was soon destroyed. A number of explanations for the demise of the moral treatment model are possible, but there is reason for consternation in the realization that our more recent regression took place in a context of adequate social resources and "scientific" thinking. The inhumane conditions and dismal hopelessness of mental hospitals during the latter half of the nineteenth century and the first half of the twentieth are no less reprehensible than the more blatantly brutal practices of the past.

Certainly the regression was in some way understandable. In one sense, the best of human intentions were thwarted by uncontrollable events. The problem was vaster than the circumscribed vision of the reformers could encompass. The immigration of hordes of foreigners and the institutionalization of hordes of chronic patients was not foreseen. Dorothea Dix's campaign to empty the prisons and poorhouses and house the unfortunates in mental hospitals resulted in conditions she would not have intended. Faced with managing sheer numbers, it was almost inevitable that a vast, authoritarian, rigid, impersonal hospital environment would evolve—one staffed by poorly trained, poorly paid attendants who understood their role as that of preventing mishaps by suppressing behavior.

But more malignant forces were also at work. The social Darwinism of the latter half of the nineteenth century bred little sympathy for the unfortunate. Dr. John P. Gray confirmed the medical community in the notion that insanity was always due to a physical cause, and Dr. Pliney Earle recalculated statistics to demonstrate that insanity was incurable. The forces of science conspired to prove the belief that the insane were a subhuman group that should perhaps be made comfortable and could perhaps be educated to behave like rational human beings (which they were not). The tighfisted economics of state legislators in collusion with hospital administrators contributed to the dismal custodial treatment of recent times (Bockoven, 1956).

In the meantime, efforts were being made to devise physical and psychological treatments to alleviate the suffering of the mentally ill, but it was not until the discovery of major psychotropic medications that new hope was born. Repelled by the degradation present in vast mental hospitals, the Great Society set out to empty these institutions and inaugurate more humane, personal, community-based treatments. Again the magnitude of the problem confounded the reformers' intentions. In the end, misery has not been alleviated, but only transferred to ill-equipped nursing homes, jails, grim hotels, lonely closets and the streets themselves (our modern "jails and poorhouses"). The ideals of "community treatment" have become a matter of empty words rather than practice.

We have resolved our discomfort by medicating the patients and anesthetizing ourselves. By scattering the patients, we have made the problem less visible. Even so, newspapers continue to call to our attention the scandalous examples of our neglect and the now unaided efforts of concerned citizens. Given our public resources, it is evident that we compare unfavorably with most of history in our not-so-benign neglect of the emotionally disturbed. The time is ripe for a modern Dorothea Dix or Clifford Beers to spark our consciousness and mobilize our resources. Whether the psychiatric and psychological communities will provide such leadership remains to be seen. Physicians (and psychologists) have hardly been overrepresented in the ranks of reformers. Reforms have mainly been the products of humanistic and religious impulses, not scientific or professional ones.

The Effectiveness of Treatment

A third history is to be found in the study of the effectiveness of our efforts to treat the mentally ill. In this effort, we are most hampered by the lack of published records. There are no orderly accounts before the nineteenth century and no outcome studies designed in ways that permit meaningful comparisons previous to the last several decades.

Nevertheless we can make some rough estimate of how effective treatments have been in the past. Regardless of the specific efficacy of a given medication or treatment procedure, it does set in motion therapeutic forces. Such "placebo" effects are clearly at work in all physical and psychological interventions and can be called into play by acts of exorcism, moral treatment, faith healing, or medical and psychological procedures. At one time, placebo effects constituted a troublesome artifact that needed to be dismissed in order to demonstrate the efficacy of a given intervention. More recently it has become a matter of study in its own right in the hopes that it may be harnassed as a beneficial force in the treatment of the patient (e.g., Cousins, 1977).

Given a shared set of beliefs and an appropriate social context in which an act perceived as therapeutic takes place, transient or permanent benefits will follow. It goes without saying that every age has had its own set of beliefs and practices consistent with these beliefs. Every age has had its own definition of abnormality, has specified certain persons as healers, and has specified certain places where healing will take place. It follows, then, that healing practitioners in all times and places have been relatively effective in alleviating human misery.

How effective an intervention will be depends on the nature and chronicity of the problem. It also depends on prevailing views concerning the given disorder. Disorders which are considered as hopeless by practitioners are not addressed as aggressively or persistently by the practitioner nor will the sufferers' resources be as effectively mobilized.

Given these observations, we can assume that persons suffering from serious emotional disturbances have enjoyed therapeutic benefits from a variety of shamans, priests, misguided physicians, and enthusiastic humanists whose only tool was the confidence that they could be effective. In point of fact, it is such persons who have provided health care for most people for most of history, and their efforts were not completely ill-informed or without virtue regardless of how outlandish they seem to us (Frank, 1961). In effect, their efforts constitute a kind of baseline against which our present efforts must be measured. This baseline of hope is a fragile asset. Public and professional attitudes such as those during the sixteenth through the eighteenth centuries and during the latter half of the nineteenth and first half of the twentieth centuries were patently countertherapeutic.

Faith healing is clearly not the complete answer to our emotional ills, but it is only within the past two decades or so that we have devised specific medical and psychological interventions that can be shown to "exceed the baseline." As we turn to a review of this literature, however, it is important to underline the point that recent breakthroughs will not represent effectiveness as opposed to ineffectiveness, but improved effectiveness over the misdirected and less focused interventions of the past.

THE EFFECTIVENESS OF TREATMENT

In the final analysis, our judgments about the value of mental hospitals and their alternatives rest on pragmatic grounds; i.e., on how effective they are at achieving certain goals. Insofar as we have learned lessons from the past, we can appreciate that one "mythology" is as good as another so long as blatant cruelty is not propagated. Shamanism, astrology, exorcism, psychotherapy, medications, and behavior modification may all be presumed to be equally viable until one approach proves its superiority in terms of effectiveness. Given our cultural bias, "scientific" approaches hold a favorable position for now, of course, but if current approaches do not demonstrate superior effectiveness, they may be swept aside by changes in the *Zeitgeist* as previous mythologies have been swept aside.

It is proper, then, that we focus on effectiveness of our approaches. Once we accept this focus, however, we discover that the term "effectiveness" introduces as many problems as it solves. Consider a person with a serious emotional problem. Effective treatment will help him or her "get better," but what does "get better" mean? It depends on who is involved in making the judgment. If the person's problem is of only secondary concern to his or her family or the society at large, she or he can contract with a therapist to reach agreed-upon goals, and the attainment of these goals constitutes effective treatment. If the family is implicated, the goals of the various family members may conflict, and "getting better" will probably be a function of changes in more than one person: "effective treatment" will have taken place when certain goals shared by the family system are reached, and such goals may well be in addition to or different from the goals initially proposed by individual family members.

When we speak of the effectiveness of a health care delivery system, we are at another level altogether. There are not two or three, but six, parties to the treatment arrangement (Erickson, 1972), each presenting its own conflicting criteria for effectiveness. The *state* (or third-party carrier) measures effectiveness in terms of reduced direct financial cost, although reduced indirect costs may be considered if such are collected and presented by interested researchers or reformers. The *community* wants protection from the bizarre and destructive behaviors of the patient. The *family* wants a respite from the patient's problems and behaviors and in some cases may hope the system can induce the patient to behave differently. The *patient* wants relief from his or her discomfort and (perhaps) some changes that will enable her or him to handle problems better. The *staff* of the mental hospital wants the patient to behave in a manner which will not disrupt established ward policies and procedures. The *therapist* wants the patient to perceive the world and respond in ways that conform with the therapist's theoretical bias. Obviously, these varying goals are often in conflict. An extreme example of a conflict between family or community goals and patients' goals is represented by involuntary commitment. Conflict between state goals and community goals are represented by shorter hospital stays which increase burdens on the community. Despite the prevalence of such conflicts, there is no place where the conflicting goals of all six parties can be negotiated (as in the case of individual or family therapy). The result is a variety of perceived meanings of the term "treatment effectiveness."

A second issue which complicates the determination of effectiveness is the heterogeneity of patient population. It is obvious that people vary in terms of the types, severity and chronicity of problems they present, yet many hospital studies and community clinics report their findings as if mental patients were a homogeneous group.

Complicating the issue further is the failure to discriminate between success as "cure" and success as effective management. Common notions of effective psychiatric treatment often imply that successful treatment means a "cure" or the resolution of problems that brought the patient into treatment. The patient is expected to emerge from treatment able to function as adequately as other persons in the society. Such expectancies stand in contrast to the notion that successful treatment establishes an effective regimen for managing a problem. To use a medical analogy, we expect a person with pneumonia to be "cured," i.e., to emerge from the hospital to take up life as if the disease process had never happened. On the other hand, in the treatment of chronic diseases such as diabetes, spinal cord injuries, arthritis and renal failure, we recognize that medical success may also be measured in terms of adequate and sometimes costly continuing management of the chronic disease.

It is true that with some emotional problems we may expect a "cure"; that is, we expect the patient will come to the end of treatment and function without difficulty and without follow-up. But with many chronic psychiatric problems, the patient may require continuing and sometimes costly management: outpatient treatment, day care, medications, sheltered workshops, and sheltered living situations. Yet our society seems more willing to underwrite costly medical management programs than to underwrite costly psychiatric management programs. This unwillingness to underwrite psychiatric management programs is probably due to a number of reasons, not the least of which may be our inability to perceive the successful management of chronic care psychiatric patients as achieving "success."

Hospital and Community Stays as Measures of Outcome

For all practical purposes, patient movement statistics currently serve as the leading measures of program success: how quickly is a patient discharged from the hospital; how long does the patient remain in the community? There are several reasons for using this way of measuring success, including comparative ease of data gathering and the current assumption that psychiatric hospitalization is an undesirable but necessary setting of last resort. If a patient is in the community, it is often assumed he or she is functioning more adequately and living under more humane and healthful circumstances than if she or he is in the hospital (cf. Rosenhan, 1973). Before such assumptions are criticized, we need to review outcome from this perspective.

Until quite recently, mental hospitals operated as custodial facilities in which patients resided for years or even for life. With the establishment of active treatment programs several decades ago, it was found that many patients could be expected to return to the community. Once release came to be the expected norm, length of stay in the hospital and tenure in the community became ways of evaluating programs.

A number of measures were devised to assess patient movement in and out of the hospital. The interested reader may gain some appreciation of this ostensibly simple, but in fact complex, methodological problem by reading Gurel (1966a), Ellsworth (1968), and Ullman (1967). Gurel (1966a, 1966b; Note 1) established accepted standards and used them over the course of a decade. His work and that of others (e.g., Ellsworth, Dickman, & Maroney, 1972; Ullman, 1967) documented major reductions in expected hospital stays and highlighted contributing administrative and policy changes. In brief, these advances were related to actions that decreased bureaucratic bottlenecks, decentralized decision making, deemphasized custodial aspects of hospital care and emphasized return to the community as the goal of hospitalization. Smaller units and improved staff-patient ratios related to increased turnover.

Other researchers went further by instituting systematic changes in treatment and assessing their impact. May (1968, 1971b; May & Tuma, 1964b) documented the impact of psychotropic medications. Sanders, Smith, and Weinman (1967), Fairweather, Simon, Gebhart, et al. (1960), and Fairweather (1964) documented the impact of various programmatic changes; Ellsworth (1968) demonstrated improvements resulting from enhancing the role of nonprofessional aides.

Encouraged by the vulnerability of patient movement statistics, other researchers set out to demonstrate the feasibility of employing time-limited programs. The Northwest Washington Hospital-Community Pilot Project (Dieter, Hanford, Hummel, & Lubach, 1965; Gove, 1965; Hanford, 1965) and a VA cooperative study (Caffey, Galbrecht, & Klett, 1971) succeeded in limiting hospital stays to three weeks when community follow-up was included. Others (Burhan, 1969; Decker & Stubblebine, 1972; Rhine & Mayerson, 1971; Weisman, Feirstein, & Thomas, 1969) reduced hospital stays to a few days. Pasamanick, Scarpetti, and Dinitz (1967) replaced hospitalization with a program of home care. A number of studies (Chasin, 1967; Erickson, 1976; Guy, Gross, Hogarty, & Dennis, 1969; Herz, Endicott, Spitzer, & Mesnikoff, 1971; Ruiz and Saiger, 1972; Wilder, Levin, & Zwerling, 1966) have established day hospitals as a viable alternative to 24-hour hospitalization for many patients.

The past two decades have seen repeated demonstrations of the fact that hospitalization can be reduced or avoided for many patients. In principle this achievement is gratifying and perhaps not so surprising given the place from which we have advanced—the huge, unwieldy, bureaucratic, understaffed, impersonal institution. Much of what has been accomplished is the result of correcting incredible inefficiencies in a neglected health care delivery system, and research has merely documented the value of instituting obviously needed reforms. Rapid changes in public policies and attitudes have in turn assisted in establishing new expectancies for the treatment of serious psychiatric problems.

In practice, however, a number of questions arise about the validity of continuing to measure success in terms of length of stay (Erickson & Paige, 1973). Once continued hospitalization is recognized to be more a function of administrative policy than of measured improvement in patient symptomatology and/or psychosocial functioning, it becomes apparent that improved "efficiency" can reflect refusal to treat certain presenting problems as readily as improved ability to treat these same problems. For example, continuing tenure in the hospital may depend solely on the presence of socially disruptive or life-threatening behaviors, while the treatment of other acute and serious emotional problems is delegated to "the community." In terms of the conflicting goals cited earlier, patient movement statistics represent the victory of the state's goals over the goals of all other parties.

Admission to and discharge from a hospital has never been a function simply of the level of pathology presented by the patient (Erickson, 1975). Many factors contribute to these decisions, including ward atmosphere, bed availability, treatment team philosophy and availability of community placements. The most systematic recent factor, however, has been to raise the criteria for hospitalization so that only the most severely disturbed patients will be kept in the hospital. This simple maneuver at one and the same time improves patient movement statistics and keeps more severely disturbed patients in the community (Blackburn, 1972; Caffey et al., 1971). The net effect of recent changes, then, has not been improved hospital treatment, but the shifting of costs in human and financial terms to the community (May, 1971a). By way of illustration, Paul and Lentz's (1977) interventions with chronic patients dealt only with the most severely disturbed and intractible patients following an untimely administrative decision which discharged most of their originally targeted population to the community. It was clearly an administrative decision, not a statement that these patients had somehow suddenly improved to the point where they had no need of the treatment offered.

Even though policies have changed so that patients are not retained over a period of years, the problem of adequate care has not been solved. Long tenures have been replaced by intermittent hospitalization as a mental hospital "career" (Friedman, von Mering, & Hinko, 1966). A number of studies show that shorter stays have been accompanied by greater numbers of readmissions (Altman, Sletten, & Nebel, 1973; Brill & Patton, 1959; Freyhan, 1958; Moon & Patton, 1965). The rate of recidivism among admissions varies from 40 percent or 50 percent (Anthony, Buell, Sharrett, & Altholff, 1972; Friedman, Lundstedt, von Mering, & Hinko, 1964) to as high as 87 percent (Rajotte & Denber, 1961).

In short, patient movement statistics have become useless or even misleading, taken by themselves. Narrowly defined cost accounting and administrative statistics coupled with uncritical assumptions and fallacious reasoning lead to the erroneous conclusion that adequate and humanitarian treatment is being given more quickly and at a lower cost (Arnhoff, 1975; Erickson & Paige, 1973). There is much evidence that this is not the case (Arnhoff, 1975), and it is clearly time to address the complex questions that were glossed over during our recent reforms. The rest of this section is, in effect, a discussion of these neglected issues expressable by the questions, "What is the probable time needed to reach the defined treatment goals as measured by assessment procedure X with patients diagnosed Y using treatment program Z?" (Erickson & Paige, 1973, p. 561) and, "What approach is most successful with which patients using whose criteria?" (Erickson, 1972, p. 77). Sorting out the issues and obtaining the data to answer these questions is no simple task.

Briefly examining the issues within the confines of patient movement statistics, it should be noted that data gathered in various studies suggest longer hospital stays may be beneficial for some patients. Researchers are far from being able to designate "optimal treatment periods" (Erickson & Paige, 1973) at this time, but it seems clear that we ought to recognize and proceed to do the research needed to enlighten our ignorance rather than to establish specific lengths-of-stay norms prematurely and arbitrarily in response to legislative and administrative pressures (e.g., Weiner & Levine, 1975). Arbitrary numbers, especially those proposed by medical staff, run the danger of being inflexibly interpreted by administrators and third-party carriers.

Some writers have suggested that longer stays are more beneficial than shorter stays with some patients (Chasin, 1967; Erickson, 1976; Erickson, Backus, Paige, & Johnson, 1972; Guy, Gross, Hogarty, & Dennis, 1969; Singer & Grob, 1975). However, such studies were not controlled and merely suggested the need for further attention to this matter. More recently, several major studies have controlled for length of stay by randomly assigning patients to shorter or longer stay groups. Mattes and his colleagues (Mattes, Rosen, & Klein, 1977; Mattes, Rosen, Klein, & Millan, 1977) followed up on 173 mixed-diagnosis patients to find a greater incidence of rehospitalization among long-stay and greater use of antidepressants among short-stay groups, but less pathology among long-stay patients, relating perhaps to greater use of follow-up psychotherapy. Herz and his colleagues (Herz, Endicott, & Spitzer, 1975; Reibel & Herz, 1976; Herz, Endicott, & Spitzer, 1976) compared 175 newly admitted inpatients who had been randomly assigned to one of three groups: standard inpatient, brief hospitalization of less than one week with transitional day care available, and brief hospitalization without day care. They found no difference between the groups at 3 and 12 weeks and found no difference in readmission rates. They did note that briefly hospitalized patients were able to return to work sooner. They recorded no differences in terms of deleterious effects on the families. At the same time, they recorded that 9 of the 112 brief-stay patients were considered "study failures" in part because of these patients' degree of impairment and the incapacity of the family and community to deal with them.

In a more ambitious project, Glick and his colleagues (Glick, Hargreaves, & Goldfield, 1974; Glick, Hargreaves, Raskin, & Kutner, 1975; Glick, Hargreaves, Drues & Showstack, 1976a; Glick, Hargreaves, Drues & Showstack, 1976b; Hargreaves, Glick, Drues, Showstack & Feigerbaum, 1977) discriminated between schizophrenic and nonschizophrenic patients, assigning the two groups to short-term and long-term treatment. The results were complex, but tended to support more extended hospitalizations for schizophrenic patients and did not tend to support more extended hospitalizations for nonschizophrenic patients.

These controlled studies reveal the kind of research questions that must be addressed before questions about the relative cost effectiveness of various treatment programs can be meaningfully answered. At the same time, the successful completion of such extraordinarily difficult projects highlights the difficulty of the task ahead. The several research projects differed widely in their definitions of short term and long term. The Mattes short-term groups stayed about as long as Glick et al. long-term group and significantly longer than the Herz et al. long-term group. In one way or another, they all demonstrated an inability to control effectively or comment upon other important variables. They do suggest, however, that the day is past when we can evaluate length-of-stay questions based on assumptions that all psychiatric patients are essentially the same, that all treatment programs are essentially the same or that there will be no interactions between types of patients and types of treatment interventions. It is becoming more apparent than ever that the type and duration of treatment must be tailored more systematically to the kinds of problems the patient presents. We are better prepared for this task than in the past because we now possess better conceptualizations and a healthier respect for the magnitude of the enterprise.

Inpatient Measures of Outcome

Once we realize we cannot reduce the question of program effectiveness to patient movement statistics, we are faced with the problem of how best to measure the value of hospitalization. As we have noticed previously, the hospital serves a complex social function, responding in various ways to the needs of six interested parties. At this point, we need to briefly highlight the observation that the mental hospital serves to provide protection as well as treatment (Ullman, 1967). Part of the hospital's value to the patient and to society is measured in its ability to serve as a humane sanctuary or asylum. Abuses of the past and of recent times (Rosenhan, 1973) should lead us to reform asylums or set up more adequate alternatives, not to abandon the notion that we must meet this need as a society.

Important as protection is, it is also obvious that the mental hospital must provide effective treatment; that is, it must record inhospital improvements in terms of symptomatology and/or psychosocial functioning. Success in this area is more often assumed than proven; i.e., in some vague and global way, the responsible clinician determines the patient is improved and ready to be discharged. His decision may indeed be correct, but his way of arriving at it is not very helpful since we do not know (nor does he) in operational terms what he is basing his decision on. Given that a variety of administrative, social and environmental factors impact his decision-making process (Erickson, 1975; Weinstein, 1964) and that professionals themselves differ regarding criteria for discharge (Katz & Woolley, 1975), we cannot assume after the fact that any one clinician is consistent over time or that one clinician or one hospital is making discharge decisions comparable to others.

The state of affairs points to a need to standardize our criteria and to develop assessment devices that can be used on a wide scale. A variety of assessment devices are available, but unfortunately none dominates the field. Correlations between these various outcome measures are lacking so that one must make a number of assumptions in comparing various reports.

It is not surprising that some of the hospital- and community-stay studies we have cited did not report inhospital improvement data. They did not see the hospital as a place to address symptom reduction or improvement in psychosocial functioning but as a place for reducing socially disruptive behaviors. On the other hand, some studies that did record inhospital improvements noted less symptomatology and/or better psychosocial functioning among longer-stay groups at discharge (Caffey et al., 1971; Erickson, 1976; Glick et al., 1975; Konick, Friedman, Paolino, & Graham, 1972). The various pharmacological and psychosocial innovations researched by May, Saunders, Fairweather, and Ellsworth also resulted in documented inhospital improvements. A seemingly endless stream of isolated reports (see Erickson, 1975) citing the value of innovations such as psychodrama, television feedback, lectures, modeling and role playing, human relations training, and even brief, friendly, casual conversations between staff and patients, tempts one to conclude that practically any reasonable innovation will result in patient improvement. The most parsimonious explanation for many of the findings would suggest that improvements are the result of unspecified factors common to all of the studies, such as the establishment of increased orderliness, explicitness and simplicity in the programs in question; physical changes of the patients' environment, increased staff attention, more positive expectancies on the part of the patients and staff; or the infusion of energy and enthusiasm into a moribund setting.

Despite their being unspecified in the research, such nonspecific factors are more than a nuisance: they represent powerful therapeutic forces that need to be understood and exploited. Until such confounding factors are controlled, clinicians may properly conclude that their hospital ought to implement a particular innovation or they may as well conclude that their hospital ought to implement a policy of continual change and innovation (Erickson, 1975).

In contrast to the episodic attention given to many innovations, two approaches have received sustained attention: "milieu" and "token economy" programs. The milieu or "therapeutic community" approach was formulated and introduced by Maxwell Jones (1953) over two decades ago. It rested on the notion that a patient is capable of taking responsibility for the functioning of the hospital unit and for understanding his or her own behavior. Milieu programs are presumably characterized by increased group activities and social interaction, expectancies and group pressure aimed at encouraging more goal-directed communication and normal functioning. The concept caught the imagination of clinicians, but their enthusiastic appropriation of the term has probably done more harm than good. The term came to refer to a variety of programs because the approach was never clearly delineated. As it became professionally desirable to have a "therapeutic milieu," the term was attached to existing hospital programs accompanied by few or no significant changes. In addition to this baleful effect, the paradoxical expectancies that are often set up as staff overtly subscribe to one treatment philosophy and covertly function on the basis of another result in confusion at best and antitherapeutic forces at worst (Sacks & Carpenter, 1974). For all its faults, the functioning of the traditional authoritarian ward was at least clear and predictable. It is little wonder that studies of the effectiveness of therapeutic communities have resulted in mixed findings (Erickson, 1975; Paul & Lentz, 1977).

Research with token economies has proceeded in a more or less orderly fashion over the last decade (see Davison, 1969; Carlson, Hersen & Eisler, 1972; Milby, 1975; Paul & Lentz, 1977, for reviews). Token economies apply principles of learning using a Skinnerian model to complete ward programs. This approach differs from milieu therapy in that it implements more systematic control over the physical and social environment and places greater emphasis on response-contingent consequences as vehicles of change rather than generalized group pressure and encouragement. A number of successful token economy programs have been reported in the literature, for the most part involving chronic patients. That behavior modification techniques can be effective in improving inhospital adjustment and ward management is scarcely open to question. However, there has been a paucity of controlled studies in this area, leaving unanswered questions regarding the role of nonspecific factors in such interventions. How effectively adaptive behaviors learned in the hospital can be generalized to the community where natural contingencies operate is open to question (Atthowe, 1973), although the finding that such behaviors may not persist would not be out of keeping with the basic presuppositions of the behavioral approach. Some behaviorists, after all, do tend to look to the environment rather than to the person for explanations and prescribe social engineering as the solution to societal and personal ills.

A reading of the token economy literature suggests it is also not without problems. As it became professionally desirable to set up "token economy" or "behavior modification" programs, a deleterious bandwagon result ensued. Less well-trained persons have implemented more poorly constructed, piecemeal, confusing and even dehumanizing programs, and the label has been attached willy-nilly to existing programs with few changes. Ethical issues arose as it became apparent that patients' interest in proferred rewards varied widely so that effective reinforcement sometimes involved introducing stringent deprivation conditions (Baker, Hall, & Hutchinson, 1974; Mumford, Patch, Andrews, & Wyner, 1975; Paul & Lentz, 1977). The reader is referred to Paul and Lentz (1977, Chapter 43) for a lengthy and informative discussion of the ethical and legal issues involved in implementing behavioral programs.

That token economy programs may be presumptuous in their conceptualization and proceed without regard to patients' wishes and perceptions is obvious (Biklen, 1976). Notably absent in the token economy literature are assessments of patient satisfaction and self-reports of improvement. Token economies, then, may well serve to exacerbate a common problem of institutional life: that of impersonal staff control. Whether many of the goals of behavior modification actually serve the purposes of institutional management or of enhancing the patients' existence and preparing them for independent living in the community is an important ethical issue. Certainly most of the programs stress changes in the simplest activities of daily living and do not address the broader decision-making, coping or cognitive strategies that are employed by persons who live independently in the community. There is evidence that combining a token economy and a milieu approach may result in better generalization into the community (Greenberg, Scott, Pisa, & Friesen, 1975). Such an approach also enhances active patient participation and control in the program. For good scientific as well as good philosophical and ethical reasons, behavioral programs should not be constructed on the assumption that patients are ciphers passively manipulated by environmental contingencies (Bandura, 1974; Erickson, 1977).

No report of inhospital treatment would be complete without reference to Paul & Lentz's (1977) monumental control study taking a token economy (social learning) approach featuring procedures drawn from basic research on learning and using tokens (plastic chips to be used to purchase commodities and privileges) as the major vehicle for reinforcing desired behaviors and comparing it with a milieu approach featuring resident involvement, communicated expectancies and group pressure. This landmark study is pivotal for a number of reasons. It is the first study to address the problem of working with the most severely debilitated chronic patients. It sets new standards of excellence for elegance and thoroughness of research design, including controlling hitherto uncontrolled but important nonspecific variables. It candidly reports all of the difficulties that occurred (which were legion) and shares the compromises that were necessary. It makes all of its procedures completely explicit to the point of publishing detailed operations manuals and schedules for both approaches under consideration. It collects data to answer every question of interest except that of patient perceptions and does this over a period of years, enabling the reader to scrutinize what was happening throughout the program. It documents significant increases in dangerous and aggressive acts as well as a decline in the effectiveness of both treatment programs following implementation of a well-intentioned but arbitrary statewide policy directive limiting the use of "time-out" (physical removal of patient to seclusion), thus adding to existing data suggesting that abstract decisions presumably protecting patient rights can in effect lead to significant losses in terms of patient welfare and the attainment of treatment goals.

The findings of this study are too voluminous to report in this chapter. In summary, the project clearly demonstrated that the token economy (social learning) approach was more effective than the milieu approach and traditional hospital treatment over all classes of functioning in the intramural setting and in terms of institutional release with hard-core, severely debilitated patients. Every resident whose physical condition allowed him to participate in the social learning program responded significantly and attained a significant release (i.e., remaining in the community for a minimum of 90 consecutive days) from the institution. This is not to say that all could be released to function independently. The vast majority of the patients still functioned at a marginal level and required community placement in protective environments. Nor is it to say that a social learning approach is necessarily the treatment of choice with less debilitated or revolving-door patients. Paul and Lentz make it clear that the relative efficacy of the token economy and milieu approaches with such patients is a matter for future research.

In concluding this section, we would report the repeated and disheartening finding that measured improvement in the hospital is not correlated with posthospital adjustment (Erickson, 1975), although Paul and Lentz's findings provide a notable exception. Follow-up studies are needed to assess which programs serve to restore or improve patients' psychosocial functioning in the community following discharge.

Follow-up Measures of Outcome

Follow-up studies presume to answer two questions: the first is concerned with whether a patient maintains or builds on the gains made in the hospital; the second, with comparing the patient's psychosocial functioning in the community with that of others. Obvious methodological and practical problems are involved in attempting to answer these questions.

The many follow-up reports do not paint a very bright picture

(Erickson, 1975). They often suggest that community adjustment is improved over prehospital adjustment in many areas and that gains in the hospital tend to be maintained. At the same time, they note losses of functioning, especially in employment, and reflect the fact that only a minority of discharged patients show as good as level of psychosocial functioning as the average person in the community. The literature suggests that hospitalization serves to restore premorbid functioning, which was often marginal, especially in the case of the chronic patient.

Those researchers who attempt to shorten hospitalization more often than not rest their case on the observation that their patients do no worse on follow-up than patients from long-stay programs, implying a kind of "we can do as badly as you for less" rationale. As we have noted, several studies have appeared suggesting that longer hospital stays may have certain long-range benefits for certain patients (Erickson, 1976; Glick et al., 1976a, 1976b; Singer & Grob, 1975), although the pertinent patient and program variables and their interactions have not been worked out.

Continuity of aftercare is a key variable in follow-up. Studies document the importance of adequate follow-up, especially if hospitalization was shorter (Erickson, 1975). It is also possible that the better showing of longer-stay programs may rest in part on greater utilization of aftercare on the part of long-stay patients (Glick et al., 1976a, 1976b).

A need for continuity of care in the case of the chronic patient has led to the increased use of a variety of sheltered living situations such as half-way houses, nursing homes, boarding houses and foster homes (Erickson, 1975; Redlich & Kellert, 1978). Ellsworth (1968) reported that 46 percent of his chronically hospitalized sample were to be found in sheltered living situations and subsequently Ellsworth et al. (1972) noted a high correlation ($r = .61$) between hospital "productivity" and the rate of special placements.

We previously noted that hospitalization historically served two functions: protection and treatment. We also noted that the emptying of hospitals has been as much or more a function of administrative actions as improvements in an ability to successfully treat patients, and further that these policy decisions have been based in large part on the assumption that the patient "in the community" is functioning more adequately, is living under more humane and healthful circumstances and is receiving more adequate treatment than if he or she were "institutionalized" in a hospital. Since many chronic patients are placed in sheltered living situations such as half-way houses, the measure to which these assumptions are realized becomes an important issue.

Some community-placement programs do reflect considered judgment and careful planning (e.g., Fairweather, Sanders, Maynard & Cressler, 1969; Atthowe, 1973; Shean, 1973). Too often, however, they represent provision for mere custodial maintenance of a patient in settings devoid of trained personnel and lacking even the pretext of a treatment program. Such living situations lack protective rationales that would even qualify them for the term "asylum" and are all the more malignant in that they hide the social problem by dispersing it. Adjustment regression occurs frequently in such settings (Ellsworth, 1968). Paul and Lentz (1977) noted that, after community placement, one-fifth of their residents declined in functioning to levels lower than those they had been at in the beginning of the project; however, the community which had once rejected these patients for such behaviors now continued to keep them, reflecting lowered community standards.

This incredible record of neglect and waste may come to a halt soon, but for the time being the high-sounding rhetoric which accompanies the movement of patients out of the hospital and into the community blinds policy makers to many grim realities. Public unrest is beginning to be reflected in the news media, but one must sadly speculate that our current inertia may not be overcome until some dramatic public tragedy or scandal occurs or some charismatic leader galvanizes public opinion to force policy changes. If and when changes do take place, it is hoped that they will not be in the direction of even more oppressive and dehumanizing policies. In any case, community placement programs now deserve the same systematic critical scrutiny as hospitals have been subject to in the past.

Conclusions

Fortunately the past several decades have left us with better tools. We now understand the need for a range of services and settings within the total mental-health-care delivery system. It has not been the conceptualization, but the implementation, of the community mental health movement mandate that has brought about the present state of affairs. In effect, we were willing to implement that part of the mandate which called for emptying large hospitals, but were not willing to underwrite that part which insisted that an adequate range of services be set up to prevent and treat serious emotional problems in the community. We implemented the easy and money-saving parts of the reform (that which administrative fiat could accomplish) but implemented the more difficult and expensive portions of the reform in a half-hearted and makeshift manner. The result is that in some ways we are worse off than before.

Nevertheless we still possess imaginative and well-formulated ideas about what could be done. In addition, we are well endowed with a wide range of psychotropic medications. That such medications are at once effective and subject to abuse and not without dangers (Bockoven

& Solomon, 1975; Gardos & Cole, 1976; Hogarty et al., 1973, 1974) is hardly open to question. Still, the judicious use of such pharmaceutical agents in the context of well-thought-out treatment programs enhances our ability to treat psychiatric illnesses.

Recent developments add to the conviction that we are on the right track in developing social learning approaches for use in the treatment of many psychiatric problems. Their potential effectiveness seems obvious given the fact that many patients, particularly chronic ones, function less adequately than others in the community. Whether their lack of needed skills is the result of never having learned skills or of disuse is not terribly important. What is important is that appropriate training and reinforcement can result in these persons learning and/or performing needed skills. Persons undergoing behavioral training have been shown to be functioning better at the time of follow-up (e.g., Ellsworth, 1968; Hanson, Rothaus, O'Connell, & Wiggens, 1970; Jacobs & Trick, 1974; Johnson, Hanson, Rothaus, Morton, Lyle, & Moyer, 1965; Sanders et al., 1962, 1967). What is even more exciting is the repeated observation that such approaches are particularly beneficial with chronic patients (Sanders et al., 1962, 1967; Ellsworth, 1968; Hogarty et al., 1973, 1974; Paul & Lentz, 1977) to the extent of overturning traditional prognostications.

Behavioral technology is at once effective, subject to abuse, and not without certain dangers. Here again, however, the judicious use of such techniques in the context of well-thought-out treatment programs enhances our ability to treat psychiatric problems. That we have only begun to understand and exploit the promise of behavioral programs is obvious from the literature. Paul and Lentz (1977) note that patients in their program were continuing to show improvement at the time the project came to an end, suggesting the limits of their approach had not been reached. They also acknowledged that limits in terms of resources prevented them from employing a variety of other already tested behavioral techniques to address specific patient problems.

The range of possible interventions that can be incorporated in sophisticated behavioral approaches is constantly expanding. "Behavior modification" or "social learning" has come a long way from the pioneer work of Lindsley and Skinner (1954) over two decades ago. We are no longer restricted to reinforcing simple skills. With Bandura's research on modeling and observational learning, our conception of psychological man has changed and we are able systematically to prepare training packages which address more complex interpersonal skills. Limits on such training seem to be a function of the ingenuity of psychologists: how acutely they can observe human interactions and how well they can capture complex social skills in paradigmatic packages to be observed, role played and systematically reinforced.

More directive therapies are now quite acceptable. So-called cognitive approaches and social learning approaches (e.g., Bandura, 1977) incorporate some of the virtues of earlier behaviorisms while avoiding some of their pitfalls and excesses. Our psychological knowledge and ethics are less at odds as we take less mechanistic views of human behavior and recognize that interpersonal influence is a reciprocal process (Bandura, 1974; Erickson, 1977).

This lengthy accolade to social learning is not meant to reflect unfavorably on other treatment approaches; it is intended to underline the understanding that with social learning approaches we enjoy a clarity and explicitness of procedure lacking in other approaches. Such clarity enables us to move in a more orderly and self-correcting manner as we address serious psychiatric problems. No doubt social learning approaches will not provide all the final answers, but they do allow us to determine more quickly and clearly when we are moving in the right direction than other types of treatment.

Finally, we are now better equipped to address the issues of treatment effectiveness than ever before because we have formulated a wider range of research methodologies and better ways of asking questions. We appreciate that the question of outcome is not a simple question which can be answered in a global way (Erickson, 1975). It is almost certainly the case that large-scale experiments employing traditional research designs are not the final answer to our problems. The high standards achieved by Paul and Lentz's landmark study are astonishing; at the same time, as the story unfolds it is not at all certain that some unpredicted event will not bring a premature end to that enterprise. Traditional designs are too expensive, inflexible and unwieldy, their completion or termination too subject to luck, to be the final answer to our evaluation probles. What will serve to obtain needed ansers in the context of uncontrollable nonlaboratory environments is not evident, but knowing we do not know is progress of sorts.

We are better equipped now than before to address issues of treatment effectiveness. We better understand the variables which must be taken into account and know the question of outcome to be a complex one. We know better the virtues and weaknesses of various research methodologies and assessment procedures. We more clearly understand what we don't know, and that is a step forward.

CURRENT ATTITUDES AND POLICIES

The mental health profession has shaped and been shaped by the social, economic, religious and philosophical temper of our times. We have seen the pendulum of history swing back and forth in the conceptualization of the role of human services, including the care of the mentally ill in our society, many times. There have been periods of reform, innovation and optimism followed by times of criticism, disillusionment and reentrenchment. Klerman (1974) observes that reforms in human services and mental health have coincided with periods of progressive social change in American society, whereas reactions, criticisms and reentrenchment have occurred with the aftermath of war or economic decline. And so it appears presently. Events in the field of mental health in the past two decades have been strongly influenced by developments in the field of medicine, law, government, finances, insurance, criminal justice, health planning and health care in general (Smith, Jones, & Coye, 1977).

The most recent reform movement began in the 1950s with the first major federal legislation dealing with mental health since the establishment of NIMH. This was followed by a host of social welfare and health care legislation which coincided with the aftermath of World War II and new developments in the social, economic and medical fields. The introduction of antipsychotic drugs in the fifties signalled a major breakthrough in the management in community settings of mentally ill persons who had previously required institutionalization. This was combined with state legislatures' desire to reduce the financial burden of the state mental hospitals. These and other events led to the establishment in 1955 of the Joint Commission on Mental Illness and Health. Its members were charged with the task on evaluating services for the mentally ill and proposing a national mental health program. The next major step in the progression was the enactment of the Mental Retardation Facilities and Community Mental Health Centers (CMHC) Construction Act of 1963. This act provided that five essential services be developed in community-based centers: inpatient care, outpatient care, emergency treatment, partial hospitalization, and consultation and education. These developments and others culminated to change both the philosophy of treating the mentally ill and the delivery of services to them. One of the major results has been to reduce the population of mental hospitals from 559,000 in 1955 to 193,000 in 1975 (Bassuk & Gerson, 1978), thereby releasing many mentally ill persons in the community for care.

The interim period between the passage of the CMHC Act in 1963 and the present has seen numerous changes in the mental health field, many of which are related to the social, political, economic and philosophical "temper of our times." Though it would be impossible to review comprehensively all the various aspects of the different movements impacting on the mental health field in the past two decades within this chapter, we will provide an overview of some of the movements which contributed to changing the face of mental health services in our society.

Civil Rights Movement

The civil rights movement of the 1950s and 1960s raised many questions about all spheres of American life, including treatment of the mentally ill. Several important issues found their way into the courts for consideration, and many more await a hearing. The issues we will focus on include the basic right to treatment and those changes involving the right of society to impose involuntary treatment on an individual.

The right to treatment is a complicated issue, with a history dating back to the 1600 Poor Laws of England. Wilensky and Lebeaux (1969) provide a historical framework for looking at this issue. They proposed two major conceptions of the social welfare institution in our society today, and term them "residual" and "institutional." Residual assistance is based on need. Such service comes into play when there is an emergency situation or when the normal channels are unable to adequately meet the needs of people. Institutional assistance is based on right, and not only serves the necessary function of meeting emergency needs in times of crisis, but also functions as a normal service to assist people in achieving their potential and self-actualization. Wilensky and Lebeaux further suggest that together these two conceptions of assistance or services represent a compromise between values of economic individualism and free enterprise versus values of security, equality and humanitarianism. However, these two differing conceptions of assistance or services appear to be more representative of a core value conflict than of a compromise (Greenblatt, 1974).

Until the 1960s the courts generally refrained from involving themselves in decisions about the treatment management of therapeutic programs, reasoning that such involvement required special expertise, which they did not have (Schwartz, 1974). This attitude appears to be changing as evidenced by legal cases focusing on the rights and treatment of the mentally ill, particularly those who are involuntarily committed and who do not have the protection of the criminal due process of the law.

The first major legal decision in recent years to focus on the right to treatment was Rouse vs. Cameron (See Budd & Baer, 1976) in 1966. The case involved a man who was confined at St. Elizabeth's Hospital after having been found not guilty by reason of insanity, and who claimed that he was receiving no treatment. The court's decision was that the purpose of hospitalization was treatment, not punishment, and that therefore, since the man had been confined longer than he would have if he had only been held criminally responsible and jailed, he had been confined without due process of the law. This case represented one of the first steps in opening the door to examinine the treatment of the mentally ill as a right versus a privilege.

The next significant case was Wyatt vs. Stickney (see Budd & Baer, 1976; Paul & Lentz, 1977), a class-action suit filed in 1970 for all institutionalized persons in the state of Alabama. The major issue in Wyatt vs. Stickney centered around confinement without treatment of an involuntarily civilly committed individual. The court found care and treatment in the state mental institutions inadequate and proceeded to outline three fundamental conditions of adequate and effective treatment in such institutions. These included: 1) a humane psychological and physical environment; 2) enough qualified staff to administer adequate treatment; and 3) individualized treatment plans. The decision further noted that a lack of funds would be an insufficient reason for noncompliance in meeting the prescribed standards for care and treatment.

The decision in the Wyatt vs. Stickney case represents a historical landmark of considerable significance in the treatment of the mentally ill in our society today. First of all, it was the first court decision to hold that mental patients committed involuntarily have a constitutional right to treatment (Leaf, 1977). Secondly, it marks a significant change in precedent with regard to the traditional "hands off" policy of the courts toward involvement in the treatment management of therapeutic programs in public mental institutions.

The entrance of the judicial system into the realm of therapeutic treatment programs promises to present a variety of dilemmas for mental health professionals and the treatment of their patients. An example can be seen in the interface of certain treatment modalities (e.g., behavior modification and social learning approaches) and the issue of the civil rights of the patients.

There appears to be little question that behavior modification techniques and social learning approaches are effective treatment for severely debilitated, chronic, mentally ill patients, many of whom are involuntarily committed (Budd & Baer, 1976; Paul & Lentz, 1977, among others). However, with recent court decisions and legal interpretations, certain social learning approaches and behavior modification techniques may become prohibited, limited or delayed so as to prevent the most effective treatment from being provided (Budd & Baer, 1976; Paul & Lentz, 1977). Among the standards set down in the Wyatt decision, there are several areas that related to behavior modification. Budd and Baer (1976) note three such provisions: 1) prohibition of the use of contingent privileges for resident labor that involves the maintenance of the institution; 2) the need to provide unrestricted access to several ward privileges that have been used as contingent in some behavior modification programs; and 3) a considerable limitation of the use of aversive techniques. Wexler (cited in Paul & Lentz, 1977, p. 457) summarizes the essence of the dilemma by noting that the items and activities that are being defined as absolute rights are the very same items and activities that the behavioral psychologists want to employ as reinforcers.

A second issue raised by the civil rights movement of the sixties focused on whether the state or society has the right to commit an individual to treatment against his or her will, and under what conditions. Historically and officially since the enactment of the original statutes in the 1840s and 1850s, the legal authority has always rested with the courts. Practically speaking, however, the unofficial authority rested with the physicians and hospital directors, and in most parts of the United States involuntary commitment was a ritualized affair. Many states, in the past, required only the signature of the physician to initiate a medical commitment. This was seen as being a modern and humane treatment as it did not require that the patient be subjected to the embarrassment and stigma of a public court hearing and was initially adopted in reaction to the former "less human" judicial commitment procedure (Steingarten, 1977). In the name of civil and human rights, we have seen the relinquishment of the medical commitment in favor of a judicial proceeding. Nearly one-half of the 50 states now have due process standards. Many states have adopted involuntary commitment laws which define specific criteria and set down legal procedure to be followed before an individual can be confined or hospitalized against his or her will. The unavoidable conclusion is that the rights of individuals in civil commitment hearings are being strengthened by the courts and state legislatures (Meisel, 1975).

The civil rights movement has had considerable impact on the treatment of the mentally ill patient. Though it has advanced the cause of civil and human rights significantly, the movement has ironically seemed to operate at cross purposes with itself. It appears that in the rush to give the mentally ill their freedom, issues of effective treatment regimes and adequate protection and safety have at times been set aside (Chodoff, 1976).

Consumerism

A second major social movement of the past decade to exert influence on the mental health field has been the consumer revolution. The initial impact of "consumerism" was on business and industry, then on the environment and finally on the professional world (Coye, 1977; Redlich & Mollica, 1976). Consumers began to insist that health be viewed as a "right" rather than a "privilege." Additionally they asked for accountability. "What kind of treatment is best for what kind of problem?" "How does it work?" "What are the risks and what are the potential outcomes?" State and federal governments are beginning to respond to this demand for accountability, but it is unclear as to what is the best method to insure individual and human rights as well as adequate care and treatment: litigation, legislation, advocacy or administrative means (Coye, 1977).

Economics

The third area to have impact on the mental health field is economics. Though the courts have mandated adequate care and treatment for those who are involuntarily committed, and consumers are demanding the right to treatment, neither Congress nor state legislatures have responded by increasing their budget expenditures accordingly. To date, the legal history of the right to treatment has been one of judicial action (Stone, 1975).

One response to the need for increased funding of mental health services has been third-party (e.g., Medicare, Medicaid, insurance companies, etc.) reimbursement for services. This has been viewed as a mixed blessing by some (Epstein, 1977) in the mental health field, as third-party payment often requires adherence to a separate set of regulations, requirements and restrictions in order for the service deliverer to qualify for payment. One of the potential risks to the profession of psychotherapy might be enforced standardization and decreased chances for developing new more innovative techniques to cope with human problems (Epstein, 1977).

Antiprofessionalism

The fourth movement to influence mental health service delivery has been "antiprofessionalism." The past two decades have seen many of the cherished values, attitudes and principles of the times challenged. One of these challenges centered on "authority," with the general trend of industrialized society to decrease it (Redlich and Mollica, 1976). The professional as an authority did not escape this challenge. As a result, we began to see a movement toward antiprofessionalism. At the same time that the authority of the mental health professional was being challenged, state hospitals were discharging large numbers of institutionalized individuals into communities ill-prepared to receive them and to respond to their various and multiple needs and demands for care (Greenblatt, 1965). There were not enough professional mental health workers to meet the demand for services, and many who were available were not particularly interested in treating the long-term previously institutionalized state hospital patients (Redlich & Kellert, 1978).

The cumulative result of the converging factors was 1) an increase in allied mental health professionals (e.g., psychologists, social workers, psychiatric nurses, etc.) (Redlich and Kellert, 1978); 2) the emergence of a new category of care providers—the paraprofessional; and 3) an increased rise in voluntarism in the mental health field. The entrance of the varying disciplines into the mental health field necessitated redefining the philosophy of treatment as exemplified by the blurring of professional roles and the introduction of the "team concept" in caring for the mentally ill.

Conclusion

Through our brief historical review of some of the various social, political and economic movements which have had their impact on the mental health field, some of the social value conflicts and contradictions in today's mental health system become more apparent. The civil rights movement and the emergence of the allied mental health professions can be equated with the values of security, equality and humanitarianism, while the present conservative economic climate is more representative of free enterprise and individualism. The consumerism movement appears to be a compromise of the two value systems, with its demand for the right to treatment, but at a fair and equitable price. Ironically but not unpredictably in view of our history, the mandate for the right to treatment is coming at a time when the political and economic climate appears to be swinging toward conservatism.

Several authors (Ochberg, 1976; Somers, 1977) have noted that it appears that we are at the end of an era which was characterized by increased emphasis on national productivity, industrial growth, technical mastery, and what seemed to be unlimited resources, and entering an era characterized by more limited resources and aspirations. The future design of mental health services will undoubtedly be shaped by the present as the conflicting and often contradictory value systems we have discussed are given priority and a new social contract is renegotiated, in part through the courts, with the mental health field.

In conclusion, the alert reader has no doubt sensed a contrast between the optimism reflected in the conclusions of the second section with regard to the development of more effective treatment approaches and the less sanguine conclusions reached here. The contrast is intentional: by highlighting it we have come full circle by recognizing (as we noted at the beginning of this chapter) that larger issues of public and professional attitudes and policies have more to do with what happens to patients than any of our specific and controllable interventions. If effective treatment approaches are to be implemented, we must justify their cost and use in the public arena. This is as it should be. Nevertheless it makes hoped-for progress more complicated and less certain. Energy will not only have to be expended in improving our treatments, but also in better educating the public about what we are doing and why.

Reference Note

1. Gurel, L. A. *A ten-year perspective on outcome in functional psychosis*. Paper presented at the fifteenth annual conference on VA Comparative Studies in Psychiatry, Houston, Texas, April 1970.

References

Alexander, F. G., & Selesnick, S. T. *The history of psychiatry*. New York: Harper & Row, 1966.

Altman, H. A., Sletten, I., & Nebel, M. E. Length of stay and readmission rates in Missouri state hospitals. *Hospital and Community Psychiatry*, 1973, *24*, 773–776.

Anthony, W. A., Buell, G. J., Sharrett, S., & Althoff, M. E. Efficacy of psychiatric rehabilitation. *Psychological Bulletin*, 1972, *78*, 447–456.

Arnhoff, F. N. Social consequences of policy toward mental illness. *Science*, 1975, *188*, 1277–1281.

Atthowe, J. M. Behavior innovation and persistence. *American Psychologist*, 1973, *28*, 34–41.

Baker, R., Hall, N. N., & Hutchinson, K. A token economy project with chronic schizophrenic patients. *British Journal of Psychiatry*, 1974, *124*, 367–384.

Bandura, A. Behavior theory and the models of man. *American Psychologist*, 1974, *29*, 859–869.

Bandura, A. *Social learning theory*. Englewood Cliffs, N.J.: Prentice-Hall, 1977.

Bassuk, E. L., & Gerson. S. Deinstitutionalization and mental health services. *Scientific American*, 1978, *238:2*, 46–53.

Biklen, D. P. Behavior modification in a state mental hospital: a participant-observer's critique. *American Journal of Orthopsychiatry*, 1976, *46:1*, 53–61.

Blackburn, H. L. Factors affecting turnover rates in mental hospitals. *Hospital and Community Psychiatry*, 1972, *23*, 268–271.

Bockoven, J. S. Moral treatment in American psychiatry. *Journal of Nervous and Mental Diseases*, 1956, *124*, 167–194, 292–321.

Bockoven, J. S., & Solomon, H. C. Comparison of two five-year follow-up studies: 1947 to 1952 and 1967 to 1972. *American Journal of Psychiatry*, 1975, *132:8*, 796–801.

Brill, H., & Patton, R. E. Analysis of population reduction in the New York state mental hospitals during the first four years of large-scale therapy with psychotropic drugs. *American Journal of Psychiatry*, 1959, *116*, 495–508.

Bromberg, W. *The mind of man*. New York: Harper and Bros., 1954.

Bromberg, W. *From shaman to psychotherapist*. Chicago: Henry Regnery, 1975.

Budd, K. S., & Baer, D. M. Behavior modification and the law: implications of recent judicial decisions. *Journal of Psychiatry and Law*, 1976, *4:2*, 171–245.

Burhan, A. S. Short-term hospital treatment: A study. *Hospital and Community Psychiatry*, 1969, *20*, 369–370.

Caffey, E. M., Galbrecht, C. R., & Klett, C. J. Brief hospitalization and aftercare in the treatment of schizophrenia. *Archives of General Psychiatry*, 1971, *24*, 81–86.

Carlson, C. G., Hersen, M., & Eisler, R. M. Token economy programs in the treatment of hospitalized adult psychiatric patients. *Journal of Nervous and Mental Diseases*, 1972, *155*, 192–204.

Chasin, R. M. Special clinical problems in day hospitalization. *American Journal of Psychiatry*, 1967, *123*, 779–785.

Chodoff, R. The case for involuntary hospitalization of the mentally ill. *American Journal of Psychiatry*, 1976, *133:5*, 496–501.

Cousins, N. The mysterious placebo. *Saturday Review*, Oct. 1, 1977, 9–16.

Coye, J. L. Michigan's system for protecting patients' rights. *Hospital and Community Psychiatry*, 1977, *28:5*, 375–381.

Davison, G. C. Appraisal of behavior modification techniques with adults in institutional settings. In C.M. Franks (Ed.), *Behavior therapy: Appraisal and status*. New York: McGraw-Hill, 1969.

Decker, J. B. & Stubblebine, J. M. Crisis intervention and prevention of psychiatric disability: A follow-up study. *American Journal of Psychiatry*, 1972, *129*, 725–729.

Dieter, J. B., Hanford, D. B., Hummel, R. T., & Lubach, J. E. Brief psychiatric treatment: A pilot study. *Mental Hospitals*, 1965, *16*, 95–98.

Ellsworth, R. B. *Nonprofessionals in psychiatric rehabilitation*. New York: Appleton-Century-Crofts, 1968. (Available through IPEV Corporation, Box 5464, Roanoke, Virginia 24105.)

Ellsworth, R. B., Dickman, H. R., & Maroney, R. J. Characteristics of productive and unproductive unit systems in V. A. psychiatric hospitals. *Hospital and Community Psychiatry*, 1972, *23*, 261–271.

Epstein, G. N. (moderator). Panel report: impact of law on the practice of psychotherapy. *Journal of Psychiatry and Law*, 1977, *5:1*, 7–40.

Erickson, R. C. Outcome studies in mental hospitals: A search for criteria. *Journal of Consulting and Clinical Psychology*, 1972, *39*, 75–77.

Erickson, R. C. Outcome studies in mental hospitals: A review. *Psychological Bulletin*, 1975, *82:4*, 519–540.

Erickson, R. C. Length of stay and adjustment and role skill changes of day hospital patients. *Newsletter for Research in Mental Health and Behavioral Sciences*, 1976, *18(1)*, 15–17.

Erickson, R. C. Walden III: Toward an ethics of changing behavior. *Journal of Religion and Health*, 1977, *16*, 7–14.

Erickson, R., Backus, F., Paige, A., & Johnson, M. Length of stay and improvement in a day hospital. *Newsletter for Research in Psychology*, 1972, *14:4*, 31–33.

Erickson, R., & Paige, A. Fallacies in using length-of-stay and return rates as measures of success. *Hospital and Community Psychiatry*, 1973, *24*, 559–561.

Fairweather, G. W. (Ed.). *Social psychology in treating mental illness: An experimental approach*. New York: Wiley, 1964.

Fairweather, G. W., Sanders, D. H., Maynard, H., & Cressler, D. L. *Community life for the mentally ill: An alternative to institutional care*. New York: Aldine, 1969.

Fairweather, G. W., Simon, R., Gebhard, M. E., Weingarten, E., Holland, J. L., Sanders, R., Stone, G. B., & Reahl, S. E. Relative effectiveness of psychotherapeutic programs; a multi-criteria comparison of four programs for three different patient groups. *Psychological Monographs*, 1960, *74* (5, Whole No. 492).

Frank, J. D. *Persuasion and healing*. Baltimore: John Hopkins, 1961.

Freyhan, F. A. Eugene Bleuler's concept of the group of schizophrenics at mid-century. *American Journal of Psychiatry*, 1958, *114*, 769–779.

Friedman, I., Lundstedt, S., von Mering, O., & Hinko, E. N. Systematic underestimation in reported mental hospital readmission rates. *American Journal of Psychiatry*, 1964, *121*, 148–152.

Friedman, I., von Mering, O., & Hinko, E. N. Intermittent patienthood: The hospital career of today's mental patient. *Archives of General Psychiatry*, 1966, *14*, 386–392.

Gardos, G., & Cole, J.O. Maintenance antipsychotic therapy: Is the cure worse than the disease? *American Journal of Psychiatry*,1976, *133*, 32–36.

Glick, I. D., Hargreaves, W. A., Drues, J., & Showstack, J. A. Short versus long hospitalization: A prospective controlled study. One-year follow-up results for schizophrenic patients. *American Journal of Psychiatry*, 1976a, *133*, 509–514.

Glick, I. D., Hargreaves, W. A., Drues, J., & Showstack, J. A. Short versus long hospitalization: A prospective controlled study. One-year follow-up results for non-schizophrenic patients. *American Journal of Psychiatry*, 1976b, *133*, 515–517.

Glick, I. D., Hargreaves, W. A., & Goldfield, M. D. Short vs. long hospitalization. A prospective controlled study: I. The preliminary results of a one-year follow-up of schizophrenics. *Archives of General Psychiatry*, 1974, *30*, 363–369.

Glick, I. D., Hargreaves, W. A., Raskin, M., & Kutner, S. J. Short vs. long hospitalization: A prospective controlled study. II. Results for schizophrenic inpatients. *American Journal of Psychiatry*, 1975, *132*, 385–390.

Gove, W. Posthospital adjustment of northwest Washington hospital-community pilot program patients. *The Bulletin* (Divison of Mental Health, Department of Institutions, State of Washington), 1965, *9*, 140–145.

Greenberg, D. J., Scott, S. T., Pisa, A., & Friesen, D. D. Beyond the token economy: A comparison of two contingency programs. *Journal of Consulting and Clinical Psychology*, 1975, *43*, 498–503.

Greenblatt, M. Therapeutic and nontherapeutic features of the environment. In M. Greenblatt, M. H. Soloman, A. S. Evans, & G. W. Brooks (Eds.), *Drug and social therapy in chronic schizophrenics*. Springfield: Charles C. Thomas, 1965.

Greenblatt, M. Class action and the right to treatment. *Hospital and Community Psychiatry*, 1974, *25*, 449–452.

Gurel, L. *Patterns of mental patient posthospital adjustment*. Washington, D.C.: Veterans Administration Psychiatry Evaluation Project, 1965.

Gurel, L. Release and community stay criteria in evaluating psychiatric treatment. In P. H. Hoch & J. Zubin (Eds.), *Psychopathology of schizophrenia*. New York: Grune & Stratton, 1966a.

Gurel, L. Release and community stay in chronic schizophrenia. *American Journal of Psychiatry*, 1966b, *122*, 892–899.

Guy, W., Gross, M., Hogarty, G. E., & Dennis, H. A controlled evaluation of day hospital effectiveness. *Archives of General Psychiatry*, 1969, *20*, 329–338.

Hanford, D. B. Appraisal of the northwest Washington hospital-community pilot programs by community resource persons. *The Bulletin* (Division of Mental Health, Department of Institutions, State of Washington), 1965, *9*, 145–152.

Hanson, P. G., Rothaus, P., O'Connell, W., & Wiggens, G. D. Some basic concepts in human relations training for patients. *Hospital and Community Psychiatry*, 1970, *21*, 137–143.

Hargreaves, W. A., Glick, I. D., Drues, J., Showstack, J. A., & Feigenbaum, E. Short vs. long hospitalization: A prospective controlled study. VI. Two-year follow-up results for schizophrenics. *Archives of General Psychiatry*, 1977, *34*, 305–311.

Herz, M. I., Endicott, J., & Spitzer, R. L. Brief hospitalization of patients with families: Initial results. *American Journal of Psychiatry*, 1975, *132*, 413–418.

Herz, M. I., Endicott, J., & Spitzer, R. L. Brief versus standard hospitalization: The families. *American Journal of Psychiatry*, 1976, *133*, 795–801.

Herz, M. I., Endicott, J., Spitzer, R. L., & Mesnikoff, A. Day vs. inpatient hospitalization: A controlled study. *American Journal of Psychiatry*, 1971, *127*, 1371–1382.

Hogarty, G. E., Goldberg, S. C., et al. Drug and sociotherapy in the aftercare of schizophrenic patients. *Archives of General Psychiatry*, 1973, *28*, 54–64.

Hogarty, G. E., Goldberg, S. C., & Schooler, N. R. Drug and sociotherapy in the aftercare of schizophrenic patients. *Archives of General Psychiatry*, 1974, *31*, 609–618.

Jacobs, M. K., & Trick, O. L. Successful psychiatric rehabilitation using an inpatient teaching laboratory. *American Journal of Psychiatry*, 1974, *131*, 145–148.

Johnson, D. L., Hanson, P. G., Rothaus, P., Morton, R. B., Lyle, F. A., & Moyer, R. Follow-up evaluation of human relations training for psychiatric patients. In E. H. Schein & W. G. Bennis (Eds.), *Personal and Organizational Change Through Group Methods*. New York: Wiley, 1965.

Jones, M. *The therapeutic community*. New York: Basic, 1953.

Katz, R. C., & Woolley, F. R. Criteria for releasing patients from psychiatric hospitals. *Hospital and Community Psychiatry*, 1975, *26*, 33–36.

Klerman, G. Current evaluation research on mental health services. *American Journal of Psychiatry*, 1974, *131*, 783–787.

Konick, D. S., Friedman, I., Paolino, A. F., & Graham, J. R. Changes in symptomatology associated with short-term psychiatric hospitalization. *Journal of Clinical Psychology*, 1972, *28*, 385–390.

Kraft, A. M., Binner, P. R., & Dickey, B. A. The community mental health program and the longer stay patient. *Archives of General Psychiatry*, 1967, *16*, 64–70.

Leaf, P. Wyatt vs. Stickney: Assessing the impact in Alabama. *Hospital and Community Psychiatry*, 1977, *28*, 351–361.

Lindsley, O. R., & Skinner, B. F. A method for experimental analysis of psychiatric patients. *American Psychologist*, 1954, *9*, 419–420.

Mattes, J. A., Rosen, B., & Klein, D. F. Comparison of the clinical effectiveness of "short" vs. "long" stay psychiatric hospitalization. II. Results of a three-year posthospital follow-up. *Journal of Nervous and Mental Disease*, 1977, *165*, 387–394.

Mattes, J. A., Rosen, B., Klein, D. F., & Millan, D. Comparison of the clinical effectiveness of "short" vs. "long" stay psychiatric hospitalization. III. further results of a three-year posthospital follow-up. *Journal of Nervous and Mental Diseases*, 1977, *165*, 395–402.

May, P. R. A. *The treatment of schizophrenia*. New York: Science House, 1968.

May, P. R. A. Cost efficiency of treatments for the schizophrenic patient. *American Journal of Psychiatry*, 1971a, *127*, 1382–1386.

May, P. R. A. Psychotherapy and ataraxic drugs. In A. E. Bergin & S. L. Garfield (Eds.), *Handbook of psychotherapy and behavior change: An empirical analysis*. New York: Wiley, 1971b.

May, P. R. A., & Tuma, A. H. Choice of criteria for the assessment of treatment outcome. *Journal of Psychiatric Research*, 1964a, *2*, 199–209.

May, P. R. A, & Tuma, A. H. The effect of psychotherapy and stelazine on length of stay, release rates, and supplemental treatment of schizophrenic patients. *Journal of Nervous and Mental Disease*, 1964b, *139* 362–369.

McNeill, J. T. *A history of the cure of souls*. New York: Harper & Row, 1951.

Meisel, A. Rights of the mentally ill: The gulf between theory and reality. *Hospital and Community Psychiatry*, 1975, *26*, 349–353.

Milby, J. B. A review of token economy treatment programs for psychiatric inpatients. *Hospital and Community Psychiatry*, 1975, *26*, 651–658.

Moon, L. E., & Patton, R. E. First admissions and readmissions to New York state mental hospitals—A statistical evaluation. *Psychiatric Quarterly*, 1965, *39*, 476–486.

Mumford, S. J., Patch, I. C. L., Andrews, N., & Wyner, L. A token economy ward

programme with chronic schizophrenic patients. *British Journal of Psychiatry*, 1975, *126*, 60–72.
Ochberg, F. M. Community mental health center legislation: flight of the phoenix. *American Journal of Psychiatry*, 1976, *133*, 56–61.
Pasamanick, B., Scarpetti, F. R., & Dinitz, S. *Schizophrenics in the community*. New York: Appleton-Century-Crofts, 1967.
Paul, G. L., & Lentz, R. J. *Psychosocial treatment of chronic mental patients*. Cambridge: Harvard University Press, 1977.
Rajotte, P., & Denber, H. C. B. Intensive follow-up study of 50 chronic relapsing psychotic female patients. In M. Greenblatt, D. J. Levinson, & G. L. Klerman (Eds.), *Mental patients in transition*. Springfield, Ill.: Thomas, 1961.
Redlich, F. & Kellert, S. R. Trends in American mental health. *American Journal of Psychiatry*, 1978, *135*, 22–28.
Redlich, F., & Mollica, R. F. Overview: ethical issues in contemporary psychiatry. *American Journal of Psychiatry*, 1976, *133*, 125–136.
Reibel, S., & Herz, M. I. Limitations of brief hospital treatment. *American Journal of Psychiatry*, 1976, *133*, 518–521.
Rhine, M. W., & Mayerson, P. Crisis hospitalization within a psychiatric emergency service. *American Journal of Psychiatry*, 1971, *127*, 1386–1392.
Rosenhan, O. L. On being sane in insane places. *Science*, 1973, *179*, 250–258.
Ruiz, P., & Saiger, G. Partial hospitalization in an urban slum. *American Journal of Psychiatry*, 1972, *129*, 89–91.
Sacks, M. H., & Carpenter, W. T. The pseudotherapeutic community: An examination of antitherapeutic forces on psychiatric units. *Hospital and Community Psychiatry*, 1974, *25*, 315–318.
Sanders, R., Smith, R. S., & Weinman, B. S. *Chronic psychosis and recovery*. San Francisco: Jossey-Bass, 1967.
Sanders, R., Weinman, B., Smith, R. S., Smith, A., Kenny, J., & Fitzgerald, B. J. Social treatment of the male chronic mental patient. *Journal of Nervous and Mental Disease*, 1962, *134*, 244–255.
Schwartz, L. H. Litigating the right to treatment: Wyatt vs. Stickney. *Hospital and Community Psychiatry*, 1974, *25*, 460–463.
Shean, G. An effective and self-supporting program of community living for chronic patients. *Hospital and Community Psychiatry*, 1973, *24*, 97–99.
Singer, J. E., & Grob, M. C. Short-term versus long-term hospitalization in a private psychiatric facility: A follow-up study. *Hospital and Community Psychiatry*, 1975, *26*, 745–748.
Smith, D. C., Jones, T. A., & Coye, J. L. State mental health institutions in the next decade: Illusions and reality. *Hospital and Community Psychiatry*, 1977, *28*, 593–597.
Somers, A. R. Accountability, public policy and psychiatry. *American Journal of Psychiatry*, 1977, *134*, 959–965.
Steingarten, J. (panelist). Panel report: Impact of law on the practice of psychotherapy. *Journal of Psychiatry and Law*, 1977, *5*, 7–40.
Stone, A. A. Overview: The right to treatment comments on the law and its impact. *American Journal of Psychiatry*, 1975, *132*, 1125–1134.
Szasz, T. S. *The myth of mental illness* (rev. ed.). New York: Harper & Row, 1974.
Ullmann, L. P. *Institution and outcome*. New York: Pergamon, 1967.
Ullmann, L. P., & Krasner, L. (Eds.). *Case studies in behavior modification*. New York: Holt, Reinhart and Winston, 1965.
Ullmann, L. P., & Krasner, L. *A psychological approach to abnormal behavior*. Englewood Cliffs, N.J.: Prentice-Hall, 1969.
Weiner, O. D., & Levine, M. S. A process of establishing norms for inpatient length of

stay in a community mental health center. *American Journal of Psychiatry*, 1975, *132*, 842–846.

Weinstein, L. Real and ideal discharge criteria. *Mental Hospitals*, 1964, *15*, 680–683.

Weisman, G., Feirstein, A., & Thomas, C. Three-day hospitalization: A model for intensive intervention. *Archives of General Psychiatry*, 1969, *21* 620–629.

White, A. D. *A history of the warfare of science with theology in Christendom*. New York: Macmillan, 1896.

Wilder, J. F., Levin, G., & Zwerling, I. A two-year follow-up evaluation of actute psychotic patients treated in a day hospital. *American Journal of Psychiatry*, 1966, *122*, 1095–1101.

Wilensky, H. L. & Lebeaux, C. N. Conceptions of social welfare. In P. E. Weinberger (Ed.), *Perspectives on social welfare*. New York: Macmillian, 1969.

Williams, C. *Witchcraft*. London: Faber and Faber, 1941.

Zilboorg, G., & Henry, G. W. *A history of medical psychology*. New York: Norton, 1941.

Part II

APPLICATIONS FROM ACADEMIC PSYCHOLOGY TO COMMUNITY PSYCHOLOGY

Overview

The preceding chapters help us place the community movement in perspective. In Chapter 1, Zax shows us how community approaches developed out of a dissatisfaction with many aspects of traditional approaches to mental disorder: the medical model, the emphasis on intrapsychic causes to the exclusion of environmental ones, the ineffectiveness of traditional psychotherapy, and so on; and how community approaches attempt to focus instead on prevention of disorder through changing environmental factors and social interactions.

The focus thus has shifted from what goes on within the person to the person's exchanges with the environment. Chapter 2, by Erickson and Hyerstay, however, points to some interesting continuities in the history of our institutionalization of the mentally disordered. In spite of the prevailing philosophy that advocates environmental causation and community approaches, the authors argue persuasively that our old attitudes of fear and disdain still prevent the mentally disturbed from receiving effective treatment. Conceptualizations and rationalizations have changed, but the basic cognitions remain the same.

These two chapters emphasize different aspects of community psychology: community psychology as a new paradigm and community psychology as a continuation of an old paradigm. Both points of view are "true"; together these views suggest that it is important to trace and understand the connection between community psychology and related areas. Zax's chapter indirectly argues that we might profitably turn to social psychology and sociology for what they can tell us about environmental causes of mental disorder, and the Erickson and Hyerstay chapter advises that we turn to cognitive approaches within psychology for what they can tell us about attitudes to the mentally ill.

The section of the book to follow carries out these suggestions. Separate chapters examine the relationship between environmental stressors and emotional reactions and between social class and mental illness. The relationship between learned helplessness and community psychology is examined, and both labeling theory and expectancy and attribution are discussed in relation to their effect on community psychology. Other areas could have been selected for inclusion as well. Behaviorism, with its focus on environmental causes, is certainly applicable to community psychology; Juliana Lachenmeyer in a later chapter (Chapter 10) details some of these applications in the context of consultation. Over all, we selectively sampled what appeared to be the most interesting and most easily applied areas.

Several of the chapters bear directly on the problem Erickson and Hyerstay posed for us as to why our attitudes toward the mentally disturbed have changed so little. In Chapter 3, Rappaport and Cleary describe the deleterious effects of labels, how assigning a name reifies a concept, and how in the process the diagnostic procedure itself can do harm. Both this chapter and Chapter 4 by Strickland and Janoff-Bulman, discuss, from different perspectives, the concept of "blaming the victim." The label "mentally ill" defines and reifies an intra-individual process; this label in turn evokes an assortment of associated attributions and expectancies about the labeled individual. Strickland and Janoff-Bulman argue that the attributions in our culture tend to be to the individual rather than to the social system even when there is much empirical evidence in support of the environmental attribution. Such attributions and expectancies often operate in self-fulfilling ways. For example, the expectancy of reinforcement from the environment (internal versus external locus of control) of community members can be affected by the punishing labels and attributions ("mentally ill," "lower class," "deviant," "welfare case," "black," etc.) society gratuitously places upon them. This process in turn limits the behavior these individuals will engage in to change the situation, and a negative state of affairs is perpetuated. It is obvious for instance that there are many ways in which the hospitalized patient being deprived of control can be both a result of the maladaptive behavior that put him or her in the hospital and the cause of future faulty adaptations to an unresponsive environment.

Sue and Zane make a similar point in Chapter 5, which considers learned helplessness. Lack of control over environmental contingencies produces a learned helplessness in the disadvantaged members of a community. Since these members feel helpless to affect their environment, their disadvantaged status is perpetuated. Sue and Zane discuss an important revision to learned helplessness involving attributions. To learn helplessness, individuals must not only be put in a situation where they cannot avoid punishment; in addition they must attribute the helplessness to themselves rather than to outside factors. Including attribution in the formulation provides community psychology with an avenue for social change. The disadvantaged need to become better aware of the social causation of their helplessness. Neither a generalized internal nor external locus of control is adequate; to make changes individuals must see that some efforts will be reinforced by the environment in spite of the fact that other types of efforts in other situations have gone ignored and unrewarded. Sue and Zane make suggestions on how to increase the sense of control of the disadvantaged.

In examining the effects of environmental stressors in Chapter 6, Sigal also points out the factor of perception of control. Thus "crowding" involves a subjective factor of perceived restriction which sheer density of people per area may or may not have. Little research has investigated the effects of subjects' perceived control of density. Crowding has been explained as producing harmful effects both through overstimulation of the autonomic nervous system or through stimulus overload. It is interesting to speculate on how much the negative effects depend on the perceived restriction. Learned helplessness, proposed as an explanation for the effects of noise, may also help explain the effects of continuous crowding. At any rate, since crowding has been so extensively researched it provides a good model as to how many other types of environmental stress may produce dysfunction.

In Chapter 7, Gibbs discusses environmental stress as an intervening variable between social class and mental disorder. She provides a psychologist's perspective of the sociological research on social class epidemiology of mental disorder. This research is important because it shows possible social causes for mental disorder, and thus suggests some direction for prevention programs. The discussion of disparity in psychological treatment according to social class relates again to our earlier point about cognitive variables. The attributions and cognitions of both professionals and clients impair treatment efforts and hamper our attempts to establish an effective community psychology.

All the authors in this section have made an attempt to relate the theory and research they discuss to practical issues and problems. This overview has focused on a few central issues, but there are obviously many areas where academic psychology can be applied to an active community mental health movement.

CHAPTER 3

Labeling Theory and the Social Psychology of Experts and Helpers

Julian Rappaport, Ph.D.
and
Catherine P. Cleary, M.A.

ADVERTISING AND THE POWER OF LABELS

Perhaps one of the surest ways to know if something "works" is to look for its adoption by the business community. The effort to create recognizable brand names with a reputation for quality, has a long and tested history. Advertising works. Manufacturers spend millions of dollars each year to keep the "image" of their product positive, and to remind us that their establishment is "our kind of place." They worry about what television programs will be associated with their label. They try to associate their product with people of note: athletes, beautiful entertainers, seemingly intelligent, happy, normal, hard-working or fun-loving people. Regardless of the exact image sought, one aim remains constant: to create an association between the image and the product. What underlies this aim is, of course, the folk wisdom that "birds of a feather flock together." The conclusion is obvious: to be like them do as they do, eat what they eat, drink what they drink, drive what they drive. This view of social reality is so endemic to our culture that an item on one of our most widely used intelligence tests asks "Why should you stay away from bad company?" The correct answer is that such people will influence your behavior and others will associate you with them. Is this true? The business world is not fooled for very long by nonpragmatic folk wisdom. There is a very clear criterion for what works, and that is whether people buy the product. The business community has found that labels have mattered.

Labels applied to people carry important information to the person labeled and to others in that person's social network. This understanding has been captured by psychologists and sociologists in various ways. Theodore Sarbin, for example, distinguishes between *achieved* and *ascribed* roles as one means by which we label ourselves and one another.

While achieved roles tend to be earned and permit positive status, ascribed roles are granted by our culture "automatically," and provide only negative or neutral status, usually related to sex, race, age or other demographic factors over which one has only limited control.

To the extent that one is forced to act in the roles ascribed there is less room to seek and obtain achieved status. For example, to the extent that women are expected to remain at home with children in order to fulfill strongly held ascribed roles, they have less time to devote to accomplishing achieved roles and status other than that granted by virtue of their sex.

In our social-scientific vocabulary there are many words that serve as a means to label, often negatively, various people (e.g., slum dwellers, culturally deprived, mental patients, juvenile delinquents). It is reasonable to hypothesize that these labels work in a fashion similar to advertising labels, albeit by creating a negative rather than a positive association. Negative labels grant people a negative ascribed status. Once labeled a person is likely to be treated negatively, so as to be degraded and further reduce the possibility of obtaining achieved status. This is the hypothesis offered by Sarbin (1970), and it is similar to what others have called a "self-fulfilling prophecy." In this view both the labeled person and others learn to expect and therefore subtly encourage behavior consistent with the label. For example, a child who scores poorly on an IQ test may become labeled as "slow" and may actually continue to do more poorly in school than if he or she is expected to do well.

One of the ways that our society perpetuates labels is to grant "labeling authority" to certain "experts" who serve in the role of modern-day priests, shamans and seers. Often these people are social scientists, physicians, educators, lawyers and judges or members of the "helping professions": psychiatrists, psychologists, social workers. For the sake of convenience this set of authorities will be referred to in the remainder of this chapter as "helpers" or "experts." There is, of course, a good deal of irony in the fact that experts and helpers can create problems for people. To say that the very people called helpers may be harmful to at least some of those they set out to help is a disturbing thought at best, and one which is developed in some detail by Thomas Szasz in a number of books and papers (e.g., *The Myth of Mental Illness* [1961], *The Manufacture of Madness* [1970], *Ceremonial Chemistry* [1974]), and more recently by Ivan Illich in *Medical Nemesis* (1976).

It has been argued elsewhere (Rappaport, 1977) that a central aim for community psychology should be to identify and change those aspects of the social structure which, in Sarbin's terminology, degrade people. If we are to take this task seriously it is essential to understand the process of labeling and the part played by social scientists and professional helpers in that process. Such understanding can enable those who are social scientists to intervene in a place where they already have a great deal of legitimacy.

Typically it is argued that the social scientist has no basis for social intervention since he or she is neither elected nor representative of the will of the public. Even if this argument were to be ignored, the social scientist often has little or only indirect political power (e.g., to suggest social policy). But what if it could be shown that some specific activity in the practices of the helpers and experts themselves were a part of the problem? *Here then would be an opportunity to correct the negative impact of at least one part of our social system by changing our own behavior, rather than trying to change the behavior of others.* "Healing ourselves" might be a necessary step before we can hope to heal others.

If we were to pursue this line of reasoning we would need to ask questions about the social psychology of experts and helpers. First we would need to discern if indeed there is such a phenomenon as the "effect of labels." For our purposes the question could be asked more specifically: "Do labels used by experts and helpers have an impact on those 'labeled'?" If the answer is "yes," then we would want to understand how the impact operates (in scientific terms, what is the mechanism?). We might then hypothesize how specific interventions would change that impact; and we might try some set of proposed interventions and systematically evaluate their outcome. Ideally these steps would lead to new proposals for social policy, and ultimately to social change.

In this chapter we attempt a considerably more modest agenda, but we do take a step toward understanding the social psychology of experts and helpers. Our aim is to show that (1) labeling theory can be a helpful way to organize a broad set of observations about the social impact of experts and helpers, and (2) the effect of labels used by experts and helpers is both real and often negative, despite good intentions.

REVIEW OF LABELING THEORY

The notion that labeling or categorizing a person can have powerful social and psychological effects on both the person labeled and those with whom he or she interacts has been a part of sociological thought for many years. It appears in the well-known anthropological studies of Malinowski (1926), and has been available for many years as a perspective through which to understand the problem of social deviance (e.g., Tannenbaum, 1951). More recently labeling has been proposed as a semiformal theory, in part as a function of Becker's *Outsiders* (1963) which has had a marked impact on modern thought concerning deviance.

> Social groups create deviance by making the rules whose infraction constitutes deviance, and by applying those rules to particular people and labeling them as outsiders. From this point of view, deviance is *not* a quality of the act the person commits, but rather a consequence of the application by others of rules and sanctions to an "offender." . . . [I] view deviance as the product of a transaction that takes place between some social group and one who is viewed by that group as a rule-breaker (Becker, 1963, pp. 9–10).

Often the literary world can powerfully capture subtle psychological realities, and in deference to that power Becker selected a quote from William Faulkner's *As I Lay Dying* as a preface to his own work.

> Sometimes I ain't so sho who's got ere a right to say when a man is crazy and when he ain't. Sometimes I think it ain't none of us pure crazy and ain't none of us pure sane until the balance of us talks him that-a-way. It's like it ain't so much what a fellow does, but it's the way the majority of folks is looking at him when he does it (cited in Becker, 1963).

Thomas J. Scheff created a more formal link between sociology, psychology, and labeling theory per se with the publication of his books, *Being Mentally Ill* (1966), *Mental Illness and Social Processes* (1967), and more recently, *Labeling Madness* (1975). Scheff outlined a theory of deviance that provides a stimulating perspective through which to view many of the problem areas of concern to clinical and community psychologists. Robert Carson, a clinical psychologist and personality theorist, has added to and elaborated on Scheff's notions, incorporating a number of additional ideas.

We shall begin here by presenting an overview of Carson's (1969) theorizing because it takes a psychological stance, proposing mechanisms to account for how a sociological reality (being labeled deviant) may have an impact on the behavior of individuals. Although his way of framing the question is more psychological than sociological, there remains an emphasis on the *social context*. Carson includes in his thinking some aspects of social learning theory (cf. Krohn & Akers, 1977), as well as exchange theory (Thibaut & Kelley, 1959), interpersonal psychology (Sullivan, 1953; Leary, 1957) and labeling theory (Scheff, 1966). It is his work which we believe is most directly useful as a frame of reference for understanding the social psychology of experts and helpers.

Carson's Psychological-Sociological Viewpoint.

It has often been recognized that the expectations one holds, as well as the reinforcement contingencies one controls, may influence the behavior of others. It has less often been recognized that the process is a mutual one, that is, one in which the behavior of one person influences the behavior of another person and in turn the original person's behavior is influenced by the reactions of the first person. In attempting to deal explicitly with this phenomenon, Robert Carson has moved the focus of the study of behavior from the single person to the dyad.

There are four basic elements in Carson's "interaction concepts of personality." First, he sees interpersonal behavior as in part composed of learned ways of avoiding anxiety and seeking security, a view originating with the psychiatrist Harry Stack Sullivan. These learned ways of avoiding anxiety and seeking security are acquired through "action learning" and "cognitive learning." By action learning Carson intends to include most of the principles useful in behavior modification and social learning theory; by cognitive learning he intends to include an emphasis on expectations and cognitions, and draws particularly on the work of Miller, Galanter, and Pribram (1960), which views the person as an active problem solver continually reformulating images of oneself and the world, and plans for one's behavior.

A second element is borrowed from Thibaut and Kelley (1959), who view behavior as an exchange between people. Carson posits that interpersonal behavior is a function of the "payoff matrix" in which persons seek to interact with others who and in ways which increase their interpersonal satisfaction. Following Leary (1957), each person is said to desire complementarity of behavior from others. In this way people are seen to seek out those whose behavior is complementary to their own and to stimulate complementary behavior in others. Over time people learn how to create desired behavior in themselves and others, and Carson suggests that this learning is cognitively mediated through the images and plans which people develop as a consequence of interpersonal problem solving. These images and plans (the third element in the theory) influence the way people see new situations, and people tend to seek a fit between their existing images and their interpersonal environments.

The fourth aspect in Carson's theory involves contractual arrangements. Through the development of (usually implicit) contracts for interpersonal behavior, people come to expect each other to behave in a particular way. These contracts are similar to the norms and roles that control social behavior more generally.

If normal behavior is to be understood in social-interpersonal terms, then deviant behavior must also be consistent with this view. Neither medical/intrapsychic explanations of deviance, which rely on variables totally internal to the person, nor external environmental explanations *alone*, can account for the social meaning of deviant behavior; and here is where Carson turns to the explanations offered by Scheff and Becker, and incorporates their sociology into his more psychological notions of interpersonal behavior.

According to both Scheff and Becker we cannot understand why a person is labeled as "mentally ill" without understanding the sociological nature of the event. The criteria for the label will be a product of convention or social custom. It will differ from one society to another. Such labels are, of course, based on a violation of norms in a given society. However, since many violations of norms are not labeled mental illness, labeling theorists make a distinction between those norms that are explicit, such as laws, and those that are part of the culture and basic to its understanding of the world; for example, unwritten assumptions about decency. In our society such "rules" include the norms of the work ethic. People who do not work are often labeled as "sick" or as suffering from some form of personal disorder. Since deliberate violation of such norms is unthinkable one searches for explanations in the supernatural, or in the morality or health of the person. Violation of such norms is termed "residual rule breaking." Residual rule breaking is a necessary but not sufficient condition to earn the label "mental illness." Many people violate such rules and are simply ignored, as for example, a wealthy or retired person who need not work.

Scheff, Becker and Carson suggest that a crucial step toward becoming "mentally ill" is the response that others have to one's deviance. Residual norm violation needs to be labeled before it becomes mental illness. For example, a person may walk along the street talking to himself and be either ignored as eccentric or labeled as hallucinatory. It is not the behavior per se, but the label, which creates social reality. If the behavior is labeled as mentally ill it may lead to other people paying a great deal of attention to it, thereby initiating a series of social actions and reactions.

Scheff suggests that labeling a behavior "deviant" calls attention to the residual norm violation and amplifies its occurrence through social feedback. That is, the attention is reinforcing and encourages continuation of the deviance. Carson goes on to add that the deviant behavior may actually serve a purpose for the person. Its persistence is explained as a behavior which gives one the best "payoff" in terms of interpersonal security; that is, for the deviant person it may be the best alternative available for coping with his or her problems in living. Rather than viewing this as sickness, it can be seen as following the same principles that govern all interpersonal behavior: maximization of interpersonal payoff given the available alternatives.

In the above sense, if being labeled "deviant" creates a limit on available alternatives, one may be said to suffer detrimental effects. For example, calling a child retarded, mentally ill, delinquent and so on, may, because of the reactions it creates in the child and in others, narrow the number and kinds of behaviors available for problem solving. Viewed in this way the problem of intervening on the behalf of a "deviant" person is that such intervention can create harm as well as good. Although it has been developed in the context of mental illness, this analysis can be applied to any form of deviance from mainstream society. As Scheff suggests:

> In order to understand the situation of the mentally ill . . . one could profit by comparing their position with that of other subordinate minorities. Psychological processes such as stereotyping, projection and stigmatization and social processes such as rejection, segregation and isolation characterize to some degree the orientation of the in-group toward the out-group regardless of the basic distinction (Scheff, 1967, p. 4).

For many people not included in the mainstream of society (be they poor, minority group members, mentally ill, delinquent, or whatever) many problems in living may be a function of a lack of available resources and alternatives, a condition which in turn may be mediated and maintained through social labeling and the roles they are forced to play as a function of those labels. If this reasoning has any validity to it, it suggests that the *experts and helpers who label people may often create as much harm as good by the very process of practicing their trade.* To raise this possibility one need not necessarily demonstrate that labeling is the original cause of the deviance, so much as the possibility that labeling may exacerbate an initial problem or prevent, rather than enhance, the likelihood that the problem will be dealt with well.

LABELING THEORY AS A SENSITIZING PERSPECTIVE

In the past ten years a number of sociologists have challenged, on both formal and empirical grounds, the adequacy of labeling theory per se as an explanation of mental illness (cf. Gibbs, 1972; Gove, 1970a, 1970b, 1975a, 1975b; Krohn & Akers, 1977). While Scheff (1975) has presented a number of interesting arguments in defense of the labeling perspective, it is generally agreed that it should probably not be thought of as a formal theory, nor can it be asserted in any simple way that labeling "causes" mental illness or other forms of deviance. On the other hand, there also appears to be general agreement that understanding the potential impact of labeling a person can have a sensitizing effect on those who are in a social position which sanctions their labeling.

The development of sensitizing theories has been suggested by Kenneth Gergen (1973) to be a crucial role for social psychology. His argument is that because the basic processes of social psychological concern are not locked into the biology of the organism they are subject to "enlightenment effects." Making people aware of influences on their behavior should aid in changing the impact of those influences. For example, one who knows that there is a tendency to act in stigmatizing ways to a person labeled "sick" may be less willing to label that person. Understanding that an IQ score serves to label a child in a way that has consequences for the child may reduce a teacher's willingness to use such scores. All of this is to argue for the use of labeling theory as a social critique.

Here we are not interested in an analysis of labeling as a formal theory or explanation of deviance, so much as with the social significance of the use of labels. Although labeling theory probably does not meet the standards of formal scientific theory, we find the perspective useful as a tool for organizing a number of seemingly unconnected observations which are of interest to those concerned with social change. The labeling perspective forces one to pay attention to the fact that it is not possible to understand people outside their social context and that *their social context includes experts and helpers.*

Observable Effects of Social Labeling

We have already noted that there is a good deal of face validity in the assertion that labeling has an impact. Evidence from one's own experience and from reflection on the experience of advertisers should not be ignored simply because it is "anecdotal." Similarly, we can all recollect how we may have stereotyped someone on the basis of appearance, or some early impression, and how this affected our interactions with that person and in turn the person's reaction to us. Many people can recall how, after a few weeks of school, a teacher either liked or disliked us and nothing we later did could change it. If we were fortunate enough to be seen as "bright," we could do no wrong. If we were unfortunate enough to be seen as a "trouble-maker" or "dull," there seemed to be little we could do to change the judgment. While this sort of introspection is looked upon with skepticism by scientists, it is reasonable to ask yourself if indeed your own experience does suggest such a phenomenon, since we shall also call on other, more theoretical and empirical evidence to supplement such introspection.

Several lines of reasoning suggest that the effects of social labeling are real and powerful. We will cite some evidence from well-controlled laboratory studies, and much from situations in which it was not possible to apply the ideal experimental design. In order to show a "treatment" (i.e., labeling) effect, the straightforward design would be to identify a population—for example, all new kindergarten students—and then randomly sample and label one-third of them dull, and one-third bright, and leave the other third unlabeled. We would then follow the students over time, and observe how others such as parents, teachers and friends interact with them. This sort of design is, of course, neither ethical nor possible in the real world, and therefore inferences from any single research project will be insufficient to demonstrate "cause." Nevertheless we can make some judgments from a review of many individual pieces of less ideal experimental and field research. Examples will be drawn from field study in the education, criminal justice and mental health systems, as well as from laboratory studies of semantic meaning, and personality and social interaction.

What should become clear from this review is that the reality of the impact of a label on the lives of those who are labeled is indeed powerful. There may be controversy over how it works, but the phenomenon itself is a social fact of life which has implications for relationships between those in authority and those in subjection to authority.

Evaluative Dimension of Words

One of the single most robust findings in psychology laboratories stems from the attempt of Charles Osgood to delineate semantic meaning: the emotional-psychological connotations that words hold for us. Dating back over twenty years (Osgood, Suci & Tannenbaum, 1957), Osgood and others have found that people tend, regardless of the denotative or dictionary definition, to see all adjectives on a scale of either good-bad, powerful-weak, or active-passive. The "first factor," which appears to account for most of the variation in connotative meaning, is the "good-bad" or evaluative dimension. It is possible for any person, object, or idea to be described in this way. Indeed, what seems to happen is that our language connotes these dimensions so powerfully that if you are asked to describe someone the chances are quite high that you will do it primarily by placing them at some point on a scale of evaluation (good to bad), regardless of the actual words you use. There are literally hundreds of studies which report this or similar results.

What does all this have to do with labeling? What we have here is only indirect evidence for the power of labels, but it is probably true that every label has implicit if not explicit connotations which are evaluative in nature and may be a stimulus for how others, once a person is labeled, treat that person. A label may also affect how a person regards her- or himself, since what is communicated is an evaluation of the person. As Kerber and Clore (1978) have recently concluded from a series of well-controlled laboratory studies examining how people use "trait attributions" (words such as, selfish, friendly, cooperative): "trait adjectives communicate *not only what another person does* in some descriptive sense, but also the affective implications of their actions . . ."

(italics added). Psychologically, the words we use to describe ourselves and others carry a great deal of connotative meaning, such that their potential for inducing powerful psychological effects is real.

A Laboratory Demonstration of Labeling

If labels do carry important connotations, then these connotations may be expected to have an impact on the behavior of those who perceive them. In a recent study by Mark Snyder and William B. Swann (1978), such an effect was demonstrated in a well-controlled laboratory paradigm. These authors showed that erroneous beliefs about a person, communicated by a label, were actually able to channel social interaction so as to cause the behavior of a labeled target to conform with the labelers' beliefs.

Snyder and Swann randomly assigned subjects in groups of three to one of three roles: a *labeling perceiver*, a *target*, or a *naive perceiver*. All sets were composed of previously unaquainted college students. Each labeling perceiver was first paired with a target in order to play a game involving a "noise weapon," with varying degrees of intensity of noise available for delivery to the opponent. Half of the target persons were told that research had shown that the loudness of noise they would deliver to their opponents would be related to their own (the target's) personal characteristics (a dispositional attribution). Half of the target persons were told that the loudness they would deliver to their opponent would be due to the way they are treated by their opponent (a situational attribution).

The labeling perceivers were told that in order to plan their strategy they should know something about their opponent. Half of the labeling perceivers were shown a false "personality trait survey" whch indicated that the target was a *hostile* person; the other half were shown one which indicated that their opponent was a *nonhostile* person.

During the game the level of noise administered to each other by the labeling perceivers and the targets was recorded. The researchers found that the labeling perceivers who were told to expect their targets to be hostile delivered a significantly higher intensity of noise to the target than those perceivers for whom the target had been labeled nonhostile. In turn, the targets labeled as hostile then tended to *reciprocate* by delivering a higher intensity of noise to their opponent than did their counterparts who were labeled nonhostile. In other words, because the perceiver believed the target to be hostile, he treated him in a more hostile fashion, causing the target to confirm the label by delivering high levels of noise back to the perceiver. Not only did the targets come to behave in accord with the label they were given, but the perceiver later interpreted the behavior of the target as due to the target's "hostile nature," despite the fact that they (the perceivers) had actually generated the high levels of noise intensity by delivering high levels to the target in the first place.

In a final part of this experiment the same labeled target person was paired with a second opponent (a *naive perceiver*) who was not given any information about the target (i.e., the target was given no label). Those targets who had been given a dispositional attribution to explain their own behavior and who were labeled as hostile in the previous interaction continued to treat their second opponent in a hostile fashion. However, those targets who had been given a situational attribution to explain their own behavior did not act in a hostile manner toward their new opponent. Consequently the originally labeled hostile targets who were given a dispositional attribution were seen by the second (naive) opponent as hostile. Those who had a situational explanation for their behavior and who did not continue to be hostile in the second interaction were not perceived as hostile.

What we can conclude from this study is that labels indeed may have a behavioral impact on those who perceive them, and may in turn create in the person labeled the very behavior implied by the label. In addition, whether or not a labeled person continues to act in a manner consistent with the label may be a function of whether or not one believes what the label says about one's self. In short, behavior is affected by the beliefs others have about us, and the beliefs we have about ourselves. These beliefs can be communicated in the form of labels which, even if not accurate initially, can actually create behavior which conforms to the label.

This is a very powerful laboratory demonstration of the impact of labels, and even though the situation is an artificial one, and the behavior is quite simple, when taken together with "real-life" examples of labeling described in the remainder of this chapter, it indicates the potential power available to those experts and helpers who are granted the authority to label others.

Experts, Helpers and Labeling

Given that labels may carry important connotations, and that these connotations can affect behavior, do experts and helpers in fact label others in some consistent fashion? It would seem that they do. Caplan and Nelson (1973), in what is probably the single best analysis of this problem from a sociology of knowledge point of view, have analyzed the ways in which experts tend to label people. Caplan and Nelson are particularly concerned with what they term a "person-blame" bias in psychological research on social problems or, in simple terms, the tendency to label individuals so as to suggest that they are always responsible for their own problems in living. Such an approach ignores situationally relevant factors external to the individual (e.g., the role of the labeler).

Going through a fairly elaborate procedure of sampling the psychological abstracts, these authors went on to discover that for the period in which they collected information, 82 percent of the classifiable psychological research dealt with black Americans in terms of personal shortcomings expressed in the form of a socially negative label. Anyone familiar with much of psychological research would have no trouble concluding that the tendency to such diagnostic labeling dominates our literature on other nonmajority groups as well.

What is perhaps even more disturbing is that even where situational labels are used, for example in much of the behaviorist writings, the labels are often construed to imply personal blame. Whether one is labeled with words like "inadequate personality," "poor ego strength," or "learning deficit," the connotations of the label suggest that there is something wrong *in* the person, and serves to justify changing the labeled individual. The labeled person is usually viewed as deficient or possessing some fatal difference from you and me. In short, while situational or social forces are alluded to, diagnosis tends to imply changing the people theselves, rather than their social and/or material situations.

We have asserted thus far that: (1) Labels have consistent evaluative connotations, (2) labels can have a behavioral impact, and (3) experts tend to use labels with a particular person-blame implication. We turn now to the question, "Can negative labels have predictable negative effects in the real world?" Note that the question is phrased here as *can*, rather than *do*. It is probably not the case that a label always leads to a given outcome, yet if we are able to show that a label can produce a given class of behavior, then we will have demonstrated that experts and helpers must be alert to the possibility that they are harmful, rather than helpful, when they "diagnose" or label, and we will have a basis for suggesting changes in social policy.

LABELING AND THE EDUCATIONAL SYSTEM

Perhaps the most well-known example of the impact of a label is the study by Rosenthal and Jacobson (1968) in which they termed labeling as the "Pygmalion Effect," after the George Bernard Shaw play about a slum child who is transformed into a well-bred, educated woman.

These researchers found that changes in measured IQ and achievement among elementary school children could in some cases be attributed quite directly to the expectations that teachers held for the children. In their ingenious study all children in an elementary school with an enrollment of 650 were given an IQ test which was represented to the teachers as a test of intellectual "blooming." Later the researchers randomly selected 20 percent of the children in each classroom and told the teachers that the test indicated that these children were about to bloom academically. All were retested after one semester, one year, and two years (after they had passed on to a new teacher).

After one year those labeled "bloomers," especially those in first or second grade, were shown to have made greater real IQ gains than the other children. Forty-seven percent increased by as much as 20 IQ points. In the second year the older children showed greater gains in IQ while the younger children failed to maintain their gains with a new teacher. IQ gains were at first most evident for children in a middle-level educational track as opposed to a fast or slow one. In addition, Rosenthal and Jacobson found that among the Mexican-American children, who constituted about one-sixth of the school's population, those who were labeled as bloomers showed the greatest IQ gain, probably as a function of increased interest in and attention paid to them. Bloomers also showed greater gains in reading and achievement tests. They were even rated by teachers as more curious and as better on personality and social adjustment measures than nonlabeled peers. Let us recall now these children were randomly selected. This evidence of the impact of a label, bloomer, given by an expert to a child's teacher, raises the serious possibility that a negative label can have the opposite effect.

Although the Rosenthal and Jacobson study has been questioned by various people on the basis of its methodology and appropriate statistical analysis (c.f. Barber & Silver, 1968) it is exemplary as a ground-breaking piece of work, and the finding does appear to have some stability and consistency. Similar results have been found for children who were in a class with the same teacher who had taught an older sibling (Seaver, 1973). In addition, expectancy effects as a function of race have also been demonstrated for student-teacher ratings of elementary school children (Rubovitz & Maher, 1973), and for ratings of employee work performance (Rotter & Rotter, 1969). Observations consistent with these data have also been reported by Weikart (1972), who collected anecdotal observations and diary reports of preschool teachers which indicated that those with high expectations for children were likely to encourage better performance.

Each of these studies is exemplary rather than conclusive, and none is definitive or shows that labeling always has an impact, but they all point to the definite likelihood that a positive or negative label can have a serious impact on later performance.

Perhaps one of the more powerful observations of the effect of labeling is found in the work of an anthropologist named Ray Rist (1970). Rist spent several years conducting an observational study of the effects of social class on teacher behavior with children from kindergarten, first and second grades. What he found was that very early in a child's career, *by the eighth day of kindergarten*, teachers placed children in labeled ability groups that reflected social class rather than performance, and that these labeled groups remained together in later school years. The most consistent commonalities in each group were indices such as father's income and occupation, and child's dress. Ability to perform school work was obviously not well sampled after one week of kindergarten, yet these children, with few exceptions, remained in their respective groups in subsequent years.

While Rist's observations were in only one elementary school, it is not unreasonable to suggest that the practice is probably more widespread. In addition to being labeled by the eighth day of class according to so-called "ability," Rist notes that the teacher's behavior as well as the child's interactions with his or her peers became consistent with the label and often influenced later achievement. In this particular study all the children as well as the teacher were black, yet the teacher's preference for middle-class behavior similar to her own reference group led not only to negative labels for children from the lower socioeconomic strata, but also to differential patterns of interaction in the classroom. The teacher's behavior tended to discourage the "lowest" group of children from participation in the class, and this resulted in similarly negative behavior on the part of their peers. The teachers actually taught less directly to those negatively-labeled children and inadvertantly made it impossible for them to improve their performance. For example, teacher time spent looking at and talking to the lowest "ability" group (all who were seated at the same table) was much less than the time spent focusing on the other groups. Not surprisingly, over time the "low ability" children tended to actually perform less well than their higher socioeconomic status peers.

Taken together, studies such as Rist's make it reasonable to conclude that whether or not we understand how it works, and whether or not the effects are universal, the possibility of positive and negative labels influencing a child's performance in school and the reaction that others, both peers and authority figures, have to the child, is very real. Such studies must raise questions about effects of IQ testing in public schools, labeling children as maladjusted, and other such activities which are common among experts and helpers.

LABELING AND THE CRIMINAL JUSTICE SYSTEM

One of the clearest ways to influence behavior is to place people in situations which call for specific kinds of activities. Often the situation is so powerful as to overcome individual differences and create consistency in behavior (see, for example, Barker, 1968; Ekehammer, 1974; Mischel, 1968; Rotter, 1954; Rotter, Chance, & Phares, 1972). One such powerful setting is prison. In prison settings there is a good deal of situational control over the behavior of those people who take on various roles. Perhaps one of role-making aspects of prison comes from a study conducted by Philip Zimbardo at Stanford University (1973). While this particular study is an analog rather than a direct observation of the prison setting itself, it does demonstrate that the social roles adopted by actors in a situation defined as prisons, where some are called guards and others are called prisoners, creates a number of perhaps surprising behaviors quite independent of who the actors are.

Zimbardo advertised in a local newspaper for volunteers to participate in a study of prison life. From a total of 231 applications he selected 75 people who appeared to be normal in clinical interviews and on personality tests. All the participants were college-age males living near Stanford University who agreed ahead of time to participate for two weeks in a situation that would involve loss of their civil rights and some personal harassment. Following their agreement to participate, without warning, local police arrested ten "volunteer prisoners," processed them, and brought them to a simulated prison. All prisoners were blindfolded and were confined by 11 "volunteer" guards. All participants had been randomly assigned to either the guard role or the prisoner role. The prison itself was designed to create an oppressive atmosphere. It had no windows, barred cells, and so on. All prisoners were given ID numbers and loose-fitting smocks rather than their own clothes. They were awakened during the night by shrill whistles for a "count." They needed permission to go to the toilet and after 10:00 P.M. they had to use a bucket in their cell. All guards were uniformed, provided with clubs, and wore reflecting glasses to prevent eye contact. The situation was one that is perhaps "normal" in the prison environment. It included 24-hour surveillance and it limited visiting privileges with friends and relatives.

Guards were free to develop rules to control the inmates while Zimbardo colllected observational data, video and audio tape recordings, diaries and interviews. From this data he describes how, over the course of only six days, rather than the two weeks that the experiment was expected to last, the prisoners first went through a period of resistance and rebellion; and then, controlled by increasingly abusive guards, became depressed, confused and withdrawn—so much so that several had to be let out of the experiment. The guards tended to become increasingly aggressive and sadistic.

What is clear from reading Zimbardo's description is that normal young college-age men, placed in a situation in which the role constraints were very powerful, where some were labeled guards and others prisoners, began to behave in surprising ways. Many expressed surprise and disbelief at finding themselves behaving in ways that they considered repugnant and frightening. Yet at this very moment some people labeled guards and others labeled criminals are engaging in exactly the same roles in real prisons. To assume that the problems in such settings are primarily due to the evil of the prisoners or the sadistic tendencies of the guards is to ignore the dehumanizing structure of the setting, the roles into which it forces its actors, and the labels and expected behaviors which are imposed on the participants.

In the criminal justice system labels are often used as explanations. We tend to view those who commit crimes as different from us—as "criminals" rather than "normal" people, and the implications of the labels for subsequent behavior may be quite profound. As Tom Wicker, a journalist who was an observer at a major prison riot wrote, "The philosophy of the 'criminal type,' has led to the conclusion that there are two kinds of people—the good and the bad—we and they. The bad *are* violent, while the good only *use* violence for "good causes" (Wicker, 1975).

One major use of labels in the criminal justice system is in the notion of "juvenile delinquency." The concept of juvenile delinquency is a perplexing one. One of its peculiar problems is that a number of behaviors that would not be illegal for an adult, such as truancy, curfew violation, running away from home or other acts of incorrigibility, are illegal for minors. These behaviors are refered to as "status offenses" because they are a crime only if one has the status of a minor. This official misbehavior often leads a young person to be labeled "delinquent" or some other euphemism with the same negative connotation such as "person in need of supervision."

What this means is that two people, one twenty-one and the other sixteen, may do exactly the same thing, but in one case it will be called a crime, and in the other it will not. That in itself may be reasonable, since it may be that certain behaviors are more age-appropriate than others. Unfortunately, the process does not stop there. Once a person is labeled as delinquent, a number of connotations associated with that label tend to be associated with the person. The tendency is for the label to become reified and the person to be seen as being different than others not so labeled.

Ask yourself what connotations you associate with the label "delinquent." Chances are that they are toward the "bad" end of the evaluative dimension and that they tend to "person blame" exactly in the sense that Caplan and Nelson suggest. The entire juvenile court system has been based on these premises. That is why identification and individual treatment are emphasized. The notion is that the child needs personal rehabilitation, presumably because there is something wrong with his or her basic personality. Without reviewing the effectiveness of such an approach in preventing crime (it is very ineffective; cf. Rappaport, Lamiell, & Seidman, in press), it is reasonable to say that the tendency to label children as delinquent may cause some harm to them by setting up negative expectations for themselves and others. What follows may be that the child becomes stereotyped, often without adequate legal evidence.

The entire problem of status offenses and labeling children as delinquent has most recently been taken up by the American Bar Association and the Institute for Judicial Administration in a twenty-three-volume proposal for juvenile law reform. As this study suggests, the labeling of status offenders as juvenile delinquents may create more problems than it solves. While it does enable the courts to officially intervene in the lives of children, it is not always clear that the label delinquent does not create more difficulties than are solved by the treatments to which people are later assigned. In an interesting analysis of this problem Edwin R. Schur (1973) presents a labeling theorist's view.

Schur suggests that calling a person (in this case, a child) criminal begins a process in which the person is treated as a criminal by social agents. Eventually the child regards him or herself as a criminal. Once begun this leads to a kind of self-fulfilling prophecy. Schur suggests that a crucial step in the "making of a delinquent" involves the *response of others* to the deviance. Once labeled "juvenile delinquent" a child is placed in a relationship to society that can serve as kind of a social trap. The child obtains what we have called ascribed status. This is especially true for children who do not have middle-class parents who will come to court or the police station and rescue their child. In our society lower-class children are more likely than middle-class children, and black children are more likely than white children, to be classified as delinquent. Schur suggests that this should alert us not to simple cause and effect relationship between labeling and crime, but to the possibility that *labeling a child delinquent may do more harm than good.*

Although it is by no means true that the suggested labeling process is shown to work in all cases, there is some empirical support that it can happen. For example, while Fo and O'Donnell (1975) found that they were successful in reducing offenses by means of providing "buddies" who were nonprofessionals trained to help children, they also found that for those youth who had no offenses prior to their referral, but for whom it was assumed that help might prevent a future offense, they actually increased the number of offenses compared to a control group. These authors raise the same question which Schur has raised: "Can an intervention program, by overidentification, labeling, and involvement of youth in legal or treatment mechanisms, actually increase the undesirable behavior?" It does seem that this is a real possibility. Seidman, Rappaport, and Davidson (1976) also found that among adolescents who were referred from the police to a volunteer program, those who were most quickly removed from contact with the legal system had a better chance of staying out of difficulty.

Among adults the problem of "crimes without victims" and the consequences of labeling consenting adults as "criminals" may lead to similar problems. Here we are specifically referring to drunkenness, disorderly conduct, vagrancy, loitering, suspicion, gambling, prostitution and other such crimes which have no victim other than perhaps the person her- or himself. Prostitution and homosexuality are excellent examples. To call such behavior criminal probably has no positive social effects, indeed it may have a negative effect by labeling the person as a criminal and creating surplus affective connotations. For example, by calling homosexuality criminal, one may cause others to treat homosexuals as criminals. This is not to suggest that one should necessarily approve or disapprove of homosexuality, but rather that there is no reason to suppose that a homosexual is not otherwise a law-abiding citizen. By labeling him or her as "criminal" and by forcing legal sanctions on homosexuals, one may force the person to behave in clandestine and maladaptive ways, perhaps leading to genuine criminal behavior. This is also the case for so-called drug addicts. Since the drug is illegal, it tends to be expensive. This in turn forces the person to engage in crime to obtain money for overpriced, illegal products.

LABELING AND THE MENTAL HEALTH SYSTEM

The mental health system, because it is founded in the traditions of medicine, is oriented around a number of assumptions which place important constraints on its practices. Central to a medical approach to treatment for illness is the notion of differential diagnosis. That is, the key to successful clinical treatment for any set of symptoms is to classify, by diagnosis, the exact type of problem presented. There is only one sensible reason for such classsification: it should lead to differential prescriptions for treatment. Disorder A is treated by Technique I. If its is misdiagnosed, then Treatment II would be applied and not work as well, or might even be harmful.

Unfortunately, in the realm of mental illness this connection between specific disorders and specific treatments is simply not the case. The traditional diagnostic labels are simply not tied to corresponding treatments. In the general case, psychiatric diagnosis and treatment is more predictable from social class than it is from the particular syndrome of behavior (e.g., Hollingshead & Redlich, 1958; Meyers & Bean, 1967). The reasons for this are very complex. It involves economics, politics, social class bias in the relationship between professionals and their clients, as well as a great deal of disagreement about exactly what mental illness is and what treatments are required.

All of these problems are background issues which require a good deal of study if one is to understand the mental health system as it presently operates. For our purposes one should simply keep in mind certain aspects of the system about which there tends to be widespread agreement in the literature. Much of this has been well summarized by Roesch and Golding (1977):

> 1. Using the current diagnostic system (*Diagnostic and Statistical Manual II*, American Psychiatric Association), trained psychiatrists and psychologists can usually agree with each other no more than 70 percent of the time, on the average, when diagnosing major, unrefined categories (neurosis vs. psychosis vs. organic syndrome vs. normal, etc.) When diagnosing at a more refined level (endogenous depression vs. chronic schizophrenia, simple, etc.), the rate of agreement drops, on the average, to a disastrous 30 percent.
>
> 2. The major sources of disagreement in such diagnostic systems are the ambiguity of the critical criteria (e.g., looseness of association, inappropriate affect, etc.) and the failure of clinicians to recognize their own judgmental biases . . . (p. 36).

What we suggest is not only that diagnosis (labeling) has no relationship to treatment, but that diagnosis itself is unreliable. The tendency, however, to diagnose and label, in medical terminology, every possible behavior or human difficulty imaginable is one which is difficult to suppress. The most recent proposals for change in the *Diagnostic and Statistical Manual*, (American Psychiatric Association, 1977), which is the labelers' handbook, are a case in point. The newest version will literally provide a label for 230 separate categories of "mental disorder," including the labeling of such problems as "reading difficulty." Even those who are unconvinced that labeling is a major cause of mental disorder have raised objections to this tendency to label all possible problems with a medical diagnosis (cf. Garmezy, 1978).

There are a variety of studies which purport to show the specific effects of labeling within the mental health system. For example, Temerlin (1968) investigated suggestion effects in psychiatric diagnosis. A film of a healthy individual being interviewed by the author was shown to 45 graduate students in clinical psychology, 25 practicing clinical psychologists and 25 psychiatrists. Before the film was shown, a "prestige" confederate remarked that the patient on the tape was "a very interesting man because he looks neurotic, but is actually quite psychotic." The film was integrated into the regular workday routine so that subjects did not know they were participating in an experiment. After viewing the film all subjects indicated their diagnosis on a sheet which listed ten psychoses, ten neuroses, and ten miscellaneous personality types, one of which was "normal or healthy personality." They were also asked to write a description of the behaviors which led them to their diagnosis. Several control groups were used in order to account for a number of potential explanations other than the impact of a suggestion by the "prestige" confederate. Data analysis revealed significant effects of the prestige suggestion. No control subject ever diagnosed psychosis, while in the experimental group a diagnosis of psychosis was made by 60 percent of the psychiatrists, 28 percent of the clinical psychologists, and 11 percent of the graduate students.

Langer and Abelson (1974) were interested in determining the effects of clinicians' beliefs on how they view their clients. They exposed professionals representing a traditional psychiatric viewpoint as well as those representing a more behavioral viewpoint to a videotaped interview. Half were told that the interviewee was a patient and the others were told that he was a job applicant. Langer and Abelson found that those who held traditional psychiatric views who were told that the interviewee was a patient rated him as significantly more disturbed than those who were told that he was a job applicant. This was not true for behavioral psychologists. The authors concluded that traditional psychologists are more susceptible to labeling bias than behaviorists.

A number of studies of admissions procedures to hospitals have found that the decision to hospitalize a person is often a function of variables such as referral source, age, and record of previous hospitalization rather than of a client's actual behavior (Mischler & Wexler, 1963). Steadman (1972) found that willingness to transfer patients from maximum security to civil hospitals was a function of age, skin color and length of hospitalization, although such variables turned out to be unrelated to later behavior. Greenly (1972) found length of hospitalization to be related to family wishes, rather than degree of psychiatric impairment; and Linsky (1970) found that the likelihood of hospitalization was predictable from one's sex, living arrangement and marital and job status. Rushing (1971) observed that those lacking socioeconomic and job status were more likely to be committed to mental hospitals. Haney and Miller (1970) found that the judgment of incompetency was predictable on the basis of who filed the court action.

A number of other authors have agreed that both incompetency to stand trial and insanity hearings are biased toward seeing incompetence and insanity (Haney & Michielutte, 1968; Scheff, 1964). Wenger and Fletcher (1969) found that the presence of legal counsel affected the outcome; and Miller and Schwartz (1966), that outcomes were a function of how the judge was approached, rather than of psychiatric symptomology.

Rather than attempting a detailed review of these and other studies we simply mention them as examples, and point out that there is a great deal of evidence to indicate that both the diagnosis and treatment a person receives in the mental health system is a function of a number of factors other than one's actual symptomology. Below we describe one study which is of particular interest in this regard.

In one of the most interesting field studies of the labeling process ever conducted, David Rosenhan describes an experiment in which sane people purposely had themselves admitted to twelve different mental hospitals (Rosenhan, 1973). These pseudopatients included people such as graduate students, physicians, a homemaker, a psychiatrist and a painter. They were men and women who changed their names and occupations but otherwise kept their own personal history when they called into a mental hospital for an appointment, and complained about hearing voices. All were admitted to the hospital. After admission they ceased feigning symptoms and behaved as normally as they were able, and followed all instructions other than swallowing their medication. These pseudopatients spent a great deal of time recording their observations. None knew when he or she would be released, and all were told that they would have to get out on their own by convincing the hospital staff that they were well. Of course none of the hospital staff knew that these were people who had purposely entered the hospital in order to observe its procedures.

The twelve hospitals were located in five different states. Some hospitals were old, and some new. They included public as well as private, university as well as federal- and state-supported hospitals. They were representative of places in which someone with an acute mental health problem would be likely to find oneself, and were not "back wards" or isolated from the mainstream of modern mental health care.

What happens to people who make such a contact with the mental health system and voluntarily allow themselves to be labelled mentally ill? All but one of the pseudopatients were admitted with a diagnosis of "schizophrenia" and none were detected as being "normal." When they were released each was labeled "schizophrenic in remission." That is, the label, once given, remained with the person. Even when released and behaving normally they were still viewed as sick, even though the so-called sickness was not directly observable.

The pseudopatients were kept in the hospital between 7 and 52 days, the average length of stay being 19 days. Many of their fellow patients guessed that these were normal people "checking up" on the doctors, but the staff never raised this question either directly or in their own notes. Rosenhan suggests that this is because the bias in the mental health system is toward seeing illness, and once a person is labeled, the label is difficult to lose. Rosenhan goes on to suggest that in the case of psychological diagnosis the tendency to see and label "illness" may create a number of detrimental social consequences, including barriers to employment, that probably impede further life adjustment. For an example of this process one need only recall the case of Senator Thomas Eagleton, who was the original democratic nominee for vice-president of the United States in 1972. Unfortunately, Eagleton was apparently once treated for psychological depression, and once it was made public that he had been a "psychiatric patient," he was forced to give up the nomination.

In an effort to begin to collect data on how the process of labeling may work, Rosenhan conducted a second experiment in which the staff of a research and teaching hospital was told that sometime during the next three months one or more pseudopatients would seek admission. Each staff member was asked to rate on a ten-point scale of confidence which of all the 193 patients admitted during that time span were psdeuopatients. Forty-one were rated with high confidence by at least one staff person to be pseudopatients. Twenty-three were suspected by at least one psychiatrist and 19 by one psychiatrist and one other staff member. Actually no pseudopatients were sent to the hospital. Rosenhan suggests that this "seeing" of pseudopatients was a function of the changed "payoff matrix" for decision making. It was very risky not to detect pseudopatients, given the embarrassment of the last experiment. However, in normal circumstances the higher risk is to find people sane, since they may go out into the community and create trouble. Hence the conservative step would be to label one as insane on minimal evidence, since this will protect the labeler.

Perhaps even more interesting is how pseudopatients were perceived when in the hospital. Rosenhan notes that once a person was designated abnormal all of his other behavior was viewed through those glasses. Indeed the label was so powerful that many of the pseudopatients' normal behaviors were either overlooked or misinterpreted. Rosenhan goes on to describe how the patients' reports of their childhood (remember that these were normal people) were interpreted to fit the current view of the dynamics of schizophrenia. Their note taking was viewed by experts and helpers as part of their pathological behavior. The staff suggested in their chart notes that it was an indication of their "paranoia."

Rosenhan goes on to speculate that such expectations, which are a part of the staff's view of people admitted to a mental hospital, may actually become a part of real patients' self-identity when they are treated this way over time. As in the Snyder and Swann (1978) study cited earlier, through this social construction of reality the patients may actually begin to exacerbate their own "crazy behavior" in order to meet expectations.

Rosenhan also presents data on how hospital systems breed disregard for patients as full human beings. He compared an attempt by pseudopatients to obtain information from various staff members to similar attempts to obtain information from a stranger in another setting. When the pseudopatient attempted to ask a question of psychiatrists, nurses or attendants, the most frequent response was for them to be literally ignored. The questions they asked were not disruptive or difficult, but simple questions asking for information, such as "When will I be presented at the staff meeting?" Rosenhan collected data similar to this as a comparison, by having a young woman walk through the halls of Stanford University and the University Medical Center, stop professors and physicians, and ask a series of questions. There was an overwhelming tendency for people to stop and talk with her in the halls.

It is clear from these reports that being granted the label "mental patient," especially if one is hospitalized, relegates one to the status of a nonperson, and makes one less likely than a complete stranger to be spoken to by "treaters." Rosenhan suggests that appropriate ways to deal with the problem other than by labeling people and sending them to a hospital might include crisis intervention and behavior therapeutic approaches which deal with problems on the spot, rather than by diagnosis (an official label) and isolation in a hospital. While these suggestions are beyond the scope of this chapter it should be understood that they are viable, practical alternatives (cf. Rappaport, 1977).

CONCLUSION

It is important for those of us who are granted labeling authority to recognize its potential effects. We regard this chapter as a statement about the social psychology of expert and helpers. Labeling theory has helped to organize a number of laboratory and field studies cutting across educational, criminal justice and mental health settings. We regard labeling theory as one which can have a sensitizing or enlightening impact on experts and helpers vis-á-vis their social power. By increasing awareness and understanding the powers which are held by authorized social-labelers, experts and helpers may better cope with the irony of creating harm as well as good.

We must not take our powers as labelers lightly. To deal with the problems raised in this chapter requires us to rethink the helper-helpee paradigm which places us in the role of expert and helper, rather than the role of servant and colleague. Were we to change our role relationships we might find ourselves trying to understand and facilitate the natural processes of help endemic to any community, rather than spending endless hours diagnosing and labeling. We might find ourselves looking for the strengths and assets, competencies and skills, in people and communities, rather than trying to find deficits and weaknesses to categorize. These are the kind of social policies which we suggested at the outset of this chapter might follow from a better understanding of the social psychology of experts and helpers. Such social policies need to be generated and tested by those who wish to take seriously the task of social change.

References

American Psychiatric Association. The task force on nomenclature and statistics. *DSM III. Diagnostic and Statistical Manual of Mental Disorders*, Third Edition, 1977.

Barber, T. X., & Silver, M. J. Fact, fiction and the experimenter bias effect. *Psychological Bulletin Monograph*, 1968, *70*, Part 2.

Barker, R. G. *Ecological psychology: Concepts and methods for studying the environment of human behavior*. Stanford, Calif.: Stanford University Press, 1968.

Becker, H. S. *Outsiders*. New York: Free Press, 1963.

Caplan, N., & Nelson, S. D. On being useful: The nature and consequences of psychological research on social problems. *American Psychologist*, 1973, *28*, 199–211.

Carson, R. C. *Interaction concepts of personality*. Chicago: Aldine, 1969.

Ekehammer, B. Interactionism in personality from a historical perspective. *Psychological Bulletin*, 1974, *81*, 1026–1048.

Fo, W. S. O., & O'Donnell, C. R. The buddy system: Effect of community intervention on delinquent offenses. *Behavior Therapy*, 1975, *6*, 522–524.

Garmezy, N. DSM III Never mind the psychologists: Is it good for the children? *The Clinical Psychologist*, 1978, *3–4*, 1,4,6.

Gergen, K. Social psychology as history. *Journal of Personality and Social Psychology*, 1973, *26* 309–320.

Gibbs, J. Issues in defining deviant behavior. In R. A. Scott & J. D. Douglas (Eds.), *Theoretical perspectives on deviance*. New York: Basic Books, 1972.

Gove, W. Societal reaction as an explanation of mental illness: An evaluation. *American Sociological Review*, 1970a, *35*, 873–884.

Gove, W. Who is hospitalized: A critical review of some sociological studies of mental illness. *Journal of Health and Social Behavior*, 1970b, *11*, 294–303.

Gove, W. Reply to Akers. *American Sociological Review*, 1972, *31*, 488–490.

Gove, W. Labeling and mental illness: A critique. In W. R. Gove (Ed.), *The labeling of deviance: Evaluating a perspective*. New York: Wiley, 1975a.

Gove, W. The labeling theory of mental illness: A reply to Scheff.*American Sociological Review*, 1975b, *40*, 242–248.

Greenly, J. R. Alternative views of the psychiatrist's role. *Social Problems*, 1972, *20*, 252–262.

Haney, C. A., & Michielutte, R. Selective factors operating in the adjudication of incompetency. *Journal of Health and Social Behavior*, 1968, *9*, 233–242.

Haney, C. A., & Miller, K. S. Definitional factors in mental incompetency. *Sociology and Social Research*, 1970, *54*, 520–532.

Hollingshead, B. B., & Redlich, F. C. *Social class and mental illness: A community study*. New York: Wiley, 1958.

Illich, I. *Medical nemesis: The expropriation of health*. New York: Pantheon, 1976.

Kerber, K. W., & Clore, G. L. *Toward an affective theory of attraction and trait attribution*. Unpublished, 1978.

Krohn, M. D., & Akers, R. L. An alternative view of the labeling versus psychiatric perspectives on societal reaction to mental illness. *Social Forces*, 1977, *56*, 341–361.

Langer, S. J., & Abelson, R. P. A patient by any other name . . . : Clinical group difference in labeling bias. *Journal of Consulting and Clinical Psychology*, 1974, *42*, 4–9.

Leary, T. *Interpersonal diagnosis of personality*. New York: Ronald Press, 1957.

Linsky, A. Who shall be excluded? The influence of personal attributes in community reaction to the mentally ill. *Social Psychiatry*, 1970, *5*, 166–171.

Malinowski, B. *Crime and custom in savage society*. New York: Humanities Press, 1926.

Meyers, J. K., & Bean, L. L. *A decade later: A follow-up of social class and mental illness*. New York: Wiley, 1967.

Miller D., & Schwartz, M. County lunacy commission hearings: Some observations of commitments to a state mental hospital. *Social Problems*, 1966, *14*, 26–35.

Miller, G. A., Galanter, E., & Pribram, K. *Plans and the structure of behavior*. New York: Holt, 1960.

Mischel, W. Personality and assessment. New York: Wiley, 1968.

Mischler, E., & Wexler, N. Decision processes in psychiatric hospitalization. *American Sociological Review*, 1963, *28*, 576–587.

Osgood, C., Suci, G. J., & Tannenbaum, P. H. *The measurement of meaning*. Urbana, Ill.: University of Illinois Press, 1957.

Rappaport, J. *Community psychology: Values, research and action*. New York: Holt, 1977.

Rappaport, J., Lamiell, J. T., & Seidman, E. Know and tell: Conceptual constraints, ethical issues, and alternatives for psychologists in (and out of) the juvenile justice system. In J. Monahan (Ed.), *The role of psychology in the criminal justice system*. Washington D. C.: American Psychological Association. In press.

Rist, R. C. Student social class and teacher expectations: The self-fulfilling prophecy in ghetto education. *Harvard Educational Review*, 1970, *40*, 411–451.

Roesch, R., & Golding, S. L. *A systems analysis of competency to stand trial procedures: Implications for forensic services in North Carolina*. National Clearinghouse for Criminal Justice Planning and Architecture. Urbana, Ill.: University of Illinois, 1977.

Rosenhan, D. On being sane in insane places. *Science*, 1973, *179*, 250–258.

Rosenthal, R., & Jacobson, L. *Pygmalion in the classroom: Teacher expectation and pupils' intellectual development*. New York: Holt, 1968.

Rotter, G. S., & Rotter, N. *Race, work performance, and merit rating: An experimental evaluation*. Paper presented at the meeting of the Eastern Psychological Association, Philadelphia, 1969.

Rotter, J. B. *Social learning and clinical psychology*. Englewood Cliffs, N. J.: Prentice-Hall, 1954.

Rotter, J. B., Chance, J., & Phares, E. J. An introduction to social learning theory. In J. B. Rotter, J. Chance, & E. J. Phares (Eds.) *Applications of a social learning theory of personality*. New York: Holt, 1972.

Rubovitz, P. C., & Maher, M. L. Pygmalion black and white. *Journal of Personality and Social Psychology*, 1973, *25*, 210–218.

Rushing, W. A. Individual resources, societal reaction, and hospital commitment. *American Journal of Sociology*, 1971, *77*, 511–526.

Sarbin, T. R. A role theory perspective for community psychology: The structure of social identity. In D. Adelson & B. Kalis (Eds.), *Community Psychology and mental health: Perspectives and Challenges*. Scranton, Pa.: Chandler, 1970.

Scheff, T. J. The societal reaction to deviance: Ascriptive elements in the psychiatric screening of mental patients in a midwestern state. *Social Problems*, 1964, *11*, 401–413.

Scheff, T. J. *Being mentally ill*. Chicago: Aldine, 1966.

Scheff, T. J. *Mental illness and social processes*. New York, Harper & Row, 1967.

Scheff, T. J. (Ed.). *Labeling madness*. Englewood Cliffs, N. J.: Prentice-Hall, 1975.

Schur, E. M. *Radical non-intervention: Rethinking the delinquency problem*. Englewood Cliffs, N.J.: Prentice-Hall, 1973.

Seaver, W. B. Effects of naturally induced teacher expectancies. *Journal of Personality and Social Psychology*, 1973, *28*, 333–343.

Seidman, E., Rappaport, J., & Davidson, W. S. Adolescents in legal jeopardy: Initial success and replication of an alternative to the criminal justice system. *Division of Consulting Psychology Newsletter*, 1977, *28*, 16–21.

Snyder, M., & Swann, W. B. Behavioral confirmation in social interaction: From social perception to social reality. *Journal of Experimental Social Psychology*, 1978. *14*, 148–162.

Steadman, H. J. The psychiatrist as a conservative agent of social control. *Social Problems*, 1972, *20*, 263–271.

Sullivan, H. S. *The collected works of Harry Stack Sullivan* (Vol. I), H. S. Perry & M. L. Gawel (Eds.). New York: Norton, 1953.

Szasz, T. S. *The myth of mental illness*. New York: Hoeber, 1961.

Szasz, T. S. *The manufacture of madness: A comparative study of the inquisition and the mental health movement*. New York: Harper & Row, 1970.

Szasz, T. S. *Ceremonial chemistry*. Garden City, N.Y.: Anchor, 1974.

Tannenbaum, F. *Crime and the community*. New York: McGraw-Hill, 1951.

Temerlin, M. K. Suggestion effects in psychiatric diagnosis. *Journal of Nervous and Mental Disease*, 1968, *147*, 349–353.

Thibaut, J., & Kelley, H. H. *The social psychology of groups*. New York: Wiley, 1959.

Weikart, D. P. Relationship of curriculum, teaching, and learning in preschool education. In J. C. Stanley (Ed.), *Preschool for the disadvantaged*. Baltimore: Johns Hopkins, 1972.

Wenger, D. L., & Fletcher, C. R. The effects of legal counsel in admissions to a state mental hospital: A confrontation of professions. *Journal of Health and Social Behavior*, 1969, *10*, 66–72.

Wicker, T. *A time to die*. New York: Quadrangle, 1975.

Zimbardo, P. G. The mind is a formidable jailer: A Pirandellian prison. *New York Times Magazine*, April 8, 1973, p. 38.

CHAPTER 4

Expectancies and Attributions

Implications for Community Mental Health

Bonnie R. Strickland, Ph.D.
and
Ronnie Janoff-Bulman, Ph.D.

Most of us consider it self-evident that what we believe about ourselves in relation to the world influences and in part determines our behavior. We perceive the events around us in many different ways and behave according to the meanings that we attribute to our environment and ourselves; we are familiar with the eternal optimist who always finds the proverbial glass of water half-full in contrast to the person who perceives the same glass as half-empty. Psychologists, in spite or perhaps because of their continued experimentation with human behavior, are not at all agreed as to how, or even if, cognitive factors, such as the perception of events, influence action. The debate as to the role of personal constructs about the world in relation to how we then respond has been a long one and is certainly not resolved.

Since social scientists do not fully understand the influence of perception, attributions of meaning, and expectancies for individual behavior, it is not surprising that even less is known about the role and influence of attributional variables for groups of people. However, psychological research and theory derived from an individual psychology emphasis may provide significant insights into processes occurring at the larger, community level. The following pages will review two cognitive constructs which have grown out of an indiviudal-oriented psychology; attributions and expectancies about control will be considered, the former derived from theory and research in social psychology, the latter from personality psychology, with its emphasis on individual differences. Both the ways in which people make attributions about the causes of behavior and the extent to which they believe in internal versus external reinforcement of control may have important implications for research and practice in the growing field of community mental health.

ATTRIBUTION THEORY

In his classic experiment on obedience, Milgram (1963, 1974) demonstrated in the laboratory that most people, when ordered to administer what they believe to be increasingly strong electric shocks to an innocent other (really a confederate of the experimenter), will continue to obey such orders. Prior to conducting his study, Milgram asked a group of psychiatrists, graduate students, professors, college sophomores and middle-class adults to predict the experimental outcome. All groups predicted that virtually all subjects would disobey, and that only 1 or 2 percent would continue to the end of the shock generator, this latter group representing a pathological fringe of the population. The psychiatrists, for example, predicted that only one subject in 1,000 would proceed to the shock marked by *XXX*. Yet fully 65 percent of the subjects, "normal" individuals drawn from the general population, administered the highest shock.

The popularity of Milgram's study has been largely due to people's person-centered approach toward human behavior; it is generally assumed that there was some factor within the subjects—perhaps some antialtruistic strain—which determined the ostensibly sadistic outcomes. However, as Milgram (1963, 1974) reports, most subjects were extremely uncomfortable and upset about continuing with the experimental shock procedures, yet obeyed nevertheless. It is extremely difficult for us to accept the finding that the situational pressures in Milgram's experiment—the presence of a 31-year-old man in a lab coat telling the subject to continue with the experiment—could induce individuals to harm (or so they thought) another person. "They focus on the character of the autonomous individual rather than on the situation in which he finds himself" (Milgram, 1974, p. 310); yet it was the situation, which on the face of it seems quite weak, which largely controlled the outcomes of the men and women involved in Milgram's experiment.

Concern over our underestimation of the situational influences on people's behavior has been addressed within attribution theory, an area of interest within the field of social psychology. Recently, there has been an increasing interest in the question of how we perceive ourselves and other people; attribution theory, in particular, is concerned with how people understand the causes or events in their lives, particularly their own and other people's behavior. Psychologists working in the area of attribution regard the "woman in the street" as an "intuitive psychologist who seeks to explain behavior and to draw inferences about actors and their environments" (Ross, 1977, p. 174).

According to an attributional perspective, the most rudimentary causal units into which we, the attributers, divide our world are the person and the environment, a dichotomy which has alternatively been described as internal-external or dispositional-situational. That is, an individual can explain behavior by attributing its cause to situational factors or personal factors, as illustrated by the statements, "Tom hit Bill because he was provoked by Bill" (external) versus "Tom hit Bill because he is an aggressive person" (internal). In making an internal or external attribution, we take into account what experience has led us to expect in various situations, including what is socially normative and appropriate behavior.

According to Kelley's (1967, 1971, 1973) Discounting Principle, if an external (situational) attribution is "sufficient" to account for an event, then no other inference (e.g., to a disposition) is made, and an external attribution is rendered. If, on the other hand, an event seems to occur "in spite of" situational factors, the event is attributed to the person (see also Jones & Davis, 1965). Thus in a "closed" classroom we would be apt to make an external (i.e., situational) attribution for the behavior of students who are calmly sitting at their desks listening to the teacher's lesson, for this would generally be regarded as appropriate classroom behavior; the fact that these students are in a classroom is sufficient to explain their behavior. However, an internal (i.e., dispositional) attribution is apt to be made for the student who is standing and shouting at the teacher in the midst of the lesson (e.g., she or he is crazy; she or he is hyperactive; she or he is completely incapable of being disciplined). In this instance, the classroom setting cannot adequately account for the student's behavior, which appears quite unexpected in this environment. The distinction between internal and external attributions is meaningfully described by Ross (1977), who proposes that situational explanations (i.e., external attributions) "do not state or imply any dispositions on the part of the actor beyond those typical of actors in general, whereas dispositional explanations (i.e., internal attributions) do state or imply unique relatively atypical or distinguishing personal dispositions" (pp. 176–177).

Attribution theorists assume that people, through the process of causal attribution, render the world more meaningful and stable. In ascribing causality to a person or situation (or some combination), we are locating stable features of environmental settings and people such that we can strengthen our own beliefs in the continuity, predictability, and controllability of our world. If we infer that Tom hit Bill because he is aggressive, we may be better prepared to deal with Tom, or we may try to insure that our paths don't cross; similarly, if we know that everyone we've spoken to about a particular English course expresses serious dissatisfactions, we are likely to make an external attribution for their poor recommendation (i.e., the course is bad) and will probably decide not to register for it. Thus, in observing behavior we seek answers to the question of "why" particular behaviors occur, and our own attributional responses affect our subsequent behavior. The ramifications of an internal versus an external attribution are perhaps most clearly observed in the case of a criminal trial in which the defendant is charged with murder. If we infer that the defendant acted in an appropriate manner, given the situation, as in the case of self-defense, we essentially are making an external attribution for the murder, and she or he will consequently be deemed not guilty; if, however, we make an internal attribution, suggesting that there is something about the defendant, and not the context in which she or he acted, which determined his or her actions, then she or he will be judged guilty of murder. A further example of the different consequences of internal and external attributions for an event derives from explanations given for the urban riots during the summer of 1967 (reported in Wegner & Vallacher, 1977). In the editorial pages of magazines and newspapers, two major categories of explanation could be found; riots were either attributed to the internal or personal properties of the actors, or they were attributed to external, situational factors. In the case of internal attributions, the rioters were perceived as deviants and criminal types, whereas in the case of external attributions, such factors as government mismanagement and an irresponsible Congress were cited as the causes of the urban disturbances. Further, those editorial writers who made internal attributions to the actors evaluated the riots as illegitimate in their newspapers and magazines, whereas those who made external attributions evaluated the riots as legitimate; the same actions were judged very differently, but the evaluative judgements were consistent with the two distinct attributions that were made to account for the riots.

The Fundamental Attribution Error

Work in the area of internal-external attributions has led theorists to propose that there exists a "fundamental attribution error." While this label was recently provided by Ross (1977), Heider (1958) discussed the bias thirty years ago. The phrase refers to a general psychological tendency to underestimate the influence of situational forces on behavior. That is, people are generally biased toward making internal rather than external attributions to explain behavior.[1] Thus, if we see a person trip on the sidewalk, we are apt not to take into account the cracks and heaves in the concrete, and conclude instead that the individual is a

[1] Generally, we are not as susceptible to this bias in explaining our own behavior as we are when inferring the causes of other peoples' behavior (e.g., Jones & Nisbett, 1971; Monson & Snyder, 1977).

clumsy person. A more powerful example of the fundamental attribution error is that offered by the preceding discussion of Milgram's obedience experiment. Those who were asked to predict the outcome of the study consistently underestimated the power of the experimental setting to induce obedience, and the predicted outcomes were thus very far from the mark. The fundamental attribution error continued to operate once the results of the experiment were publicized, for once again people underestimated the environmental control of the experimental subjects and assumed that there must have been something about the people who participated (i.e., internal attribution) which could account for their "despicable" obedience. Social psychology professors confront this same attitude in the classroom when they present the results of the Milgram experiment, for, with very few exceptions, students confidently assert that they would never have gone to the end of the shock board; and yet Yale students responded with approximately the same level of obedience as the nonstudent population when Milgram ran the study with this intelligent, aware population (Milgram, 1974).

While the fundamental bias exists, its source remains somewhat of a mystery. It may derive from a desire to render other people's actions, in particular, predictable; if we make dispositional, internal attributions, we are essentially preparing ourselves for future interactions with people by presuming stable traits internal to others. The attributional error may derive as well from a more perceptual, less motivationally-based bias. People and the environment may represent a figure-ground type of picture, in which changes are ascribed to the figure (person) rather than the broader background factor, the ground (environment). While the source of the attributional bias remains an open question, its actual existence can be well documented.

In social-psychological experiments it has been found that attributers draw relatively confident inferences about a person's dispositions and private opinions, even when these inferences are drawn, for example, from an essay which the person wrote in response to an experimenter's request in a "no choice" condition (Jones & Harris, 1967); that is, the person is told by the experimenter which side of the argument to take, and yet the attributer assumes this represents the other's true opinion. The situation is once again causally underestimated. The immense impact of Darley and Latané's (1968) work on the phenomenon of bystander intervention in an emergency seems also to stem largely from our tendency to unwittingly underestimate situational influences on behavior. These researchers were interested in the problem of the lack of helping behavior in emergencies, a problem epitomized by the 1964 Kitty Genovese case in Queens, New York. Kitty Genovese was murdered outside her apartment building while 38 of her neighbors looked on but did nothing to help. In responding to this situation, people, including the media, generally cried out about the problem of apathy in our cities; in the case of Kitty Genovese, her neighbors were apathetic, noncaring people. Darley and Latané's research, however, suggests that these attributions were not accurate; the source of the problem lay not within the personal dispositions of the people involved, but rather in the situational factors surrounding the incident. In a series of ingenious experiments, Latané and Darley demonstrated that the larger the group of bystanders, the less likely the intervention in an emergency. There is a "diffusion of responsibility" that occurs, by which the amount of responsibility an individual feels is a function of the number of people present. The more people there are, the less one's individual responsibility. Thus in the case of Kitty Genovese, there was a feeling that somebody else must have called the police already; Darley and Latané's results suggest that if only one person witnessed the murder, it is far more likely that the police would have been called early, rather than after it was too late, as was the case. The situation affects our behavior more than we generally recognize.

Blaming the Victim. The phenomenon referred to as "blaming the victim" is in many ways a special case of the fundamental attribution error. Instead of attributing the cause of a victim's misfortune to external factors, people instead make an internal attribution and thus blame the personal characteristics of the victim. Within social psychology, Lerner (1970; Lerner & Matthews, 1967; Lerner & Simmons, 1966) has demonstrated this phenomenon in the laboratory, for in his experiments innocent victims are derogated by observers. While Lerner presents his findings as support for his proposed "need to believe in a just world," his results are also consistent with an attributional bias perspective.

In a book entitled *Blaming the Victim*, Ryan (1971) examines the problem of blaming the victim from a social policy perspective. Ryan presents a very cogent argument, contending that victims of social, economic and racial injustice in this country are actually blamed for their circumstances and problems by those who have managed to escape such victimization and have decent jobs, houses and schools for their children. The latter, Ryan suggests, are neither insensitive nor unconcerned about the victims; in fact, they probably sincerely want to put an end to poverty, discrimination, slums and exploitation, but they unwittingly engage in blaming people rather than larger social institutions, the true source of the problems. The nonvictimized, according to Ryan, have been misled by myths and untruths, and have accepted an ideology of "blaming the victim," to the grave detriment of those who have been unable to escape victimization.

A study by Caplan and Nelson (1973) powerfully illustrates that psychologists, too, are far from immune from the fundamental bias and the "blaming the victim" phenomenon. Although Caplan and Nelson were specifically interested in the social implications of psychological research, and not in the question of attributional biases, they did choose to examine the extent to which psychological researchers attributed causality for a social problem to person-centered variables (i.e., internal attribution). They focused on the problems of black Americans and located all research dealing with black Americans that was abstracted in *Psychological Abstracts* during a six-month period in 1970. They found that approximately 82 percent of the research interpreted the problems of black Americans as due to person-centered causes. Caplan and Nelson discuss some of the larger consequences that result from such an attributional perspective, including releasing the government and social agencies from blame, freeing social institutions from feeling responsible for ameliorating the problem, and focusing treatment on changing people rather than changing institutions. While such implications may not represent the reasons for such attributions, the work of Caplan and Nelson argues that they are functionally the result of such attributions. The fundamental attribution error, then, is not a bias without the potential for powerful social consequences.

Social Roles. While "blaming the victim" is a special case of the fundamental attribution error in that it focuses on the attributions made for a special population (i.e., victims), another special case of the fundamental attribution error focuses on a particular aspect of the situation which is underestimated, that of social roles (see Ross, 1977). Our interpersonal interactions are often shaped by the roles we play, yet roles do not derive from our personal dispositions, but are in important ways external to the person. Thus, while a person "carries" his or her personal dispositions and tendencies with him or her (although she or he may or may not act on them), she or he probably plays different roles which are consistent with the situational context of an interaction. So at school Susan is in a student role, at home she is in a daughter role, with her roommate she is in a friend role. Thus, in making an attribution to one's role we are in essence making an external rather than an internal attribution, and, as in the general case, of internal-external attributions, we underestimate the power of roles.

The significance of roles in determining behavior, and the underestimation of this influence, was demonstrated in a study of prison behavior conducted by Zimbardo, Haney, Banks, and Jaffee (1973). Zimbardo et al set up a mock prison in the basement of a building at Stanford University and recruited Stanford male undergraduates to take part in the study. Students were given psychological tests and were screened to insure that those who participated were psychologically healthy. The 21 undergraduates selected from 75 volunteers were randomly assigned to the role of prisoners (10) or guards (11), and without being told beforehand when it would occur, one day the "prisoners" were picked up at their homes by local police and brought to the mock prison at Stanford. Zimbardo et al. tried to make the prison as psychologically similar to a real prison as possible (e.g., prisoners wore stockings over their heads rather than having their heads shaved), yet nobody in the study expected the experience to be as "real" as it was. Several prisoners had breakdowns and had to leave early (the first after 36 hours), and eventually the study had to be ended prematurely; it was initially scheduled for 14 days, but was terminated on the sixth day. Most dramatic of all was the extent to which the students quickly and naturally engaged in role-consistent behavior. While the prisoners initially tried to rebel, they soon became a seemingly apathetic lot, obeying the whims of the guards; the guards, in the meantime, were quite brutal, waking prisoners in the middle of the night and asking them to do situps, punishing the prisoners severely for small "errors," and acting in what appeared to be a sadistic manner. In relating their experiences in the prison after the completion of the study, both the prisoners and guards stated that they were not simply "acting" in roles; rather they were prisoners and guards. This sense is reinforced when one sees the slide show of the study compiled by Zimbardo and his colleagues; the experience was an extremely powerful one, and the roles in which the students were randomly placed resulted in a complete metamorphosis of normal, healthy, college students. Nothing in the personality tests administered prior to the study could predict the differentiation of behavior between prisoners and guards. The roles to which they were assigned determined the differences which, from an observer's perspective, looked very much like personality (i.e., dispositional) differences. The powerful impact of the roles was not expected.

While roles have a powerful influence on behavior in general, they also provide differential power in social interactions, leading to self-presentations determined by roles rather than personal characteristics. An experiment by Ross, Amabile, and Steinmetz (1977) found strong support for our underestimation of the effects of roles on self-presentation. In the study subjects were assigned to the roles of "questioner" or "contestant," and the task was a quiz game on "general knowledge." The subjects assigned to the questioner role were asked to compose a set of questions for the contestants; contestants responded to the questions and questioners provided feedback as to how they did. Both questioners and participants were then asked to rate the questioners' and contestants' general knowledge. What is of particular significance is the fact that the random assignment of students to roles actually resulted in a "role-conferred advantage" for the questioners and a "role-conferred disadvantage" for the contestants. Questioners were able to draw from their own store of knowledge in asking questions of the participants, questions which were likely to be difficult and esoteric, and not likely to be known by the contestants. If given the chance, contestants could no doubt have drawn difficult questions from their selective knowledge base, yet this was not a part of the contestant role. While subjects were aware of the random assignment to roles, as well as the "unequal" nature of the quiz game, they were nevertheless consistently biased in their evaluations of contestants' and questioners' general knowledge; both questioners and contestants rated the questioner as having more general knowledge than the contestant, an evaluation shared by uninvolved observers as well.

In discussing the implications of these findings, Ross (1977) writes:

> There are, of course, countless other contexts in which formal or informal social roles may constrain interpersonal encounters and, in so doing, bias both the data available to the intuitive psychologist and the interpersonal judgements that follow from that data. Thus the employer may dwell upon his personal triumphs, avocations, and areas of knowledge and may avoid mention of his failures, whereas his employee enjoys no such freedom. The physician, likewise, is relatively free to assume with his patient whichever role—stern parent, sympathetic friend, or detached scientist—he wishes. Similarly, the more dominant partner in a personal relationship can disproportionately dictate the rules and arenas for self-presentation and that partner's choice is likely to be self-serving. . . . Individuals who enjoy positions of power by accident of birth, favorable political treatment, or even their own efforts also tend to enjoy advantages in self-presentation. Such individuals, and especially their disadvantaged underlings, may greatly underestimate the extent to which the seemingly positive attributes of the powerful simply reflect the advantages of social control (pp. 195–196).

Not only do roles largely determine our behavior, then, but the differential social power inherent in roles places constraints on the extent to which a self-presentation will be successful. Since encounters are controlled by those in relative positions of power, given their social roles, the encounter will generally be self-serving for these people. Their own self-presentational success is likely to render the disadvantageous position of the powerless even more devastating.

Community psychology and community mental health. The significance of the fundamental attribution error for community psychology and community mental health lies in its implicit warning against facile, internal attributions for people's problems. Since the growing field of community mental health is eager to serve groups which have too often been ignored by traditional psychology, particularly Ryan's "victimized" populations, awareness of our general attributional tendencies may help protect against an unwitting interpretation of problems in terms of person-centered causes. Racial, economic, and social injustice force particular roles and circumstances on people, and problems which derive from these roles and circumstances are all too often regarded and treated as psychological in nature, emanating from mental deficits within the individual.

The very phase "mental illness" connotes a disease which must be treated by focusing one's ameliorative efforts on the individual. Psychologists, who have traditionally attributed the causes of mental disorders to the personal dispositions of their clients, have no doubt been unwitting perpetrators of the fundamental attribution error. Community mental health, with its focus on the context in which an individual is embedded, is, from the perspective of attributional biases, just the type of corrective needed within the mental health field to adjust for the overwhelmingly person-centered approaches which have dominated the discipline to date.

Regarded as a "third mental health revolution," the field of community mental health involves a radical change in the conception of mental malfunctioning. As Korchin (1976) writes:

> As a consequence of the first revolution, the mentally disturbed emerged as sick people worthy of humane concern; from the second, their conditions were conceived as psychologically determined and psychologically treatable. The thrust of the third mental health revolution lies in the quest for prevention of emotional disorders through social and community interventions aimed at their social determinants (p. 473).

Given the power of the situation over people's behavior, as well as our general tendency to underestimate these external factors and overestimate personal dispositions, the new field of community mental health is an accomplishment in the evolution of clinical psychology. It implicitly and explicitly concerns itself with the external world of the individual, assuming that the cause of an individual's problem lies largely in the situational forces outside of the person. It is assumed that changes at the level of social institutions, including schools and families, can be effective in fostering the mental health of individuals, and the emphasis is thus on social and community interventions, which are "system-oriented" rather than person-oriented. This is a significant therapeutic feature of the community mental health movement, and is entirely consistent with recommendations that would follow from an awareness of the fundamental attribution error.

Social psychological research on attribution theory suggests that there are powerful biases operating in our causal inferences regarding the behavior of others; the area of community mental health is clearly a very positive step in the right direction, that of overcoming our general tendency to underestimate the importance of the situation when explaining behavior.

EXPECTANCIES ABOUT INTERNAL-EXTERNAL CONTROL OF REINFORCEMENT

The same arguments about locus of causality of events and problems of attribution bias that occur among social psychologists have also been of concern to personality theorists. Personality theory, especially in this country, first developed with an emphasis on individual differences and the identification of motives, needs and behaviors that are unique to one person in comparison with another. Psychologists, like the people they were trying to describe, attributed stable, ongoing personal characteristics to individuals and, at least historically, assumed that the locus of causality of events rests within the individual. For example, although aware of the press of environmental events, Murray (1938) described a number of individual needs, one of which was eventually elaborated into the "need for achievement" (Atkinson, 1958). Men who gave substantial achievement themes when asked to respond to projective tests were also found to be involved in successful, productive professional activities. They were ambitious, hard-working, and persisted at tasks which would lead to eventual reward. Most of the achievement research was conducted with males and few investigators could identify achievement motivation among women; another attributional error could have been occurring. Because women were not giving achievement themes to the same projective material and in the same conditions to which men responded, they were thought to have little, or no need for achievement, an assumption in line with prevailing beliefs about sex roles. Later research demonstrated that women too could be characterized as achievement-motivated, depending on sex-role orientation and the situation to which they were asked to respond (Alper, 1974). Horner (1972) further identified another need variable for women which she called "fear of success."

Following the Second World War, a number of psychologists were interested in understanding how some of the people of Germany could have become involved in the atrocities of the Holocaust. In contrast to the experimental work of Milgram on obedience and response to authority, Adorno and others (Adorno, Frenkel-Brunswick, Levinson, and Sanford, 1950) used more of a case study or clinical approach. They looked at projective and interview material given by a number of highly ethnocentric and anti-Semitic people. On the basis of these responses, Adorno and his colleagues described the potential fascist, whom he called the "authoritarian" personality. These individuals were characterized as rigid and intolerant of ambiguity as well as being particularly sensitive to dominant and submissive roles.

During the 1950s and 1960s, when the general public became concerned about bureaucracy and "group-think," psychologists went on to describe a number of other "needs" or "traits," all of which were thought to reside within the individual. These included need for affiliation, dependency, conformity and approval-motivation. Analysts were talking about oral and anal personalities. Although there was a growing recognition of the influence of environment and situational demands, most personality theorists were still assuming that causality of events lay within the individual. This was not surprising, of course. One was hard-pressed to identify even simple human behaviors, much less to open the door to describe the myriad situational events that face each of us daily. Still, psychologists became increasingly perturbed about the number of unanswered theoretical and practical questions which surrounded general personality theories with a trait emphasis. Is behavior stable over time? When do people change? When do personal needs become predominant and when do they fade into the background? And, of major importance, what about the influence of the environment? Doesn't the situation in which one finds oneself, shape responses? For a while personality theorists argued as to which was most important in understanding behavior, the individual or the situation. Others believed that human behavior could best be predicted through an interactional model which took both individual characteristics and situational demands into account.

Social Learning

Among the first interactional personality theories was a social learning approach developed by Julian Rotter (1954). Rotter proposed that the potential of a behavior occurring in a particular situation is a function of the individual's expectancy of the occurrence of reinforcement and the value of that particular reinforcement to the individual (Rotter, 1954; Rotter, Chance, & Phares, 1972). Basically behavior is a function of both expectancy and reinforcement in any particular situation. This theoretical approach was an integration of two diverse but exceptionally influential trends in American psychology, namely cognitive or field theories, which emphasized perceptual and cognitive mediating variables, and stimulus-response or reinforcement approaches, which focused on environmental contingencies. Several other theorists (Bandura, 1971; Mischel, 1973) have also developed similar models and there seems to be growing acceptance of the importance of understanding both individual difference variables, particularly those related to expectancies, beliefs systems and attitudes, as well as the nature of the environment and the stimulus conditions that shape responses.

One of the most important expectancy variables that emerged within Rotter's social learning theory was that of internal-external locus of control of reinforcement (IE). In the mid-fifties Rotter and his colleagues, especially Phares and James, began to investigate the fundamental question of whether and how expectancies influence behavior. They found that typical learning curves, including performance and extinction, varied depending upon whether or not human subjects believed that reinforment occurred as a function of their own skills or abilities or as a result of luck or chance. For example, Phares (1962) continually presented nonsense syllables, some of which were accompanied by an electric shock to the finger, to subjects whose perceptual threshholds to these syllables were noted. Some of these subjects were then told that they could terminate the shock by learning which button on a control panel controlled the shock for each syllable. Others were told that if they pressed the correct button the shock would terminate but that the connection between the buttons and syllables would be continually changing so that terminating the shock was entirely a matter of guessing and no learning was possible. In the first instance, subjects thought they could control the shock if they learned which button was linked to which syllable. In the second, subjects believed that the shock was beyond their control and would occur by chance. As Phares predicted, subjects in the skill, or control, condition improved their recognition threshold for the syllables to a significantly greater degree than did subjects in the chance condition. Phares was thus able to demonstrate that people who believe that they can control a situation, in contrast to those who feel that they have no control, are more likely to exhibit adaptive perceptual behavior which will enable them to cope with potentially threatening situations. Individuals who perceive contingencies between their own responses and subsequent events behave differently from people who see no relationship between their own actions and eventual reward.

The early work of Phares (1957), James (1962) and Holden and Rotter (1962) involved manipulation of skill and chance instructions in different tasks. In other experiments (Rotter, Liverant, & Crowne, 1961; Blackman, 1962; Bennion, 1961) the nature of the task itself was manipulated; for example, a hand steadiness task was compared to an extrasensory perception (ESP) task. In each of these instances, the results of the skill-chance classification of situations, whether by instruction or by the nature of the task, demonstrated different learning and extinction patterns. When subjects expected that they would control outcomes, they appeared to generalize from past experiences and developed improved strategies which resulted in greater learning. In chance conditions, subjects learned less and "this decrement in learning seems directly attributable to the effects of expectancy of belief that, in a given situation, they do not control the relationship between behavior and reinforcement" (Phares, 1976, p. 30).

If expectancies generated by skill and chance situations have an impact on simple learning tasks, then it is important to know if these expectancies might also be operating in a more general way when people are involved in their daily activities. Moving from a situational manipulation, a logical next step would be to determine the degree to which individuals usually believe that the events that occur in their lives are a function of their own skill and/or personal characteristics (internal expectancies), or whether the things that happen to them are a result of luck, fate, chance or powers beyond their personal control and understanding (external expectancies). Testing instruments were then developed to assess these generalized expectancies about IE (Rotter, 1966). Now we have returned to an individual expectancy variable which should be predictive of behavior in certain situations. Again, this locus of control expectancy is an individual reflection of reality and is not necessarily accurate. Thus, like other attributional and cognitive mediating styles, beliefs about control may be subject to biases and error.

Although the early IE measuring instruments had some limitations (for example, many people who reported themselves to be internal also appeared to be giving answers that were socially desirable), they did give investigators an opportunity to consider the relationship of the continuum of IE expectancies to behaviors logically related to beliefs about control. The impact of IE beliefs should be most noticeable in novel or ambiguous situations since specific environmental demands and unique expectancies can override the impact of generalized cognitive mediating variables. A young man who is constantly dominated by a strong father may have learned that he is not likely to get his way in the family when his wishes are at odds with his father's. When trying out for the school track team, however, he may expect that he will be successful if he practices and improves his running skills.

The early IE research was conducted within two broad methodologies: basic experimental laboratory research and field studies. This integration of theoretical findings from the laboratory and practical implications from field settings, including schools, prisons and hospitals, probably contributed to the increasing importance of the IE dimension in personality research. A further advantage inherent in this research was that the IE construct had first been described within an interactional social learning theory and so escaped some of the problems associated with trait theories. The popularity of IE was also probably a function of the importance and concern that most of us feel with regard to the way we control our lives. Beliefs about locus of control of reinforcement are learned like other behaviors, are appropriate in certain situations and not in others, and are modifiable. The general research on IE has been extensively reviewed elsewhere (Lefcourt, 1966; 1976; Phares, 1976; Rotter, 1966; 1975; Strickland, 1977, 1978) so we will now turn our attention to some of the specific research findings and their implications for community psychology.

Research Findings. Within our North American culture, beliefs about locus of control would be expected to have influence both with regard to the advantaged social groups who make attributions about the disadvantaged as well as the recipients of these attributions. Conversely, the disadvantaged have their own sets of beliefs about the "spoiled rich," the "honky" and so on. From our earliest history lessons, we have been taught that individuals within this "land of opportunity" who are willing to work hard can "make it" in our society. Public education has been provided for our nation's children and job possibilities are thought to be bountiful for adults. We all know the stories of Abe Lincoln, Henry Ford and even Jimmy Carter. In point of fact, many individuals within our society have struggled and come to realize some financial and professional success. Successive generations complete more years of schooling and per capita income steadily increases for most people. So it is probably not surprising that the larger society looks upon its disabled, disadvantaged, and dissident population with some suspicion. The minority is often a threat to the majority, or at least a nagging reminder that everyone does not enjoy the good life. One would expect the perceptions about control of reinforcement might be quite different according to one's position as a member of the "haves" or the "have nots." Indeed, this does appear to be the case.

As in most psychological research, responses to the IE assessment instruments were standardized on college students. Later innumerable other populations were added, including ordinary adult subjects, children and almost every imaginable social and economic group. In the early sixties, college students generally gave mean responses on the Rotter scale of 8 with a standard deviation of ±4, (the range on the scale is 0–23, with higher scores representing more external responses). Scores of noncollege adult populations were quite similar to those of the college students. As the decade of the sixties progressed, however, students became significantly more external in their responses, so that by the early seventies, mean scores were 12 (sd=4) (Rotter, 1975). This increasing turn toward externality presumably represented perceptions that life events were increasingly beyond one's control, an expectancy that may have been quite realistic in view of the war in Southeast Asia and the increasing unrest of college students and others who were perturbed with the political leadership in this country. The events of Watergate further reinforced the feelings that powerful others were manipulating the government to their own ends with little respect for the concerns of the citizens. Interestingly enough, IE responses have stayed around the 12 range during the seventies, with perhaps some indication that responses may be dropping toward internality as the decade draws to a close (Hochreich, Note 1). Generally, whether scores are changing or not, most groups of white middle-class adults, including college students, give similar mean scores while less advantaged groups are usually more external in their responses. This is true for people of low socio-economic status, for black populations, for psychiatric patients and for some people with chronic physical handicaps (see MacDonald, 1978 for a selected bibliography). Only one group that might be expected to be external gives IE scores similar or more internal than the general white middle class. The elderly, although their responses are tempered by the living situations in which they find themselves (Wolk, 1976), often give relatively internal responses when answering IE assessment instruments. Some researchers who have conducted these investigations suggest that the elderly learned their general expectancies about control at a time when society was even more reinforcing of individual action and personal skill than it is now (Duke, Shaheen, & Nowicki, 1974). Over all, then, it does appear that expectancies about control are related to age, to social and economic class placement as well as to certain other group characteristics such as acceptance and assimilation. The more subtle question is, what do these control expectancies mean in relation to the ways the socially advantaged and disadvantaged view each other? And, of more importance, does perceived control affect the ways these groups treat each other?

At this juncture of our research endeavors, these questions are not clearly answered. External individuals apparently feel helpless in effecting appropriate change and believe themselves to be powerless, or at least feel alienated from the political process. If one is trying to describe "typical" internals, however, certain inconsistencies arise. For example, individuals who hold an internal control of reinforcement orientation appear to be somewhat conservative and traditional in their political beliefs (Fink and Hjelle, 1973; Thomas, 1970; Silvern and Nakamura, 1971), yet this same reliance on self-sufficiency and individual as opposed to group or government efforts appears to be related to social protest and attempts to take action to improve aversive life situations. For example, during the early days of the civil rights movement in this country, Gore asked a large number of black college students to indicate the degree to which they were willing to commit themselves to significant social action. She asked students if they were willing to sign a petition, to march on the state capitol in a protest rally, or to actually take part in a "freedom ride" across the Southern states that were still actively resisting integration. She found that internal students were significantly more likely than external students to indicate that they would involve themselves in the more dramatic social actions such as a freedom ride (Gore and Rotter, 1963).

A problem with this research was that Gore and Rotter used the verbal report of the black students and did not actually observe them in protest situations. Strickland (1965) had the opportunity to approach members of the Southern Student Non-violent Coordinating Committee (SNCC), when they were holding an annual meeting in 1963 in the city of Atlanta. Members of this early civil rights organization were involved in voter registration across the South and were daily threatened and harassed by white community members who were not sympathetic to their efforts. One SNCC member had been arrested 62 times, and the mean number of arrests for all of the activists was 5. These people, who were daily working in conditions of poverty and to whom physical harm was a constant threat, helped black people register to vote at a time when the civil rights movement had not yet attracted much white support and before an arrest for civil disturbance had become a badge of honor. The mean IE score for 53 black SNCC workers and activists was 7.45, significantly more internal than the responses (M=9.64) of a control group of 105 nonactive black college students.

The interactions of beliefs about control and involvement in change are complex, however. The early assessment instruments were quite global and were not specific as to unique control beliefs such as self- versus situational control. The Gurins and their colleagues (Gurin, Gurin, Lao, & Beattie, 1969) modified the Rotter IE scale and developed scoring systems for personal and ideological control. They found that blacks were not significantly different from whites in their beliefs about personal control, but blacks did report that they felt they had less control over institutional sources of reinforcement than did whites.

As the civil rights movement progressed and as protest took a more violent turn, different people appeared to be attracted to the movement and more specific beliefs about IE could be identified. For example, in 1973 individuals who espoused a militant as opposed to a more moderate revolutionary stance were significantly more external than internal in their beliefs about locus of control (Sank & Strickland, 1973). Ransford (1968) interviewed 312 black males who were heads of households in the Watts section of Los Angeles during the time of the riot there. The more external of the group viewed violence as necessary for achieving racial justice. Of the 16 men who admitted participating in the riot, 15 were external.

So while we have evidence that belief systems are related to involvement in social movements, at least for black people, we must also be cautious in interpreting these data as representing any point-for-point simple phenomenon. The intricacies of the relationship are likely dictated, as mentioned earlier, by specific situational demands and perceived opportunities for change. These very complex relationships are also demonstrated in other social and political movements. For example, women involved in women's liberation activities are generally more internal than control groups (Pawlicki & Almquist, 1973) yet this involvement may represent differing personal interpretations of internal versus external control orientations. Thus Sanger and Alker (1972) found active feminists to be more internal in their sense of personal control and more external on beliefs about the Protestant Ethic and feminist ideology than were uninvolved women. Levenson and Miller (1976) demonstrated that for liberal students, beliefs in control by powerful others was positively related to increased activism while these results were reversed for more conservative students. Militant lesbians expected more control by powerful others and less personal control in their lives than did members of a relatively inactive women's liberation group. Similarly, students who attended a regional conference of Students for a Democratic Society expected greater control by powerful others than did political science majors who belonged to a nonactivist liberal group. Evidently the prevailing cultural mores about the desirability of engaging in certain actions and the popularity of a movement make a difference as to the kinds of people who will become involved, the activities in which they will engage, and the degree to which differing beliefs about control influence their behavior. What is important about these findings for the purposes of the present chapter, however, is the demonstration that IE beliefs are important, although in a very complicated way, in terms of the likelihood of engaging in social action to change one's life situation. Those people who are responsible for initiating community help agencies would be well advised to note carefully both the realistic conditions under which the community members live as well as the community members' beliefs about the possibility of change occurring as a function of their own behavior. The integration of outsiders into a community, even when they come with the best intentions, is beset with problems.

The notion that community members may be resistant to change, even when this change is supposedly in their best interests, is, of course, not a new one. This resistance may occur for any number of reasons. Community members may have been misled in the past. Politicians may have made promises which they did not keep; businesses may have failed; community members themselves may have been overly disappointed after having expectations that certain events which never came to pass, would in fact occur. One might also consider, however, that community resistance might be predicted on the basis of belief systems. Basic research with the IE dimension has demonstrated that internals, who apparently like to do things for themselves, do not care to be told how to behave or how to perform, especially if they feel they are being subtly or surreptitiously manipulated. For example, Gore (1962) showed TAT cards to individuals, telling them she was testing for creativity, and tried to influence them to produce longer stories by subtle and covert nonverbal cues. She would smile and emphasize one particular card as she handed it to the person, saying, "Now, try *this* one." Internals gave stories which were significantly shorter for this card than for the others, thereby demonstrating an unwillingness to be manipulated. Other research on verbal conditioning in which the experimenter attempts to influence the verbal responses of subjects through head nods and subtle verbal cues has also showed that not only do internals fail to repeat the desired responses during acquisition, but they actually give the proper response only during extinction, when they are no longer being reinforced (Getter, 1966; Strickland, 1970). Evidently when internals perceive themselves as being manipulated by external forces they resist social influence, do not conform (Crowne & Liverant, 1963) and continue to make their own judgments even when these responses go against the obvious desire of the external authority or the judgment of peers. Lefcourt (1976) also reports that in psychological research internals are less likely to follow the instructions and manipulations of an experimenter, while externals readily capitulate. If internals do resist social influence and prefer to take responsibility for their own actions, then it is important that community change agents recognize the prevailing social norms and influence of the locus of control beliefs when they actually work with community members to change or enhance living conditions.

Implications for Community Psychology. When behavior or system change is a crucial aspect of a community psychology approach another important consideration should be raised. Too often in the past, psychologists have been guilty of looking for simplistic answers to complicated questions. At one time mental health workers were trying to discover the "best therapist," the "best client" and the "best therapeutic technique" as if there were one best approach for everybody. We know now (Kiesler, 1966; Gomes-Schwartz, Hadley & Strupp, 1978) that there are probably many different kinds of therapeutic techniques and therapists who can be helpful to diverse kinds of clients. There is no one best approach that will work for everyone. We are faced with matching clients who have particular problems with the therapists and therapeutic techniques which will be most effective.

We also know that congruence of expectancies about internal versus external control and situational demands may lead to the most effective behavior change (Strickland, 1978). For example, Cromwell, Butterfield, Brayfield, & Curry (1977) considered recovery rates for 229 hospitalized patients who had suffered heart attacks. The experimenters manipulated nursing care, participation in various activities, and information about heart attack while the patients were in intensive care and on the hospital wards. No patients who were involved in congruent combinations of locus of control beliefs and participation in self-treatment (internals with high participation and externals with low participation) returned to the hospital or died ($p < .06$) within 12 weeks following their hospital stay. The small number of patients who did return to the hospital ($N = 12$) or who did die ($N = 5$) had all been involved in incongruent conditions: that is, they were externals who participated in considerable self-help or internals who were given information from the outside rather than being allowed to seek out information on their own. Cromwell and his colleagues suggest that patients whose hospital treatment was incongruent with personal expectancies may have resisted a decision to return to the hospital when critical symptoms of another heart attack appeared. Other findings in the health area also suggest that a matching of control beliefs and situations is important. Congruence of expectancies and situational demands, such as structure matched with external beliefs of self-initiation of performance and internality, appear to enhance biofeedback of blood pressure manipulation (De Good, 1975), smoking modification (Best & Steffy, 1975) and responses to psychotherapy (Abramowitz, Abramowitz, Roback, & Jackson, 1974; Kilmann, 1974; Kilmann, Albert, & Sotile, 1975).

The matching of expectancies and situational demands should probably also be employed in relation to community change. Some communities whose members may feel powerless, alienated and uninformed about the political process may benefit most from community help agents who provide structure and external strength. Others may need the outside change agent to act as more of a catalyst so that community members themselves may seize the opportunity to effect change within their own communities. Many activist internal individuals will resent and resist outside influence. Expectancies about control will likely make a difference in how community change agents are received and how community change will occur. The worth of the community psychologist may be enhanced as he or she comes to understand and appreciate attributions and expectancies about locus of causality and control in the life of the individual and the community.

Reference Note

1. Hochreich, D.J. Changing IE score. Personal communication, 1977.

References

Abramowitz, C. V., Abramowitz, S. I., Roback, H.B., & Jackson, C. Differential effectiveness of directive and nondirective group therapies as a function of client internal-external control. *Journal of Consulting and Clinical Psychology*, 1974, *42*, 849–853.

Adorno, T. W., Frenkel-Brunswik, E., Levinson, D. J., & Sanford, R. N. *The authoritarian personality*. New York: Harper, 1950.

Alper, T. G. Achievement motivation in college women: A now-you-see-it-now-you-don't phenomenon. *American Psychologist*, 1974, *29*, 194–203.

Atkinson, I. W. (Ed.). *Motives in fantasy, action, and society*. Princeton: Van Nostrand, 1958.

Bandura, A. *Social learning theory*. Morristown, N.J.: General Learning, 1971.

Bennion, R. C. Task, trial by trial score variability of internal versus external control of reinforcement. Doctoral dissertation, Ohio State University, 1961.

Best, J. A., & Steffy, R. A. Smoking modification procedures for internal and external locus of control clients. *Canadian Journal of Behavioral Science*, 1975, *7*, 155–165.

Blackman, S. Some factors affecting the perception of events as chance determined. *Journal of Personality*, 1962, *54*, 197–202.

Caplan, N., & Nelson, S. D. On being useful: The nature and consequences of psychological research on social problems. *American Psychologist*, 1973, *28*, 199–211.

Cromwell, R. L., Butterfield, E. C., Brayfield, F. M., & Curry, J. L. *Acute myocardial infarction: Reaction and recovery*. St. Louis: Mosby, 1977.

Crowne, D. P., & Liverant, S. Conformity under varying conditions of personal commitment. *Journal of Abnormal and Social Psychology*, 1963, *66*, 547–555.

Darley, J., & Latané, B. Bystander intervention in emergencies: Diffusion of responsibility. *Journal of Personality and Social Psychology*, 1968, *8*, 377–383.

De Good, D. E. Cognitive control factors in vascular stress responses. *Psychophysiology*, 1975, *12*, 399–401.

Duke, M. P., Shaheen, J., & Nowicki, S. The determination of locus of control in a geriatric population and a subsequent test of the social learning model for interpersonal distance. *Journal of Psychology*, 1974, *86*, 277–285.

Fink, H. C., & Hjelle, L. H. Internal-external control and ideology. *Psychological Reports*, 1973, *33*, 967–974.

Getter, H. A. A personality determinant of verbal conditioning. *Journal of Personality*, 1966, *34*, 397–405.

Gomes-Schwartz, B., Hadley, S. W., & Strupp, H. Individual psychotherapy and behavior therapy. *Annual Review of Psychology*, 1978, *29*, 435–471.

Gore, P. S. Individual differences in the prediction of subject compliance to experimenter bias. Doctoral dissertation, Ohio State University, 1962.

Gore, P. M. & Rotter, J. B. A personality correlate of social action. *Journal of Personality*, 1963, *31*, 58–64.

Gurin, P., Gurin, G., Lao, R., & Beattie, M. Internal-external control in the motivational dynamics of Negro youth. *Journal of Social Issues*, 1969, *25*, 29–53.

Heider, F. *The psychology of interpersonal relations*. New York: Wiley, 1958.

Holden, K. B., & Rotter, J. B. A nonverbal measure of extinction in skill and chance situations. *Journal of Experimental Psychology*, 1962, *63*, 519–520.

Horner, M. S. The motive to avoid success and changing aspirations of women. In J. M. Bardwick (Ed.), *Readings on the psychology of women*. New York: Harper & Row, 1972.

James, W. H. Internal versus external control of reinforcement as a basic variable in learning theory. Doctoral dissertation, Ohio State University, 1962.

Jones, E. E., & Davis, K. E. From acts to dispositions: The attribution process in person perceptions. In L. Berkowitz (Ed.), *Advances in experimental Social Psychology* (Vol. 2). New York: Academic Press, 1965.

Jones, E. E., & Harris, V. A. The attribution of attitudes. *Journal of Experimental Social Psychology*, 1967, *3*, 1–24.

Jones, E. E., & Nisbett, R. The actor and the observer: Divergent perceptions of the causes of behavior. In E. E. Jones, D. E. Kanouse, H. H. Kelley, R. E. Nisbett, S.

Valins, & B. Weiner (Eds.), *Attribution: Perceiving the causes of behavior*. Morristown, N.J.: General Learning, 1971.

Kelley, H. Attribution theory in social psychology. In D. Levine (Ed.), *Nebraska Symposium on motivation* (Vol. 15). Lincoln: University of Nebraska, 1967.

Kelley, H. Attribution in social interaction. In E. E. Jones, D. E. Kanouse, H. H. Kelley, R. E. Nisbett, S. Valins, & B. Weiner (Eds.), *Attribution: Perceiving the causes of behavior*: Morristown, N. J.: General Learning, 1971.

Kelley, H. The process of causal attribution. *American Psychologist*, 1973, *28*, 107–128.

Kiesler, D. J. Some myths of psychotherapy research and the search for a paradigm. *Psychological Bulletin*, 1966, *65*, 110–136.

Kilmann, P. R. Direct and non-direct marathon group therapy and internal-external control. *Journal of Counseling Psychology*, 1974, *21*, 380–384.

Kilmann, P. R., Albert, B. M., & Sotile, V. M. Relationship between locus of control, structure of therapy and outcome. *Journal of Consulting and Clinical Psychology*, 1975, *43 (4)*, 588.

Korchin, S. *Modern clinical psychology*. New York: Basic, 1976.

Lefcourt, H. Internal versus external control of reinforcement: A review. *Psychological Bulletin*, 1966, *65*, 206–220.

Lefcourt, H. *Locus of control: Current trends in theory and research*. Hillsdale, N. J.: Lawrence Erlbaum, 1976.

Lerner, M. J. The desire for justice and reaction to victims. In J. R. Macaulay & L. Berkowitz (Eds.), *Altruism and helping Behavior*. New York: Academic Press, 1970.

Lerner, M. J., & Matthews, G. Reactions to suffering of others under conditions of indirect responsibility. *Journal of Personality and Social Psychology*, 1967, *5*, 319–325.

Lerner, M. J., & Simmons, C. Observer's reaction to the "innocent victim": Compassion or rejection? *Journal of Personality and Social Psychology*, 1966, *4*, 203–210.

Levenson, H., & Miller, J. Multidimensional locus of control in sociopolitical activists of conservative and liberal ideologies. *Journal of Personality and Social Psychology*, 1976, *33*, 199–208.

MacDonald, A. P. Internal-external locus of control: A selected bibliography for those concerned with the counseling and education of high risk students. U. W. Systemwide Center for the Study of Minorities and the Disadvantaged. Office of the Graduate School, University of Wisconsin/Milwaukee, 1978.

Milgram, S. Behavioral study of obedience. *Journal of Abnormal and Social Psychology*, 1963, *67*, 371–378.

Milgram, S. *Obedience to authority*. New York: Harper & Row, 1974.

Mischel, W. Toward a cognitive social learning reconceptualization of personality. *Psychological Review*, 1973, *80*, 252–283.

Monson, T. C., & Snyder, M. Actors, observers, and the attribution process: Toward a reconceptualization. *Journal of Experimental Social Psychology*, 1977, *13*, 89–111.

Murray, H. A. et al. *Explorations in Personality*. New York: Oxford, 1938.

Pawlicki, R. E., & Almquist, C. Authoritarianism, locus of control, and tolerance of ambiguity as reflected in membership and nonmembership in a women's liberation group. *Psychological Reports*, 1973, *32*, 1331–1337.

Phares, E. J. Expectancy changes in skill and chance situations. *Journal of Abnormal and Social Psychology*, 1957, *54*, 339–342.

Phares, E. J. Perceptual threshold decrements as a function of skill and chance expectancies. *Journal of Psychology*, 1962, *53*, 399–407.

Phares, E. J. *Locus of control in personality*. Morristown, N. J.: General Learning, 1976.

Ransford, H. E. Isolation, powerlessness, and violence: A study of attitudes and participation in the Watts riot. *American Journal of Sociology*, 1968, *73*, 581–591.

Ross, L. D. The intuitive psychologist and his shortcomings: Distortions in the attribution process. In L. Berkowitz (Ed.), *Advances in experimental social psychology* (Vol. 10). New York: Academic, 1977.

Ross, L. D., Amabile, T. M., & Steinmetz, J. L. Social roles, social control, and biases in social-perception processes. *Journal of Personality and Social Psychology*, 1977, *35*, 485–494.

Rotter, J. B. *Social learning and clinical psychology*, Englewood Cliffs, N.J.: Prentice-Hall, 1954.

Rotter, J. B. Generalized expectancies for internal versus external control of reinforcement. *Psychological Monographs*, 1966 *80*, (1, Whole No. 609).

Rotter, J. B. Some problems and misconceptions related to the construct or internal versus external control of reinforcement. *Journal of Consulting and Clinical Psychology*, 1975, *43*, 56–67.

Rotter, J. B., Chance, J. E., & Phares, E. J. *Applications of a social learning theory of personality*. New York: Holt, Rinehart & Winston, 1972.

Rotter, J. B., Liverant, S., & Crowne, D. P. The growth and extinction of expectancies in chance controlled and skill tasks. *Journal of Psychology*, 1961, *52*, 161–177.

Ryan, W. *Blaming the victim*. New York: Vintage, 1971.

Sanger, S. P., & Alker, H. A. Dimensions of internal-external locus of control and the women's liberation movement. *Journal of Social Issues*, 1972, *28*, 115–129.

Sank, Z. B., & Strickland, B. R. Some attitudes and behavioral correlates of a belief in militant or moderate social action. *Journal of Social Psychology*, 1973, *90*, 337–338.

Silvern, L. E., & Nakamura, C. Y. Powerlessness, social-political action, social-political views: Their interrelation among college students. *Journal of Social Issues*, 1971, *27*, 137–157.

Strickland, B. R. The prediction of social action from a dimension of internal-external control. *Journal of Social Psychology*, 1965, *66*, 353–358.

Strickland, B. R. Individual differences in verbal conditioning, extinction, and awareness. *Journal of Personality*, 1970, *38*, 364–378.

Strickland, B. R. Internal-external control of reinforcement. In T. Blass (Ed.), *Personality Variables and Social Behavior*. Hillsdale, N.J.: Lawrence Erlbaum, 1977.

Strickland, B. R. Internal-external expectancies and health-related behaviors. *Journal of Consulting and Clinical Psychology*, 1978, *46*, 1192–1211.

Thomas, L. E. The I-E scale, ideological bias, and political participation. *Journal of Personality*, 1970, *38*, 273–286.

Wegner, D. M., & Vallacher, R. R. *Implicit Psychology: An introduction to social cognition*. New York: Oxford, 1977.

Wolk, S. Situational constraint as a moderator of the locus of control-adjustment relationship. *Journal of Consulting and Clinical Psychology*, 1976, *44*, 420–427.

Zimbardo, P. G., Haney, C., Banks, W. C., & Jaffee, D. The mind is a formidable prison: A Pirandellian prison. *New York Times Magazine*, April 8, 1973, 38–60.

CHAPTER 5

Learned Helplessness Theory and Community Psychology

Stanley Sue, Ph.D.

and

Nolan Zane

The application of a psychological theory based upon experimental laboratory research on animals and small samples of human beings to a large social group or community is hazardous. Assuming that the theory is well grounded in research with sound internal validity, the major problems are over (1) the external validity—the extent to which the theory can be generalized to other situations or subjects—and (2) the theoretical validity or the logical bearing of the research to the theory and to the theory's application (Mahoney, 1978). Furthermore, the concept of community is difficult to define, and in its complexity, critical or rigorous tests for a theory are not easily constructed. As indicated by Cowen (1978), "Communities are many things. One thing they are not is an ideal laboratory for antiseptic psychological studies. Their extraordinary complexity, omnipresent flux, action-service orientation, and susceptibility to day-to-day pressures present real and formidable barriers to 'Mr. Clean'. . .studies" (p. 803).

The purpose of this chapter is modest. We hope to show how learned helplessness theory can be applied to community processes. While the ultimate test of the theory's appropriateness lies in the development of empirical research approaches, our task at present is to argue the relevance of concepts involving control and helplessness in community processes. Specifically, three major propositions are advanced. First, laboratory findings concerning learned helplessness consistently demonstrate the importance of having control or perceptions of control over one's life. These findings seem applicable to social groups or communities. Second, the very "essence" of community involves control. Where individuals in a particular community lack control, psychological well-being and the psychological sense of community may be diminished. Third, if helplessness theory is useful in conceptualizing or describing community phenomena, then intervention strategies derived from the theory may suggest means for developing community resources. We feel that the theory not only provides a means of conceptualizing certain community processes but also offers directions for intervention.

LEARNED HELPLESSNESS THEORY

In order to examine the relationship between the theory and community phenomena, we would like to describe the origin of the theory and some recent research on the effects of helplessness and its relevance for social groups.

Experimental Studies

Learned helplessness theory was originally formulated by Martin Seligman (1975) who, along with his colleagues, conducted a series of interesting experiments on dogs. He found that when experimentally naive dogs were placed in a two-compartment shuttlebox, they could learn to escape electric shock administered in one compartment by jumping into the other, no-shock (safe) chamber. After a number of trials, these dogs made conditioned avoidance responses by immediately jumping into the safe chamber when they were placed in the shock chamber. However, Seligman discovered that dogs exposed to certain conditions often failed to learn escape and avoidance behaviors. These dogs were first restrained in a Pavlovian hammock in which they were classically conditioned with tones followed by inescapable shocks. That is, a tone was sounded and then the dogs were administered powerful shocks. Restrained in the hammock, the dogs could do nothing to avoid or escape the aversive stimulus. After this experience with inescapable shocks, the dogs were then placed in the shuttlebox experiments where, through trial and error, they could learn to escape and avoid shocks by jumping from one chamber to another. Surprisingly, most dogs exposed to shocks in the Pavlovian hammock failed to learn escape responses in the shuttlebox. Rather, in response to the shocks, these dogs ran around and then lay down, passively whining in the shock chamber. The dogs had learned to be "helpless." Similar performance deficits following exposure to uncontrollable events have been reported for rats (Maier & Testa, 1975; Seligman & Beagley, 1975), cats (Thomas & Dewald, 1977), and fish (Padilla, 1973).

The subsequent negative effects of uncontrollable events involving a variety of stimuli have also been studied in humans. Subjects exposed to uncontrollable loud noise demonstrate little persistence in a frustrating task (Glass & Singer, 1972; Sherrod, Hage, O'Halpern, & Moore, 1977), exhibit carelessness in proofreading (Glass & Singer, 1972), experience difficulty solving anagrams (Hiroto & Seligman, 1975; Cole & Coyne, 1977), volunteer little aid to those requesting it (Sherrod & Downs, 1974) and fail to escape in a subsequent noise avoidance test (Hiroto, 1974; Hiroto and Seligman, 1975). Experience with unsolvable puzzles has led to performance difficulties in subsequent anagram solving (Benson & Kennelly, 1976) and aversive noise avoidance (Jones, Nation, & Massad, 1977). Uncontrollable shock resulted in increased latency in a shock avoidance task (Thorton & Jacobs, 1970; Thorton & Powell, 1974). The above studies present convergent evidence of the deleterious effects of learned helplessness in humans.

Before we continue this discussion, the focus of the chapter in relation to the various empirical approaches to learned helplessness must be clarified. Seligman (1978) distinguishes between three research aims of the learned helplessness enterprise: the production and explanation of learned helplessness in animals, the etiology and effects of learned helplessness in humans and the applicability and utility of learned helplessness as a model of depression. We are primarily concerned with the second concern; specifically, the antecedents and consequences of the expectation of uncontrollability and their relation to community processes. As Seligman has noted and as is apparent in the previously-mentioned studies, the phenomenon can be produced reliably in humans with fairly predictable consequences for subsequent behavior.

Four other points should be noted. First, perception of control or noncontrol is important. Glass and Singer (1972) exposed college students to irritating and loud noises. Half of the subjects (perceived control group) were told that by pressing a button, they could terminate the noise. However, they were asked by the experimenter not to push the button. The other subjects (perceived noncontrol group) were not told the button was available. Although no one in the perceived control group pressed the button, everyone in it performed better on subsequent tasks and was less irritated by the noise than the perceived noncontrol group which was actually exposed to the same amount of noise. The difference in performance was attributed solely to difference in the perception of control.

Our second point is that control implied predictability: if I do *x*, then *y* will occur. Where events are unpredictable, an increase in helplessness may occur. Seligman (1968) showed that hungry rats trained to press a bar for food respond differently according to whether the occurrence of an aversive stimulus is predictable or not. Those rats that received "predictable" shocks were given signals prior to the onset of electric shocks. The "nonpredictable" group of rats was given the same number of signals and shocks although the two were not contingently arranged (i.e., shocks were not always preceeded by signals which, in turn, were not always followed by shocks). The predictable group suppressed bar pressing and showed fear only in the presence of the signal. The unpredictable group stopped bar pressing altogether (in the presence or absence of the signals), showed chronic fear and developed massive ulcers.

Third, we should note that subjects who have direct experiences with noncontrol in laboratory settings perform similarly to those who have an external locus of control as measured by the IE Scale (a measure of powerlessness as a personality trait) and to those who have a cognitive set of uncontrollability (e.g., subjects told that a particular task is governed by chance rather than skill), as demonstrated by Hiroto (1974). Finally, helplessness theory has been used to conceptualize the experiences of certain social collectives such as minority groups (Seligman, 1975; Sue, 1977b).

The Initial Theory and Its Reformulation

Theory of Learned Helplessness. On the basis of the work in this area, Seligman (1975) formulated the theory of learned helplessness. Essentially the theory has three elements: information, cognitive expectancy and behavior. To begin with, human beings or animals receive information concerning the relationship between their voluntary responses and outcomes. In some cases, actions lead to outcomes; in others, outcomes are independent of, or unaffected by, actions. In these latter cases, responding and reinforcement are unrelated, so that the probability of the outcome is the same whether or not a given response occurs. In essence the outcome is uncontrollable. Information is received from direct experiences with the contingent or noncontingent relationship or from indirect experiences with the relationship (e.g., through observational learning or simply being told about the nature of the relationship). What makes the theory a cognitive-learning perspective is the element of cognitive expectancy. Information itself is insufficient to account for learned helplessness since the information is processed into a cognitive representation of the contingency (i.e., one's expectation). Thus a fourfold table is created as indicated in Figure 5-1.

In cells *a* and *d*, one has realistic perceptions of control or noncontrol. In cells *b* and *c*, perceptions of control or noncontrol are inaccurate. Presumably in cells *c* and *d*, where there are perceptions of noncontrol,

FIGURE 5-1. Perception and Control

		Actual Control	
		Yes	No
Perception of Control	Yes	a	b
	No	c	d

whether or not these perceptions are accurate, feelings of helplessness develop. Finally, perceived control or noncontrol has effects on behaviors and emotions. Learned helplessness may result in (1) poor motivation, apathy and passivity; (2) cognitive disruption and the failure to learn that events can be controlled; and (3) emotional disturbance such as anxiety and depression.

Information is necessary for perceptions of control or noncontrol. Yet information may be insufficient to account for perceptions. The lack of a one-to-one correspondence between information and perception suggests that other factors are important in the formation of cognitive expectancy. Indeed, Seligman believes that *prior experiences* with controllability modify one's interpretation of current information. Another factor is *discriminative* control. Even after exposure to noncontrol, pervasive expectancy of helplessness may not develop if the person can adequately distinguish situations in which control is possible or not possible. Finally, the relative *importance* of events influences expectancy and feelings of helplessness. The transfer of helplessness from one situation to another may be affected by the importance of outcomes. Helplessness derived from important or significant events may transfer more readily to less important events, but not vice versa. These three conditions—prior experiences, discriminative control and importance of events—demonstrate the complex association between cognitive expectancy and information.

Reformulation of the Theory. Abramson, Seligman, and Teasdale (1978) have proposed a reformulation of the learned helplessness theory to resolve two major shortcomings. The old theory did not distinguish between an expectation of noncontingency in which the individual believes that only some people (namely, relevant others such as peers) but not the individual himself can control outcomes, and one in which the person believes *all* persons cannot control outcomes. The former is an example of personal helplessness while the latter represents a case of universal helplessness. Helplessness effects can be quite general or specific, depending on the extent to which they occur in a variety of situations. Such effects also vary in duration. Some cases are long-lived or recurrent while others are short-lived or nonrecurrent. The old theory did not specify the conditions which determine the generality and chronicity of helplessness. In the revised model, Abramson et al. (1978) explain in greater detail the process by which the perception of noncontingency results in the expectation that future events will be noncontingent. Once a person perceives that the desired outcome remains independent of his or her actions, he or she makes an attribution as to the cause for the perceived noncontingency. This attribution influences the form of the subsequent expectation of future noncontingency, which leads to the symptoms of helplessness. As in the early model, the

FIGURE 5-2. Events Involved in Helplessness

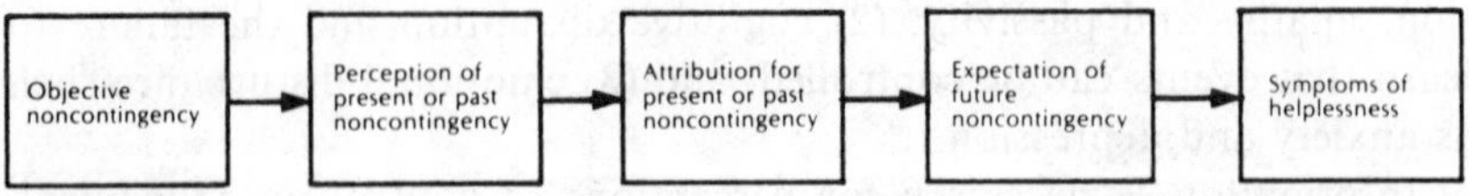

expectation of noncontingency is the decisive factor in determining helplessness symptoms. However, the reformulation posits that it is the attribution that the individual makes in accounting for perceived past or present noncontingencies that determines the type of expectation made. Causes can vary along at least three orthogonal dimensions; internal-external, global-specific, and stable-unstable. Personal helplessness involves internal attributions while universal helplessness involves external attributions. If a person perceives certain outcomes as having a greater or lesser likelihood of happening to him or her than to relevant others, he or she will attribute such outcomes to internal causes. However, if he or she believes that certain outcomes are just as likely to happen to him or she as to relevant others, he or she will implicate external causes. This distinction between internal and external attributions based on the personal-universal helplessness dichotomy yields the prediction of a fourth deficit of human helplessness: lowered self-esteem. It is hypothesized that internal attributions will result in lower self-esteem than external attributions. In addition an individual can make a global or specific attribution referring to whether or not the cause affects a wide variety of outcomes. He or she can make a stable or an unstable atttibution referring to whether or not the cause persists over time. Figure 5-3 presents examples of various attributions which differ along the internal-external, global-specific and stable-unstable dimensions. Thus the specificity and stability of the cause selected in the attribution will determine the generality and chronicity of the expectation of future helplessness, and the internality of the cause will determine extent of self-esteem decrement due to helplessness. In some cases the initial attribution selection may not influence the subsequent expectation when new information intervenes between the former and latter and changes the latter.

Although it is too early to determine the empirical validity of the reformulated model, it already has stimulated some thoughtful feedback. In their critique of certain aspects of the reformulation, Wortman and Dintzer (1978) have identified the following problems: People may not make attributions after every outcome. Recent reviews of attribution studies question the validity of the assumption that attributions are clearly related to subsequent behavior. People may hypothesis-test

FIGURE 5-3. Examples of Attributions with Different Dimensional Aspects

	Internal		External	
Dimension	Stable	Unstable	Stable	Unstable
Global	Lack of intelligence	My assertiveness threatens men sometimes	Men discriminate against women	Men discriminate against women sometimes
Specific	Lack of administrative ability	My assertiveness threatens him sometimes	My boss discriminates aganst women	He discriminates against women sometimes

Situation: Female secretary who has been consistently denied promotion to administrative position by male employer.

alternative attributions rather than selecting an attribution immediately following the noncontingency perception. The uncertainty of the attribution may determine whether people behave in a helpless manner or seek out new information resulting in the facilitation effect found in several studies. Other types or levels of attributions may be important (e.g., mechanical causality of the event itself versus philosophical causality; immediate causality versus prior causality—namely, causes that cause the immediate cause; and outcome causality versus reaction-to-outcome causality. Preliminary findings appear to be inconsistent with predictions of the new model. Factors such as perceived controllability of the cause and whether or not the cause was anticipated may be just as important or more important than the three proposed factors. Other factors besides attributions and expectations of control may influence reactions to uncontrollable outcomes (e.g., Was the outcome expected? Can the outcome be meaningfully understood? Can the outcome improve or worsen regardless of one's behavior? What is the perceived cost of influencing the outcome? Can the outcome recur in the future?). The relationships between the cognitive, motivational and affective components have not been delineated. Finally, the conditions under which people react to uncontrollable outcomes with helplessness as opposed to renewed efforts to exert control (facilitation effects) have not been specified.

The reformulation and its critique make it evident that the mechanisms by which the perception of uncontrollability results in helpless behavior remain unclear. Despite this ambiguity, the discussion has generated several significant changes in the conceptualization and understanding of the learned helplessness phenomenon. First, learned helplessness can no longer be considered a homogeneous phenomenon, across individuals and situations, that is an inevitable consequence of uncontrollable outcomes. Depending on the types of cognition (which include attributions, outcome perceptions, cost expectancies, etc.) invoked by the individual, the expectation of future noncontingency and subsequent symptoms of helplessness will vary in form, duration and generality, if they occur at all.

Second, it appears that the assessment of attributions and outcome perceptions can facilitate the identification of specific characteristics of helplessness expectations and symptoms for that individual or group of individuals. This in turn will aid in the development of treatment plans for the alleviation of helplessness. In other words, the mediating cognitions, be they attributions or not, must be assessed to accurately determine what type of helplessness is involved, whether or not subsequent deficits are serious enough to warrant an intervention and what type of intervention will be most effective.

The third point involves the recognition that learned helplessness does not necessarily follow the perception of uncontrollable outcomes. This has important implications for programs designed to immunize people against helplessness deficits. Such programs must focus on certain procedures that create life experiences or cognitive styles and skills that maximize the occurrence of facilitation effects rather than helplessness in response to uncontrollable outcomes. This immunization strategy differs somewhat from that proposed by the old model. Where the old strategy advocated successful control experiences to minimize the effects of helplessness, the new strategy opts for experiences and expectations that maximize the possibility of an alternative response to uncontrollable outcomes—renewed efforts to affect outcomes. The implications of these advances in helplessness theory for the community will be discussed later in the chapter.

RELATIONSHIP OF THE THEORY TO COMMUNITY

Control as a Vital Ingredient

Thus far, we have argued that (1) learned helplessness influences psychological well-being and (2) helplessness or powerlessness in which outcomes are independent of actions can be caused by different conditions. For helplessness theory to have meaning in the study of communities, it must be shown that control and power are important in the concept of community. Indeed, it is our belief that a community cannot be defined without reference to control and power.

As indicated earlier, a precise definition of community is problematic. The physical setting or geographic boundary, mutually dependent social relationships, social cohesion, a "psychological sense," common values and traditions and so forth, have all been stressed in the concept of community (Bloom 1977; Panzetta, 1971). Individuals in a community negotiate, exchange, or develop mutual dependency with each other and with community institutions. For Sarason (1976b), the concept of community involves related and unrelated networks of relationships along vocational, religious, political, recreational, neighborhood, charitable, educational and other dimensions. These networks may be informal and may involve no actual face-to-face contacts.

While an exact definition of community is difficult to arrive at, one essential feature of the concept is the dimension of control and power. In communities individuals have influence on or are influenced by other individuals as well as by norms, traditions, economy, interest patterns, common goals, the political structure, communication patterns, institutions or a multitude of other processes. This is implicit when the definition of communities involves mutually dependent social relationships, social cohesion and networks. By control, power and influence, we are referring to Seligman's notion of the relationship between actions and outcomes. Those individuals who have power can affect outcomes; those who are powerless and helpless find that outcomes are independent of their actions. In this view, power obviously has meaning only in direct reference to individuals or groups of individuals. Although social scientists often analyze the "power" of big business, of the mass media, of government and of other institutions, we prefer to look at power in terms of the relationship between actions and outcomes for members of a community. If institutions regulate the lives of people, it simply means that people have a difficult time affecting outcomes.

Obviously persons in a particular community vary in the degree of power and control they have and in their willingness to exert that control. Some have a great deal of influence while others have no impact on outcomes. For example, the politician, authoritative scholar and the wealthy may exert considerable influence compared to the average citizen. French and Raven (1959) have classified the sources of individual power as rewarded, coercive, legitimate, referent, and expert. Communities themselves vary in the degree to which members are able to affect outcomes. Individuals may not have appreciable power in (1) a disorganized, anomic community, (2) a dictatorship or (3) a community controlled by a larger regulatory body (e.g., a local community dominated by state government). Finally, persons and institutions may differ in the areas of power and control. Through hard work and motivation, one may be able to perform well and affect job outcomes; if, however, promotions are based largely upon factors other than performance, the person may have little effect on career outcome. The federal government may dictate that a community desegregate; neverthless the citizens in the community may be free to choose the particular desegregation plan.

A Loss in the Sense of Community

If control and power are necessary ingredients in the psychological sense of community, then loss of control might well diminish one's sense of community. Such a proposition has been argued by a number of investigators. We would like to examine this proposition and to indicate how helplessness theory can conceptualize the situation.

In his analysis of increasing governmental control, Sarason (1976a) noted:

> The central state (and its governmental apparatus), by its very nature and dynamics, inevitably becomes a force alien to the interests of its people, and the stronger the state becomes, the more it enslaves people in the sense that they are required, they are forced, to do things they do not want to do; i.e. there is a dilution in personal autonomy . . . The more powerful the state becomes, the more its people look to it as the fount of initiative and succor, the more is the psychological sense of community diluted. That is to say, the more the lives of people are a consequence of decisions made by Kafkaesque officialdom, the more are they robbed of those communal bonds and responsibilities upon which the sense of rootedness is built (p. 251).

In the situation described by Sarason, the greater the government control, the greater the feelings of helplessness, which in turn diminish a sense of community and relatedness. Dunham (1977) has also argued that the loss of control is associated with a loss in the sense of community. In his view social control and relationships have in the past been rooted in basic, primary, personalized and simple structures. These structures included the family, the church and the local neighborhood. Because of industrialization, mass communication and geographic mobility, the simpler institutions no longer exert influence on social control. Peoples' lives are now more regulated by the bureaucratic state, corporations, schools, labor unions and welfare agencies. Furthermore Dunham believes that ideals of personal freedom and fairness and democratic values have led to a situation in which what were considered private and personal troubles are now thrust into public issues. Issues concerning race, gays, poverty, unemployment, abortions and the like have been translated into public issues. Society is becoming increasingly fragmented and unstable. For example, the push to widen democracy by such means as integration and busing has also meant threats to the social order, often in the form of protest and violence. Thus individuals have less control over their lives because of the shift to larger and more complicated regulatory influences and because of an increase in conflict and public exposure to interest groups. The consequences are a loss in the sense of community and increased feelings of alienation.

Implications of Alienation. There are three implications that seem to be common to the analyses by Sarason and by Dunham. First, individuals in our society increasingly have lost control and have perceptions of noncontrol over their lives. Larger regulatory bodies such as the federal government have supplanted smaller and more local institutions. Second, the loss of control is associated with nonpredictability of the relationship between actions and outcomes. For Sarason, individuals are at the mercy of governmental whims. Dunham believes that the price paid for societal changes is instability and lack of order. Third, both perceive a loss in the psychological sense of community. The notion of a relationship between one's perception of control and one's sense of community seems to receive support in two studies.

In an interesting simulation game of urban land development, Kaemmerer and Schwebel (1977) divided subjects into roles as citizens or planners. According to game rules, subjects were to adopt their respective roles and to develop their urban community by working together. Four conditions were created: (1) high information from both planners and citizens, (2) high information from planners and low information from citizens, (3) low information from planners and high information from citizens, and (4) low information from both. The results suggested that the greater the amount of information one conveys, the greater the sense of community and the perceptions of control. Carr, Dixon, and Ogles (1976) conducted 120 interviews of persons in a community in order to find attitudinal correlates to involvement in a neighborhood organization designed to improve the community life. In contrast to nonmembers of the organization, members were more likely to feel the neighborhood was a good place to live, to have greater identification with the neighborhood, and to believe that residents could be effective or influential in improving the livability of the community. Obviously the cause-effect relationship between loss of control and a diminished psychological sense of community is difficult to establish. Nevertheless the studies cited do suggest that perceptions and expectations of the inability to influence outcomes in a community will result in a loss in the psychological sense of relatedness and community.

Lack of faith and trust in the service delivery system may also be the result of helplessness. Helplessness often generates passivity so that persons come to rely increasingly upon governmental intervention. Yet the intervention itself may be a part of the problem. Levine (1978a) states, "The very solution to a problem of individual helplessness, the public provision of care, may itself become a part of the problem by exacerbating feelings of helplessness and producing alienation" (p. 1). In two articles, Levine (1978a, 1978b) poignantly describes his personal experience in trying to obtain Medicare reimbursement for services his father-in-law received for a mid-thigh amputation and a heart attack.

Denial of their initial claim, inability to find out the reasons for the denial despite repeated requests, getting the bureaucratic runaround, months of appeals and further problems even after an administrative law judge ruled in favor of the appeal, were encountered.

Sue (Sue, 1977a; Note 1) also believes that helplessness theory is relevant to the analysis of client utilization patterns of community mental health services. A client who uses services usually has the belief or expectancy that "If I use mental health services, I may feel better." Clients would probably not use services if this action-outcome expectancy were not present. In his analysis of the exceedingly high premature termination (i.e., dropout) rates for ethnic minority clients using community mental health services, Sue (Note 1) concludes that many of these clients with different subcultural values find services strange, unpredictable, foreign and inconsistent with their backgrounds. That is to say, mismatches between ethnic clients and service systems increase the clients' belief that outcome (i.e., psychological well-being) is independent of action (i.e., using mental health services). These clients may then feel quite alienated and drop out of treatment. Interestingly, feelings of helplessness may come from two opposite mental sets. After repeated experiences with prejudice and discrimination, some ethnic minority group members may already have low expectations for favorable outcomes at mainstream mental health services. These individuals avoid services or come in for help only as a last resort, after all other resources have failed. If they are unable to receive treatment harmonious with their life styles or expectations, this only reinforces their beliefs that services are unresponsive. On the other hand, some ethnic minority members may actually have high expectations for positive outcome. The powerlessness felt by ethnic minority groups often forces them to seek aid from local, state or federal governmental sources. Those persons with high expectations for favorable outcome are frequently disappointed and disenchanted when they are mismatched with services. A number of community psychologists have stressed the importance of good person-environment or person-organization matches (Kelly, Snowden, & Munoz, 1977; Price & Blashfield, 1975).

Implications from Helplessness Theory

If there have been changes in the forces controlling contingencies within communities and for individuals, is it possible to predict how individuals in particular communities will respond? Indeed if learned helplessness theory is valuable in conceptualizing community processes, it should aid in the understanding and the development of novel predictions concerning community phenomena. While investigators have loosely implicated noncontrol and feelings of helplessness in community settings, the association cannot really be stated with any degree of confidence. There is no evidence that noncontrol results necessarily in poor motivation, cognitive defects and emotional disturbance. For example helplessness can presumably sap motivation and lead to apathy, passivity or alienation; yet we now witness in society an apparent increase in activity. Dunham (1977) himself believed that the rise of protest groups, open marriages and communes was partly in *response* to the interpersonal vacuum created by changes in power relationships. For the past several years, one cry from liberal and conservatives alike is for control of community institutions. Blacks and other groups are demanding control of their schools; antibusing forces are angry over their inability to send children to neighborhood schools; the passage of the widely publicized Proposition 13 in California was seen as a tax "revolt" against inflation, bureaucracies and lack of control over government spending. The civil rights leader Jesse Jackson has repeatedly stressed before black students, "We can be as good in academics as in athletics, but we've got to believe we are somebody. Repeat after me, 'I am somebody. I may be poor, but I am somebody. I may be on welfare, but I am somebody. Nobody can save us, for us, but us" (Learning to excel in school, p. 45). Jackson's plea is for hard work and discipline among blacks. While some believe that Jackson may place unfair responsibility on the deprived for their deprivation, his message has the effect of increasing feelings of pride and personal contol. That is, the inspirational part of his message is that blacks can and must take personal action to affect their own outcomes. More apparent activity can also be seen in the multitude of political and special-interest groups such as right-to-life advocates, gays, ERA groups and opponents, ethnic and racial alliances and so forth.

Cognitive Mediators

Given that power is relevant to the concept of community, that power has shifted from small and local institutions to larger ones and that individuals have less influence in controlling their personal lives, these conditions represent an increase in objective noncontingency. According to the reformulated helplessness theory, objective noncontingency is not sufficient to cause helplessness. There are cognitive mediators (i.e., *perception*, *attribution*, and *expectation*) that determine the relationship between objective noncontingency and helplessness. Furthermore individuals may possess personal helplessness (e.g., the belief that one does not have the leadership skills to effect changes) or universal helplessness (e.g., the belief that no one can effectively fight city hall). The key to understanding and predicting reactions to noncontrol is in the cognitive mediators.

Is there any evidence that people today perceive that they have less control over outcomes than in the past? To answer this question, it is necessary to have data on beliefs concerning actions and outcomes over time. We simply do not have good empirical data of this kind. Anecdotal reports, retrospective observations, sociological analyses and indirect evidence (such as that cited earlier) suggest that individuals perceive that they have less control over their lives, particularly in areas such as influencing national policies, the economy, the educational system, wages, price controls and employment practices. We also believe that perceptions of noncontrol may be reflected in the increased externalization of blame for social ills. For example violence in society is attributed to television programming, the inability of many students to read and write is blamed upon the educational system and teachers, and the economy is believed to be under the control of labor unions and big business. While these views may be valid, our point is that increased externalization of blame may be correlated with perceptions of noncontrol.

The second mediating process—the first being perception—is attribution. Here attributions can be placed on the dimensions of internal-external, stable-unstable and global-specific. They are important in predicting and influencing expectations, which in turn influence the type of helplessness that develops. It is likely that those who perceive noncontrol and who attribute the noncontrol to internal, stable and global factors develop expectations of powerlessness and feelings of pervasive helplessness. In contrast, loss of control that is attributed to external, unstable and specific forces is less likely to result in broad and pervasive feelings of helplessness. While Abramson et al. (1978) stress the importance of attributions in influencing the type and severity of helplessness expectancies, we believe that attributions may also aid in the understanding of why certain groups become active and attempt to gain power despite perceptions of increased helplessness. Abramson et al. speculated that uncontrollable events may result in a "facilitation" effect in which compensatory attempts to reassert control develop. While they believe that leaving the situation perceived as helpless may encourage efforts to regain control, the specific conditions that underlie the facilitation effects are unclear. If one of the possible outcomes of exposure to noncontrol is increased attempts to gain control, this is a much "healthier" response for individuals and communities than the development of helplessness characteristics. At this point, we would like to suggest possible reasons for the facilitation effect using attributional variables.

Facilitation Effects First, attribution for changes appears to be of an external kind. The loss of the sense of community discussed by Sarason (1976a) and Dunham (1977) refers to the increasing influence of government regulations, big and impersonal bureaucratic institutions, the mass media, and so on. These are more readily attributed to factors within the environment than to factors within the person. That is, one is likely to believe that institutions have changed rather than the person's own attitudes, behaviors and attributes. Lao (1970) and Rappaport (1977) maintain that a distinction should be made between personal control and control ideology.

Personal control is the belief that one can control outcomes in one's own life. Control ideology refers to how much control one believes people possess in a particular community. Control ideology is divided into systems blame and individual blame. An example of the former would be when blacks attribute their status to a discriminatory system; in the latter, blacks would attribute their status to poor motivation among themselves. (At first glance, personal control and control ideology may seem very similar to the respective concepts of personal helplessness and universal helplessness proposed by Abramson et al. (1978). The similarity of the two sets of concepts seems to be due to the fact that internal self-attributions underlie both personal control and personal helplessness, while external attributions [to others or to the system] underlie both control ideology and universal helplessness. We believe that Lao (1970) and Rappaport's (1977) analysis involves mediational-cognitive aspects of control while Abramson et al's concept of helplessness refers to an end product of mediational processes.)

The meaningfulness of the personal control and control ideology distinction was tested by Lao (1970). When the Rotter IE Scale was administered to black students, students were divided into high versus low personal control beliefs and into individual versus systems blame (control ideology) on the basis of their scores. Findings indicated that in contrast to students low in personal control beliefs, high scorers exhibited better academic performance, more academic confidence and higher educational expectations. Main effects for control ideology were not significant on these academic measures. However, on measures of participation in civil rights activities and of preference for social action strategies, students who blamed the system scored higher than those who blamed individuals (i.e., their own reference group). Personal control was not significantly related to control ideology. Lao's study is important in our discussion of attribution. It suggests that while one may believe and acknowledge that external forces are to blame for one's plight, this belief may serve to enhance activism (i.e., a facilitation effect). The findings also show that attributions themselves do not necessarily lead to helplessness, a point made by Abramson et al. (1978).

The second reason for the facilitation effect is that individuals may attribute their noncontrol in society to stable or to unstable (or transitory) factors. Expectations of helplessness are less likely to develop if the attribution is to unstable phenomenon. For example, persons who feel that government leaders are not responding to their needs may be heartened by the fact that new elections will soon take place. Attempts to regain control may be enhanced if noncontrol is attributed to transitory factors that can be controlled. Wortman and Dintzer (1978) argue that controllability of the causal factor may be more important in predicting helplessness than internal-external, stable-unstable or global-specific attributions. While persons may believe that their lives are totally dominated or controlled by government regulations, they may also feel that the regulations can be changed. One may believe that television has a profound impact on the values and behaviors of individuals, yet this person may also conclude that television programming is substantially influenced by organized groups such as the PTA. Dunham's observation that groups (e.g., protesters and communes) have formed in order to regain a sense of community and that personal problems (e.g., racial prejudice, unemployment, abortions, etc.) have been made into public issues in an attempt to widen democracy may also be explained by desires to gain control and to influence policies. Rapid changes in political leadership, the relatively large number of incumbents who failed to be reelected to local and federal offices in recent elections, the success of special interest groups in gaining media coverage and influence, and the like, all may add impetus to the belief that causes of one's problems can be modified. Note that we are distinguishing between the controllability of a causal agent and the agent's control. A trial attorney may feel quite helpless in the presence of a dominating and prejudicial judge, yet he or she may also feel that it is possible to have that judge replaced. We believe that the facilitation effect is influenced by (1) perceptions about the controllability of the causal agent, (2) access to the factors controlling the causal agent, and (3) the aversiveness of the causal agent in fostering feelings of helplessness. If civil rights sympathizers feel that discriminatory laws or practices can be controlled, that they have relevant personal skills or have access to influential groups that control the laws, and that the helplessnes generated by these laws is quite aversive and important to them, they may become civil rights activists. Thus increases in the perceptions of noncontrol due to a causal agent are not necessarily related to inactivity.

A third concern in our discussion of the facilitation effect is that despite perceptions of noncontrol, one may continue to be active, especially if attributions are specific rather than global. The belief that noncontrol is situation-specific implies that helplessness will not occur across situations. Seligman (1975) originally postulated that prior experiences with controllability, discriminative control (distinguishing situations where control or noncontrol is possible) and the importance of events are significant factors to consider. These factors may determine whether attributions are global or specific. In a community where individuals (1) have for a long time experienced an inability to influence outcomes, (2) cannot distinguish where control is possible, and (3) have suffered from noncontrol in important areas of life, passivity and alienation are likely to develop.

Finally, the reformulated helplessness theory states that attributions are predictive of the expectations that develop and that expectations determine the type and severity of helplessness. New evidence may intervene between the initial formulation of an attribution and expectancy so that the expectation is altered. For example, despite the fact that many black youths may have developed quite internal, stable and global attributions of noncontingent control, new information, inspirational messages and demonstrations that control is possible can change expectancies. Such a change is difficult but possible. Jesse Jackson's exhortation to black youths to take control of their lives is, perhaps, based upon a belief in the modifiability of expectations. Moreover mass media coverage of demonstrations and special interest group influences in policies may give hope to those who perceive noncontrol. That is, media coverage can serve to inspire as well as to educate persons on the value of organizing to attain power.

Reflections

It may be wise at this point to summarize our major points, to indicate the utility of our helplessness theory application to community phenomena and to engage in some critical evaluation. We feel that the application of helplessness theory has utility in viewing community phenomena. For years individuals have demanded "power to the people" and "community control"; social scientists have discussed alienation, powerlessness, institutional control, increasing federal encroachment on individual life styles, big business influence and so on. While analyses of control and community processes often fit our intuitive sense and our experiences, it is obvious that social scientists must provide greater empirical and theoretical contributions. Increased predictive precision, better means of testing cause and effect relationships and implications for prevention and intervention are needed. The potential contribution of helplessness theory is that of specification. Learned helplessness allows us to conceptualize loss of control as no longer a nebulous, homogeneous phenomenon but as one that can vary in its consequences.

We believe that there has been a change in contingent relationships so that traditional institutions such as family, churches, neighborhoods and other small and local networks have increasingly lost their influence on people's lives. It is in these more intimate institutions that people have in the past felt some degree of involvement and control. Individuals may then perceive less action-outcome contingencies. We have not empirically demonstrated this loss of control perception. In fact, one fruitful line of investigation would be to assess those specific areas in which control and noncontrol are perceived. What is also unclear is whether individuals have in reality little possibility for control over their lives or whether societal changes have occurred so fast that stable alternative institutions can but have not yet developed.

Many investigators feel that perceived noncontrol in communities means that there is (1) a loss in the psychological sense of community (including relatedness, intimacy, mutual influence and sharing) and (2) an increase in feelings of helplessness and alienation. While loss in the sense of community is likely (particularly in one's relationship to smaller and local institutions), we disagree with views that noncontrol inevitably leads to helplessness and to deficits in motivational, cognitive and affective spheres. As mentioned previously, helplessness theory may be of value in better specifying the consequences of perceived noncontrol. Powerlessness may result in helplessness (which can itself vary in form, duration, generality and severity), lack of helplessness or even in facilitation effects, depending upon the cognitive mediators. Attributions, beliefs in the controllability of the causal agent, and expectations aid in the explanation of reactions to noncontrol. If some reactions to noncontrol are more psychologically adaptive and if we understand the factors behind these reactions, implications for prevention and treatments can be derived. As noted by Dohrenwend (1978), community psychologists are concerned with the early elements in the stress process, the preexisting mediating factors in the person or environment, and within-person or -environment factors that promote or prevent the occurrence of stress. Helplessness theory may be of benefit in these tasks.

At the beginning of this chapter we stated that the application of helplessness theory to community settings is difficult. Helplessness theory and its reformulation have not been adequately tested. The reformulation is rich in ideas and implications, although some propositions are vague and are subject to criticism. For example the theory must better specify what causes individuals to develop certain attributions. Wortman and Dintzer (1978) propose a number of other mediational factors that may be important in helplessness. Furthermore our community analysis is focused upon community processes and reactions of individuals or groups. We have not examined, at another level of analysis, different communities and reactions of communities. Communities vary in areas of control and noncontrol, and it may be wise to compare communities in terms of variables such as production output, economy, decision-making processes and utilization of services.

Directions for Research and Intervention

Research. Suggestions for research directions have been made in various parts of this chapter. We feel that it is important to determine perceptions of control over time for individuals in various communities. Precise areas of control and noncontrol should be assessed. In the past, researchers have used global instruments to evaluate community needs or beliefs about control and power. Helplessness theory suggests that global instruments such as the IE Locus of Control Scale may not be of value in predicting reactions to helpless experiences unless consideration is made of specific factors such as attributions, controllability of causes and certainty of attributions. Reactions to noncontrol are quite complex and varied. Factors that determine the facilitation effect should be investigated since this reaction is a relatively healthy one, assuming that control is possible. We have suggested possible variables in the facilitation effect: degree of perception of the controllability of the causal agent, access to the controllability factors, and the aversiveness and importance of the outcome related to the causal agent. It would be interesting to test these variables. Finally, the formation of new psychological communities should be evaluated. Perhaps because of mass media and institutional "bigness," new and meaningful institutions may be developing to foster a sense of community. Ethnic identity and alliances between members of different ethnic minority groups throughout the nation may be an example of this process.

Intervention. We believe that helplessness theory has direct implications for prevention and intervention in three main areas: primary prevention, immunization and alleviation. Primary prevention occurs when the incidence of a disorder in a population is reduced, presumably by (1) eliminating the etiological agent, (2) immunization, or increasing personal and environmental resources to resist the agent, and (3) isolating the agent from members of the population. The first two techniques are especially relevant to our discussion. Since action-outcome noncontingency is a stressor, elimination of the noncontingency should be a major goal. Rappaport (1977) argues that in order to decrease feelings of helplessness and alienation, it is necessary to make structural changes in society so that objective success where actions lead to outcomes is possible. Iscoe and Spielberger (1977) make a similar plea that community psychologists change communities to meet human needs. No one can really disagree with the value in changing contingencies so that people have greater control over their lives. However, increasing control in the short term may also result in decreasing control in the long run. Let us take voting behavior as an illustration. Votes determine the outcomes of elections. To the extent that more people vote, the effect of a single voice or vote is diluted. As another example, special interest and lobbying groups have a substantial impact on local and national policies. If more people see the contingent relationship between lobbying action and policy outcome and form lobbying groups, each group will have decreasing power because of the increase in the number of groups. Societal supplies, services and goods are limited; increasing demand may decrease control of particular groups. We are definitely not suggesting that objective contingency between actions and outcomes be less than a primary goal. We are simply pointing to complicating factors that need to be carefully considered. Community institutions and the mental health delivery system can surely be made more responsive so that individuals receive better and more appropriate services and outcomes.

Increasing personal and community resources may also reduce the incidence of helplessness and alienation. Assuming that individuals will encounter experiences of noncontrol, these resources can immunize or prevent helplessness. One main point throughout this chapter has been the importance of mediating cognitions and expectancies. Under the right conditions, helplessness will not develop. Abramson et al. (1978) outline various strategies to prevent, treat or alleviate helplessness. These tactics include reducing the likelihood for aversive outcomes, and increasing the likelihood for desired outcomes; making the preferred outcomes less preferred; changing expectancies of noncontrol to those of control; and changing unrealistic attributions toward more external, unstable and specific ones. Communities and institutions can play a critical role in facilitating some of these strategies.

First, people can be encouraged to join citizen and action groups in their community. Wortman and Dintzer (1978) indicate that interaction with others often has the effect of altering attributions of persons exposed to uncontrollable life events. Associating with similar others can help victims realize that the life crises are not the product of their own inadequacies. We also believe that citizens' groups can develop into social-change advocacy groups that engage in a meaningful process of control. The meaningfulness of the process must be distinguished between objective control of outcomes. Earlier we mentioned that an increase in the number of action or lobbying groups may in the long run result in less control of any particular group. Nevertheless the value of such groups may lie in giving people the opportunity to feel they are participating in (not absolutely controlling) the decision-making process. They are also valuable in the development of a psychological sense of community and relatedness, and in their self-help nature.

Another way to facilitate change is for communities to make an attempt to foresee it so that new programs and institutions can develop to alleviate feelings of noncontrol. If busing in a community is inevitable, plans should be devised so that the quality of schools involved are improved and so that parental concerns regarding safety are addressed. A third factor in effecting changes is research. On the basis of research findings, communities should organize their intervention programs in terms of certain priorities. Perceptions of noncontrol in *important* areas of life and the attributions given should receive first attention. That is, the outcomes that are the most valued in a community would be the primary areas of focus. Finally, human services should be more flexible in individualizing care and in fostering self-help. We believe that mismatches between clients and type of service may be responsible for feelings of noncontrol. Those services that are nontraditional or that are not within our mainstream delivery system to the extent that they respond to the unique needs of a particular community should be given encouragement.

The intervention strategies outlined form an incomplete listing of the possibilities suggested by helplessness theory. The theory has acted as a stimulus for us in the development of ideas. We hope that other strategies can be generated, applied and tested in the community.

Reference Note

1. Sue, S. Mental health in a multiethnic society: The person-organization match. Paper presented at the American Psychological Association Convention, Toronto, September, 1978.

References

Abramson, L.Y., Seligman, M. E. P., & Teasdale, J. D. Learned helplessness in humans: Critique and reformulation. *Journal of Abnormal Psychology*, 1978, *87*, 49–74.

Benson, J. S., & Kennelly, K. J. Learned helplessness: The result of uncontrollable reinforcements or uncontrollable aversive stimuli? *Journal of Personality and Social Psychology*, 1976, *34*, 138–145.

Bloom, B. L. *Community mental health: A general introduction.* Monterey, Calif.: Brooks/Cole, 1977.

Buchwald, A. M., Coyne, J. D., & Cole, C. S. A critical evaluation of the learned helplessness model of depression. *Journal of Abnormal Psychology*, 1978, *87*, 180–193.

Carr, T. H., Dixon, M. C., & Ogles, R. M. Perceptions of community life which distinguish between participants and nonparticipants in a neighborhood self-help organization. *American Journal of Community Psychology*, 1976, *4*, 357–366.

Cole, C. S., & Coyne, J. C. Situational specificity of laboratory-induced learned helplessness. *Journal of Abnormal Psychology*, 1977, *86*, 615–623.

Cowen, E. L. Some problems in community program evaluation research. *Journal of Abnormal Psychology*, 1978, *46*, 792–805.

Dohrenwend, B. S. Social stress and community psychology. *American Journal of Community Psychology*, 1978, *6*, 1–14.

Dunham, H. W. Community as a process: Maintaining the delicate balance. *American Journal of Community Psychology*, 1977, *5*, 257–268.

French, J. R., & Raven, B. H. The basis of social power. In D. Cartwright (Ed.), *Studies in social power*. Ann Arbor: University of Michigan Press, 1959.

Glass, D. C., & Singer, J. E. *Urban stress: Experiments on noise and social stressors*. New York: Academic Press, 1972.

Hiroto, D. S. Locus of control and learned helplessness. *Journal of Experimental Psychology*, 1974, *102*, 187–193.

Hiroto, D. S., & Seligman, M. E. P. Generality of learned helplessness in man. *Journal of Personality and Social Psychology*, 1975, *31*, 311–237.

Iscoe, I., & Spielberger, C.D. Community psychology: The historical context. In I. Iscoe, B. L. Boom, & C. D. Spielberger (Eds.), *Community psychology in transition*. Washington, D. C.: Hemisphere, 1977.

Jones, S. L., Nation, J. R., & Massad, P. Immunization against learned helplessness in man. *Journal of Abnormal Psychology*, 1977, *86*, 75–83.

Kaemmerer, W. F., & Schwebel, A. I. Citizen participation in community planning: A simulation of the citizen-planner information exchange process. *American Journal of Community Psychology*, 1977, *5*, 249–253.

Kelly, J. G., Snowden, L. R., & Munoz, R. F. Social and community interventions. *Annual Review of Psychology*, 1977, *28*, 323–361.

Lao, R. C. Internal-external control and competent and innovative behavior change among Negro college students. *Journal of Personality and Social Psychology*, 1970, *14*, 263–270.

Learning to excel in school. *Time Magazine*, July 10, 1978, 45–46.

Levine, M. President's column. *Division of Community Psychology Newsletter*, 1978a, *11*, 1–2.

Levine, M. President's column. *Division of Community Psychology Newsletter*, 1978b, *11*, 1–3.

Mahoney, M. J. Experimental methods and outcome evaluation. *Journal of Abnormal Psychology*, 1978, *46*, 660–672.

Maier, S. F., & Testa, T. J. Failure to learn to escape by rats previously exposed to inescapable shock is partly produced by associative interference. *Journal of Comparative and Physiological Psychology*, 1975, *88*, 554–564.

Padilla, A. M. Effects of prior and interpolated shock exposures on subsequent avoidance learning by goldfish. *Psychological Reports*, 1973, *32*, 451–456.

Panzetta, A. F. The concept of community: The short-circuit of the mental health movement. *Archives of General Psychiatry*, 1971, *25*, 291–297.

Price, R. H., & Blashfield, R. K. Explorations in the taxonomy of behavior settings: Analysis of dimensions and classification of settings. *American Journal of Community Psychology* 1975, *3*, 335–352.

Rappaport, J. *Community psychology: Values, research, and action*. New York: Holt, Rinehart and Winston, 1977.

Sarason, S. B. Community psychology and the anarchist insight. *American Journal of Community Psychology*, 1976a, *4*, 246–261.

Sarason, S. B. Community psychology, networks, and Mr. Everyman. *American Psychologist*, 1976b, *13*, 317–328.

Seligman, M. E. P. Chronic fear produced by unpredictable shock. *Journal of Comparative and Physiological Psychology*, 1968, *66*, 402–411.

Seligman, M. E. P. *Helplessness: On depression, development and death*. San Francisco: Freeman, 1975.

Seligman, M. E. P. Comment and integration. *Journal of Abnormal Psychology*, 1978, *87*, 165–179.

Seligman, M. E. P., & Beagley, G. Learned helplessness in the rat. *Journal of Comparative and Physiological Psychology*, 1975, *88*, 534–541.

Sherrod, D. R., & Downs, R. Environmental determinants of altruism: The effects of stimulus overload and perceived control on helping. *Journal of Experimental Psychology*, 1974, *10*, 468–479.

Sherrod, D. R., Hage, J. N., Halpern, P. L., & Moore, B. S. Effect of personal causation and perceived control on responses to an aversive environment: The more control, the better. *Journal of Experimental Social Psychology*, 1977, *13*, 14–27.

Sue, S. Community mental health services to minority groups: Some optimism, some pessimism. *American Psychologist*, 1977, *32*, 616-624 (a).

Sue, S. Psychological theory and implications for Asian Americans. *Personnel and Guidance Journal*, 1977, *55*, 381–389 (b).

Thomas, E., & Dewald, L. Experimental neurosis: Neuropsychological analysis. In J. D. Maser & M. E. P. Seligman (Eds.), *Psychopathology: Experimental models*. San Francisco: Freeman, 1977.

Thorton, J. W. & Jacobs, P. D. Analysis of task difficulty under varying conditions of induced stress. *Perceptual and Motor Skills*, 1970, *31*, 343–348.

Thorton, J. W., & Powell, G. D. Immunization to and alleviation of learned helplessness in man. *American Journal of Psychology*, 1974, *87*, 351–367.

Wortman, C. B., & Dintzer, L. Is an attributional analysis of the learned helplessness phenomemon viable? A critique of the Abramson-Seligman-Teasdale reformulation. *Journal of Abnormal Psychology*, 1978, *87*, 75–90.

CHAPTER 6

Physical Environmental Stressors

Janet Sigal, Ph.D.

The effects of physical environmental stressors as potential contributory factors to mental illness are of concern to the community psychologist. If it can be shown through accumulated evidence that the presence of these stressors in the environment can be linked to the incidence of mental illness, or even to the deterioration of social relationships, the occurrence of aggressive behavior or other socially negative effects, then the amelioration or elimination of these stressor conditions should form a part of the prevention emphasis of community psychology.

This chapter will review representative studies related to the potentially detrimental consequences of brief or continued exposure to aversive physical environments. Crowding, noise and air pollution were selected as sample stressors, with particular emphasis upon crowding, primarily because of the voluminous literature in the area. Recent publications such as Baum and Epstein's (1978) text as well as Stokols's (1977) book provide excellent and thorough coverage of much of the crowding literature. This author will concentrate on sample laboratory, field and correlational studies which can directly or indirectly be linked to the concern for mental health and coping. The concept of designing environments to provide potentially more satisfying lives for individuals will also be considered as part of prevention.

CROWDING

Definitions

The controversy over the definition of crowding might seem odd to the ordinary person, who can certainly clearly distinguish between a crowded subway at rush hour and an empty university library at 8:00 A.M. on a weekday. However, despite one possible interpretation of the controversy as reflecting the psychologist's tendency to needlessly transform a relatively simple concept into a complex controversy to confuse the layman, there does appear to be a genuine basis for the controversy. As Freedman (1975) has suggested, some situations are not simplistic and clearcut.

For example, although a person intuitively knows that a crowded subway is different from a delightful party with several people in his or her one-room apartment, the precise nature of the definitional distinction remained unclarified until Stokols's (1972) paper. Stokols claimed that density is a "physical condition . . . involving spatial limitation" (p. 275). Along these lines, Altman (1978) defined density as the "number of people per unit of space" (p. 16). On the other hand crowding, according to Stokols (1972), is an "experiential state . . . in which the restrictive aspects of limited space are perceived by the individuals exposed to them" (p. 275).

In effect the density concept is objective, and the crowding concept is subjective. Clearly the subjective state is a more important concept in this chapter. Although this distinction has been generally accepted by psychologists performing research in the area, often measures of "perceived crowding" (Stokols, 1972, p. 276) have not been included in these studies.

Another conceptual distinction which has stemmed from research is the differentiation between spatial density or "the behavior of groups of the same number in spaces of differing sizes" (Loo, 1973, p. 222) and social density or "the behavior of groups of differing numbers in the same sized space" (Loo, 1973, p. 222).

Finally, Galle, Gove, and McPherson (in Moos & Insel, 1974) identified four types of density measures to be used in housing studies: 1) "the number of persons per room; 2) the number of rooms per housing unit; 3) the number of housing units per structure; 4) the number of residential structures per acre" (p. 142).

In specifying these distinctions, Galle et al. (1974) indicated that some density measures could be more psychologically meaningful than others. For example, they suggested that although most people would identify a low-rise tenement building in a slum area as being crowded (high "room density"), few people would qualify a large luxury condominium in Florida or a large luxury apartment house on New York's Fifth Avenue as representing crowded conditions. The latter two examples would reflect high within-housing unit and high neighborhood density, rather than high room density.

Stress or Arousal Theoretical Approach to Crowding

In terms of theoretical orientations, according to Altman (1978) the majority of important and current theoretical approaches to the study of crowding effects emanate from a basic "equilibrium/homeostatic model" (p. 19) of stimulation. These theories assume that individuals respond best and cope most successfully with an "optimal level of stimulation" (Altman, 1978, p. 19). Once an excessive amount of stimulation bombards the individual, such as in crowded settings, this "stimulus overload" produces possible concomitant stress responses or arousal, and attempts to cope with the overload.

Stress responses have been identified by Lazarus (1966) as including: 1) "reports of disturbed affects; 2) motor-behavioral reactions; 3) changes in the adequacy of cognitive functioning and 4) physiological changes" (p. 29). In terms of responses produced by crowding, the first stress response might involve discomfort, for example. The second response might trigger aggression or dislike in others; the third, decreased performance, particularly on complex tasks; and the fourth, variations in indices such as heart rate and blood pressure.

D'Atri (1975), in an often-cited experiment, examined the role of crowding conditions in producing stress reactions. The study utilized three different prisons to test the hypothesis that prisoners confined in dormitories, as compared with prisoners in individual cells, would show increased evidence of stress or arousal. Using both blood pressure and pulse rate as stress measures, D'Atri found a significant "positive correlation between degree of crowding" (in dormitories as compared with cells) and physiological responses of elevated blood pressure readings (p. 240). A difficulty in one of the prisons was that dormitory residents had generally been in prison for a more extended term than prisoners in individual cells in the same institution. Although this difference could present methodological difficulties, the same relationship apparently did not obtain in the other prisons. One other relevant finding by D'Atri indicated a nonsignificant tendency for prisoners with heightened crowding feelings to exhibit more stress symptoms.

This experiment was particularly interesting because of the direct measures of physiological responses to presumed stress-inducing crowding conditions. As D'Atri pointed out, the study was only correlational. Also, as Evans (1978) suggested, social and spatial density were not clearly separated in the D'Atri procedure. In addition D'Atri himself criticized the study because "inmates were not . . . assigned in a random fashion" (p. 250) in the various prisons used in the study. Another obvious difficulty in terms of generalization related to the special nature of the inmate sample. D'Atri indirectly referred to this characteristic by saying that crowding could be perceived as involving more potential danger to inmates. Although this observation could be related to the interference theory approach, which will be described in a subsequent section, this particular source of stress determinant would probably not be much of a factor in considering the effects of crowding in, for example, a high-rise building.

Nevertheless overall the D'Atri study, by definitely supporting the thesis that crowding can induce stress in a field setting involving longer-term exposure, thus is less subject to the artificiality criticism often leveled at laboratory experiments on crowding effects.

In a related prison study McCain, Cox, and Paulus (1976) examined the relationship between type of incarceration domicile and frequency of what might be considered stress-associated illness. Subjects were volunteers who resided either in one- or two-man cells or dormitories in a prison or county jail, and who had lived in the same place for a minimum of 30 days. In support of the stress approach, and consistent with the D'Atri research, McCain et al. found that a higher number of "illness complaints" (p. 284) (for example, "backpain, nausea . . . sinus . . . chest pain" p. 285) occurred in both prison and county jail inmates who were living in dormitories, than occurred in single-cell subjects.

As a result of the controls in the study, the use of a field setting once again, and the extended duration of crowding conditions, these findings lend strong support to the thesis that "crowding can induce traumatic psychological stress," which contributes to the development of psychosomatic symptoms.

Aiello, Epstein, and Karlin (1975) obtained somewhat more indirect support for the stress or arousal interpretation. Two particularly interesting aspects of the study's design distinguish it from other research. First, various measures of responses to crowding conditions were obtained, including physiological measures, questionnaire responses and performance measures on "simple and complex tasks." Second, "long-term crowding effects" were assessed in a field experiment utilizing a sample of students who were comparable on all background characteristics. These male and female subjects were living in double rooms which housed either two or three students, the latter because of a lack of sufficient dormitory space. The students received their rooms on a random basis ("randomly assigned to living conditions," p. 4).

Although the results did not indicate any direct overall physiological effects of crowding conditions, the lack of negative findings may be partially attributed to the limited number of subjects from whom these measures were obtained, as the experimenters stated in the article. Crowded females in particular, however, revealed somewhat greater evidence of "physical and psychological" symptoms (p. 8). In addition, triple-room subjects did demonstrate the predicted effects of "improved performance on a simple task and impaired performance on a complex task" (pp. 8, 9). If arousal was produced by crowding, this arousal should facilitate simple and inhibit complex tasks as explained by a drive or arousal theory. Affective responses indicating greater perceived space restrictions and greater unhappiness with the residence for triple-room individuals reinforce the pattern of obtained results just described.

The Aiello et al. results once again support the contention that crowding can produce an environment which is stressful for people over a period of time, and suggest, as Aiello and his coauthors note, that lab experiments concerning crowding have external validity. The study is an improvement over the D'Atri (1975) and McCain et al. (1976) prison studies because of the more representative nature of the sample. Living in a crowded urban area for several years, however, might produce more adaptation than was observed in the Aiello et al. experiment. In addition, college subjects are not as representative a sample as could be desired. The use of a variety of measures, however, and some good methodological points make the Aiello group's research one of the more impressive supportive studies in this expanding and controversial area.

Contradictory Reports. Two investigations apparently contradicted the hypothesis that crowding is a stressor that may adversely affect productivity. The first investigation, by Emiley (1975) involved spatial density. Male subjects completed a complex task in either crowded or uncrowded conditions. Crowding had no effects on either self-reported stress or task performance. Two explanations advanced by Emiley might serve to clarify the issue. The first explanation suggested that since subjects were involved in a complex and interesting task, they may have "tuned out potentially negative aspects" (p. 273) of their crowded environment. Furthermore, as the author stated, the crowding was of limited duration in a controlled, otherwise pleasant or neutral setting, as contrasted with more naturalistic crowding studies. Still another difficulty was that only self-reported stress measures were used.

The second, related study was by Sundstrom (1975). It also generally found nonconfirmatory results, but was again subject to the lab experiment artificiality criticism and the inadequacy of self-reported stress measures objection.

Alternative Theoretical Orientations and Supporting Evidence

Stimulus Overload Theory. A current adherent of the second or "stimulus overload" interpretation of crowding is Milgram (in Moos & Insel, 1974). He suggested that city residents and workers may attempt to cope with the overload problem by "disregard of low priority inputs" (p. 191) and by reducing the number of other individuals with whom they interact in a significant manner. For example, Milgram points out that in overcrowded areas, strangers may help one another less frequently in emergency situations, not because people are apathetic, but because they cannot empathize with or assist all the potential victims with whom they come into contact in the course of their daily urban life.

McCauley, Coleman, and DeFusco (1978) attempted to investigate some of the implications of Milgram's "stimulus overload" interpretation of urbanite behavior. The experimenters suggested that one method in which people may cope with the overload presented by the complexity of the urban setting (particularly as represented by the larger numbers of people) is to limit eye contact. Specifically McCauley et al. hypothesized that eye contact in an urban area would occur less frequently than in suburban areas. In their field experiment, male and female stooges were employed to establish continuous eye contact with suburban commuters as they boarded their trains in the morning and as they arrived at the urban stations. The same process occurred in reverse in the evening as commuters returned home. The hypothesis was confirmed.

McCauley et al. interpreted these results as reflecting "short-term adaptation to the city environment" (p. 221) or as a way of reducing urban stimulus overload by means of "decreased eye contact with strangers" (p. 221) in a manner similar to withdrawal from social interaction. In general the McCauley et al. research was well controlled although somewhat trivial in nature, and indicated that some tenets of the Milgram stimulus overload interpretation have been substantiated.

Interference Theory. An alternative minitheoretical approach to explaining crowding stress was formulated by Schopler and Stockdale (1977). These experimenters postulated that it is a person's "perception" that other individuals will "frustrate" his or her achieving a particular desired end which creates stress for the individual. This so-called "interference" theory implies that social density provides much more potential for "goal-interference" than spatial density, because there are many more individuals who can compete for the desired goals or resources.

For example, space would be a difficulty for a class of 30 students in a smaller as opposed to a larger room. If, however, you compare 30 students with 110 students (social density), then competition for "increasing scarcity of 'fixed' resources" (Schopler & Stockdale, 1977, p. 83)—such as the teacher's recognition of different students' questions and interference with learning due to increased noise level—becomes a significant determinant of an individual's feeling of being crowded.

Heller, Groff, and Solomon (1977) performed a laboratory experiment related to the interference theory presented above. The experimenters tested the effects of spatial density and the amount of actual "physical interaction" (p. 185) required in the performance of a relatively simple task. Subjects were required to add numbers after collecting and arranging pages of a booklet in a particular order. The collating was either performed by individuals seated at separate desks or by each subject picking up the various pages at different desks scattered around the room ("high physical-interaction," p. 186). Although the "physical-interaction" variable did not influence subjective perceptions of crowding differently from the density manipulation, the extensive "physical interaction" group performed more poorly on this relatively simple task than the group with a minimum amount of "physical interaction." The experimenters interpreted the results both in terms of "interference-theory," "goal-blocking" (p. 189) and overstimulation approaches. A related real-life example of the differences between varying amounts of physical contact would be a densely populated cafeteria or self-service restaurant (perceived subjectively as more crowded) versus a densely-populated restaurant with waiter service.

Personal Distance Theory. Worchel and Teddlie (1976), however, implied that the interference theory is not broad enough, since it cannot explain why people feel crowded even when sitting in one place. The experimenters proposed the following two-component approach to crowding: crowding occurs when there is a "state of arousal created by violations of personal space . . . followed by the attribution that other people are the cause of this arousal" (p. 32). Worchel and Teddlie suggest that social versus spatial density may not be as crucial a distinction as that between little versus great interpersonal distance.

In conjunction with this crowding interpretation, several investigators have indicated that violation of personal space conventions produces discomfort (possibly stress) among individuals. In this area Efran and Cheyne (1974) performed a laboratory experiment in which some subjects ("violation" group) were forced to walk between two confederates who were talking in a hallway. These subjects demonstrated considerably more evidence of arousal as reflected by nonverbal cues, such as "head and gaze down . . . eyes closed . . . and negative mouth gestures" (p. 223), as compared with subjects who walked from one room to another without encountering any people.

Despite some possible suspicion-producing aspects of the experimental procedure and the lack of physiological indications of arousal on a heart-rate measure, this study can be seen as support for the Worchel and Teddlie (1976) theory. Efran and Cheyne (1974) also suggested that what seem to be rather "trivial" everyday interactions can produce stress and arousal, particularly in crowded settings, a contention which is relevant to the thesis of this chapter.

Aiello, DeRisi, Epstein, and Karlin (1977) performed a lab experiment which was related both to the stress arousal approach and to the Worchel and Teddlie (1976) personal space explanation of crowding. Using all female subjects, the experimenters first obtained baseline measures of "Skin Conductance Level" (SCL; p. 274) and a measure of subjects' habitual personal distances in an informal interaction with a female experimental stooge. In a subsequent session, groups of four subjects (spatial density) were placed in restricted-space rooms (close distances) or larger rooms for thirty minutes with no interaction permitted.

In the initial stage of this waiting period, crowded subjects in general displayed higher amounts of SCL, but individuals who had been identified as demanding "greater distances with people" (p. 280) in interpersonal settings and enounters displayed the greatest stress when placed in the smaller room. Questionnaire responses indicated that self-reported discomfort and "somatic" symptoms supported these findings. The study demonstrated that the personal space invasion hypothesis can explain part of the crowding effect and that there are personality differences in subjects' responses to crowding.

The study was limited, however, by the short duration of crowding as discussed by Aiello et al., and by the artificiality of the lab session including some possible suspicion-producing aspects to the manipulations. In addition only female subjects were used and spatial, not social, density was introduced. The results do manage to shed light on short-term crowding effects. Aiello et al. did suggest that the short-term crowding experience could be related to real-life, short-time crowding such as that experienced by subway commuters, although other concomitant stress-producing stimuli such as noise, odor and heat were eliminated in the lab experiment.

In support of this cautious generalization, a 1978 CBS news report revealed that commuters on the subway or train demonstrate higher blood pressure levels during and following the commuting experience than prior to commuting, and that for subjects with predispositions to stress-related illnesses, these elevated levels can persist and may be potentially harmful for the individual commuter.

Density Intensity Theory. A final theoretical orientation to be considered in this section is Freedman's (1975) "density intensity" (p. 89) approach. Freedman might be considered the advocate of the theory that "crowding does not necessarily produce stress." Freedman suggested that density by itself does not affect an individual in a consistent manner, even when one distinguishes between social and spatial density. If a person is enjoying a particular activity or setting (for example, attending a play), the more people there are, the more enjoyment he or she derives. If a person is uncomfortable in a particular setting (for instance, when a claustrophobic person is in an elevator), the more people present, the greater his or her discomfort. This approach could explain the differential reaction to the party versus the subway setting described earlier.

A crucial point about the Freedman theory is that "increasing density does not produce stress or arousal, but it does make the presence of the other people . . . more important . . . and whatever the individual's reactions, they will be stronger" (p. 96). Freedman, Klevansky and Ehrlich's (1971) findings that increasing density per se had no effects on simple or complex task performance supported Freedman's theoretical approach.

In conclusion it is apparent that the stimulus overload and stress approaches are more consistent with the concerns of the community psychologist. If it can be shown that crowding does produce stress or arousal, as indicated by some of the research discussed, this stressful or unpleasant state is a condition which should be prevented or at least ameliorated by intervention techniques. As far as supporting one interpretation or the other goes, at the present time it seems that both stimulus overload and arousal may be significant aspects of crowding responses and that a complex condition such as crowding can probably be analyzed in terms of several components (e.g. "interference" as well as "personal space invasion").

Density and "Pathology"

Galle, Gove, and McPherson (in Moos & Insel, 1974) in an often-cited research study, investigated the correlation between various measures of "population density" and indices of "pathology" in Chicago. Using a gross index of density, "number of persons per acre" (p. 138), the experimenters correlated this measure with indices such as "juvenile delinquency" based on court records, and incidence of mental illness based on "admissions to mental" institutions (p. 139). Although the authors demonstrated some positive relationships between these variables, when essential controls for "social class and ethnic" variables (p. 141) were included, these correlations became extremely small.

After evaluating the density measure as too broad, Galle et al. correlated each of the density measures mentioned earlier ("number of persons per room; . . . rooms per housing unit; the number of housing units per structure; and the number of residential structures per acre"; p. 142) with the pathology indices. The experimenters found that the concentration of individuals per room was highly related to pathology such as juvenile delinquency, whereas the concentration of "rooms in each housing unit" was related to mental illness incidence (that is, persons living by themselves were more likely to be hospitalized). Galle et al. suggested that these relationships, which existed even when social class and ethnic variables were partialed out, were reasonable, since these aspects of density related most to "interpersonal press" (p. 147) or social and psychological aspects of crowding. In effect this analysis conforms to the general theoretical and definitional orientation which suggests that crowding is an experience or a feeling state which is psychological in nature. In addition the experimenters suggested that the"persons per room" crowding condition was related to overstimulation and an absence of "privacy" (p. 147), which is also consistent with the theoretical orientations previously described.

Although these results appeared to substantiate the hypothesis that overcrowding on an interpersonal level can have deleterious consequences, Galle et al. qualified these results by first underscoring the obvious correlational nature of the research which precluded any causal inferences. More important for this discussion, the experimenters also concluded that the relationship between density and incidence of mental illness is difficult to interpret. The researchers suggested that contrary to the concept that single living produces or contributes to institutionalization for mental illness, individuals with a tendency towards mental illness may seek out single living conditions because of their inability to cope with the demands of relationships with others in a home environment.

Over all, then, this correlational study does not strongly support the contention that crowding conditions contribute to mental illness, but does suggest that overcrowding can have negative interpersonal consequences. It should be noted parenthetically, however, that admissions to mental institutions may not be a totally satisfactory measure of incidence of mental illness.

Freedman, Heshka, and Levy (1975) disagreed with the limited and cautious conclusions reached by Galle et al. Freedman and his coworkers, within the framework of Freedman's "density-intensity" approach, which does not assume an inherently negative effect of "population density," criticized the Galle study on methodological and statistical grounds.

On the basis of this analysis and Freedman's theoretical orientation, Freedman et al. tested the "pathology" hypothesis using "338 health areas" (p. 542) in New York City. The experimenters correlated the "number of persons per residential area" (p. 543) and "the average number of persons per room in all household units" (p. 543), density measures with measures of "juvenile delinquency," mental institution admissions and "psychiatric terminations" (p. 542), presumably in patient outclinics. Although initial correlations indicated some relationships between density measures and pathology, further statistical analysis utilizing multiple correlations revealed that neither measure of density accounted for a large proportion of the variance in most of the pathology measures used. The only exception was a small association between density and "psychiatric terminations" (p. 546).

Again proceeding somewhat cautiously in terms of limiting causation generalization from correlational research, Freedman suggested that these results disputed the common assumption that population density automatically produces detrimental effects. Instead the authors implied that the study's results can be interpreted as possible support for the intensification of prevailing situational conditions by density interpretation.

It is obviously difficult to compare directly the Freedman research with previous studies because of the increased sophistication in the former's statistical analysis. In addition the same criticism of the mental health criteria used in the Galle et al. study could be applied to Freedman's research. Over all it does again appear that the relationship between density and mental illness, if it indeed exists at all, is extremely complex. Instead density might conceivably be an issue which is not particularly relevant for incidence of mental illness measures. Although Freedman's "number of persons per room" measure was not associated with mental illness, this "interpersonal press" measure can contribute to decreased interpersonal functioning in a less global sense, as will be subsequently discussed.

Along the lines of the Freedman et al. thesis, but from a broader perspective, Srole (1972) has argued that the hypothesis in which urban areas are associated with higher incidences of mental illness was promulgated by researchers who were "anti-urbanites." Srole cited evidence which seemed to indicate that urbanites might have slightly lower incidences of symptoms related to mental illness than those living in more rural areas. However, as Srole pointed out, these figures have not controlled for other factors such as SES. It would be more cautious, therefore, to assume no significant difference in "symptoms of psychological distress" between urban and rural dwellers (p. 580).

It is also interesting that Srole reinforced the Galle et al. contention that urban dwellings may be the result, to a large degree, of "self-selection." The crowded urban area, therefore, may not precipitate mental illness but urban areas may attract individuals who are deviant and prone to pathological symptoms because these individuals feel safer in the seemingly more liberal urban environments.

At any rate, Srole's discussion did not support the concept that urban living is conducive to the development of mental illness. Of course the studies Srole described did not utilize crowding or density measures. In addition, the incidence of mental illness and prevalence of "distress" symptoms were measured in varied ways.

To conclude this discussion of correlational studies, it seems apparent that physical measures of density will not clearly be related to either pathological symptoms or incidences of mental illness. As indicated in the definition section, crowding is experienced by individuals, and only correlational studies which have measured "perceived crowding" have shown relationships between this measure and psychological symptoms. As reviewed by Sundstrom (1978) Booth's study found a relationship between "subjective household crowding" and "psychiatric impairment" (Sundstrom, p. 67). Sundstrom also suggested that "neighborhood density" in several studies was not apparently related to mental illness in any consistent, significant manner.

Social and Behavioral Consequences of Crowding

Social Density and Interpersonal Attraction. In a relatively early study Griffith and Veitch (1971) investigated the effects of high and low degrees of social density on attraction measures in a lab setting. Subjects in same-sexed groups filled out questionnaires in either very crowded conditions or uncrowded conditions. Following this exposure to crowding, subjects then indicated their like or dislike of a hypothetical "anonymous stranger" (p. 94), whose attitudes were described to them. The experimenters found that high social density produced significantly more dislike of the stranger than did low social density, a result reflecting the potential detrimental effect of high density on interpersonal relationships.

There were, however, several difficulties with the study, including the artificiality and short-term nature of the crowding experience. Griffith and Veitch themselves suggested that mixed-sex groups and groups of friends might respond differently to crowded conditions from same-sex stranger groups. Still another major difficulty concerned the fact that subjects did not engage in any interaction, and attraction was measured in terms of a hypothetical individual. However, according to the interference theory described earlier, if physical interaction had been required, the negative attitudes might have been exacerbated.

Spatial Density and Interpersonal Attraction. Some of the difficulties associated with the Griffith and Veitch study were resolved in the experiment by Ross, Layton, Erickson, and Schopler (1973), who investigated the effects of spatial density on liking relationships. The major improvement over the Griffith and Veitch study was accomplished by having subjects in the Ross et al. lab experiment interact with one another in an attempt to produce group decisions on problems. The experimenters found that whether the exposure to crowding was of short or long duration, crowded males responded negatively to each other; females in larger, uncrowded rooms also responded negatively to one another. These results were interpreted in terms of the personal space invasion explanation described earlier. The finding of relatively "mild stress" (p. 75) reactions could be attributed to the short period of exposure to crowding conditions (the maximum time was 20 minutes) and again to the lack of physical interaction. The study does, however, support the thesis that crowding for some subjects can produce negative feelings toward other individuals.

Social versus Spatial Density. The fact that both the Griffith and Veitch, and Ross et al. studies produced evidences of aversive consequences of crowding is interesting, since the first study utilized social density and the latter, spatial density. Eoyang's (1974) questionnaire study, performed in the naturalistic setting of a trailer camp, seemed to indicate that social density was an extremely important factor in determining a resident's perception of his or her living space. It was Paulus, Cox, McCain, and Chandler (1975), however, who clarified the issue of the relative importance of social versus spatial density with a prison setting. The experimenters definitely found that higher social density in dormitories was significantly related to increased negative feelings about these living conditions, whereas spatial density differences had no consistent effect. These results seem to indicate that within a real-life setting social density produces more negative effects than spatial density.

As a conclusion to this discussion on interpersonal attraction, the Baron, Mandel, Adams, and Griffen (1976) study on social density in college dormitories should be mentioned. The experimenters utilized a large variety of measures to differentiate between "doubles" and "triples" subjects and basically found that triples (as in the Aiello, Epstein, & Karlin [1975] study discussed earlier) were more unhappy with their environment and more unhappy with their roommates than doubles. Baron et al. however, also revealed that triple subjects, who appeared to get along better with their roommates, seemed to perform more poorly academically. If this result can be replicated, the inference to be drawn is that great care should be taken to design an environment more conducive to academic study. The experimenters suggested that the "social overstimulation" (p. 445) and integration difficulties bombarding the triple subject would entail greater effort in developing a good coordination with a roommate, and that this effort might detract from the student's attention to his or her studies.

Spatial Density and Aggression. With a related but slightly different focus, Ginsburg, Pollman, Wauson, and Hope (1977) investigated the effects of "spatial density" on aggression among male elementary school subjects. Hidden cameras recorded the type and amount of aggressive behavior during free-play settings in a large or small playground. Although a repeated-measures design was utilized, the study did include several good controls and obtained high reliability ratings of the videotaped aggressive-behavior sequences.

Contradictory to some previous studies, the experimenters found a higher incidence of aggression among children in the smaller playground setting. On the other hand, the fights in that small space were of shorter duration than those in the larger playground. A greater mean number of children also participated in the separate fights in the smaller playground than occurred in the larger playground. These results seemed to indicate that restricted space is associated with higher levels of fighting or aggression.

The study is, of course, limited in terms of generalization because the sample was composed only of children and because of the use of only male subjects, the lack of any supervision or activities which might have reduced the amount of aggression, and the use of a predominantly middle-class sample from a relatively small town. All of these deficiencies should be viewed in the light of the major advantage of external validity, since the study did not involve unnatural settings or manipulation.

Spatial Density and Helping Behavior. The opposite side of the behavioral coin from aggression might be considered to be altrustic or helping behavior. It is interesting that the Ginsburg et al. study found that the majority of additional children who entered a two-child fight in the smaller play area did so to help the fight victim, thus partially explaining why the small playground area fights did not last as long as those in the large play area. These results seemed to imply that spatial density might increase helping behavior or altruism.

Bickman, Teger, Gabriele, McLaughlin, Berger, and Sunaday (1973) directly investigated the relationship between density in student university housing and helping behavior. Using the overall unit or dorm rather than the more common room unit as the density measure, the experimenters selected "high density" dorms (p. 472) with an average of over 500 residents, "medium density" dorms with about 150 students, and "low density" dorms with an average of about 60 students, in a few colleges. Both the rate of return of stamped addressed envelopes apparently "lost" in the dorms, and another nonreactive measure of contributions of milk containers to a resident student's art class confirmed Bickman et al.'s hypothesis that higher density settings would produce lowered helping rates.

In addition, student questionnaire responses reported more negative feelings towards fellow residents in high density dorms, a finding consistent with the studies discussed previously. High density residents also found the dorms to be "more impersonal, unfriendly and cold" (p. 487), as compared with low density residents. The answers suggested Milgram's concept of stimulus overload discussed earlier, as a possible interpretation of the results. The fact that the students appeared to "adapt" to their high density settings, according to the authors, did not preclude the possibility that these settings might have serious significant aversive consequences in terms of overall interpersonal relationships and trust. The study's advantages lie primarily in the use of a naturalistic field setting with a relatively homogeneous sample. Although the experiment can be criticized in terms of the difficulties with the dropped envelope procedure, questionnaire responses did support the experimental results. Over all, the results seemed to indicate possible detrimental effects of density on a relatively trivial low-cost helping response.

Learned Helplessness. High density or crowding has been tentatively linked to the development of "learned helplessness," a situation in which subjects feel that the rewards they obtain are unrelated to their efforts or inputs (see Chapter 5 for an extensive discussion of learned helplessness). If individuals have had experiences in which they lacked social control over rewards, they "no longer learn to perform adaptively when their outcomes are . . . contingent upon their responses" (Rodin, 1976, p. 571). Rodin suggested that if people are raised in very crowded environments, they may develop learned helplessness because the restricted environment means the individual has less "control" over his or her activities.

In a complex set of lab experiments, Rodin demonstrated that younger high density-exposed predominantly black children did not choose to "control" their own rewards as much as low density children. Also when subjects were first given a problem which did not lend itself to successful resolution, they were less likely to be able to cope with a second problem which was more readily resolvable. This inability to cope was particularly apparent for children raised under high density conditions. While it was true that some difficulties with the study existed as described by Rodin—notably the obvious problem of extraneous factors associated with high residential density which might have contributed to the learned helplessness type syndrome—the investigation was interesting and relevant.

Another study related to the learned helplessness effect or lack of control phenomenon was performed by Baum, Aiello, and Calesnick (1978), using university dorm students. The experimenters examined attraction and task performance differences among "long-corridor" subjects (those in more crowded living conditions) and "short-corridor" subjects. The hypothesis that long-corridor subjects would be more unhappy with their situation and would experience a greater "reduction in perceived control" (p. 1,009) over interaction was confirmed. In addition, Baum et al. found that long-corridor individuals first responded "competitively" in a game setting but after a while began to "withdraw" within that setting, a response compatible with the development of the learned helplessness syndrome. These results, observed with a relatively representative sample and over an extended period of time, reinforce the concept that crowding experiences can be related to the mechanism of learned helplessness. The fact that the performance measure was obtained in an artificial setting is offset by the questionnaire responses relating to perceived crowding and feelings toward living conditions, which were consistent with the performance responses.

Crowding and Prevention

In reviewing the research on crowding, the preponderance of evidence suggests that crowding does have deleterious effects on individuals, whether in terms of stress, difficulty in interpersonal relationships or functioning, decreased helping and increased aggression, lack of control or learned helplessness and possibly mental pathology.

The research findings can be subject to various interpretations. On the one hand, a crowding expert might suggest that the commuter traveling on crowded subways or railroads, or one who lives in a crowded environment, is subject to mental illness, high blood pressure or psychosomatic symptoms. This position is probably overly simplistic. The opposite viewpoint, whose strongest advocate is Freedman (1975) states that density per se has no negative aversive effects. Again this extreme view (although not quite as simple as presented here) does not appear realistic, particularly since much of the research upon which Freedman's position is based was performed in the laboratory with its concomitant artificiality problems.

A more appropriate view would be the more moderate position which suggests that crowding is an aversive state capable of making one adapt and cope with the aversive setting. Certain individuals may be more sensitive to this aversive condition. For example the Paulus, Cox, McCain, and Chandler (1975) study discussed previously, found that "the greater the length of confinement in a crowded environment, the more the inmates (prisoners) valued low levels of crowding" (p. 89). The Baron, Mandel, Adams, and Griffen (1976) study described earlier, obtained the same results with college students. Furthermore, stronger predispositions towards the development of mental illness, psychosomatic symptoms and illness complaints might affect various individuals differently and these effects may be exacerbated by aversive crowding settings.

Yet even for those individuals who are not predisposed towards these illnesses, the concept of prevention and amelioration of aversive crowding conditions can alter unpleasant surroundings and promote more positive social relationships and functioning. Prevention in this area is apparently related to designing of environments, and this author would like to suggest that community psychologists become more actively involved in planning and design.

Clearly the ideal situation is related to the planned community discussed by Zax and Specter (1974). Realistically, however, prevention and planning will probably most often be restricted to smaller arenas. For example a field experiment by Stokols, Smith, and Prostor (1975) studied the effects of the use of immovable five-foot dividers versus more flexible lower dividers ("ropes") versus no partitions, on subjective judgments of crowding and other nonreactive measures. The study was well controlled and conducted in a public agency, providing a somewhat representative sample of subjects. Contrary to the authors' predictions, the "architectural intervention" of immovable partitions did not lower feelings of crowding and, in fact, produced increased incidences of "tension."

The experimenters suggested that partitions voluntarily imposed by an individual in his or her living space might reduce negative affect, but in a public setting, because they lack "control" over the partitioning, subjects may become upset by the "clutter" (p. 808) and the "herding" (p. 808) feeling induced by partitions. An additional problem concerned the ineffectiveness of the partitions in reducing eye contact. Implications from the study include the necessity to obtain subject reactions to techniques designed to ameliorate crowding feelings.

On a more significant level, Griffin, Mauritzen, and Kasmar (in Moos & Insel, 1974) urged that psychiatrists (or community psychologists) coordinate efforts with architects to create better environments in mental institutions. Griffin et al. reviewed evidence suggesting that adding new furnishings, putting down carpeting, painting, and repositioning chairs in institutions can encourage more contact among residents. In addition one study reviewed by the same authors suggested that the extended passageways in mental institutions can produce hallucinations among patients and, in particular, the "sense of time and distance becomes distorted" (p. 225).

Along these lines of reasoning Wolfe (1975) examined patterns of utilization of rooms by disturbed children in a children's mental institution. By observation Wolfe determined that the ideal or optimal situation appeared to be small private rooms. She found that increasing group size decreased use of bedrooms, and that a small double room produced the least use among subjects. The important point again is that in order to decide on the appropriate design for any institution, observational studies should be performed to determine behavioral effects of different architectural plans. Wolfe also suggested that certain stereotyped views—for example, that private rooms would encourage withdrawal—might have to be revised. Considering that most daytime activities would involve social contacts, perhaps the disturbed children have the same need for privacy that ordinary children do.

Housing. Finally, in terms of housing, students, at least according to Bickman, Teger, Gabriele, McLaughlin, Berger and Sunaday (1973), seem to prefer low-rise to high-rise dormitory buildings. Suites and short hallways, both of which minimize social density, should be more conducive to feelings of control over the social environment and good personal relationships with roommates and dormmates. As a point of reference, one of the most popular living quarters at the large eastern university where this author teaches is a complex of reconverted low-rise apartment houses.

Housing design and planning were also discussed by Ittelson, Proshansky, Rivlin, and Winkel (1974) in their environmental psychology book. The authors reviewed Newman's (1972) research in which he found that public housing residents prefer smaller buildings because they can be more responsive to and interact more with their neighbors. Also the lower buildings are seen as safer. It is felt that if there are too many hidden corners and extended hallways, "surveillance" (p. 269) is more difficult. Newman suggested that this type of residence be placed in various areas of a city, and that large concentrations of high-rise, low-cost housing create unfavorable living conditions.

To reinforce Newman's analysis, Ittelson et al. discussed a San Francisco low-rise housing project constructed mostly for blacks. The project consisted of "town houses" (p. 271) which were also designed to insure maximum "privacy," along with social interaction in public areas. The architects designed this project in conjunction with future residents. One only has to visit low-cost high-rise buidings in crowded ghetto areas to discover the importance of planning and of utilizing the services of experts such as community psychologists as well as the input from future residents.

NOISE

Definition and Theoretical Orientation

As I have been writing this chapter, I have been continually disturbed and irritated by the drilling of a Con Edison crew outside my window. To add to my irritation, the management of my high-rise apartment building has decided to replace the garage floor, a project which also involves drilling. This situation will sound familiar to any urban resident; nor does the suburban resident escape, since motorcycles, airplanes, unmuffled lawn mowers as well as garbage trucks can disturb the poor homeowner's peace.

Fortunately for the sake of this chapter and the productivity of urban office workers, task performance does not seem to be continuously and adversely affected by exposure to noise. There are, however, certain negative effects of noise pollution, and noise can be conceptualized as a stressor. After defining noise and briefly considering theoretical orientations to it, some deleterious consequences of noise pollution will be considered.

Noise has been defined as "any unwanted sound" or "any sound that is physiologically arousing and harmful, subjectively annoying, or disruptive of performance" (Glass & Singer, 1972, p. 15).

In their text on noise as a stressor, Glass and Singer basically adopt the homeostatic equilibrium arousal model discussed earlier in connection with crowding. There is, however, more emphasis on adaptation to noise as a stressor than on adaptation to crowding conditions. Glass and Singer identified the measure of adaptation as "the organism's decreased response sensitivity following repeated exposure to aversive stimulation" (p. 8).

Although this adaptation may prevent immediate negative consequences of exposure to noise, there are "psychic costs," both from the noise exposure and the adaptation, which may not emerge until long after the noise exposure.

Both the arousal-stress and stimulus-overload interpretations are most directly applicable to the noise exposure setting. Since these approaches were considered in detail with respect to crowding effects, very little additional discussion of these theories is necessary in this section. The only comment that seems appropriate at this point is that, although subjects do adapt to noise, clearly a high degree of "overload" on the noise continuum would produce performance decrements, particularly on a difficult task.

Social, Behavioral and Physiological Effects of Noise

Noise and Perceived Control. In an experiment which serves as a paradigm for noise research, Reim, Glass, and Singer (1971) investigated a variety of factors related to noise effects. Using "long-term" city residents, a sample which increased the generalization potential of the study, the experimenters exposed subjects to noise presented at either regular or irregular intervals while subjects engaged in task activity. Some of the subjects in the second ("perceived control") group were instructed that it would be possible to eliminate the aversive sound but that the experimenter preferred them to continue the noise exposure. An additional control group performed the activities without the noise exposure.

Results demonstrated that noise produced few performance deficits on relatively easy activities in any of the three experimental groups. Subjects seemed to "adapt" to the noise as indicated by the physiological measures used. A post-noise performance measure, however, indicated "negative aftereffects" (p. 53) of noise presented at irregular intervals, but these effects disappeared when individuals were given a perceived "sense of control over noise" (p. 49). Reim et al. interpreted these results in terms of regular-interval noise and irregular-interval noise with "perceived control" conditions permitting individuals to concentrate less on adapting to the noise and more on the task. Following the noise, fewer "psychic costs" would have been incurred in these two groups than in the irregular noise condition, thus averting postnoise negative effects. The study supports previous research indicating that motivation to continue engaging in insoluble tasks is decreased only for irregular-interval noise where there is no "perceived control."

The selection of the sample was excellent, but generalization to real-life conditions was somewhat limited due to the artificial nature of the laboratory setting. Over all, the conclusion to be drawn is that noise does not necessarily have negative effects on subjects engaging in simple tasks, but increased demands during noise exposure can produce negative effects subsequent to that exposure.

A conceptual follow-up study was performed by Sherrod, Hage, Halpern, and Moore (1977). The experimenters investigated the relative importance of the learned helplessness and "enhanced competence" (p. 15) explanations of why perceived control decreases negative effects of noise exposure. In a lab experiment, male subjects performed relatively easy tasks and a more difficult task requiring increased concentration, while being exposed to either an unpleasant noise condition or a pleasant sound control condition. Subjects in the unpleasant noise groups were divided into the following subgroups: 1) No choice with respect to noise exposure; 2) choice of playing the noise tapes or not; 3) choice of stopping the noise that had already been playing; 4) combination of 2 and 3. All subjects were urged to leave the noise on while performing the task, and most agreed.

The results first indicated that subjects thought the unpleasant noise was "more stressful" (p. 20) than the pleasant noise, thus supporting the stress-arousal interpretations of reactions to noise exposure. Sherrod et al. also demonstrated that both complex task performance during noise exposure and "frustration tolerance" (p. 17) on the "postnoise . . . task" (p. 24) were positively affected by "perceived control." Both conditions 3 and 4 exhibited increased performance as compared with the other unpleasant noise groups. These results, according to the experimenters, suggested that the perceived control effect can be best explained by the learned helplessness approach. Learned helplessness feelings would be lessened by the ability to produce positive outcomes (group 3). Reduction of learned helplessness feelings apparently plays a greater role in decreasing negative effects of noise pollution than the increased competence approach ("I can choose whether or not to turn on the sound"). Subjects in conditions 3 and 4 are encouraged to try harder.

From a slightly different viewpoint, the noise-ending "control" (group 3) could be associated with drive or arousal reduction, although in this case the reduction is only potential, since subjects are urged not to turn off the noise. In some manner, this potential drive reduction may generate positive responses, which may result in counteracting the negative effects of noise pollution.

The Sherrod et al. study was generally well controlled, and the experimenters effectively ruled out alternative interpretations of the results. As the authors themselves indicated, however, the question of external validity is at issue in this laboratory experiment.

Noise and Somatic Complaints. An experiment by Pennebaker, Burnam, Schaeffer, and Harper (1977) examined the implications of the perceived control concept for the prevention of debilitating somatic complaints. Subjects in the Pennebaker et al. lab experiment reported significantly greater frequency of bodily symptoms (for example, "racing heart," "chest pains," "dizziness;" p. 173) after exposure to irregular noise than did subjects who had perceived control over this irregular noise. This result was similar to the McCain, Cox, and Paulus (1976) study which showed increasing frequency of symptoms following crowding exposure. The Pennebaker investigation supports this chapter's thesis that noise is a stressor which can adversely affect an individual.

Further support for the deleterious effects of noise exposure can be obtained from an interview study conducted in Detroit and Los Angeles by Cameron, Robertson, and Zaks (1972). These experimenters reported that "noise-exposure" (p. 71) was associated with self-reported and second-person reported symptoms. In particular, machine noises were apparently most disturbing. Although interview studies are subject to bias criticisms, and a sampling technique using residents with telephones is not as representative a method as could be desired, this study strongly supports the findings of the Pennebaker et al. investigation. These results have implications for prevention which will be discussed in a subsequent section.

The previous two studies described suggest health-related problems associated with noise exposure. In an interesting recent discussion, Glass, Singer, and Pennebaker (1977) suggested that "a hyperactive style of coping with the experience of uncontrollability" [associated with irregular noise-exposure and learned helplessness at least conceptually] is . . . [believed] related to long-term impairments of cardiovascular functioning" (p. 149). Although it is too early to draw conclusions, preliminary research does seem to indicate aversive effects of negative noise exposure.

Noise and Aggressive and Helping Behaviors. As in the crowding research, less serious consequences of noise, such as the effects on both aggression and helping behavior, have been investigated. Geen and O'Neal (1969) exposed subjects to either "white noise" or to an absence of noise as subjects shocked a confederate. Some of the subjects first watched a film in which a boxer was attacked. White-noise individuals shocked the confederate more than the control group, particularly if they had seen the film. The film and shock measure strongly encouraged subjects to respond aggressively. This response was maximized by the white-noise arousal. Clearly generalization from this study to real-life violence is possible, although it is questionable because of some artificial aspects of the research. The aggression measure is not representative of real-life aggression, and the subjects were college students. In terms of this chapter's thesis, it would also have been more germane if the film had been eliminated and the effects of noise alone had been investigated. These results, however, do suggest a possible relationship between noise and aggression or violence in society.

Sherrod and Downs (1974), in a lab experiment, looked at the effects of noise on helping or prosocial behavior. Subjects performed a difficult activity while listening to unpleasant sound or to pleasant sound (control group). Some of the negative noise group subjects were instructed that it would be possible to eliminate the sound, if desired, but the experimenter preferred that the subjects not exercise this option (which they termed "perceived control"; P. 472). The other negative noise group individuals did not have "perceived control" over the noise. Subsequent to this noise exposure, a confederate of the experimenter accosted subjects outside the lab and asked them to assist on a project. The most help was given by subjects in the control group, then by the "perceived control" noise subjects, with the least amount of help from those in the negative noise, no "perceived control" group. These results were interpreted by Sherrod and Downs in terms of the "increased competence" and "stimulus overload" explanations described earlier in the chapter.

To eliminate the artificiality and potential subject suspicion of procedure difficulties inherent in Sherrod and Down's lab experiment, Mathews and Canon (1975) manipulated noise exposure in an ingenious field experiment. Individuals walking in a residential university area were presented with a stooge victim who needed help with some books he had dropped. One group of subjects viewed the victim under high-noise conditions created by a loud mower being used by another stooge on an adjacent lawn. Other subjects saw the stooge victim under ordinary neighborhood low-noise conditions. Subjects exposed to low noise helped the stooge more than those exposed to high noise. Mathews and Canon interpreted their results in terms of the decreased or "restricted attention" (p. 571) to the environment of high-noise groups. Thus subjects would not be responsive to a victim even in this low-cost trivial helping setting. Although discounted by the experimenters, it appears to this author that the lack of help from the high-noise group might be a result of the individuals feeling motivated to remove themselves from the irritating noise setting. This experiment once again demonstrated the potential negative effects of noise on interpersonal interaction settings in a manner which exhibited increased external validity.

Finally, along these lines Ittelson, Proshansky, Rivlin, and Winkel (1974) reviewed research which suggested that a high level of noise pollution in natural environments is associated with "stress and withdrawal on the part of the residents" (p. 267).

Noise Pollution and Prevention

Although less extensive than the crowding research, experimentation on noise pollution suggests that this stimulation, particularly in excessive amounts, can produce stress responses and other assorted negative effects. The noise literature is relatively consistent, but somewhat less convincing, than the crowding literature, partly because of the overreliance of the former on laboratory experimentation. The subjective and psychological nature of noise determination also contributes to the confusion concerning conclusions and implications about prevention. One final difficulty relates to the conservation-progress controversy. Most people will agree that attending a discotheque five nights a week can damage hearing. Complaints about noise producers such as the SST, on the other hand, are not shared by all involved individuals. Residents of Queens, New York who live in close proximity to the airport where the Concorde lands are united in their protests, but are attacked vigorously by English and French citizens who are directly involved in the production of the SST.

The author suggests that community psychologists become involved with the development of effective, enforceable antinoise legislation. An alternative approach would be to develop incentives to encourage manufacturers and other noise polluters to eliminate noise in their areas. For example, at the university where this author teaches, there is a "quiet dorm" in which sound volume is regulated and making noise is prohibited at certain specified times. In another example, a recent New York Times travel article (1978) was entitled "Where to go for a 'quiet' time." (p. 16). Thus, a restricted prevention approach might be explored in various areas, as well as the differential effectiveness of positive and negative incentives in preventing sound pollution.

Finally, with respect to the perceived control issue, it is difficult to understand how these experimental findings can be applied to real-life settings. Perhaps noise complaint bureaus could be set up to investigate noise complaints, but with the general ineffectiveness of these bureaucratic agencies, it is doubtful that complainants would experience any relief following report of these polluters.

AIR POLLUTION

Rotton, Barry, Frey, and Soler (1978) defined air pollution as the "interaction of chemical substances with the atmosphere" (p. 58). These authors, as well as Heimstra and McFarling (1974), noted that very little psychological research has been performed relevant to air pollution. As a result this chapter will devote very little space to this stressor.

As Heimstra and McFarling (1974) pointed out, responses to air pollution are subjective. Many individuals are unconcerned about air pollution, or if they are concerned, feel helpless about controlling or eliminating it. The authors point out that like noise pollution, eliminating air pollution could mean increasing taxes in order to develop adequate air pollution controls.

In terms of psychologically-oriented research, Baron and Byrne (1977) suggested that individuals exposed to air pollution have been shown to exhibit decreased productivity. Rotton et al. (1978) experimentally exposed some subjects to smelly rooms and found that these subjects "liked" hypothetical described stimulus people less than subjects in control groups. The "odor" room individuals were also more unhappy than the control subjects. Although interesting, the accuracy and generalizability of the findings was decreased by the laboratory setting. As a final note, the experimenters indicated a distaste for performing this type of research since "the odors tend to cling to one's clothes" (p. 68). Before any conclusions can be reached regarding prevention and pollution, additional research is necessary.

SUMMARY AND IMPLICATIONS

This chapter has reviewed several field and lab experiments as well as correlational research related to the effects of physical environmental stressors on behavior. These stressors, particularly crowding conditions, have been shown to produce arousal, somatic symptoms and aversive social and behavioral consequences. A variety of theories and approaches, including the "stimulus overload," the "stress/arousal" and the "learned helplessness" explanations, have been proposed to account for the data.

Since the majority of studies seem to indicate some negative effects of physical stressors, the community psychologist should become involved in programs and planning designed to prevent and alleviate these conditions and settings.

References

Aiello, J. R., DeRisi, D. T., Epstein, Y. M., & Karlin, R. A. Crowding and the role of interpersonal distance preference. *Sociometry,* 1977, *40*, 271–282.

Aiello, J. R., Epstein, Y. M., & Karlin, R. A. Field experimental research on human crowding. Paper presented at the Eastern Psychological Association Convention, New York, April 1975.

Altman, I. Crowding: Historical and contemporary trends in crowding research. In A. Baum & Y. M. Epstein (Eds.), *Human response to crowding.* Hillsdale, N.J.: Lawrence Erlbaum, 1978.

Baron, R. A., & Byrne, D. *Social psychology: Understanding human interaction* (2nd ed.). Boston: Allyn & Bacon, 1977.

Baron, R. M., Mandel, D. R., Adams, C. A., & Griffen, L. M. Effects of social density in university residential environments. *Journal of Personality and Social Psychology*, 1976, *34*, 434–446.

Baum, A., Aiello, J. R., & Calesnick, L. E. Crowding and personal control: Social density and the development of learned helplessness. *Journal of Personality and Social Psychology*, 1978, *36*, 1,000–1,011.

Baum, A., & Epstein, Y. M. (Eds.). *Human response to crowding.* Hillsdale, N.J.: Lawrence Erlbaum, 1978.

Bickman, L., Teger, A., Gabriele, T., McLaughlin, C., Berger, M., & Sunaday, E. Dormitory density and helping behavior. *Environment and Behavior*, 1973, *5*, 465–490.

Cameron, P., Robertson, D., & Zaks, J. Sound pollution, noise pollution, and health: Community parameters. *Journal of Applied Psychology*, 1972, *56*, 67–74.

D'Atri, D.A. Psychophysiological responses to crowding. *Environment and Behavior*, 1975, *7*, 237–252.

Dumphy, R. J. Notes: Where to go for a 'quiet' time. *New York Times*, November 12, 1978.

Efran, M. G., & Cheyne, J. A. Affective concomitants of the invasion of shared space: Behavioral, physiological, and verbal indicators. *Journal of Personality and Social Psychology*, 1974, *29*, 219–226.

Emiley, S. F. The effects of crowding and interpersonal attraction on affective responses, task performance, and verbal behavior. *Journal of Social Psychology*, 1975, *97*, 267–278.

Eoyang, C. K. Effects of group size and privacy in residential crowding. *Journal of Personality and Social Psychology*, 1974, *30*, 389–392.

Evans, G. W. Human spatial behavior: The arousal model. In A. Baum & Y. M. Epstein (Eds.), *Human response to crowding.* Hillsdale, N.J.: Lawrence Erlbaum, 1978.

Freedman, J. L. *Crowding and behavior.* San Francisco: Freeman, 1975.

Freedman, J. L., Heshka, S., & Levy, A. L. Population density and pathology: Is there a relationship? *Journal of Experimental Social Psychology*, 1975, *11*, 539–552.

Freedman, J. L., Klevansky, S., & Ehrlich, P. R. The effect of crowding on human task performance. *Journal of Applied Social Psychology*, 1971, *1*, 7–25.

Galle, O. R., Gove, W. R., & McPherson, J. M. Population density and pathology: What are the relations for man? In R. H. Moos & P. M. Insel (Eds.), *Issues in social ecology: Human milieus.* Palo Alto: National, 1974.

Geen, R. G., & O'Neal, E. C. Activation of cue-elicited aggression by general arousal. *Journal of Personality and Social Psychology*, 1969, *11*, 289–292.

Ginsburg, H. J., Pollman, V. A., Wauson, M. S., & Hope, M. L. Variation of aggressive interaction among male elementary school children as a function of changes in spatial density. *Environmental Psychology and Nonverbal Behavior*, 1977, *2*, 67–75.

Glass, D. C., & Singer, J. E. *Urban stress: Experiments on noise and social stressors.* New York: Academic, 1972.

Glass, D.C., Singer, J. E., & Pennebaker, J. W. Behavioral and physiological effects of uncontrollable environmental events. In D. Stokols (Ed.), *Perspectives on environment and behavior: Theory, research and applications.* New York: Plenum, 1977.

Griffin, W. V., Mauritzen, J. H., & Kasmar, J. V. The psychological aspects of the architectural environment: A review. In R. H. Moos & P. M. Insel (Eds.), *Issues in social ecology: Human milieus.* Palo Alto: National, 1974.

Griffitt, W., & Veitch, R. Hot and crowded: Influences of population density and temperature on interpersonal affective behavior. *Journal of Personality and Social Psychology,* 1971, *17,* 92-98.

Heller, J. F., Groff, B. D., & Solomon, S. H. Toward an understanding of crowding: The role of physical interaction. *Journal of Personality and Social Psychology,* 1977, *35,* 183–190.

Heimstra, N. W., & McFarling, L. H. *Environmental psychology.* Monterey: Brooks/Cole, 1974.

Ittelson, W. H., Proshansky, H. M., Rivlin, L. G., & Winkel, G. H. *An introduction to environmental psychology.* New York: Holt, Rinehart & Winston, 1974.

Lazarus, R. S. *Psychological stress and the coping process.* New York: McGraw-Hill, 1966.

Loo, C. Important issues in researching the effects of crowding on humans. *Representative Research in Social Psychology,* 1973, *4,* 219-226.

Mathews, K. E., Jr., & Canon, L. K. Environmental noise level as a determinant of helping behavior. *Journal of Personality and Social Psychology,* 1975, *32,* 571–577.

McCain, G., Cox, V. C., & Paulus, P. B. The relationship between illness complaints and degree of crowding in a prison environment. *Environment and Behavior,* 1976, *8,* 283–290.

McCauley, C., Coleman, G, & DeFusco, P. Commuters' eye contact with strangers in city and suburban train stations: Evidence of short-term adaptation to interpersonal overload in the city. *Environmental Psychology and Nonverbal Behavior,* 1978, *2,* 215–225.

Milgram, S. The experience of living in cities. In R. H. Moos & P. M. Insel (Eds.), *Issues in social ecology: Human milieus.* Palo Alto: National, 1974.

Newman, O. *Defensible space.* New York: Macmillan, 1972.

Paulus, P., Cox, V., McCain, G., & Chandler, J. Some effects of crowding in a prison environment. *Journal of Applied Social Psychology,* 1975, *5* 86–91.

Pennebaker, J. W., Burnam, M. A., Schaeffer, M. A., & Harper, D. C. Lack of control as a determinant of perceived physical symptoms. *Journal of Personality and Social Psychology,* 1977, *35,* 167–174.

Reim, B., Glass, D. C., & Singer, J. E. Behavioral consequences of exposure to uncontrollable and unpredictable noise. *Journal of Applied Social Psychology,* 1971, *1* 44–56.

Rodin, J. Density, perceived choice, and response to controllable and uncontrollable outcomes. *Journal of Experimental Social Psychology,* 1976, *12,* 564–578.

Ross, M., Layton, B., Erickson, B., & Schopler, J. Affect, facial regard, and reactions to crowding. *Journal of Personality and Social Psychology,* 1973, *28,* 69–76.

Rotton, J., Barry, T., Frey, J., & Soler, E. Air pollution and interpersonal attraction. *Journal of Applied Social Psychology,* 1978, *8,* 57–71.

Schopler, J., & Stockdale, J. E. An interference analysis of crowding. *Environmental Psychology and Nonverbal Behavior,* 1977, *1,* 81–88.

Sherrod, D. R., & Downs, R. Environmental determinants of altruism: The effects of stimulus overload and perceived control on helping. *Journal of Experimental Social Psychology,* 1974, *10,* 468–479.

Sherrod, D. R., Hage, J. N., Halpern, P. L., & Moore, B. S. Effects of personal causation and perceived control on responses to an aversive environment: The more control, the better. *Journal of Experimental Social Psychology,* 1977, *13,* 14–27.

Srole, L. Urbanization and mental health: Some reformulations. *American Scientist,* 1972, *60,* 576–583.

Stokols, D. On the distincition between density and crowding: Some implications for future research. *Psychological Review,* 1972, *79,* 275–277.

Stokols, D. (Ed.). *Perspectives on enviornment and behavior: Theory, research, and applications.* New York: Plenum, 1977.

Stokols, D., Smith, T. E., & Prostor, J. J. Partitioning and perceived crowding in a public space. *American Behavioral Scientist*, 1975, *18*, 792–814.

Sundstrom, E. An experimental study of crowding: Effects of room size, intrusion, and goal blocking on nonverbal behavior, self-disclosure, and self-reported stress. *Journal of Personality and Social Psychology*, 1975, *32*, 645–654.

Sundstrom, E. Crowding as a sequential process: Review of research on the effects of population density on humans. In A. Baum & Y. M. Epstein (Eds.), *Human response to crowding*. Hillsdale, N.J.: Lawrence Erlbaum, 1978.

Wolfe, M. Room size, group size, and density: Behavior patterns in a children's psychiatric facility. *Environment and Behavior*, 1975, *7*, 199–224.

Worchel, S., & Teddlie, C. The experince of crowding: A two-factor theory. *Journal of Personality and Social Psychology*, 1976, *34*, 30–40.

Zax, M., & Specter; G. A. *An introduction to community psychology*. New York: Wiley, 1974.

CHAPTER 7

Social Class, Mental Disorder and the Implications for Community Psychology

Margaret S. Gibbs, Ph.D.

Community psychology arose from a dissatisfaction with the effectiveness of traditional forms of treatment. Community psychology must therefore be closely linked to the epidemiology of mental disorder, that is, the study of the occurrence of mental disorder within a population. Before we can plan interventions for the community, we must know what the chief psychological problems are within the community, where they are concentrated and how they are presently treated. To obtain all this information is a staggering task, but epidemiology has already made one major contribution to community psychology.

One major impetus of the community mental health movement was the discovery that mental disorder both exists in disproportionately high levels in the lower classes and is less likely to be treated there. A considerable body of knowledge has been built up relating social class to mental disorder and its treatment. It is the purpose of this chapter to discuss this knowledge as it relates to community psychology. Epidemiology has also found interesting variations in the distribution of mental disorder according to race and to sex. These findings are less conclusive, however, and therefore more difficult to apply. This chapter will deal only with the social class data for this reason.

Problems in method make even the social class literature difficult to interpret, and these problems must be briefly presented. The plan of the chapter is the following. There will be a selective historical overview of the social class epidemiology of mental disorder. In this section, studies which illustrate some of the major problems in experimental method will be presented. Some of the proposed explanations for the correlation between lower class membership and mental disorder will be discussed with regard to the implications these explanations hold for our efforts to prevent mental disorder in the community. The second half of the chapter deals with the evidence for bias in the psychological treatment offered to the lower classes. The implications of this evidence for developing effective community treatment programs are drawn.

Historical Overview

The study of the epidemiology of mental disorders has shown through the years both a tendency toward greater methodological sophistication and a tendency to change positions with the tide of social and political sentiment.

One of the earliest epidemiological studies, by Odegaard (1932), found Norwegians who migrated to Minnesota to have a higher rate of schizophrenia than those who did not migrate. Odegaard's interpretation, that those genetically more prone to schizophrenia are more prone to migrate, can be seen as an early variant of the "downward drift" hypothesis. The downward drift hypothesis, when applied to social class, states that the mentally disturbed *become* lower class, i.e. drift downward, as opposed to the idea that social class variables directly affect mental health. The debate about the direction of causality, begun so early, touches a central issue about the limitations of epidemiology. Correlational findings between social class and mental illness cannot in themselves indicate causality. What the investigator chooses to postulate as an intervening variable will depend on prevailing psychological and political philosophy. For instance, irrespective of the merits of downward drift as an explanation (Harkey, Miles, & Rushing, 1976; Turner, 1968), it clearly tends to justify the social and political status quo.

A look at the work of Dunham provides an illustration of how shifts in hypotheses can occur. A pioneer in epidemiology, Dunham participated with Faris in their early study examining schizophrenia within different areas of the city of Chicago (Faris & Dunham, 1939). They hypothesized that social isolation was the factor accounting for the high rates of schizophrenia found at the center of the city. In 1976 Dunham stated, "This hypothesis was a rather far-fetched inference and stemmed more readily from existing socialization theory than it did from our several distribution patterns" (Dunham, 1976, p. 151). Dunham's later (1965), more sophisticated research into schizophrenia and the center city found smaller differences than did the earlier work, as well as some support for downward drift (also Dunham, Phillips, & Srinivasan, 1966). Dunham recently concluded from a review of the area that "social class is not an etiological factor in the development of schizophrenia" and that "no social psychological factor has been conclusively demonstrated to play a role in the development of schizophrenia" (1976, p. 155).

Certainly not all investigators would agree with Dunham. His recent attitude may be seen, however, as part of a more general waning of interest in the kind of epidemiological studies of social class that were popular ten and twenty years ago. There are many exceptions to the following generalization, but it appears that social class as an etiological factor in mental disorder became an increasingly popular hypothesis as social welfare philosophies also became increasingly popular, reaching a zenith in the sixties and early seventies. Today the mood of the country is more conservative and less concerned with social welfare. Corresponding to this shift in political philosophy there seems proportionately less research on social class and mental disorder. Of that carried out, it is interesting that many studies find results contrary to those found earlier as to the importance of social class (Crocetti, Spiro, & Siassi, 1976; Derogatis, Yevzeroff, & Wittelsberger, 1975; Singer, Garfinkel, Cohen, & Srole, 1976; Tischler, Henisz, Myers, & Boswell, 1975; Weinstein & Brill, 1971).

Incidence and Prevalence

Of course, the greater recognition of problems of method in epidemiology is also related to the lessening of enthusiasm for such studies today. Some of the problems have been apparent from the beginning. Epidemiology in the field of medicine, where it originated, tends to focus on the *incidence* of a disease, that is, the number of *new* cases of the disease in a population within a specified period of time. Obviously it is easier to determine the number of new cases of smallpox or pneumonia than it is to determine the incidence of compulsive neurosis. Mental disorders usually have slower, less definite onsets than do physical diseases. First admission to a mental hospital is sometimes used as a measure of incidence for mental disorders; one of the lessons we have learned from epidemiology itself, however, is that only a small fraction of cases of mental disorder end up in a mental hospital (Srole, 1975). Since there is no good measure of incidence, workers within the mental health field tend to use *prevalence* measures, the number of *existing* cases of a disorder in a population within a specified period of time. Prevalence depends both upon incidence and upon the duration of a disorder. Once we consider the duration of a disorder, new problems arise. First, mental problems seldom run a recognized consistent course as do physical diseases. Mental disorder tends to fluctuate in intensity depending on circumstances in the environment (Subotnik, 1972). Second, even when some consistency can be found in duration of disorder, different mental disorders have different durations. One cannot look at the prevalence of "mental disorder" per se, since this would involve combining the apples and oranges of, for instance, cyclical depression and stress reactions, which have very different durations.

Third, the duration of a disorder depends upon the treatment received for it, which depends upon the treatments available. This point deserves some amplification, and it is worthwhile to consider the findings of Hollingshead and Redlich (1958) in this connection. Hollingshead and

Redlich carried out an exhaustive study of cases of mental disorder in treatment in the New Haven area. They discovered a striking negative correlation between the prevalence of mental disorder and social class, with the preponderance of disorders in the lower classes. A comparison of incidence and prevalence figures showed the following. The incidence of neurosis was about the same for both classes, but the prevalence of neurosis was higher in the upper classes; the incidence of psychosis was higher in the lower classes, but the prevalence of psychosis was much higher in the lower classes. Thus, looking at incidence alone, psychosis (primarily schizophrenia) occurred more frequently in the lower classes, but there was also evidence of an interaction between social class and duration of disorder. In this case the interaction quite clearly related to treatment availability. Examination of treatment assignment showed a definite pattern. Upper class patients, regardless of diagnosis, were more likely to be assigned to psychotherapy. Lower-class patients were more likely to receive only custodial treatment in a mental hospital. Thus the reason for the disparity between incidence and prevalence of psychosis was that the lower-class cases were remaining untreated in the hospitals. The reason for greater prevalence of neurosis in the upper classes appeared to be that these people were receiving treatment for it and were thus more likely to be "counted" in the prevalence figures. Myers and Bean (1968), in a ten year follow-up of the patients in the New Haven sample, showed that this trend became more exaggerated with time, so that the higher the class, the less likely the person was ever to be hospitalized, and the more likely to be in outpatient treatment. When an upper-class case did become hospitalized, as compared to a lower-class patient, the likelihood of discharge was higher for each readmission and the likelihood of receiving psychotherapy during hospitalization was higher.

The demonstration of the interaction between treatment availability and social class was a good deal more than an exercise in the problem of obtaining accurate prevalence figures. It indicated a pattern of social injustice. Hollingshead and Redlich's findings about the incidence of schizophrenia in the lower classes became assimilated into this pattern in the public mind, although Hollingshead and Redlich themselves were cautious about interpreting the correlation they had found. The attention their study received was a reflection of the growing social concern of the sixties and the beginning of the community mental health movement; the study itself also contributed immeasurably to this mood and the growth of the movement.

The Hollingshead and Redlich study did also show the serious weakness of determining prevalence through surveying treatment cases. It became clear that to control for treatment availability, all members of a population must be surveyed. The proportion of the population needing treatment but going undetected became an important issue. An early exploration of this issue was made by Eaton and Weil (1955), who painstakingly surveyed the Hutterite community, a cohesive religious community in which not one case of psychological treatment existed at the time of the study. Eaton and Weil found 3 percent of the population to be psychologically disordered, with a surprisingly high prevalence of manic-depression and low prevalence of schizophrenia. They related these figures to the strong sense of group responsibility and cohesiveness of the community.

Later studies found less cohesive societies to have far larger percentages of impairment. Gurin, Veroff, & Feld (1960) reported that one in five of their sample of Americans acknowledged that they had felt at some time in their life (lifetime prevalence) an "impending nervous breakdown." The Leighton survey of Stirling County within Nova Scotia (Leighton, Harding, Macklin, Macmillan, & Leighton, 1963) reported over half of the inhabitants to have a diagnosable psychiatric disorder. The study which had the most influence, however, was probably the midtown Manhattan study of Srole, Langner, Michael, Opler, & Rennie (1962), because of the size of the effort and the attention to instrumentation and obtaining a representative sample. Srole et al. administered an extensive, well-designed, structured questionnaire via an interview to 1,660 residents constituting a cross-section of the midtown population. The researchers concluded that 23.4 percent of the population showed psychological impairment and that 50 percent of the lowest social class was impaired. Only about one quarter of the impaired were in treatment, with the untreated group skewed toward the lower classes. The midtown Manhattan study underlined the social injustice findings of Hollingshead and Redlich. In addition, it showed the enormous need within the country for psychological assistance which appears when a population as a whole is surveyed. This also had a tremendous impact on the community mental health movement, since it made clear that existing mental health services could not meet community needs.

Diagnosis of Mental Disorder and Social Class

Another feature of the Srole et al. study should be discussed. We have been talking about the relationship between mental disorder and social class as though both of those terms had well-understood operational definitions. Nothing could be further from the truth. In fact, the three studies reported in the last paragraph each used a different criterion for mental disorder: subjective distress, the psychiatric diagnostic system and a six-point continuum of observer-rated impairment. There is very little likelihood that all three studies measured the same phenomenon.

The midtown group in particular attacked the problem of the definition of mental disorder (Srole, 1975), and concluded that the usual approach of assigning categories within the psychiatric diagnostic system was inadequate. Not only did the diagnostic system lack reliability and validity, but there were special problems in diagnosing individuals who were not in treatment. Significant impairment might exist that did not fit within the diagnostic system, the traditional diagnostic interview might not be appropriate for individuals who were not self-referred with specific symptoms, and the cost of hiring experienced psychiatrists and psychologists to do all interviews would have been prohibitive. The midtown group made admirable efforts to develop scales that could measure functioning and that later proved to be susceptible to computer analysis through weighting the predictor items (Srole, 1975). This approach also avoided any adherence to the medical model and avoided the "apples and oranges" problem mentioned previously of trying to compute the prevalence of mental disorders with different durations.

The midtown approach, however, involves a certain loss of information. To be facetious, calling it all fruit does not really resolve the difference between apples and oranges. Whatever the defects of the diagnostic system, certain broad categories, especially the organic disorders and the psychoses, seem to exist as separate entities. Diagnosis of these categories can be made relatively reliably (Spitzer & Wilson, 1975). In addition, it appears as though these categories are relevant to the social class distribution of mental disorder. There are indications that organic deficit in children is class related, with a concentration of CNS pathology in the lowest classes (Amante, 1975; Amante, Van Houten, Grieve, Bader, & Margules, 1977; John, 1963), although much research remains to be carried out.

As to the psychoses, most epidemiological studies have been performed on hospitalized, nonorganic patients who are primarily psychotic, as this is the group of disordered most easily identified. Fried (1969) reports on 34 such studies, 29 of which show the highest rate of psychoses and/or hospitalization to reside in the lowest status group. As already discussed, however, these findings are confounded by treatment availability, which we know to be class linked. Dohrenwend and Dohrenwend (1969, 1974a; Dohrenwend, 1975) restrict themselves to field studies surveying a population or a representative cross-section of a population in order to avoid this problem. They report that psychosis as a whole is not class linked. This may well be because of the disparity for manic-depression. Of seven studies dividing psychosis into manic-depression and schizophrenia, all seven found manic-depression to be highest in other than the lowest class. Five of the seven found schizophrenia highest in the lowest class. There is some reason to question the validity of the two aberrant studies, both of which were conducted in Japan (Dohrenwend & Dohrenwend, 1974a). Personality disorder was the only other specific diagnostic category found more frequently in the lowest classes.

The importance of breaking down mental disorder into the specific diagnostic categories lies in our efforts to use epidemiology to provide direction for community mental health. That is, we need to find the causal variables accounting for the correlation between class and mental disorder, and what we know about specific disorders may be useful in this pursuit. For instance, at least some of the connection between CNS pathology in children and social class appears fairly obvious because we know of the impact of poor nutrition and poor prenatal, obstetrical and pediatric care upon the CNS, and we know these variables themselves to be class linked (Birch & Gussow, 1970; Pasamanick & Knobloch, 1961). That is, although the evidence could be a good deal more extensive and conclusive, because we know something about CNS pathology in children we can make fairly confident recommendations for community mental health. Certainly any comprehensive primary prevention program will include an emphasis on providing proper nutrition and medical care for its target population.

Although personality disorder appears to be class linked, what we know about personality disorders cannot provide such clear direction for prevention. Personality disorder is a diagnosis with notoriously poor reliability (Spitzer & Wilson, 1975). It includes a variety of diagnoses which are posited to have widely different causes and symptoms. For instance, an individual with an antisocial personality disorder and one with an obsessive-compulsive personality disorder would probably have very little in common either theoretically or practically. The little that personality disorders are supposed to have in common is their relative lack of anxiety and the tendency toward maladaptive patterns of behavior which cause problems for others. Thus such types of "antisocial" behaviors might be observed in members of the lowest social classes simply because such members have most cause to feel antisocial and least to lose by such behavior. In addition, any kind of social class bias in clinical judgments, to be discussed later, might tend to show up particularly in personality disorder diagnoses because of the vagueness of such diagnoses. Behaviors which are appropriate for the lowest social classes but inappropriate for the rest of society may also be diagnosed here. For instance, reliance on welfare with no attempts to find self-employment in an otherwise functioning individual could be erroneously diagnosed "passive-aggressive personality disorder" either through a misunderstanding of the individual's opportunities or through bias. In sum, it appears that few implications for community mental health can be drawn from the findings linking social class to personality disorders.

The most intriguing and perplexing correlation is that between schizophrenia and social class. Here we are hampered in drawing inferences by our lack of knowledge of the disorder. Indeed epidemiological work becomes important in what it can tell us about schizophrenia as well as the reverse. What is most perplexing is the finding that across cultures schizophrenia is a remarkably similar syndrome occurring with remarkable similarity in frequency (Dunham, 1965; Murphy, 1976; Tsuang, 1976) at the same time that there is so much evidence that it varies with social class. That is, while there are certainly cross-cultural differences in schizophrenia, the similarities are marked, which makes the class differences obtained seem more important. The finding of cross-cultural similarities is used to support genetic theories of schizophrenia, while social class differences seem to imply functional explanations. While most theorists today are willing to grant both biological and social factors in the etiology of schizophrenia (Meehl, 1962), until we know better the nature of the disorder it will be difficult to unravel which social factors are causative. As will become apparent later in the chapter, most of the theories linking social class and mental disorder have little to do specifically with schizophrenia. Nevertheless, discovering the causes for the specific connection between schizophrenia and social class remains a detective problem begging to be solved.

Defining Social Class

We have been discussing the ambiguities of the term "mental disorder"; it is only fair that we should also pay some attention to the ambiguities of the term "social class." First it should be mentioned that many writers today favor the term "socioeconomic status" (SES) over social class. Social class is a vaguer term and to speak of people as lower class can sound more derogatory than to speak of them as having lower socioeconomic status. On the other hand, SES is not really an operational definition any more than social class. This author prefers "class" because it appears that a class system does exist in our society, with important implications for its members; any other term tends to obscure the existence of that system.

In defining social class, occupation, income and education are the usual criteria. Since occupation and income are highly correlated as variables, often only one of the two is used, as in the Hollingshead and Redlich (1958) study. Hollingshead and Redlich started with three criteria to determine empirically class level: occupation, education and residence area. They later found residence area added little to the discrimination power of their rankings and dropped this as a factor. They give a complete description of the typical life style within each of their five classes in New Haven, from the Class I Old Yankee families, Class II business and professional families, Class III white-collar families, Class IV blue-collar families, to Class V families of semiskilled and unskilled laborers. Interesting anthropological comparisons are given of housing (Class I's modal house has 12 to 15 rooms; Class IV lives in two- or three-family houses), reading tastes (Class III can be identified by the *Reader's Digest*) and educational patterns (women are more educated than their husbands in the lower classes; the reverse is true in the upper classes). There is something vaguely disquieting about reading these descriptions. Factual and nonevaluative as they are in every way, they indicate a definition of social class that mirrors social values.

Weber (1946) long ago pointed out that there are three possible bases for defining social class: status, money and power. The contemporary term SES indicates that we have chosen the first of these three bases as our criterion. This is particularly true when income is omitted as one of the variables defining status, as it is in the Hollingshead and Redlich study. For instance, teachers belong to Class II in Hollingshead and Redlich's schema although they may be making less money than plumbers or carpenters (Class IV), and may have less power than a Class IV union representative. To what class do a pimp or a Mafia godfather belong? Money and power as criteria give different answers than does status.

A simple definition of status might be that to which society accords honor, that which is socially desirable. Living in a two-family house and reading the *Reader's Digest* is not especially socially estimable, although it is not directly undesirable. There is, of course, nothing wrong with using status as an indicator of social class. It may be, however, that it poses special measurement problems when social class is to be compared with mental disorder.

Confounding of Class and Mental Health Measurement

In short, an argument can be made that status and mental health are inextricably confounded, that mental health assessments are based on status as much as social class assessments are. Let us examine the ways in which status may affect judgments of mental functioning.

Edwards (1957) has perhaps been the most persuasive voice arguing that seemingly objective measures of mental disorder actually are measuring the response set of social desirability. He has compiled impressive arrays of the correlation between objective tests such as the MMPI and his own scale of social desirability. Edwards has stressed mainly that persons may appear healthier than they are through striving to give a good impression. Megargee (1966) has shown, however, that while social desirability is a response set, it is also a factor in "real" mental health; i.e., an objectively healthier group scored higher on social desirability in his study than a less healthy group with a stronger motive to present itself favorably. Healthy mental functioning is inescapably a socially desirable and socially estimable quality.

The MMPI, so often relied upon for objective measurement of mental disorder, provides some clues to the relationship beween social class and mental health. Interesting correlations exist between the validity scales on the test and class. The Lie scale (L), for instance, consists of fairly transparent items that are untrue for most people and thus indicate an attempt to present the self in a more favorable light (for example, "I never put off until tomorrow what I can do today."). Endorsement of such items leading to L scale elevation is more frequent in the lower classes, and is explained as a function of less education, more naivete, and less tolerance of psychological deviance in the lower classes (Graham, 1977). By the same token, it was predicted that upper class individuals would score lower on K, the defensiveness correction scale on the MMPI (Dahlstrom, Welsh, & Dahlstrom, 1972), because of tolerance toward deviation. Items on this scale are more subtle than the L scale and were derived empirically as the items endorsed by subjects whose actual functioning appeared more pathological than their MMPI clinical scales would indicate. (For example, "Criticism or scolding hurts me terribly," answered "false" is scored on the K scale.) It was discovered that, contrary to what had been predicted, upper-class individuals scored higher on K. Since K corrections are necessary on five of the eight clinical scales, it appears that upper-class individuals in general may score lower on these scales than their actual functioning would indicate.

It is not clear, however, that upper class subjects are simply more defensive. The K scale is a complex one and brings to mind the connection between social desirability and mental health reported previously. Moderate elevations on K are correlated with adaptive capacities and functioning, with low scores indicating a failure of the defenses. It does not appear possible to separate defensive self-presentation in a favorable light from actual functioning in terms judged favorable in society.

One possible explanation for the upper-class K elevations may lie in different meanings of its items for upper- and lower-class members. Gynther (1972) has pointed out that blacks show MMPI elevations disproportionate to their actual functioning because of their tendency to endorse items atypical for whites. For instance, "I believe I am a condemned person" is an item showing differential endorsement and having different meanings for blacks and whites. Further study (Davis & Jones, 1974) indicated disproportionate elevations only for poorly educated blacks, so that a class difference was interacting with a racial difference.

More research like Davis and Jones' is needed to validate measures of pathology for different social classes. It is possible that differential interpretation of interview and questionnaire items by the lower classes may account for some of the obtained differences in level of pathology. Carr and Krause (1978), for instance, found, as Mechanic (1970) suggested, that lower-class subjects are more likely in a socially desirable way to deny that they feel aggression. This affects both the response style of acquiescence and the measurement of mental impairment on the Langner scale.

The more general issue, however, is whether measures of functioning do not also measure status. Any inventory, no matter how carefully developed, may actually operate as a K scale or social desirability scale. The correlation between such measures and SES would not then be surprising.

Vaillant's recent (1977) study of a sample of healthy, successful American men is interesting in this connection. The range of both social class and psychological functioning was very restricted in the study, and when variables show strong correlations within such a restricted range it is worthwhile to pay attention to them. Vaillant found that income was one of the best predictors of psychological health within the index he developed. Other predictive factors included a listing in *Who's Who*, steady career advancement every five years, and social mobility; i.e., occupational success (income, responsibility and status) greater than their father's. Such items correlated with many others reflecting social adjustment, subjective satisfaction with life, absence of psychiatric treatment and good physical health. While such findings about status may be distasteful, they are not truly surprising, however superficial the manifestation and our judgments about status may be. Status is a measure of the amount of contribution an individual is judged to make to society, and in some sense this is a measure of functioning.

Similarly, at all class levels a person's psychological functioning will be reflected in social status. It is possible that this would hold less true in cultures less achievement-oriented than our own. With Western cultures, however, ever since Freud said that the healthy person is one who can love and can work, in evaluating functioning we tend to include the difficulty of the individual's occupational activities. These difficulties are perceived as related to the status of the occupation. For example, the mayor of New York City is popularly said to have the second toughest job in America, although probably most individuals would rather be mayor than, say, a coal miner.

What are the implications of confounding the measurement of social class and mental health? To the extent that psychological functioning "truly" includes status, as Vaillant would argue, there is some support for a "downward drift" theory: i.e, if an individual cannot earn status his or her functioning is not as good as that of the individual who can. On the other hand, as we become aware of the cultural relativism of our measures of psychological functioning we must become aware of the pervasiveness of social class discrimination. That is, our actual judgment of disorder is class biased, given the economic barriers within our society to social mobility. Since social desirability and true adaptive functioning do not seem to be separable, both these types of argument have some merit. Perhaps the safest conclusion is that the barriers of a class system include barriers to the level of psychological functioning a person will be judged to have in that system. Removing the barriers of the class system should improve both the measured and the real mental health of the culture.

NEW DIRECTIONS: DETERMINATIONS OF CAUSALITY

Current research in epidemiology has changed its focus and is attempting to determine what are the intervening variables between mental disorder and social class. Even if one agrees with the author that mental health and social class correlate partly because their measurement is confounded, it remains a worthwhile effort to discover which class barriers operate most effectively against both social mobility and mental health. Discovery of these factors is essential to effective primary prevention.

Much of the progress in determining causal factors is related to advances in statistics. Computer technology makes factor-analytic and analysis of covariance designs readily available. For example, the Dohrenwends (1969, 1974a; Dohrenwend, 1975) have worked out a covariance scheme whereby downward drift may be contrasted with social causation theories. If social causation is the major explanatory factor in the incidence of mental disorder in the lower classes, then mental disorder should be proportionally greatest in those segments of the lower classes where class barriers are most firmly entrenched—for instance, ethnic minorities against whom prejudices exist. If, on the other hand, downward drift is the causative factor, then mental disorder should be proportionally greatest in groups, such as white segments of the lower classes, in which social mobility is more possible. Many such group comparisons will be necessary before definite conclusions can be drawn, but the mere possibility of obtaining an answer to this old question is exciting.

Economic Change

A covariance technique applied within a time series was responsible for Brenner's (1973) fascinating findings relating rates of psychiatric hospitalization to economic change, as measured through the unemployment rate. Since unemployment rates are higher in the lower classes, an explanation is provided for lower-class mental disorder. Since 1973, Brenner has linked other economic indices, per capita income and inflation, to mental disorder, and has also shown physical illness and rates of crime to be related to economic change (Herbert, 1978). The implications of these findings on both a political and a primary prevention level are obvious.

Liem and Liem (1978), in discussing Brenner's results, warn against the "ecological fallacy" of assuming that factors that operate on an ecological level are also causative at the level of the psychology of the individual. That is, they assert that Brenner's data need to be strengthened by showing that individuals do become emotionally disturbed after losing employment. They do, however, themselves cite several studies which show loss of self-esteem in individuals who become unemployed.

One way in which economic factors may act to influence the mental health of the individual, and the way that Brenner himself hypothesizes, is through the stress created by economic change. For instance, Catalano and Dooley (1977) report a sizable correlation between unemployment and other "life events" that are known to be stressful.

Stress of "Life Events"

Holmes and Rahe (1967) first developed in a systematic way the idea that life events, both desirable (e.g., marriage) and undesirable (e.g., death of a family member) create stress and cause illness, both physical and emotional. Langner and Michael (1963) had earlier shown the relationship between stress factors in the lower classes and psychological impairment, using the midtown Manhattan data. By now a sizable body of research has been built up to support the theory that positive and negative life events themselves are stressful and are related to a number of types of impairment (Dohrenwend & Dohrenwend, 1974b).

In addition, life event scores have been found to be higher in the lowest class and the relationship between life events and psychological impairment to be highest in the lowest class (Dohrenwend, 1973). While Myers, Lindenthal, and Pepper (1974) did not find more life events in the lower classes, they found more negative life events in the lower classes. Mueller, Edwards, and Yarvis (1977) review the Dohrenwend results, a study of their own and two others relevant to the issue, and conclude that it is undesirable events rather than the stress of change in any life event that causes psychological impairment. This is somewhat contrary to the formulation of Holmes and Rahe, but would tie in with the Myers et al. (1974) data in explaining the greater psychological impairment in the lower classes. The difference between whether the lower classes experience more life events or more negative life events may be resolved through the use of a new life events scale proposed by Dohrenwend, Krasnoff, Askenasy, and Dohrenwend (1978) which uses more events than the Holmes and Rahe scale (1967), and better stratifies positive and negative events. A further improvement consists of separating life events which are simple stressors (death of a loved one) from events which to some extent may be consequences as well as causes of emotional disorder (divorce, unemployment).

Social Relationships

Myers, Lindenthal, and Pepper (1975), in their life event research, suggested that the extent of integration within the society mediates the impact of stress on the individual. Thus married employed individuals were more likely to be low on impairment in spite of many life events. Eaton (1978) has further analyzed the Myers data using highly sophisticated panel regression techniques. Eaton's results show that it is not only that the married have less mental disorder, but the *relationship* between life events and mental disorder is smaller for them. He feels this provides evidence for the notion that marriage itself provides emotional support. In addition Eaton shows that life events are relatively independent of each other over a two-year period and that life events correlate with higher levels of disorder when the individual experienced fewer life events earlier in life. That is, life events may be more stressful when the individual is not accustomed to them. Gore (1978) has also found lack of social supports to relate to higher cholesterol level, more symptoms of illness and more emotional response in the unemployed.

Summarizing to this point, it may be that the lower classes have more mental disorder because they experience more life events and/or more negative life events, particularly of an economic nature, and that they have fewer social relationships to sustain and support them through these stresses. Liem and Liem (1978) recommend this kind of explanation at multiple levels of analysis. A complete understanding of the relationship would involve reconciling and showing the interaction between these multiple levels. Thus economic change causes stress itself and creates other stressful life events that impact on the lower-class individual, who tries to deal with them on the basis of coping styles that are themselves related to subcultural values and influences. Ideally we should be able to show that some coping styles are less effective than others and more conducive to mental disorder, especially schizophrenia. Any attempts to make such connections are as yet very tentative. There is, however, additional evidence with regard to the nature of the negative life events occurring in the lower classes and to the coping styles in terms of social supports open to them.

Myers and Roberts (1959) investigated the question of whether specific psychological disorders in the different classes could be linked to specific types of stresses. They compared 25 Class III patients to 25 Class V patients, with half of each group being neurotic and half psychotic. In Class III they found stress was related to upward mobility striving and the frustration that occurred when the individual was unable to attain success. In Class V the stresses involved much greater alienation from any community goals or institutions. The stress of lifelong economic insecurity was linked to feelings of neglect throughout life, from parents as well as social institutions. Patients cited a lack of love from parents and a defensive relationship to parents in which anger could not be expressed without retribution. While such analysis was descriptive, Myers and Roberts did document that Class V members belonged to fewer social organizations and had fewer friends and less informal visiting outside and within their neighborhood.

Shinn (1978) provides some indirect support for Myers and Roberts in her review of 54 studies about father absence and its detrimental effects on cognitive development. Father absence is more common in the lower classes. Few studies have systematically investigated such class effects. However, in exploring several possible causes for the detrimental effect on cognitive development, those that Shinn finds supported seem class linked. Sex-role identification does not play an important role, while the most important variable appears to be the diminished amount of interaction between child and parent. The financial hardship resulting from father absence also appears to be important as a factor in the findings of inferior cognitive performance.

Myers and Roberts's and Shinn's work seems to fit the notion of a vicious circle of alienation. Children growing up without attention and love from parents, without either financial or emotional security, are cognitively damaged and do not have the necessary trust (Erikson, 1950) to themselves reach out to form social contacts. Their adaptation to the severe financial stresses they encounter will be poor, both because of lowered cognitive capacities and fewer social supports. Mental disorder is possible as a consequence of inability to adapt to stress. Social mobility is unlikely, and "downward drift" may occur. Adaptation to the rearing of their own children is likely to be distant and uninvolved and thus the cycle is perpetuated.

Social Integration

Such a description, although it includes more emphasis on intrapsychic reactions, brings back the concept of social integration mentioned before in connection with Faris and Dunham (1939). While social disorganization and disintegration are difficult concepts to operationalize there appears to be some support for their importance, on a cultural level as well as on the level of individual alienation. As mentioned, Eaton and Weil (1955) attributed the low rate of mental disorder among the Hutterites to the strong group bonds provided by the religious community. Leighton et al. (1963) interpreted the high rates of disorder found in Stirling County to be related to a lack of community cohesion and integration. Mintz and Schwartz (1964) reported low rates of mental disorder where the density of an ethnic population is high, implying a cohesive subculture, while the rate of mental disorder is high where such density is low and uprooting has taken place. While some of the studies lack the sophistication of method seen in more recent epidemiological research, there is clearly some support for the use of integration as an explanatory concept in the relationship between social class and mental health.

IMPLICATIONS FOR PRIMARY PREVENTION

A multilevel analysis of the relationship between social class and mental disorder, incomplete and tentative as it may be at this point, suggests that intervention will have to be performed at several levels as well. Some possibilities for intervention include the following.

Political and Social

Brenner's (1973) exploration of economic factors suggests that more awareness is needed of the impact of unemployment and inflation on mental health. More active lobbying for economic measures favorable to the lower classes is needed.

The lower classes apparently need to experience fewer stressful life events and more social supports in dealing with these events. While many laws and policies may need to be implemented to strengthen and support the social fabric of the lower classes, a few specific examples follow.

1) Welfare laws that encourage father absence need to be abolished.

2) Child-care assistance to counter the effects of neglect is needed, including better day-care facilities.
3) Better public health services are necessary.
4) Public housing and slum projects should plan for the intactness and integrity of the neighborhood.

Perhaps most relevant both to the impact of stress and to the need for greater social integration in the lower classes is the fostering of self-interest power groups within the lower classes themselves. Any real political change helpful to the lower classes is unlikely unless people themselves cause it, according to Alinksy's (1970) analysis of the operation of self-interest within society. This seems especially true given today's conservative political philosophy. Not only is change more likely to occur through self-initiated action, but the integration and social support of the community is strengthened through such action.

Psychological

Crisis intervention seems tailor-made for easing the stress created by life events. Eaton's (1978) findings about the effects of prior stress on the reaction to current stress support Caplan's "innoculation" notion: exposure to stress in a form in which it can be handled is beneficial to handling future stress. The reader to referred to Chapter 9, which discusses crisis intervention, for a further consideration of the concept and its effects.

SOCIAL-CLASS TREATMENT EFFECTS AND THEIR IMPLICATIONS

In the preceding discussion we have been emphasizing the possible causes of greater mental disorder in the lower classes. It is apparent that these causes remain uncertain and complex. Whatever they are, however, the mere fact that there is greater disorder in the lower classes means that more intervention is required here, and that community mental health programs must address more of their secondary prevention attempts toward the lower classes. Several questions arise when we consider the treatment of lower-class mental disorders:

1) Is there or is there not evidence of treatment inequality?
2) If so, what are the reasons for it?
3) How do these reasons relate to the directions our secondary prevention efforts should take?

Let us examine these questions in order.

Evidence of Treatment Inequality

We have already cited the early Hollingshead and Redlich (1958) findings that lower-class patients were assigned to custodial hospital care while upper-class patients received psychotherapy. Myers and Bean (1968) found that over a ten-year period the effects of such treatment disparity magnified and intensified the relationship between prevalence of mental disorder and social class. Srole et al. (1962) reported that lower-class patients were usually treated in public facilities while upper-class patients were treated in private facilities or by private practitioners. There were 62 percent more psychiatric patients in the upper classes, although as we have discussed there was much more mental disorder in the lower classes.

Hollingshead and Redlich felt that economic factors alone could not be held responsible for treatment differences. Such differences occurred even in public institutions. When payment was required, upper-class patients sometimes actually paid less than lower-class patients. Schaffer and Myers (1954) also showed that economic factors are not central. They investigated patient assignment in a low-cost clinic, for patients with incomes less than $5,000, which specialized in analytically oriented psychotherapy. The majority of Class II and III patients were accepted, while 66 percent of Class IV and 97 percent of Class V patients were rejected. This appeared to be independent of the diagnostic category of the patient. Brill and Storrow (1960) also found a relationship between acceptance for treatment in a low-cost clinic and higher social class.

It is certainly possible that some community mental health facilities, devised to meet the needs of the whole community, avoid social-class treatment effects. Tischler, Henisz, Myers, and Boswell (1975) report that in a catchmented mental health area social class accounted for only 2 percent of the variance in relation to use of mental health services, although the young, unmarried and unemployed were more likely to use services. That such results can be found today makes it more imperative that we look to the causes of inequity in treatment when they do exist.

Reasons for Treatment Inequality

As with the study of the prevalence of class-related psychological disorder, the study of class-related psychological treatment has moved from establishing correlations to searching for causes. The causes for treatment inequality reduce themselves roughly to two: bias on the part of largely middle-class practitioners and characteristics of lower-class patients which make them less appropriate for psychological treatment.

Social-class biases in mental health practitioners. Abramowitz and

Dokecki recently (1977) provided an excellent review of studies on possible social-class, race, sex and value bias in clinical judgment. They found most consistent results for social class. They assert the soundest method for studying clinician bias is by means of an analogue experiment in which clinicians are presented with case material in two forms, identifying the patient as middle- or lower-class, while all other information is held constant. Nine of 14 such analogue studies found less favorable clinical judgments given to lower-class as opposed to middle-class patients. Abramowitz and Dokecki remark on idiosyncracies of the remaining five studies that could attenuate such a relationship. They refuse, however, to conclude that clinician bias exists, which is perhaps an indication itself both of today's greater methodological sophistication and of greater caution about drawing inferences that suggest political or social change. Abramowitz and Dokecki point out that since lower-class patients may in fact be more prone to pathology or have to adapt to a more stressful environment, clinicians may simply be responding accurately to additional information when they rate a lower-class patient less favorably. This is somewhat similar to the notion presented earlier that class and mental health judgments are confounded. It should be pointed out, however, that in the case of these analogue studies, the social-class label is embedded in a context of many other cues about functioning. That is, in these studies the symptoms and adaptive qualities that might be presumed to vary systematically with class are equated for members of the two classes. The simple label of "lower class" must convey a great deal of information about pathology to acquit clinicians of at least some amount of prejudice. For instance, if we substitute "black" for "lower class" we can also agree that a black environment presents special stresses not experienced within a white environment. Were clinicians, however, so uniformly to judge black patients more disturbed than white regardless of equation of all other information about functioning (clinicians do not, according to Abramowitz and Dokecki), it would be hard to avoid inferring some bias.

Abramowitz and Dokecki's caution in inferring clinician bias can be supported from the point of view of confounded measurement. It does seem, however, that psychologists must also be especially cautious about conclusions that tend to justify their profession. It would be unfair to imply such self-justification to Abramowitz and Dokecki. A recent analogue study not included in their review, however, performed by Crocetti, Spiro, and Siassi (1976), leaves itself more open to charges of self-justification. They conclude that neither diagnosis nor treatment recommendations were affected by class bias, but their data do not support this conclusion. Diagnosis was analyzed in terms of percentages of predetermined "correct" diagnoses. The psychiatrist subjects chose correct diagnoses in only about 50 percent of the cases, both for upper-

and lower-class cases. Without knowing the favorability of the remaining half of the chosen diagnoses, obviously nothing can be concluded about possible bias.

Recommended treatment is reported in six different categories for the 264 cases. The authors do not specify what statistics were used, and it is unclear how they produced the significance levels reported. It appears as though, contrary to their conclusion, long-term psychotherapy *is* significantly more often recommended for upper-class cases. There are 81 cases for whom long-term therapy is recommended; the percentages in the table indicate 49 upper-class and 30 lower-class cases (totalling 79 cases), while the percentages given in the text of the article would indicate 49 upper-class and 31 lower-class cases (totalling 80 cases) were given such recommendations. Using the latter figure and the reported figure of 133 upper-class and 131 lower-class cases, $X^2=5.43$, d.f.$=1$, $p<.025$. The numbers in the other five treatment recommendation classifications are too small for effective analysis. If we combine those treatments which do not involve individual or family treatment—that is, hospitalization, group therapy and drugs—we find that such recommendations are more often made for lower-class cases (32) compared to upper-class cases (16) with $X^2=6.85$, d.f.$=1$, $p<.01$.

The Crocetti study does not really warrant such extensive discussion and the lack of significance the researchers report is probably a result of carelessness in reporting or calculation. However, the study illustrates the need for care in order to avoid the criticism that social science research is performed to fulfill social and professional functions at the expense of the data.

There is some correlational evidence supporting the idea of clinician bias. Nash, Hoehn-Saric, Battle, Stone, Imber, and Frank (1965) found class was related positively to the therapist's judgments about patient attractiveness, ease of rapport and good prognosis. Each of these variables predicted length of treatment. McDermott, Harrison, Schrager, and Wilson (1965) found that in children of blue-collar families with psychiatric records, serious symptomatology was more often perceived in families where the father's work was unskilled as compared to skilled. Also such children were seen more often as coming from unstable homes, although the true incidence of broken homes was greater when the father's work was skilled.

As Abramowitz and Dokecki (1977) point out, such correlational evidence can only be suggestive and supportive. This evidence does support, however, the other strong indications of class bias in clinical judgment presented by Abramowitz and Dokecki. Such indications suggest that we need 1) better selection and education of therapists to increase understanding and appreciation of lower-class problems and viewpoints and 2) more input from lower-class individuals and groups on community mental health programs and therapies. We will discuss these possibilities later.

Lower class characteristics as they affect psychological treatment. While it appears clear from what we have presented that fewer lower-class individuals with problems receive psychotherapy, it is not so clear what happens to them when they do receive it. Backeland and Lundwall (1975) recently provided an extensive review of drop-outs from therapy and their characteristics. Garfield's (1977) criticisms of the review do not apparently affect the section on social class. They first provide support for the idea that drop-outs show about the same as or a slightly lower level of later adjustment than do therapy continuers. This is not the case, however, for the severely disturbed individual—psychotic, alcoholic or addicted—who is more likely later to need hospitalization than is an equally disturbed individual who continues in therapy. As we know from other evidence that the lower-class patient *is* more likely to be seriously disturbed, Backeland and Lundwall's analysis makes lower-class drop-outs a cause for concern.

In analyzing the characteristics of drop-outs, Backeland and Lundwall find that in 35 of 57 studies, lower-class patients were more likely to drop out of therapy than middle- or upper-class patients. They also present some other data that may help explain the reasons that more lower-class patients drop out. Studies of adults in individual psychotherapy showed a social-class effect in 16 of 18 clinics that emphasized psychoanalytically oriented psychotherapy. Three which did not use psychoanalytically oriented treatment showed no social-class effects. Social isolation and lack of affiliation is positively associated with dropping out in 19 of 19 studies. Twenty of 42 studies find that the less socially stable (occupationally, maritally, residentially) the patient, the more likely he or she is to drop out. As we have discussed previously, these characteristics have been linked to social class.

In addition, lack of "psychological mindedness" has been related to dropping out in 24 of 26 studies. This ties in with the expectancies of lower-class patients about therapy. Six out of 6 studies found drop-outs occurred more frequently when patient and therapist expectancies did not mesh. We will discuss this issue in more detail shortly.

Finally, in support of our previous section on therapist bias, therapist characteristics were correlated with dropping out in 35 of 35 studies. Some of these therapist characteristics included ethnocentrism, dislike of the patient, reluctance to give medication, permissiveness, introversion and detachment. Backeland and Lundwall report that the therapist who loses patients is most likely to give short shrift to the lower socioeconomic status patient.

Whether the lower-class patient who continues in therapy without dropping out receives the same benefit as the middle- or upper-class patient is a separate but related question. Luborsky, Auerbach, Chandler, and Cohen (1971) reviewed the psychotherapy literature and found low social class influenced treatment outcome adversely. Lorion (1973) cites four reports that state there is no relationship between social class and success in therapy. Heitler (1976) mentions six mostly impressionistic reports that the lower-class patient does not benefit as much as the middle- or upper-class patient. Conclusions seem less warranted as to the amount of benefit attained in therapy by the lower-class patient who stays. Fewer studies have been performed, outcome and dropping out have not always been measured separately and criterion measures for outcome may themselves be subject to social class effects; i.e., lower-class patients may benefit in different ways that require different types of outcome measures.

Assuming that lower-class patients might in some cases benefit from therapy as much as middle- or upper-class patients makes the drop-out problem more intense. The area of therapist-patient expectancies about therapy is perhaps the most interesting because expectancies appear more easily manipulated than some of the other variables that may be involved, such as social isolation or occupational stability. In spite of Wilkins's (1973) claim that positive expectancy of therapeutic gain has not been proven to be an active therapeutic agent, more recent research, primarily in well-designed behavioristic studies, seems more conclusive, especially when the strength and the effectiveness of the expectancy manipulation in the experiment is taken into account (Kazdin & Wilcoxon, 1976; Lick & Bootzin, 1975). In addition, there are the findings summarized by Backeland and Lundwall (1975) about the importance of matching patient and therapist expectancies.

What does the lower-class patient expect from therapy and how does this correspond with what he will receive? Reiff (1966) describes several conflicts between what he perceives as the mental health professional's and the working person's views of emotional disorder and treatment. He states that the professional sees mental health and disorder on a continuum, so that the psychotic, neurotic and essentially normal person differ in degree, not kind. For the worker to have his or her problems in living seen as similar to the "illness" of the psychotic is upsetting and stigmatizing. Not "psychologically minded," the worker wants concrete here-and-now solutions to the problem. Workers perceive themselves as victims of circumstances, not as victims of themselves. They have difficulty understanding the role of a therapist who offers essentially the helping services of a friend yet expects payment.

Documentation of Reiff's theoretical ideas has been provided in several places. Overall and Aronson (1963) found lower-class patients tended to expect a medical orientation in therapy, with the therapist active but permissive. A significant relationship was found between having inaccurate expectancies and dropping out of therapy. Hornstra, Lubin, Lewis, and Willis (1972) found community mental health applicants, primarily lower class, expected services that required little commitment and provided fast abatement of symptoms. They wanted primarily advice and medication and felt that talking regularly about their problems would do little good. To enlarge on Reiff's analysis, when working-class patients do see their problems as "illness," they evidently expect a medical treatment. Lorion (1974) reviews several such studies of lower-class expectancies and concludes that inaccuracy of expectancies in the lower classes is widespread. There are studies with negative or equivocal results. Weinstein and Brill (1971) found few differences in "subjective" versus "objective" causes listed by middle- and lower-class hospitalized patients in response to the question, "What are the main causes of your mental illness?" It is possible, however, that upper- and middle-class patients might have held more psychologically sophisticated beliefs as to the relationship between external and internal causes of illness.

One hopeful set of results has been provided by Fischer and Cohen (1972). They found favorable attitudes toward seeking professional help for problems in a group of students to be independent of social class background (occupation of father). Instead, the more education of the students (high school versus college; under-class versus upper-class in college), the more positive the attitude toward seeking professional help. Although lower-class misperceptions about therapy appear to extend far beyond mere willingness to seek help, Fischer and Cohen's results do indicate the changeability of mental health attitudes through education.

Education of both therapist and patient appears important in dealing with the disparity of their expectancies. In addition new types of therapy that could better meet lower-class attitudes and expectancies seem necessary.

Treatment Implications

It appears as though both therapist and patient variables operate in the inequality of treatment received by upper- and lower-class patients. Lower-class patients do not always understand or accept the assumptions of long-term psychotherapy, and drop out of the process. Middle-class therapists do not understand or accept the needs of lower-class patients, and through this misunderstanding and/or bias are not able to meet them. Four different types of changes in our secondary prevention efforts have been suggested previously to deal with this inequality, and these will be examined in turn.

Better selection and education of therapists. More awareness of the problems and attitudes of the lower classes and minority groups should obviously be incorporated into training programs for mental health professionals. Candidates with ethnocentric and class-centered values could be preselected out or identified early for special programs. Self-awareness and role-playing techniques in groups may help such students to identify themselves and change. More practicum and internship experiences in lower-class settings could be beneficial if supervised carefully to make candidates more aware of strengths and assets of their lower-class patients.

Jones and Seagull's (1977) discussion of the relationship between black clients and white therapists can be transposed to apply to lower-class clients as well. Jones and Seagull point out the dynamics that impede sensitivity and of which students need to become aware. They suggest that power is an important element in the therapy relationship, both in terms of the therapist's need to maintain it and the client's need to exert power through what may appear to be "passive," "unsophisticated" interactions. Both "trying too hard" because of guilt feelings and lack of similarity to lower-class clients can hamper the middle-class professional. Smith, Burlew, Mosley, and Whitney (1978) assert that for counselors to succeed with social minorities, they must have TSMKS, Therapist's Sensitivity and Minority Knowledge Style, and the authors detail ten characteristics of such sensitivity. These include understanding of group language, of the client's community, of client mistrust from a history of being excluded by society, and of the literature about therapy and assessment of minority groups (which include lower-class members).

Lower-class involvement in community mental health. The use of the paraprofessional follows logically from the need for greater congruence between expectancies of therapist and patient. Paraprofessionals can themselves be members of the lower class, able to communicate and understand their fellows and their needs and goals.

One problem with the use of paraprofessionals is the potential for their abuse. Schaffer and Myers (1954) found that not only did acceptance of an individual for treatment correlate with social-class level, but that higher-class patients were more likely to be treated by higher-status therapists, with medical students treating primarily lower-class patients. While this finding has not always been replicated, a rather alarming result was obtained by Sue, McKinney, Allen, and Hall (1974). They found that in a survey of a community mental health clinic in Seattle, black clients were significantly more likely to be assigned to paraprofessionals. While this could simply be due to a "good" matching of therapist-client expectancies, Sue et al. found that there was seldom a mention of race in the intake and that no such explicit matching was discussed. The possibility exists, then, of paraprofessionals coming regularly to treat minority and lower-class members in a kind of discriminatory system.

Such a system would not be discriminatory were paraprofessionals able to receive the training and professional status that Rieff (1966) recommends. Goldstein (1973), among others, has made a laudatory attempt to develop appropriate training techniques for the paraprofessional. Given the gradual drying-up of job opportunities within mental health, however, it is unlikely that paraprofessionals will be allowed many opportunities by professionals to become their equals in the field.

This same kind of political issue affects other types of lower-class entry into community mental health. Community input to any real decision-making process is likely to be limited because of professional reluctance to relinquish power. Rieff (1974) considers the control of knowledge itself a form of power, and feels the helping professions will not voluntarily relinquish this power to nonprofessionals. He feels society must compel the helping professions to share their knowledge. Any such relinquishing of professional power into the hands of the community where it would have much impact seems at the moment unlikely.

Modification of lower-class expectancies and behavior. We have seen that the lower-class view of mental problems and therapy is often unrealistic. In addition, unrealistic expectancies seem to be a contributory factor in the large number of lower-class drop-outs from therapy. Education about the mental health profession's views of disorder and therapy would seem to be appropriate.

Public education on a large scale would certainly appear to be in order. Most of the emphasis in education, however, has been put on changing the attitudes of the individual client before she or he embarks on therapy. Goldstein (1971) has long argued that we should put our knowledge of persuasion from social psychology to the purpose of changing attitudes in and about therapy. Heitler (1976) has reviewed studies of preparatory techniques for someone about to begin therapy. These techniques vary in nature, including simple instructions on finding out about how competent and warm one's therapist is, film models with and without instruction and comment, taped excepts of "good" patient behavior, and role-induction interviews which clarify for the individual patient the goals and roles of therapy for her or him. All these methods have been found to make therapy more effective as measured by, for instance, quality and quantity of communication, increased motivation and expectancy, better therapy outcome on several measures, and reduction in the number of drop-outs. Only studies by Heitler (1973) and Strupp and Bloxom (1973) dealt specifically with lower-class patients. No study seems to have shown that lower-class patients benefit more from such procedures than middle-class patients do.

Goldstein (1973) has attempted to show the relationship between therapist bias and lower-class therapy attitudes through the construct of "therapeutic attractiveness." That is, he feels that lower-class attitudes toward therapy make the lower-class client unattractive both as a person and as a therapy candidate, so that the therapist directly and indirectly rejects the client. The Nash et al. (1965) study previously cited and other research cited by Goldstein support such a point of view. Lower-class induction procedures, then, should focus on making the candidate more attractive to the therapist as well as the reverse. Heitler in his 1976 review did not find such increase in the attractiveness of the client necessary to the effectiveness of the prepatory induction. A recent study by Jennings and Davis (1977) used Goldstein's structured learning procedures to teach interview skills to lower-class children and adolescents hospitalized with a nonpsychotic diagnosis. As compared with a placebo control, these children showed better post-training measures on two of the four interview skills taught and were more attractive to the interviewer. Children in the experimental group did not perceive the interviewer as more attractive.

While mutual attractiveness may or may not be central to effective therapy, the Jennings and Davis study demonstrates that structured training of interview behavior is effective. It should be noted that in several of the studies Heitler (1976) cites, the intent of the experimenters was also to teach appropriate interview behavior through modeling and instruction. It is not clear whether behavior or expectancies form the most appropriate focus for attention, or to what extent they are each involved in the other.

One criticism that can be made of this entire approach of educating the lower-class patient is that it implies preexisting lower-class values and behavior are inferior to those held by mental health professionals. While this is indeed implied, it is also true that the mental health profession has built up a body of knowledge over the years. Lower-class attitudes may represent a different truth that should be incorporated into the profession. At the present time, however, if lower-class individuals are to be able to take advantage of what exists, some such education of their expectancies and behaviors seems useful and appropriate.

Alternate approaches to therapy with the lower classes. The development of therapy approaches empirically shown to be effective with the lower classes seems the most legitimate and practical of solutions to the problem we have been discussing. Special therapies for the lower classes are open to the criticism of discrimination, of course (Heitler, 1976), just as in the case of discriminatory use of the paraprofessional. One can envision a biased therapist arguing that lower-class patients respond best to custodial hospital care! Such criticisms lose their force, however, if a method has been shown experimentally to be effective and the treatment of choice.

Goldstein and Stein (1976) have persuasively made the argument that assignment of treatment modality should be made prescriptively. They believe that we need more interactive research designs in therapy outcome, investigating what is the most appropriate treatment modality for patient *a* with symptom *b* of social class *c* to be treated by therapist *d*, etc. Few studies of this type have been performed and fewer still have used social class as a variable. Those that have, indicate that social class does interact with effectiveness of treatment modality.

Love, Kaswan, and Bugental (1972) performed an interesting experiment using children with severe social and behavioral problems. Eighty percent of the children had academic difficulties or were underachievers, with grades used as the primary criterion measure. Children and their families were assigned to three types of therapy; traditional child psychotherapy with about 12 mean number of contact hours per child; parent counseling, the giving of information and advice about child-rearing to the parents, with about 6 mean number of contact hours per family; and information feedback, a procedure designed by the authors which involved viewing and rating family and school videotapes with the goal of self-initiated changes in family behavior, with about 8 mean number of contact hours per family. For lower-social-class families, parent counseling led to an improvement in children's grades. For upper-class families, information feedback improved children's grades. Children in child therapy showed a significant decrease in grades in all classes.

The Love et al. study clearly underlines the need for fitting the therapy modality to the social class. One can see in light of our previous discussion why parent counseling with its direct, short-term focus would mesh well with lower-class expectancies. In addition the study points out the potential for family therapy. While the focus on the child alone proved detrimental for all classes, family therapy seems particularly appropriate for lower-class members. As Aponte explains so well in Chapter 12, a family approach allows one to better attack the social system in which the individual with the problem is embedded. Outcome research is needed on family therapy with the lower classes, but it seems likely that this approach will prove to be effective.

Behavior therapy also holds promise. It should be noted that Goldstein's (1973) structured learning approach involves not only changing therapy behavior but also provides a role-playing approach to therapy itself that is tailor-made for the lower-class patient. Sloane, Staples, Cristol, Yorkston, and Whipple (1975, 1976) compared a more traditional behavior therapy to analytically oriented psychotherapy on a number of different dimensions, one of which was social-class effectiveness. Neither therapy approach proved more effective over all than the other, and both were more effective than a waiting list control. Psychotherapy, however, was less effective with lower-class patients than with upper-class ones. Behavior therapy did not show this effect and in general seemed applicable to a broader range of patients. Staples, Sloane, Whipple, Cristol, and Yorkston (1976) discuss client and therapist perceptions in the same experiment. Behavior therapists were more active, had more interpersonal contact and were perceived as more authoritarian. Those patients better liked by their therapists showed more improvement in psychotherapy, but liking did not affect the results of behavior therapy. Behavior therapy, then, may better meet the expectancies of the lower-class patient and may better circumvent the interpersonal attractiveness issue presented by Goldstein. Such hypotheses would be more clearly supported had Staples et al. included social class explicitly in their analysis of the data.

The approach described by Smith and Glass (1977) ought also to have prescriptive relevance. Combining many studies of therapy outcome as to their effect size makes comparisons possible between studies. Social class is a variable which should be examined through this technique. Indeed, if we have learned anything through our epidemiological survey, we have learned that social class needs to be examined more often as a variable in therapy outcome research.

SUMMARY AND CONCLUSIONS

Lower social class and mental disorder appear to be linked through a variety of causes: measurement of both through social status, amount of stress, social support and cohesion and, particularly, inequity of treatment. Broad-range prevention programs are desperately needed to attack the problems of stress and support. The mood of the country and the expense of the programs seems to make their implementation unlikely, however. The inequity of treatments seems more easily attacked. Modification both of lower-class treatment expectancies and of treatments to accommodate lower-class needs has been demonstrated to be effective, and both types of approaches can and should be increasingly employed.

References

Abramowitz, C. V., & Dokecki, P. R. The politics of clinical judgment: Early empirical returns. *Psychological Bulletin*, 1977, *84*, 460–476.

Alinsky, S. The professional radical, 1970. *Harpers*, 1970, *240*, 35–42.

Amante, D. Visual motor malfunction, ethnicity, and social class position. *Journal of Special Education*, 1975, *9*, 247–259.

Amante, D., Van Houten, V. W., Grieve, J. H., Bader, C. A., & Margules, P. H. Neuropsychological deficity, ethnicity, and socioeconomic status. *Journal of Consulting and Clinical Psychology*, 1977, *45*, 524–535.

Backeland, F., & Lundwall, L. Dropping out of treatment: A critical review. *Psychological Bulletin*, 1975, *82*, 738–783.

Birch, H. G., & Gussow, J. D. *Disadvantaged children: Health, nutrition, and school failure.* New York: Harcourt, 1970.

Brenner, M. H. *Mental illness and the economy.* Cambridge, Mass.: Harvard, 1973.

Brill, N., & Storrow, H. Social class and psychiatric treatment. *Archives of General Psychiatry,* 1960, *3*, 340–344.

Caplan, G. *Principles of preventive psychiatry.* New York: Basic Books, 1964.

Carr, L. G., & Krause, N. Social status, psychiatric symptomatology, and response bias. *Journal of Health and Social Behavior,* 1978, *19,* 86–91.

Catalano, R., & Dooley, D. Economic predictors of depressed mood and stressful life events in a metropolitan community. *Journal of Health and Social Behavior,* 1977, *18*, 292–307.

Clausen, J. A., & Huffine, C. L. Sociocultural and social-psychological factors affecting social responses to mental disorder. *Journal of Health and Social Behavior,* 1975, *16*, 405–420.

Crocetti, G., Spiro, H. R. & Siassi, I. Psychiatry and social class. *Social Psychiatry,* 1976, *11*, 99–105.

Dahlstrom, W. G., Welsh, G. S., & Dahlstrom, L. E. *An MMPI handbook: Volume I: Clinical interpretation.* Minneapolis, Minn.: University of Minnesota, 1972.

Davis, W. E. & Jones, M. H. Negro vs. caucasian psychological test performance revisited. *Journal of Consulting and Clinical Psychology,* 1974, *42*, 675–677.

Del Gaudio, A. C., Stein, L. S., Ansley, M. Y., & Carpenter, P. J. Attitudes of therapists varying in community mental health ideology and democratic values. *Journal of Consulting and Clinical Psychology,* 1976, *44*, 646–655.

Derogatis, L. R., Yevzeroff, H. & Wittelsberger, B. Social class, psychological disorder and the nature of the psychopathologic indicator. *Journal of Consulting and Clinical Psychology,* 1975 *43*, 183–191.

Dohrenwend, B. P. Sociocultural and social-psychological factors in the genesis of mental disorders. *Journal of Health and Social Behavior,* 1975, *16*, 365–392.

Dohrenwend, B. P., & Dohrenwend, B. S. *Social status and psychological disorder: A causal inquiry.* New York: Wiley, 1969.

Dohrenwend, B. P. & Dohrenwend, B. S. Social and cultural influences on psychopathology. In M. R. Rosenzweig & L. W. Porter (Eds.), *Annual review of psychology,* Vol. 25. Palo Alto, Calif.: Annual Reviews, 1974a.

Dohrenwend, B. S. Social status and stressful life events. *Journal of Personality and Social Psychology,* 1973, *28*, 225–235.

Dohrenwend, B. S., & Dohrenwend, B. P. *Stressful life events: Their nature and effects.* New York: Wiley, 1974b.

Dohrenwend, B. S., Krasnoff, L., Askenasy, A. R., & Dohrenwend, B. P. Exemplification of a method for scaling life events: The PERI Life Events Scale. *Journal of Health and Social Behavior,* 1978, *19,* 205–229.

Dunham, H. W. *Community and schizophrenia.* Detroit: Wayne State University, 1965.

Dunham, H. W. Society, culture and mental disorder. *Archives of General Psychiatry,* 1976, *33*, 147–156.

Dunham, H. W., Phillips, P., & Srinivasan, B. A research note on diagnosed mental illness and social class. *American Sociological Review,* 1966, *31*, 223–227.

Eaton, J. W., & Weil, R. J. *Culture and mental disorders.* Glencoe, Ill. Free Press, 1955.

Eaton, W. W. Life events, social supports, and psychiatric symptoms: A re-analysis of the New Haven data. *Journal of Health and Social Behavior,* 1978, *19*, 230–234.

Edwards, A. L. *The social desirability variable in personality assessment and research.* New York: Dryden, 1957.

Erikson, E. H. *Childhood and society.* New York: Norton, 1950.

Faris, R. E. L., & Dunham, H. W. *Mental disorders in urban areas.* Chicago: University of Chicago, 1939.

Fischer, E. H., & Cohen, S. L. Demographic correlates of attitude toward seeking professional psychological help. *Journal of Consulting and Clinical Psychology, 1972, 39*, 70–74.

Fried, M. Social differences in mental health. In J. Kosa, A. Antonovsky, & I. K. Zola (Eds.), *Poverty and health: A sociological analysis.* Cambridge, Mass. Harvard, 1969.

Garfield, S. L. Further comment on "Dropping out of treatment." Reply to Backeland and Lundwall. *Psychological Bulletin,* 1977, *84*, 306–308.

Goldstein, A. P. *Structured learning therapy: Toward a psychotherapy for the poor.* New York: Academic Press, 1973.

Goldstein, A. P., & Simonson, N. R. Social psychological approaches to psychotherapy research. In A. E. Bergin & S. L. Garfield (Eds.), *Handbook of psychotherapy and behavior change.* New York: Wiley, 1971.

Goldstein, A. P., & Stein, N. *Prescriptive psychotherapies.* New York: Pergamon, 1976.

Gore, S. The effect of social support in moderating the health consequences of unemployment. *Journal of Health and Social Behavior*, 1978, *19*, 157–165.

Graham, J. R. *The MMPI: A practical guide.* New York: Oxford, 1977.

Gurin, G., Veroff, J., & Feld, S. Americans view their mental health. *Monograph Series No. 4, Joint Commission on Mental Illness and Health.* New York: Basic Books, 1960.

Gynther, M. D. White norms and black MMPI: A prescription for discrimination. *Psychological Bulletin,* 1972, *78*, 386–402.

Harkey, J., Miles, D. L., & Rushing, W. A. The relation between social class and functional status: A new look at the drift hypothesis. *Journal of Health and Social Behavior*, 1976, *17*, 194–204.

Heitler, J. Preparation of lower-class patients for expressive group psychotherapy. *Journal of Consulting and Clinical Psychology,* 1973, *41*, 251–260.

Heitler, S. Preparatory techniques in initiating expressive psychotherapy with lower-class, unsophisticated patients. *Psychological Bulletin*, 1976, *83*, 339–352.

Herbert, W. Mental health parley focuses on economy. *APA Monitor*, 1978, *9(7)*, 1.

Hollingshead, A. B., & Redlich, F. C. *Social class and mental illness.* New York: Wiley, 1958.

Holmes, T. H., & Rahe, R. H. The Social Readjustment Rating Scale. *Journal of Psychosomatic Research,* 1967, *11*, 213–218.

Hornstra, R., Lubin, B., Lewis, R., & Willis, B. Worlds apart: Patients and professionals. *Archives of General Psychiatry,* 1972, *27*, 553–557.

Jennings, R. L., & Davis, C. S. Attraction-enhancing client behaviors: A structured learning approach for non-Yavis. *Journal of Consulting and Clinical Psychology,* 1977, *45*, 135–144.

John, V. P. The intellectual development of slum children: Some preliminary findings. *American Journal of Orthopsychiatry,* 1963, *33*, 813–822.

Jones, A., & Seagull, A. A. Dimensions of the relationship between the black client and the white therapist: A theoretical overview. *American Psychologist,* 1977, *32*, 850–855.

Kazdin, A. E., & Wilcoxon, L. A. Systematic desensitization and nonspecific treatment effects: A methodological evaluation. *Psychological Bulletin,* 1976, *83*, 729–758.

Kurtz, N., Kurtz, R., & Hoffnung, R. Attitudes toward lower- and middle-class psychiatric patients as a function of authoritarianism among mental health students. *Journal of Consulting and Clincial Psychology,* 1970, *35*, 338–341.

Langner, T., & Michael, S. *Life stress and mental health: The midtown Manhattan study.* London: Free Press, 1963.

Leighton, A. H., Lambo, T. A., Hughes, C. C., Leighton, D. C., Murphy, J. M., & Macklin, D. B. *Psychiatric disorder among the Yoruba.* Ithaca, N.Y.: Cornell University, 1963.

Leighton, D. C., Harding, J. S., Macklin, D. B., Macmillan, A. M., & Leighton, A. H. *The character of danger.* New York: Basic Books, 1963.

Lick, J., & Bootzin, R. Expectancy factors in the treatment of fear: Methodological and theoretical issues. *Psychological Bulletin,* 1975, *82*, 917–931.

Liem, R., & Liem, J. Social class and mental illness reconsidered: The role of economic stress and social support. *Journal of Health and Social Behavior,* 1978, *19*, 139–156.

Lorion, R. P. Socioeconomic status and traditional treatment approaches reconsidered. *Psychological Bulletin,* 1973, *79*, 263–270.

Lorion, R. P. Patient and therapist variables in the treatment of low-income patients. *Psychological Bulletin,* 1974, *81*, 344–354.

Love, L. R., Kaswan, J., & Bugental, D. E. Differential effectiveness of three clinical interventions for different socioeconomic groupings. *Journal of Consulting and Clinical Psychology,* 1972, *39*, 347–360.

Luborsky, L., Auerbach, A. H., Chandler, M., & Cohen, J. Factors influencing the outcome of psychotherapy: A review of quantitative research. *Psychological Bulletin,* 1971, *75*, 145–185.

McDermott, J. F., Harrison, S. I., Schrager, J., & Wilson, P. Social class and mental illness in children: Observations of blue collar families. *American Journal of Orthopsychiatry,* 1965, *35*, 500–508.

Mechanic, D. Problems and prospects in psychiatric epidemiology. In E. H. Hare & J. K. Wing (Eds.), *Psychiatric epidemiology.* London: Oxford, 1970.

Meehl, P. E. Schizotaxia, schizotype, schizophrenia. *American Psychologist,* 1962, *17*, 827–838.

Megargee, E. I. The Edwards SD Scale: A measure of adjustment or of dissimulation? *Journal of Consulting Psychology,* 1966, *30(6)*, 566.

Mintz, N. L., & Schwartz, D. T. Urban ecology and psychosis. *International Journal of Social Psychiatry,* 1964, *10*, 101–118.

Mischel, W. On the future of personality measurement. *American Psychologist,* 1977, *32*, 246–254.

Mueller, D. P., Edwards, D. W., & Yarvis, R. M. Stressful life events and psychiatric symptomatology: Change or undesirability? *Journal of Health and Social Behavior,* 1977, *18*, 307–317.

Murphy, J. M. Psychiatric labeling in cross-cultural perspective. *Science,* 1976, *191*, 1019–1028.

Myers, J. K., & Bean, L. L. *A decade later: A follow-up of Social Class and Mental Illness.* New York: Wiley, 1968.

Myers, J. K., Lindenthal, J. J, & Pepper, M. P. Life events and psychiatric impairment. *Journal of Nervous and Mental Disease,* 1971, *152*, 149–157.

Myers, J. K., Lindenthal, J. J., & Pepper, M. P. Social class, life events, and psychiatric symptoms: A longitudinal study. In B. S. Dohrenwend & B. P. Dohrenwend (Eds.), Stressful life events: Their nature and effects. New York: Wiley, 1974.

Myers, J. K., Lindenthal, J. J., & Pepper, M. P. Life events, social integration and psychiatric symptomatology. *Journal of Health and Social Behavior,* 1975, *16*, 421–427.

Myers, J. K., & Roberts, B. H. *Family and class dynamics in mental illness.* New York: Wiley, 1959.

Nash, E. H., Hoehn-Saric, R., Battle, C. C., Stone, A. R., Imber, S. D., & Frank, J. D. Systematic preparation of patients for short-term psychotherapy II: Relation to characteristics of patient, therapist and the psychotherapeutic process. *Journal of Nervous and Mental Disease,* 1965, *140*, 374–383.

Odegaard, O., Emigration and insanity: A study of mental disease among the Norwegian-born population of Minnesota. *Acta Psychiatrica et Neurologica,* 1932, Supplementum 4.

Overall, B., & Aronson, H. Expectations of pychotherapy in patients of lower socioeconomic class. *American Journal of Orthopsychiatry,* 1963, *33*, 421–430.

Pasamanick, B., & Knobloch, H. Epidemiological studies on the complications of pregnancy and the birth process. In J. Caplan (Ed.), *Prevention of mental disorders in children.* New York: Basic Books, 1961.

Reiff, R. Mental health manpower and institutional change. *American Psychologist*, 1966, *21(6)*, 540–554.

Reiff, R. The control of knowledge: The power of the helping professions. *Journal of Applied Behavioral Science*, 1974, *10*, 451–461.

Schaffer, L, & Myers, J. Psychotherapy and social stratification. *Psychiatry*, 1954, *17*, 83–93.

Shinn, M. Father absence and children's cognitive development. *Psychological Bulletin*, 1978, *85(2)*, 295–324.

Singer, E., Garfinkel, R., Cohen, S. M., & Srole, L. Mortality and mental health: Evidence from the Midtown Manhattan Restudy. *Social Science and Medicine*, 1976, *10*, 517–525.

Sloane, R. B., Staples, F. R., Cristol, A. H., Yorkston, N. J., & Whipple, K. *Psychotherapy versus behavior therapy.* Cambridge: Mass. Harvard, 1975.

Sloane, R. B., Staples, F. R., Cristol, A. H., Yorkston, N. J., & Whipple, K. Patient characteristics and outcome in psychotherapy and behavior therapy. *Journal of Consulting and Clinical Psychology*, 1976, *44*, 330–339.

Smith, M. L., & Glass, G. V. Meta-analysis of psychotherapy outcome studies. *American Psychologist*, 1977, *52*, 752–760.

Smith, W. D., Burlew, A. K., Mosley, M. H., & Whitney, W. M. *Minority issues in mental health.* Reading, Mass.: Addison-Wesley, 1978.

Spitzer, R. I., & Wilson, P. T. Nosology and the official psychiatric nomenclature. In A. M. Freedman, H. I. Kaplan, & B. J. Sadock (Eds.), *Comprehensive textbook in psychiatry II.* Vol. I. Baltimore: Williams and Wilkins, 1975.

Srole, L. Measurement and classification in socio-psychiatric epidemiology: Midtown Manhattan Study (1954) and Midtown Manhattan Restudy (1974). *Journal of Health and Social Behavior*, 1975, *16*, 347–364.

Srole, L., Langner, T. S., Michael, S. T., Opler, M. K., & Rennie, T. A. C. *Mental health in the metropolis: The Midtown Manhattan Study.* New York: McGraw-Hill, 1962.

Staples, F. R., Sloane, R. B., Whipple, K., Cristol, A. H., & Yorkston, N. Process and outcome in psychotherapy and behavior therapy. *Journal of Consulting and Clinical Psychology*, 1976, *44*, 340–350.

Strupp, H., & Bloxom, A. Preparing lower-class patients for group psychotherapy: Development and evaluation of a role-induction film. *Journal of Consulting and Clinical Psychology*, 1973, *41*, 373–384.

Subotnik, L. Spontaneous remission: Fact or artifact? *Psychological Bulletin*, 1972, *77*, 32–48.

Sue, S., McKinney, H., Allen, D., & Hall, J. Delivery of community mental health services to black and white clients. *Journal of Consulting and Clinical Psychology*, 1974, *42*, 794–801.

Tischler, G. L., Henisz, J. E., Myers, J. K., & Boswell, P. C. Utilization of mental health services. II Mediators of service allocation. *Archives of General Psychiatry*, 1975, *32*, 416–418.

Tsuang, M. T. Schizophrenia around the world. *Comprehensive Psychiatry*, 1976, *17*, 477–481.

Turner, R. J. Social mobility and schizophrenia. *Journal of Health and Social Behavior*, 1968, *9*, 31–37.

Vail, A. Factors influencing lower-class black patients remaining in treatment. *Journal of Consulting and Clinical Psychology*, 1978, *46*, 341.

Vaillant, G. E. *Adaptation to life.* New York: Little, Brown, 1977.

Warheit, G. J., Holzer, C. E., & Arey, S. A. Race and mental illness: An epidemiological update. *Journal of Health and Social Behavior*, 1975, *16*, 243–256.

Watkins, B. A., Cowan, M. A., & Davis, W. E. Differential diagnosis as a race related phenomenon. *Journal of Clinical Psychology,* 1975, *31*, 267–268.
Weber, M. Class, status, party. In H. H. Garth & C. W. Mills (Eds.), *From Max Weber: Essays in sociology.* New York: Oxford, 1946.
Weinstein, R. M., & Brill, N. Q. Social class and patients' perceptions of mental illness. *Psychiatric Quarterly,* 1971, *45*, 35–44.
Wilkins, W. Expectancy of therapeutic gain: An empirical and conceptual critique. *Journal of Consulting and Clinical Psychology,* 1973, *40*, 69–71.

[illegible]

Part III

CONCEPTUAL AND EMPIRICAL STRATEGIES FOR COMMUNITY CHANGE

Overview

This section of the book focuses on strategies of intervention. All the chapters emphasize the good of the community rather than the individual, and in varying degrees each emphasizes environmental change.

No book on community mental health would be complete without reference to Caplan's (1964) three-fold conceptualization of prevention: primary, secondary and tertiary prevention. Primary prevention involves an attempt to lower the rate of new cases of mental disorders in a population by taking measures to counteract harmful factors before they lead to mental disorders: advocacy, changing environmental stressors and teaching coping skills would be examples of primary prevention. The focus is on the risk factors in the community, identifying environmental factors and their relationship to stress. Chapters 6 and 7 on environmental stressors and epidemiological variables are related to primary prevention as is Chapter 11 on advocacy.

Secondary prevention is an attempt to reduce the rate of mental disorder by identifying cases in the population at risk. Secondary prevention focuses on changing factors that lead to new cases, but usually in practice involves reducing the duration and/or severity of existing cases. This is done by early detection and early treatment. Identification should occur before problems become major. In order to have early detection, diagnostic tools must be refined so as to identify onset earlier from fewer and less severe signs and symptoms. Rappaport (1977) notes that a system can only treat as many cases as it can identify. He cautions that if one is to label an individual as maladjusted, one should have some positive alternatives; intervention should not occur where "spontaneous recovery" is likely. Also it should be added that if one is going to predict on the basis of fewer signs and symptoms, these predictions should be based on adequate research, or the rate of diagnostic error will increase along with its social consequences (For further discussion of the problems of labeling see Chapter 3 by Rappaport and Cleary.) The following chapters can be conceptualized as dealing with aspects of secondary prevention: Chapters 9, 10 and 12 on crisis intervention, consultation and family therapy.

Tertiary prevention aims to reduce the rate of mental disorder within a community. This corresponds to rehabilitation on a large scale (see Chapter 2 by Erickson and Hyerstay). The implication of tertiary prevention is that as few individuals as possible should be taken out of their homes or out of the community. For those that are taken out, the period that they are away should be as brief as possible.

Let us look at the contribution of the individual chapters in Part III. Chapter 8 by Albee, "A Competency Model of Prevention," makes a strong argument against the continued use of the medical model of mental illness. Rather than emphasizing its inadequacy in explaining or predicting behavior, as has been done often in the past, Albee looks at the consequences of the application of this model. He uses both historical examples and applications from everyday life. He espouses a competency model and cites several examples of its use.

Chapter 9 by McGee, "Crisis Intervention," carefully defines what is meant by the term. He discusses the historical development of crisis intervention, several conceptual models, the settings in which it occurs, the process of crisis intervention and an evaluation of crisis intervention service.

Juliana Lachenmeyer in Chapter 10, "Consultation and Programmatic Change," reviews mental health consultation as a process of intervention. She also summarizes and discusses the status of behavioral community intervention programs and briefly refers to organizational development as a strategy for within-organization change.

Knitzer in Chapter 11, "Advocacy and Community Psychology," traces the historical roots of advocacy. She looks at the underlying assumptions of this approach to change, the types of advocacy, the strategies of advocacy, the models of advocacy and finally the relationship of advocacy to community psychology.

Aponte in Chapter 12, "Family Therapy and the Community," presents the view often found among family therapists that behavior patterns have direct links to structures in systems other than those represented by the person or persons who are acknowledged as having the problem: families should be treated, not individuals. He extends this argument. Societal institutions have limited family action in many areas; therefore, one must look at the entire ecological context in which problems are generated and maintained. He presents a case illustration and discussion.

All the chapters in this section deal with intervention in community mental health. All place greater emphasis on the environment. Even the competency model deals with what the individual can do to cope with stress in the environment and suggests a definition of mental disorder that involves a reaction to the environment. Advocacy argues for political efforts to change the environment. Consultation involves efforts to help those within community mental health organizations in their relations with one another and with their clients. Family therapy is both a response to problems and a redefinition of those problems. Crisis intervention involves a recognition of urgency, certain types of problems and the realities of what resources are available to deal with them.

References

Caplan, G. *Principles of preventive psychiatry.* New York: Basic Books, 1964.
Rappaport, J. *Community psychology: Values, research and action.* San Francisco: Holt, Rinehart & Winston, 1977.

CHAPTER 8

A Competency Model to Replace the Defect Model[1]

George W. Albee, Ph.D.

Frequently a revolution in scientific thinking occurs when some widely accepted premise, some "historical truth," is seen finally as inaccurate or incorrect. Our minds explore the crowded spaces created by the walls of fixed ideas until eventually we question why the walls are there at all. With the expanse of space that comes into view as the old conceptual walls are torn down, completely new kinds of explorations are possible. The simple step of abandoning an old, habitual pattern of thinking often leads to a whole new way of dealing with a problem.

TWO MODELS

Primary Prevention and the Defect Model

The sickness or defect or illness explanation of disturbed behavior has been ascendant for a century. It has been questioned repeatedly over the years, but only recently has the intellectual climate become nurturant to the seeds of disbelief. Now the harvest of doubt is ready to be gathered.

One of the most important factors forcing our reevaluation of the "illness model" is a growing concern with the primary prevention of emotional disturbance. To prevent something we must first identify or describe what it is that we wish to prevent; then we must identify the causative forces that lead to the undesirable state or process, and try to remove them—or as another strategy, we must do other things that "strengthen the host" to resist successfully the causative agent.

The illness model has come to be seen increasingly as inappropriate to meaningful efforts at primary prevention. Mental illnesses are not objective facts. They are not identifiable diseases to be confirmed in the

[1] An earlier version of this chapter was prepared for the Vermont Conference on the Primary Prevention of Psychopathology: Competence and Coping Skills in Adulthood, June, 1978.

A volume based on the proceedings of that conference is to be published by the University Press of New England. The present chapter is used with permission of the Vermont Conference on Primary Prevention.

laboratory through diagnostic tests. There is, with rare exceptions, no organic pathology to be discovered. These conditions are not easily identified and are not reliably diagnosed. They do not follow the usual public health paradigm of prevention where an identifiable disease is traced back to a predictable cause that can be removed or defended against. Rather we are concerned with problems in living, problems often created by blows of fate, by the damaging forces of a racist, sexist, ageist society where preparation for competent adaptation is minimal.

One revealing consequence of this state of affairs is resistance and opposition from psychiatry to efforts at primary prevention. The most frequent argument holds that "We do not yet know enough about mental illness's organic causes to prevent them—and anyway we must spend our limited financial resources helping those who suffer" (Carstairs, 1958; Henderson, 1975; Eisenberg, 1975). The opposition to prevention in psychiatry is not much different, however, from attitudes in other areas of medicine—prevention has very low priority generally.

A widely-touted myth says that the medical profession is actively interested in prevention. The facts lead to a contrary conclusion. Of the billions of dollars spent in recent years for research into the causes and cure of cancer, for example, only a small fraction of 1 percent has been devoted to research into prevention. This astounding allocation of the lion's share of research money for a search for "cures" is in direct and stark contrast to the generally agreed upon fact that 80 to 90 percent of all cancer is environmentally caused and therefore theoretically preventable. The most underfunded and underpaid branches of medicine have long been the areas concerned with public health; schools of public health are nearly always at the bottom of the totem pole at major universities in terms of status and funding. This curious neglect of prevention research is all the more strange because of the generally accepted fact that most of the triumphs of medicine for the past century have resulted from discoveries leading to the prevention of diseases rather than to their cure. Recently one of my radical friends, listening to my puzzled preoccupation with these facts, pointed out to me that when strange and paradoxical social situations existed, Lenin was wont to ask, "Who benefits?" Is it too cynical to suggest that physicians are more interested in treatment than in prevention because it is to their economic benefit to treat? Or that a selection process screens out of medicine people with a prevention orientation? Medicine is most interested in the treatment of illness. Psychiatry is interested in furthering and defending the argument that emotionally disturbed people are sick. It is in the self-interest of the latter field to hold to these views. (But we *know* that socially acceptable reasons will be found in support of these views.)

Henderson (1975), writing in the *Bulletin of the Menninger Clinic*, sees a "fading" of community psychiatry, decries "the magical notion of 'primary prevention' " (p. 235), and sees "the striking advances of biological medicine" (p. 235) in both treatment and prevention. Persons are naive when they talk about prevention (says Henderson) because there are "only a few conditions in psychiatry (brain syphilis and PKU perhaps) that are well . . . [enough] understood to be preventable" (p. 235). He concludes: ". . . it makes little sense to divert millions of dollars from treatment to a 'woolly' notion of primary prevention" (p. 236).

One of the senior gurus in American psychiatry, Leon Eisenberg (1975) has examined the mental hygiene movement and concludes that "Seven decades later, there is no evidence of even modest success from a multitude of earnest efforts" (pp. 118–119). Eisenberg feels it is "absurd" to think mental hygiene programs can eliminate mental illness (p. 119). Rather, each of the variety of separate "psychiatric disorders," each with a separate cause, must be approached separately if prevention is the goal.

Surprisingly the general public has not been fooled into accepting the illness model despite the best efforts of the propagandists for psychiatry over the years. Most people simply do not believe that "mental illness is an illness like any other."

In spite of 100 years of increasingly massive attempts at "educating" the general public about "mental illness," the person in the street, in contrast to the highly educated, does not interpret most disturbed behavior as illness. Back in the late fifties the Joint Commission on Mental Illness (sic) and Health (Action for Mental Health, 1960) reported on an extensive nationwide sample survey done by Shirley Star to determine what is recognized by most people as "mental illness." On the basis of 3,500 interviews Star concluded that there is a large "tendency to resist labeling anyone as mentally ill" (by the general public) except as a last resort.

In interviews with a cross-section of the populace her staff described six separate patterns of disturbed behavior. These were fairly detailed sketches of the behavior that would ordinarily occur in those persons labeled paranoid schizophrenic, simple schizophrenic, chronic anxiety neurotic, compulsive phobic, alcoholic and juvenile delinquent. After listening to the descriptions of each of these kinds of behavior the 3,500 interviewees were asked to tell whether there was anything wrong with the person, whether the person was mentally ill, and whether it was serious.

For five of the six disturbed people described, a majority of those interviewed was unwilling to label the behavior "mental illness" and was able to give more commonsense explanations. Only in the case of the behavior of the so-called paranoid schizophrenic was a majority inclined to label the person mentally ill.

If the general public has not been sold on the sickness explanation, and if our research data fail to support this explanation, then why do we continue to feature the illness model in our professional intervention centers and in our professional training programs? If emotional problems are learned in a social context, why do we continue to pretend that people with these problems are sick? If emotional problems have been, and continue to be, shown to result from the interaction of environmental stress and learned ability to cope with stress (competence), why is our clinical model still medical? Who benefits?

Bertrand Russell suggested that anything worth stating is worth overstating. Clearly I will be following that principle!

Primary Prevention and the Competency Model

First let me state my own position. I believe the competency model demands an egalitarian political and moral philosophy. If we believe that every person, female and male, of whatever race, nationality, age, or ethnic origin deserves every possible opportunity to maximize their competence and coping skills, then we must free ourselves of the prejudices that are so much a part of Western thought. We must accept the position that everyone has the potential for growth and the right to personally develop the greatest possible competence to deal with stress.

This moral position is, and will be, highly threatening to the authoritarians and to those who accept a defect model. I want to argue that a competency model is incompatible with the position that certain persons are emotionally defective, that certain groups are defective because of genetic or organic factors, that women are inferior to men, blacks inferior to whites, southern Europeans inferior to Nordics, and that there is something inherently different about Jews, Orientals, French Canadians, Bantus, or any other group. I am not arguing against the concepts of individual differences and statistical variability. I am arguing against prejudice, ethnocentrism and elitism.

A competency model will be opposed, subtly or overtly, by those who favor meritocracy, divine right or separate and unequal kinds of interventions for separate groups. A competency model is anticategorical and antielitist. I should warn readers that acceptance of a competency model will be dangerous to their comfort. There are many powerful forces that are threatened by such a model; and as these forces have the power to punish those espousing it, it will be dangerous if we go too far down this road. There is a safe dilettante position we can play: the artificial competency training of persons who are imbedded in an authoritarian system that is loaded with injustice. This is comparable to polishing brass on the *Titanic*. But if one accepts the position that most emotional distress develops as a result of the unequal battle between individual resistance to stress, competency to deal with stress on the one hand and the overwhelming injustice and dehumanization that are part of our consumer-oriented industrial society on the other, then clearly the strategy is to strive to change the society and its values if we are to make a competency model more promising for success in prevention.

My thesis argues that excessive industrialization requires the dehumanization of work, submergence or elimination of individuality, of individual creativity, of a sense of identity and of personal competence.

We are merely dealing with a small part of the problems when we try to build competencies into children who are destined to take their places as workers in the endlessly boring and routinized jobs in manufacturing, sales, service, and agribusiness. The modern industrial state has defined human existence into rigid roles emphasizing efficient production and mindless consumption. In the process competent individuality has been all but lost (Albee, 1977).

I hope I am not exhibiting the "Old Oaken Bucket Delusion" when I suggest, for example, that life on the family farm may have provided one of the best environments for the development of individual competency and clear personal identity. Jefferson and his contemporaries based their views of democracy on the independent, self-sufficient, small-farm way of life. We have become what Jefferson most feared—a people crowded into cities. Three-quarters of us live on 2 percent of the land. Two hundred years ago 90 percent worked on the land. In 1950 there were five and a half million farms in the United States. Half of these no longer exist. Surely I need not spell out the nutritional horrors and health hazards that have resulted from the industrialization of agriculture, nor the degradation of the lives of five million migrant farm workers.

Let me try to make clear my position on prevention. In developing a model for primary prevention we should focus our attention on the following formula:

$$\text{Incidence} = \frac{\text{Organic Causes and Stress}}{\text{esteem and social support systems}}$$

Figure 8-1.

I should point out that this model can accommodate efforts in the organic and psychotherapeutic modes as well—it depends on whether the focus is on an individual or a population. The point is that building competence through increasing coping skills will reduce incidence—so long as we do not assume the presence of an unmodifiable organic defect, as long as we have some control over excessive social and economic stress and as long as we do not have a society that destroys self-esteem and/or social support systems. But focusing on competence, important as it is for prevention, must be part of a larger effort at social and political change.

If the primary prevention of emotional distress can be accomplished through the reduction of stress and the development of competence, why do we continue to direct all of our clinical efforts at treating symptoms? Why do we focus on secondary prevention? Again, who benefits?

In the face of all of the arguments in opposition to the sickness (medical, illness, defect) model, to what forces can we attribute the continued ascendancy of the sickness explanation of mental and emotional problems? I believe that one answer for the persistence of a defect model is to be found in the same ethnocentrism and racism that historically were part of the widespread ideological justification for slavery, for the jailing of paupers, for the exploitation of women and for the ghastly treatment of foreign-born "lunatics." I am *not* suggesting that all psychiatrists (and others) who hold for the illness model are sexists and racists. But the appeal of the model, in the absence of convincing empirical support, rests in large measure on the attitudes that perpetuate racism and sexism. The best argument for the inhumanity of slavery, the denial of rights to women and paupers and the warehousing of lunatics, was that these people were members of an inferior species and had no more rights than other subhuman species or beasts of burden. It was, and is, argued that each member of these groups possesses a personal defect that defines him or her as inferior.

Let us look for a moment at some history.

HISTORICAL BACKGROUND OF THE DEFECT MODEL

As a result of the potato famine in Ireland in 1850 hundreds of thousands of poverty-stricken and illiterate Irish peasants were dumped into the eastern cities of the United States. While they did not have to endure the degradations of slavery that were the lot of blacks in the South, the Irish were horribly exploited as cheap labor, as were the Chinese imported to build the railroads and the Japanese imported to work the pineapple fields of Hawaii. (Meanwhile the American Indians were being slaughtered and/or herded into reservations to make way for the expansion of the industrial society under the thoughtful leadership of the great robber barons of the nineteenth century). All of these groups were defined as members of inferior races; they were incompetent to participate in civilized society, and they could not be made competent.

The widespread conviction that the Irish were constitutionally inferior, and that Irish lunatics were incurable, can be read in Edward Jarvis's *Idiocy and Lunacy in Massachusetts of 1855*. This report to the Massachusetts legislature (recently reprinted by Harvard University

Press) is perhaps the best and most clear-cut delineation of psychiatric opinion of that day. Native-born Yankees were curable through gentle, kindly and humane treatment, but the coarse and uncouth Irish, who had higher rates of lunacy and idiocy, were made of weaker stuff and had to be housed permanently in separate insane asylums where they would not contaminate the Yankees who had only temporary aberrations. The development of psychiatry in the U.S. can be traced directly to the newly-formed Association for Superintendents of Hospitals for the Insane. More and more insane asylums sprang up across the land over the next half century to house increasing numbers of mentally disturbed. Most of these were bewildered peasants, first from Ireland, and then from Scandinavia, Eastern Europe and Southern Europe. Most recently the inmates are overrepresented by blacks and by Puerto Ricans and Chicanos. The interested psychologist should read the *American Journal of Insanity* from about 1860, when it came under the editorship of John P. Gray, who began to preach the message that a defective brain in a constitutionally inferior body was the cause of insanity. (Phyllis Chesler [1973] and Albert Deutsch [1944] have added comparable explanations of the frequent incarceration of women, members of another inferior species who could be institutionalized if a husband or father said they were deranged.)

The Census of 1840

Albert Deutsch (1944) reviewed some of the "scientific" evidence about the anatomical and mental peculiarities of the "Negro." He pointed out how the proslavery forces were comforted by the 1840 census. An attempt was made to count all insane persons and idiots. This count was reported separately in statistical tables for white and colored inhabitants of the various states and regions. The results of the sixth U.S. census revealed an interesting phenomenon. The rate of idiocy and lunacy among "free Negroes" was some eleven times *higher* than it was among Negroes who were slaves! In Maine, for example, every fourteenth Negro was afflicted with insanity or a mental defect. In contrast, in Louisiana, where slavery was firmly entrenched, only one Negro in 4,310 was so afflicted!

Southern Senator John C. Calhoun spoke eloquently on the floor of Congress: "Here is proof of the necessity of slavery. The African is incapable of self care and sinks into lunacy under the burden of freedom. It is a mercy to him to give him a guardianship and protection from mental death" (quoted in Deutsch, p. 473).

It is to his eternal credit that psychiatrist Edward Jarvis, studying the 1840 census while bedridden with a broken leg, found many discrepancies in the data and published a criticism of the census. He questioned the accuracy of the figures about blacks but his criticism was ignored or rejected by Calhoun and his group in the Senate.

Jarvis was the leading psychiatrist at the time of the 1840 census; he pointed out the false implications of the published data, stating:

> Slavery is more than 10-fold more favorable to mental health than freedom . . . the slaves are consoled with the assurance that although another man's will governs them, that their minds are not bound with insane delusions, nor crushed in idiocy, as are those of their brethren who govern themselves . . . The apparent exemption of the slaves from one of the most terrible disorders that has visited humanity and the ten-fold inability of the free black to the same, may become not only a fundamental principle in medical science but also one of the elementary principles in political economy (Jarvis, 1855, pp. 74–75).

These errors indeed found their way into the mass media and into the psychiatric literature. The *American Journal of Insanity* in 1851 asked "Who would believe, without the fact in black and white, before his eyes, that *every 14th* colored person in the State of Maine is an idiot or lunatic" (Italics in original)?

In spite of his admirable efforts at correcting the census figures for mental conditions among blacks, Jarvis was not immune to the defect model. In his classic study of *Idiocy and Lunacy in Massachusetts*, he obtained names of all idiots and lunatics from the town clerks throughout the state and constructed detailed tables for his epidemiological study. After poring over these figures he reported that ". . . we find that the pauper class furnishes, in ratio of its numbers, 64 times as many cases of insanity as the independent class" (pp. 52–53). Reviewing other studies from England and Wales, Jarvis concluded that the proportion of lunacy among the poor was about 40 times as great as among those not supported by public charity. Then Jarvis went on to state the intimate connection between poverty and lunacy. He said:

> In this connection it is worthwhile to look somewhat at the nature of poverty, its origin, and its relation to man and to society. It is usually considered as a single outward circumstance—the absence of worldly goods; but this want is a mere incident in this condition—only one of its manifestations. Poverty is an inward principle, enrooted deeply within the man, and running through all his elements; it reaches his body, his health, his intellect and his moral powers as well as his estate . . . hence we find that, among those whom the world calls poor, there is less vital force, a lower tone of life, more ill health, more weakness, more early death, a diminished longevity. There are also less self-respect, ambition and hope, more idocy (sic) and insanity, and more crime, than among the independent (p. 52).

Jarvis found, as noted earlier, that it was the Irish who supplied the largest proportion of insane, paupers and idiots, and he found that they have "greater irritability, are more readily disturbed . . ." and that "unquestionably much of their insanity is due to their intemperance, to which the Irish seem to be peculiarly prone."

In summarizing his findings, Jarvis argued that persons placed in institutions for the insane should be with members of their own social class, not mixed indiscriminately—rich and poor, native-born and foreign. He argued at some length for separate state hospitals for "State paupers."

The underlying fatal flaw or defect that afflicts the pauper group, the inferior classes, cultures, races and women, was used to explain higher rates of feeblemindedness and insanity in these groups but it also has been used as the excuse for the subjugation and exploitation of these inferior peoples. Indeed this belief in defect, enthusiastically supported by both psychiatry and psychology throughout their history, actually led to laws providing for mass programs of sterilization, and even to malign neglect and to extermination. Perhaps these words are too strong for the sensitivities of delicate defenders of the purity of our sciences. Let us look and see if they are justified.

Two Models of Mental Illness

In recent decades two major streams have mixed within American psychiatry. The sickness or defect explanation for psychosis, and the requirement of medical training for the practice of psychoanalysis, have made allies of the "organic" psychiatrists and the "analytic" psychiatrists, and have led to the inevitable medical domination of intervention at both levels of disturbance (psychosis and neurosis).

The greatest perpetrators of evil in our society are not masked desperados planning the Great Train Robbery. The real villains are the manicured and talcum-powdered pillars of their church and their society, respected and admired by their community. They rarely see their victims, and may not even be conscious of the evil they do as they make abstract decisions, manipulate budgets and protect and enhance the affluence of themselves and their peers. They use those ideologies that support the Establishment in economics, in social and political philosophy and in explaining dehumanization and emotional distress.

I think the illness model of mental disturbance is evil. It restricts the field of therapy to a small elite band by setting artificially high nonfunctional educational criteria for helpers. If one works directly with "sick patients" then one must have prestigious training and high status. This model demands that every person receiving help be given a medical diagnosis—a damaging label that can be a self-fulfilling prophecy and that may be a lifelong scarlet letter. It ensures that the large sums of money that a trusting society thinks it is appropriating for the relief of human suffering wind up in the pockets of a small and powerful elite group whose underlying purpose is to support the status quo. It denigrates and ridicules efforts at prevention that suggest the importance of social change and competence building.

The medical model has other faults. It focuses our attention on one-to-one patchwork symptom reduction as the best way to help. Finding ways to prevent cancer would destroy one of the major American growth (!) industries. Accepted epidemiological doctrine says that no mass disorders afflicting humankind have even been eliminated by one-to-one intervention with afflicted persons. In the case of genuine diseases the principle always operates. Smallpox, typhoid fever, polio and measles were not dealt with successfully by training enough physicians to treat sufferers individually. These scourges afflicting humankind were brought under control by discovering their causes and by effective efforts at primary prevention. A similar analogy can be drawn for emotional problems. They are so common, so damaging to effective living and so endemic that we cannot expect to have enough professional people to intervene with each disturbed person on a one-to-one basis; rather we ought to devote our efforts to documenting the social origins of psychopathology and to making the social changes necessary to reduce the incidence of these problems and to increase the competency of people to deal with problems in living. The defect model diverts our attention from the social origins of disturbance and it camouflages the need for radical social change.

While I am at it I have another complaint about psychiatry and the medical model; it too relates to prevention.

DRUGS AND THE DEFECT MODEL

One of the several major myths that has been promulgated with great intensity in recent years has it that the deinstitutionalization of persons who have been locked in the state hospitals for years is a result of dramatic discoveries in psychiatry and improvements in the field of psychotropic medication. This is unmitigated nonsense, but it affects our attitude about prevention.

If the decarceration of hundreds of thousands of inmates of mental hospitals has not been the result of the effectiveness of the new psychotropic drugs, then what indeed has led to the decarceration? Scull (1977) gives the answer to this question with devastating clarity. It is *cheaper for the states.* With the gradual shift in the cost of public welfare to the federal government, the states, particularly the ones with conservative administrations, discovered that it is far less expensive to take people out of mental hospitals that are supported by state monies and put them into communities where they can be supported by Medicare, daycare and welfare. No matter that these poor unfortunates are herded into the poverty-stricken ghettos of the city slums where they are preyed on by others. No matter that they must lead lives of terror, subject to the rapaciousness of profiteering group-home and nursing-home operators. In short, the "revolution in the care of the mentally ill" touted by the mass media as a triumph of modern psychiatric and pharmacological research is little more than a way for the states to cut their losses and shift the burden onto the federal government. Scull (1977) points out: "The pervasiveness, intensity, and mutually reinforcing character of the pressures to adopt a policy of decarceration are shown to be intimately connected to the rise of welfare capitalism" (p. 12).

Mechanic (1969) also has shown that the accelerating tendency in England to release mental cases from institutions was observed before the introduction of the psychotropic drugs. He summarizes a number of studies that make it clear "that the tremendous change that took place is due largely to alterations in administrative policies" (see Scull, p. 82). Data on the length of hospitalization make it clear that before the marketing of chlorpromazine the average duration of stay in mental hospitals in England had already dropped significantly. At the Vermont State Hospital the number of schizophrenics admitted was essentially the same between 1948 and 1958, but the number of schizophrenics discharged increased four times during this period—before drugs were in use!

Scull (1977) documents in other ways, with incisive criticism, the current fiction that drugs are responsible for decarceration. He cites several examples of the nonsense written in support of the position that the drugs did it. He reviews studies that underscore the lack of real therapeutic value of the psychotropic drugs for hospitalized psychotics. He concludes:

> But if phenothiazines are ineffective for substantial portions of the target population, and if in any event the types of maintenance doses generally prescribed are largely ineffective, how can anyone seriously contend that the advent of drug therapy is the main reason for the decline in mental hospital populations (the more so since the drugs are apparently the *least* effective with the groups whose release has been *most* crucial to the running down of mental hospital populations—the old, chronic cases?) (p. 88)

Scull further describes the recent history of the "massive medical commercial exploitation of new drugs on the basis of flimsy scientific evidence" (p. 89). He cites the example of amphetamines, which have earned untold millions of dollars for the profit-seeking drug companies as a result of their vigorous promotions to and by the medical profession. He describes the comparable exploitation of the psychotropic drugs which have been pushed enthusiastically through physicians, and through articles in the popular media, on the basis of the thinnest possible evidence of their usefulness and value.

The point of this seeming digression is that it is argued frequently that prevention efforts must await the more careful delineation of the underlying organic causative mechanisms whose existence is already established by the effectiveness of drugs in treating mental conditions.

Clearly persons given psychotropic drugs become lethargic and tractable. There is a reduction in the amount of assaultive and other aggressive acting-out behavior in persons under the influence of heavy psychotropic medication. Such persons often lose interest in their surroundings. As the psychotropic drugs became more widely used on the back wards, the use of other forms of physical restraints dropped off. But the drugs are not curative. They do not establish an organic causation.

Drugs and Deviance

In another frightening proposal in the frightening world of organic psychiatry the psychopharmological drugs are being proposed as having usefulness in altering behavioral deviance in the areas of crime and delinquency (Klerman, 1974, pp. 87–88). And if that is not enough, consider the suggestion of Brill and Patton (1966, p. 294), who believe we are "in urgent need of a mass therapy for conduct and personality disorder, social incapacity, economic dependence, unemployability and vagabondage . . . " They see these conditions as an indication of "the large number of psychiatric casualties whose primary and presenting symptoms are those of gross economic and social incapacity . . . " They observe that "the problems of these people clearly lie within the field of psychopharmacology." These are leaders of American psychiatry speaking! Are we really to treat crime and unemployment with drugs? Who benefits?

It does not seem to me to do violence to the whole complex pharmacologic issue to suggest that many members of the psychiatric profession have become the conscious agents of social control. They dispense drugs that immobilize but do not cure, and they impose chemical restraints on human beings just as inhumane and barbarous as those who in earlier days chained the insane and the enemies of society in rank dungeons.

Of all the professions that have been developed to provide for the social control of deviants, psychiatry has been most successful. By allying itself with medicine and by labeling deviants as having actual diseases based on underlying (as yet undiscovered) organic conditions and defects, psychiatry has achieved great social power. Persons adjudged insane can be deprived of their liberty without a trial, on the basis of psychiatric testimony about their dangerousness—while the research evidence has established clearly the unreliability of this prediction.

Stone, a professor of psychiatry and law at Harvard, has reviewed the research evidence on the prediction of dangerousness. Stone concludes: "It can be stated flatly on the basis of my own review of the published material on the prediction of dangerous acts that neither objective actuarial tables nor psychiatric intuition, diagnosis, and psychological testing can claim predictive success when dealing with the traditional population of mental hospitals" (1975, p. 33).

IQ AND THE DEFECT MODEL

So far I have had some highly critical things to say about psychiatry. Let me give equal time to the evils of psychology. May I commend to your reading Leon Kamin's incisive book, *The Science and Politics of IQ* (1974). Kamin documents in incredible detail the lengths to which prominent American psychologists were willing to go to prove their tenacious beliefs in the inheritance of a fixed entity called intelligence, the inferiority of non-Nordics, and of other groups who were so inferior genetically that they threatened to destroy the very existence of the early sturdy stock of the United States. The roster of these psychologists is a *Who's Who* in American psychology. These people were leaders of the APA, and their intellectual offspring are still at work in our most prestigious universities today. Terman (1917), for example, was convinced that both Spanish-Indian and Mexican families in the Southwest and negros (sic) had deficient intellects.

Repeatedly we find psychologists were arguing that poor people are poor because they are defective and not for reasons of environmental origin. Terman favored eugenic solutions and he observed pointedly that organized charities often allow these feebleminded individuals to survive when otherwise they would not be able to live and reproduce. Henry Goddard (1917), in an invited address at Princeton, spelled out all the reasons why workmen with low intelligence did not merit the same living standards as persons on higher mental levels. Robert Yerkes, another president of APA, was active in the eugenics movement. His group educated Congress and the state legislatures on the importance of passing sterilization laws.

Kamin concludes: "The mental testers pressed upon the Congress scientific IQ data to demonstrate that the 'new immigration' from Southeastern Europe was genetically inferior" (p. 12). The evidence from the mental testers was used to change the pattern of immigration to shut off, in so far as possible, immigration from Southern and Eastern Europe. Goddard, in 1912, went to Ellis Island with his Binet test under his arm and administered this and other performance tests to a representative sample of what he referred to as the great mass of average immigrants. He found that "83% of the Jews, 80% of the Hungarians, 79% of the Italians, and 87% of the Russians were 'feeble minded'" (Kamin, p. 16).

The Army Alpha Test

But the most convincing evidence came from the psychological testing of soldiers during World War I. Yerkes, then APA president, and his consultant Edward Lee Thorndike (a later president of the APA) were largely involved, although it was a book by Carl Brigham (1923) of Princeton University that brought the evidence to the educated public. In brief, Brigham's book, based on the tests of soldiers in World War I, found a clear-cut relationship between the proportion of Nordic, Alpine and Mediterranean blood and performance on intelligence tests. Brigham's book was praised by the chairman of the Senate committee considering a change in the immigration law.

Brigham says, near the end of his "scientific" review: "We must face a possibility of racial admixture here that is infinitely worse than that faced by any European country today, for we are incorporating the negro into our racial stock, while all of Europe is comparatively free from this taint . . . The decline of American intelligence will be more rapid . . . owing to the presence here of the negro" (pp. 209–210).

The foreword of the book was written by Robert Yerkes. (It may be of some historical interest to note that Brigham designed the Scholastic Aptitude Test and served as Secretary of the College Entrance Examining Board. Later he was elected Secretary of the APA.)

Because the Army IQ tests had shown that Jews, negroes (sic), Poles, Italians, Spanish-Mexicans, French Canadians, and other "brunette nationalities" performed at the feebleminded level in at least 80 percent of the cases, the immigration laws were changed to defend, late as it was, the purity of the native-born white Protestants. As Kamin points out, "There is nowhere in the records of the Congressional hearings—nowhere—a single remark by a single representative of the psychological profession to the effect that the results of the Army testing program were in any way being abused or misinterpreted" (p. 24). Indeed the Army testing program was officially organized by the American Psychological Association and Robert Yerkes.

Kamin points to the interesting parallel between the statements made about the Italians by Pintner in his 1923 text *Intelligence Testing* and the statements made today about blacks. Jensen (1969) argues that "Negroes" average about one standard deviation (15 IQ points) below the average of the white population. Is it not highly probable that this finding is as valid as the earlier observations by psychologists that 83 percent of Jewish immigrants were feebleminded or that the average IQ of the Italian was 84?

The most frightening thing about all of this was the sober and owlish assurance given by these early psychologists that they were presenting objective scientific facts. They had convincing evidence, they said, that intelligence was a fixed entity, that it was inherited, and that certain ethnic and racial groups were simply genetically inferior. They appear to have been totally unconscious of their biases and prejudices, that these biases preceded their data collection and their interpretation of the data from the testing of World War I soldiers. Brigham's book, in particular, was not criticized for the obvious fact that the correlation was strong between intelligence and the length of time that the persons tested and their forebears had been part of mainstream American culture.

The Army Alpha test administered during World War I contained, for example, a multiple-choice question asking the name of the Brooklyn Baseball Club; another asked for the name of the company that manufactured revolvers in the United States, and so on. Failure to answer such questions by immigrant Jews and Italians meant that they had defective genes for intelligence! The higher-scoring groups had had time to get acculturated to the motivations, language, facts and values of the dominant American society. Why did no one point out this obvious fact?

Are our contemporary psychologists as blinded by *their* values? And who benefits?

The Jensen position is a modern version. It is antithetical to a competency model. Jensen's monograph (1969) argued that compensatory education may be considered a failure. For him, some people simply don't have it. Jensen has acknowledged that his conclusion, if true, amounts to a death sentence for the ideal of egalitarianism, a powerful influence in contemporary Western society.

Jensen says:

> There is an increasing realization among students of the psychology of

> the disadvantaged that the discrepancy in their average performance cannot be completely or directly attributed to discrimination or inequalities in education. It seems not unreasonable, in view of the fact that intelligence variation has a large genetic component, to hypothesize that genetic factors may play a part in this picture. But such an hypothesis is anathema to many social scientists. The idea that the lower average intelligence and scholastic performance of Negroes could involve, not only environmental, but also genetic, factors has indeed been strongly denounced, e.g., Pettigrew (1964). But it has been neither contradicted nor discredited by evidence.
>
> The fact that a reasonable hypothesis has not been rigorously proved does not mean that it should be summarily dismissed. It only means that we need more appropriate research for putting it to the test. *I believe such definitive research is entirely possible but has not yet been done* (Italics added; p. 82).

These paragraphs bear careful study. What Jensen is saying is that there are hints and clues that support the position that there are differences in intelligence between the races that are due to genetic factors. But he makes it clear that definite scientific evidence in support of this hypothesis has not yet been accumulated. He urges more research on the question.

But having disposed of this scientifically necessary qualification he goes on to reach conclusions and give recommendations for changes in social policy as if the difference had been scientifically established. Actually, in a truly scientific approach one never rejects the null hypothesis until the evidence is in, and then only in terms of stated probability limits. The psychologists referred to seem to be rejecting the null hypothesis (that would state that there are no differences between races that cannot be accounted for by environmental differences), but with no real certainty. This is a cardinal scientific sin!

The "organic model" of retardation, like the organic model of "mental illness," is contradicted by a great many facts. The first of these is that it is very, very hard to find "mildly retarded" children before schooling begins. Frequently someone decides to do early intervention with mildly retarded preschoolers in order to see if such efforts can reduce the child's later learning problems in school. In most efforts of this sort it turns out to be impossible to locate "mildly retarded" preschoolers! If pediatricians in public clinics, or family doctors, or public health nurses, or welfare workers are asked—all of these professionals can identify the more seriously retarded children in the community. But no one knows (with reliable knowledge) who the mildly retarded are. So researchers must work with groups of "high-risk" children—say, all the children of mothers with low IQs—to find *some* children who later will receive the label in schools.

Another fact is that the IQs of inner-city children often decline while they are in school, and they wind up being called "mildly retarded" when they get to junior high or high school—having gone through regular classes in elementary school. Lane and Albee (1970) found that inner-city school children tested as part of a routine group testing program in the Cleveland schools showed a decline in IQ from second to sixth grade that averaged more than 10 points! These children were in the normal range in second grade and were at the borderline or mildly-retarded level four or five years later. Obviously this had to be pseudo-retardation.

Intelligence and Social Roles

Jane Mercer (1973) has reported a careful study of the social role performance of children with IQ's below 69 in the schools of Riverside, California. She compared Anglo (white middle-class) children with black and Mexican-American children. Basically she found that the Anglo children called educable mentally retarded (EMR) were failing in their *social* roles. Children from the two other ethnic groups classified as EMR were *not* failing socially. Most important, she found a low correlation between behavior described as adaptive or competent and measured intelligence. Sixty percent of the Chicano (Mexican-American) children who had "failed" their intelligence tests were able to pass a measure of good adaptive behavior. They were quite competent. Ninety percent of the black children in this same EMR group were also able to pass a measure of adaptive behavior. Mercer suggests that the educable mentally retarded should be divided into three groups. The first group would include those children damaged by organic identifiable factors (a relatively small number). The second are those normally retarded because of the operation of polygenic inheritance (a large group). The third are those who are culturally different from the norm. It is in this third group that objective measures of intelligence and objective measures of adaptive competent behavior do not agree. Mercer found that at least half of the Mexican-American adults who might have been classed as mentally retarded in school were leading effective, competent lives—they had married, were gainfully employed, and were adapting successfully to their environment.

Women do as well on intelligence tests as men. Those who argue that tests are color-blind and class-blind, and therefore that they open up opportunities for everyone, must face the fact that women are paid consistently less than men in the same jobs. Because roadblocks are erected against women in a great number of occupations those women who do succeed in these jobs are usually better qualified intellectually than men in the same jobs. Yet the women's income is lower. Obviously factors other than test scores are used to establish pay scales. When it suits the purpose of the employer to use tests to discriminate against minority groups, tests are used—"just not qualified for the intellectual demands of the job." When women do well on the tests, some other basis for discrimination is found.

The Fatal Flaw. There is a common pervasive value assumption underlying certain common psychiatric and psychological explanations of the conditions once called lunacy and idiocy and now referred to as mental illness and mental retardation. This widely held assumption holds that persons who are not members of the middle- and upper-class groups are biologically inferior, and further, that higher rates of idiocy and lunacy found in these inferior groups are the results of constitutional defect. The defect (or fatal flaw) is not limited however, to members of these inferior races and cultures. It also applies to women. Similarly, appropriate "effective treatment" goes largely to affluent white males—the "elect." Lest this accusation be regarded as having only historical relevance, we need only look at the report of the latest President's Commission on Mental Health (1978) to see how our underlying values limit appropriate high-quality "treatment" to affluent males.

In a review, Albee (1978) says the following:

> Who are the underserved and unserved? They are described in several places in the Commission's report. They include children, adolescents and the elderly—all of whom are identified repeatedly as underserved. These three groups together represent "more than half" of the nation's population. Then there are the minority groups that include 22 million black Americans, 12 million Hispanic Americans, 3 million Asian and Pacific Island Americans, and one million American Indians and Alaska natives. All of these groups are underserved or, in many instances, inappropriately served by persons insensitive to cultural differences or incompetent in appropriate languages. While clearly these identified groups of 38 million persons overlap somewhat with the earlier groups identified as underserved we are not yet at the end of the statistical complexities. Five million seasonal and migrant farm workers are largely excluded from mental health care. Elsewhere we discover that women also often do not receive appropriate care in the mental health system. Neither do persons who live in rural America, or in small towns, or in the poor sections of American cities. Neither do 10 million persons with alcohol-related problems, nor an unspecified number of persons who misuse psychoactive drugs, nor the very large number of children and parents involved in child abuse nor 2 million children with severe learning disabilities, nor 40 million physically handicapped Americans, nor 6 million persons who are mentally retarded. While the Commission made some very brave statements about the recent improvements in the availability of mental health care in this society, it seems clear that this improved care must have been available largely to

those groups not identified as being underserved—they could only be white educated males living in the affluent sections and suburbs of major American cities.

COMPETENCY MODELS AND PREVENTION

The model we adopt affects directly the kind of people we help and the kind of institutions we develop for intervention and prevention. These in turn dictate the kind of people we use to deliver care. With a social-developmental model focused on social reform and competence-building, our state hospitals and public clinics would be replaced by social intervention centers, largely staffed by people at the bachelor's level—people such as special education teachers and social welfare workers, potentially available in vastly greater supply than psychologists and psychiatrists. For prevention, more highly trained professionals would be needed as teachers, researchers and, especially, as radical social activists proselytizing for changes in our society to make it more supportive, less dehumanized.

The massive deterioration of the fabric of industrial society and its institutions results in a complex tangle of pathology. The pathology includes especially the destruction of the emotional integrity of the family. Let me emphasize here something with which readers are probably already familiar. Many significant research breakthroughs have already been made. Many of the discoveries are already in. We know, for example, that the emotional climate which surrounds the infant and young child is of critical importance in determining his or her future—including the kind, the severity, and perhaps even the biological concomitants, of later disturbance.

Such knowledge is dangerous. We usually shut our eyes to its implications. We go on trying to fix up damaged adults in one-to-one relationships when a more proper professional function would be to spend a considerable portion of our energies trying to fix up our society in ways that will increase the strength and stability of the family, thereby affecting positively the mental health of generations to come.

Managing Stress

Most efforts at prevention focus on the forces that have produced disturbance. Another approach for investigators is to try to define and measure "adaptive potential." This approach argues that certain individuals develop highly skilled patterns of competent adaptation to a wide range of situations. Offer and Sabshin (1963) made a study of adolescents without gross psychopathology—they all showed a high level of mastery of developmental tasks and effective coping skills in their relationships with others. Grinker, Grinker, and Timberlake (1962) studied mentally healthy young males and found that "homoclites" (optimally adjusted men) tended to be self-confident goal-seekers with a strong sense of self-worth, warm family relationships and an action orientation. This model would suggest that preventive efforts be focused on the development of competence and coping skills in contrast with the more life-history-oriented model which focuses on the elimination of pathological experiences. Obviously the two models are not separate and even complement each other.

Poser (1970) has discussed a behavioral model for prevention. This approach focuses attention on the role of learning processes in the development of adaptive and maladaptive behavior. The approach suggests specific learning experiences can be identified and that behavioral approaches effective in leading to behavioral change can also be identified. Some persons may actively learn to behave in a maladaptive way while others may passively learn, through modeling, ineffective social and interpersonal skills. Both groups are then more vulnerable to later stress situations and so are at higher psychological risk. This approach stresses more careful delineation of specific behavioral problems and draws heavily on the concepts of behavioral psychology.

Other examples in this area include the work of Seligman (1975), whose work on learned helplessness has had such a widespread impact. Seligman suggests that giving individuals early experience with stress situations that they can learn to control may reduce their susceptibility to later feelings of helplessness in uncontrollable aversive situations. Suinn, Jorgensen, Stewart, and McGuirk (1971) gave groups "anxiety management training" and Meichenbaum (1975) used a cognition training procedure that he called "stress inoculaton" as a defense against later anxiety.

All of these approaches involve some form of practice in the management of stress so as to increase the person's ability to deal competently with later stress.

Forced Incompetence

Others have dealt at greater length with the issue of competence. Let us, however, keep in mind that competent persons often are turned into incompetent persons as a result of the operation of social and economic forces outside of their control. Forcing persons into an incompetent role or lifestyle when in fact they are competent in another role or lifestyle, must be a major source of stress contributing to emotional disturbances and other forms of psychopathology. I will cite a couple of examples:

In many parts of the United States, particularly in southern states, laws are written in such a way that competent black farmers are being forced off the land they have long regarded as their own, land that has been in their family for several generations. There is a "proper" legal mechanism involved. The fact is that in the past black farmers have often died without a will so that their land has been inherited and shared by children and/or other relatives. After two or three such generations the legal title to the land is so clouded that persons and corporations coveting the land (the value of which is increasing rapidly) can use any of several stratagems to force a sheriff's sale. As a result, many competent black farmers and their families are being forced out of a way of life in which they are self-respecting and self-supporting, and into cities where they have few saleable skills and where they are forced to go on the welfare rolls. Critics of the "growing welfare burden" do all sorts of dehumanizing things to add to the stresses placed on these families, with resulting emotional disturbance, crime, delinquency and premature pregnancy.

Here is a second example. Impoverished women throughout our society, and especially throughout the Third World, are being encouraged to bottle-feed their infants with powdered formula. Propaganda and social pressure for bottle-feeding by women who are perfectly competent to breast-feed their infants is fostered and augmented by the formula manufacturing companies, who often have "arrangements" with local physicians and governmental health educators. These officials give new mothers free samples of powdered infant formula that last long enough for the mother's breast milk to dry up, after which she is then obligated to pay a significant portion of the family income for the formula. In areas where water supplies are contaminated, infants often receive disease-laden formula, or they are given inadequate quantities of the powdered milk as their mothers seek to stretch the formula because of its excessive cost. As a consequence, thousands of infants are failing to thrive, dying or not developing proper central nervous system growth. A major source of stress, of course, is the sickness and death of these infants, so again we see competent people turned into incompetent people as a result of social pressures and economic manipulation.

Many serious, sober and far-from-radical observers today believe the problem at the heart of our social malaise is the primacy of corporate profits over long-range planning for the publc good. Short-run success is all that is important to the mindless corporation. In pursuit of these immediate rewards our environment is devastated, our people are brainwashed into becoming mindless consumers or thrill-seeking robots and the pleasures of human contact have been subordinated to the pleasures of material consumption.

Blaming the Victims

One of the most serious mental health problems of any industrial society, and perhaps particularly of the uncontrolled, unplanned, devil-take-the-hindmost conglomerate-corporation industrial society, is the lack of joy in work. Most industrial jobs, whether on the assembly line or in management, have become so monotonous, boring and meaningless as to throw an intolerable load on people's leisure-time activities and on conspicuous consumption as a source of satisfaction. Eric Fromm (1972) suggests that one of the most important sources of aggression today is to be found in persons with what he terms a "bored character." These individuals, who represent a very large portion of our adult society, lack any profound interest in people or in life as a consequence of their feelings of powerlessness. Fromm feels that many people have become controlled by meaningless jobs, and they fall under extreme social pressure to consume worthless and meaningless goods. People, having nothing else to do, have become compulsive consumers, using up the enormous outpouring of the industrial machine.

One of the most fearsome aspects of this situation is the seeming hopelessness of the system to change itself. Enormous corporations and conglomerates defy government control. The cost of running for federal office has grown to the point where successful candidates must be supported by these giant corporate powers in order to be elected. The conglomerates and cartels are more powerful than governments, and power structure extends around the earth.

Blame is one of the most useless human activities. I do not propose to blame corporations or the people that run them for the dehumanization that is such a prominent part of the conglomerate society. But we must all point to them as a major source of our pollution, environmental and human, and then seek coldly and rationally to change the system.

Back in the early days of this century, before the psychodynamic-sickness model had assumed its current total primacy, there was little ambiguity among mental health professionals about where Evil was to be found. It was clearly recognized that human beings were damaged, dehumanized and destroyed by the mindless and indifferent forces of free-enterprise industrialization. And it was clear that social causes of emotional disturbance demanded social action as a remedy.

Jane Addams in 1910 was merciless in her criticism of professionals who failed to recognize the relationship between industrialization and poverty. She urged her own field of social work to come together with "the Radicals" to fight for better social conditions. In her view social work, to achieve its goals, had to engage in social and political action. It was no accident that the economic reforms and labor legislaton proposed in the 1912 platform of Theodore Roosevelt's Bull Moose Party read like Jane Addams's program for social action. She was on the platform and seconded his nomination.

When did we switch from an evil-is-in-the-system social reform philosophy to the more conservative evil-is-inside-the-person individual treatment philosophy? Probably sometime in the decade of the 1920s. Psychiatry and social work focused on individual need, on psychic determinism and on the one-to-one intervention method. The early involvement of social workers in social action—storming the citadels of the establishment, organizing the poor, working with the unions, leading and encouraging tenant strikes—gave way to the ascendant psychiatric notion that evil is inside the person, and that if we can get the person across a desk from us we can somehow patch him or her up.

Our training programs all teach this model, which serves as a support for reaction. If evil is inside the person, then we do not need to change anything except him or her, and the damaging status quo is left intact.

Let us recognize that these training fictions influence the moral attitudes and ethical values of professional workers, and these significantly influence both the form of intervention and prevention we choose to use, and the way we are perceived by society. The fundamental professional decision is whether we represent the client or whether we represent the agency, institution and society that pay our salary.

The professional worker in the human services fields is faced with severe personal role conflicts which are continuing and inescapable. Each professional worker must decide to whom he or she is responsible, to the establishment, or to the victim. Professional workers are overwhelmingly drawn from the middle class, and notoriously timid about fighting for social change. Middle-class professionals are educated in middle-class colleges and universities and are exposed to an endless indoctrination which rewards conformity and control and punishes extremism and originality. The lock-step system of education from the earliest school years through college and professional training continuously weeds out rebels and deviants so that professionals completing their training are a highly selected group of middle-of-the-roaders. Yet once one begins to work with the emotionally disturbed, the so-called insane, the rebels against the system, the alcoholics, the drug addicts, the juvenile delinquents and criminals, one begins to see that many of these problems are caused by the faults and defects of the economic system. Is this knowledge enough to counteract our years of training in conformity? Is it enough to affect our attitudes toward prevention?

The professional must continuously decide whether he or she is a defender of the established order or whether he or she must become an advocate for the victims of that order. Those who opt for the traditional pattern of pinning diagnostic labels on disturbed people and explaining their deviant behavior in terms of a sickness originating in a defective brain, or endocrine system, or chromosomal defect, are clearly defenders of the status quo, particularly in the absence of any compelling evidence for such a defect explanation. This whole approach has been well-labeled by William Ryan (1971) as *Blaming the Victim.* The poor are to blame for their poverty, and the insane are to blame for their insanity and the criminals are to blame for their rebellion.

On the other hand, the professionals who see disturbed people as victims of an exploitative and dehumanizing system are quickly made visible and are themselves labeled as radicals or rebels with emotional problems (probably caused by some internal defect). We need unanimity in these matters, or we will be picked off one by one!

Kenneth B. Clark (1974) has pointed out that "any form of rejection, cruelty and injustice inflicted upon any group of human beings by any group of human beings *dehumanizes* the victims overtly and in more subtle ways dehumanizes the perpetrators" (p. 144). He called on psychology to stop avoiding the moral and survival problems of the human race and to try to enhance the human capacity for creativity and progress. He argued that it is imperative for psychology to seek to control the destructive forces within society.

Professionally we also know that a person with the strongest hunger for power, with power needs that lead to an insatiable drive for authority and control over others, is not ordinarily the most empathic person. If those who avidly seek positions of power are drawn from the more neurotic, then perhaps we should apply what we know about intervention in neurosis (which is to make the unconscious conflicts conscious). This suggests that we continue to interpret to political leaders the causes of their most dehumanizing actions, and that we seek to secure whatever legal checks and balances we can to minimize the damage they do to those who cannot help or protect themselves.

Professionally we also know something about the development of empathy, that feeling we experience when we put ourselves in the place of others. Those with a mature and well-developed conscience are capable of empathy. Empathy is the source of most humanistic actions and concerns. Yet we know too that empathy is most likely to appear when specific, real and concrete objects for empathy are clearly perceivable. Many bomber pilots in Vietnam found it hard to empathize with abstract people who might or might not have been in jungle villages thousands of feet below their planes. Neither can polluters feel empathy for unknown people who might be damaged hundreds of miles distant, or several generations hence. Knowing this, it seems to me that we must help find ways to make known the sufferings of people—those who are the victims of human actions and policies.

By all of this I am suggesting that we should consider assuming more active efforts to change society. (I make this suggestion with some trepidation because I anticipate protest from those who will point to our lack of enough firm knowledge, at the grandiosity implicit in this proposal, and at the inappropriateness of small and precious groups attempting such a formidable task. But our social problems are all human problems, and we are the experts!)

We must do more than simply make our knowledge available to the decision makers of our society. As practitioners of an ethical social science, we must advocate, assert, urge and proselytize. Each of us must decide how he or she can best contribute to the reduction of the dehumanizing forces in our society and the enhancement of the human competence that is possible. But we must first agree that the problem is in the system, not in the victim.

References

Action for Mental Health. Final report of the joint commission on mental illness and health. New York: Basic, 1961.

Albee, G. W. Emerging concepts of mental illness and models of treatment: the psychological point of view. *American Journal of Psychiatry*, 1969, 7 (*125*), 870–876.

Albee, G. W. The protestant ethic, sex, and psychotherapy. *American Psychologist*, 1977, *32*, (2), 150–161.

Albee, G. W. A manifesto for a fourth mental health revolution? A review of the Report of the President's Commission on Mental Health, 1978. *Contemporary Psychology*, 1978, 8 (23), 549–551.

Brigham, C. C. A study of American intelligence. Princeton: Princeton University Press, 1923.

Brill, H., & Patton, R. E. Psychopharmacology and the current revolution in mental health services. *Proceedings of the Fourth World Congress of Psychiatry* (Part One). Amsterdam: Excerpta Medica Foundation, 1966, 288–295.

Carstairs, G. M. Preventive psychiatry—is there such a thing? *Journal of Mental Science*, 1958, *104*, 63–71.

Chesler, P. *Women and madness.* New York: Avon, 1973.

Clark, K. B. *Pathos of power.* New York: Harper & Row, 1974.

Deutsch, A. The first U.S. census of the insane (1840) and its use as pro-slavery propaganda. *Proceedings of the New York Medical History Society*, February 2, 1944.

Eisenberg, L. Primary prevention and early detection in mental illness. *Bulletin of the New York Academy of Medicine*, 1975, *1 (51)*, 118–129.

Fromm, Erich. The Erich Fromm theory of aggression. *The New York Times Magazine*, February 27, 1972.

Goddard, H. H. Mental tests and the immigrant. *Journal of Delinquency*, 1917, *2*, 271.

Grinker, R. R. Sr., Grinker, R. R. Jr., & Timberlake, J. A. Study of "mentally healthy" young males (homoclites). *A.M.A. Archives of General Psychiatry*, 1962, *6*, 405–410.

Henderson, J. Community tranference review: with notes on the clinic-community interface. *Journal of the American Academy of Psychoanalysis*, 1974, *2*, 113–128.

Henderson, J. Object relations and a new social psychiatry: The illusion of primary prevention. *Bulletin of the Menninger Clinic*, 1975, *1*, *(39)*, 233–245.

Jarvis, E. *Idiocy and Lunacy in Massachusetts. Report of the Commission on Lunacy, 1855.* Boston: William White, Printer to the State, 1855. Cambridge, Mass.: Harvard University Press, 1971.

Jensen, A. R. How much can we boost I.Q. and scholastic achievement? *Harvard Educational Review*, 1969, *39*, (1), 1–123.

Kamin, L. *The science and politics of I.Q.* Potomac, Md.: Erlbaum, 1974.

Klerman, G. Psychotropic drugs as therapeutic agents. *Hastings Center Studies*, 1974, *2 (1)*, 81–93.

Lane, E. A., & Albee, G. W. Intellectual antecedents of schizophrenia. In M. Roff, and D. Ricks, (Eds.), *Life history research in psychopathology*. Minneapolis: University of Minnesota Press, 1970.

Lemkau, P. U. Freud and prophylaxis. *Bulletin of the New York Academy of Medicine*, 1956, *32*, 887–893.

Mechanic, D. Some factors in identifying and defining mental illness. *Mental Hygiene*, 1962, *46*, 66–74.

Mechanic, D. *Mental health and social policy*. Englewood Cliffs, N.J.: Prentice-Hall, 1969.

Meichenbaum, D. Self-instructional methods. In F. H. Kanfer and A. P. Goldstein (Eds.), *Helping people change*. New York: Pergamon, 1975.

Mercer, J. Labeling the mentally retarded. Berkeley: University of California Press, 1973.

Offer, D., & Sabshin, M. The psychiatrist and the normal adolescent. *American Medical Association Archives of General Psychiatry*, 1963, *IX*, 427–432.

Pettigrew, T. *A profile of the Negro American*. Princeton, N.J.: Van Nostrand, 1964.

Pintner, R. Intelligence testing: Methods and results. New York: Holt, 1923.

Poser, E. G. Toward a theory of behavioral prophylaxis. *Journal of Behavioral Therapy and Experimental Psychiatry*, (1970), *1*, 39–43.

Ryan, W. *Blaming the victim*. New York: Pantheon, 1971.

Scull, A. *Decarceration*. Englewood Cliffs, N.J.: Prentice-Hall, 1977.

Seligman, M. *Helplessness: On depression, development, and death*. San Francisco: Freeman, 1975.

Stone, A. A. *Mental health and the law: A system in transition*, (DHEW Publication No. [ADM] 76–176). Washington, D.C.: U.S. Government Printing Office, 1975.

Suinn, R. M., Jorgensen, G. T., Stewart, S. S., McGuirk, F. D. Fears as attitudes: Experimental reduction of fear through reinforcement. *Journal of Abnormal Psychology*, 1971, *3*,*(78)*, 272–279.

Terman, L. S. Feeble-minded children in the public schools of California. *School and Society*, 1917, *5*, 161–165.

CHAPTER 9

Crisis Intervention

Thomas F. McGee, Ph.D.

Shortly more than one decade ago, crisis intervention was viewed as an innovative therapeutic concept which was especially relevant to the emerging field of community mental health. During the past decade, theoretical viewpoints about the concept of crisis intervention have developed rapidly. This has been accompanied by a continuing development in empirical knowledge, and crisis intervention is now widely accepted and commonly utilized in a multiplicity of health and mental health settings. There is little doubt that crisis management has exercised an important influence on the practice of contemporary psychotherapy. This influence is particularly significant when one considers the extremely broad range of conditions which lead many individuals to seek mental health assistance. It is probable that many individuals who seek some form of mental health assistance do so initially as a result of crisis situations which are related to personal, familial, interpersonal, vocational or societal factors.

The body of theoretical and empirical knowledge which has emerged about crisis intervention during the past two decades has clarified our understanding of this concept. However, there have been difficulties developing a clear delineation of the concepts of crisis and crisis intervention. Schulberg and Sheldon (1968) have indicated that the concept of crisis intervention remains ambiguous, and that it is more attractive to those concerned with the immediate delivery of mental health services than to researchers and theorists. Korchin (1976) makes a similar observation and notes that crisis intervention represents an orientation to therapeutic practice and a way of thinking rather than a systematic body of knowledge, theory and practice. In view of these observations, it is not surprising that a number of ambiguities exist regarding crisis intervention, particularly at a theoretical level.

Despite these ambiguities, crisis intervention approaches have continued to grow in scope and utilization, and it is possible to present a relatively coherent, empirically based definition of crisis intervention. Such a definition takes cognizance of crisis theory, the history of crisis intervention and empirical developments about crisis intervention which have occurred during the past two decades.

Crisis intervention can be seen as a therapeutic approach which is goal directed, goal limited and usually short term. It is used primarily with individuals experiencing a crisis with which their coping mechanisms are inadequate to deal effectively. In crisis intervention the therapeutic focus is on the stress related to the crisis, its immediate causes, and on the individual's reaction to that stress. Crisis intervention implies that the crisis intervener rapidly assesses the nature of the crisis and explores the adaptive and maladaptive aspects of the individual's reaction to the crisis. Although the focus of intervention is primarily on current events in the individual's life, a careful appraisal is made of the individual's reactions to previous crises. In crisis intervention the crisis intervener or therapist attempts to become directly allied with the strengths and resources of the client/patient. At least four characteristics differentiate crisis intervention from other forms of psychotherapy. These are: 1) crisis intervention is oriented toward the resolution of immediate problems, 2) crisis intervention is usually limited to relatively few contacts, 3) crisis intervention is characterized by a relatively high level of therapist activity and availability, 4) crisis intervention includes relatively direct efforts to enlist the individual's interpersonal assets, such as family, friends and vocational resources, in the process of intervention.

HISTORICAL DEVELOPMENT OF CRISIS INTERVENTION

Throughout human history many types of crises have been identified. These have included personal, interpersonal and impersonal crises, and there is little doubt that crisis experiences form an important part of everyone's life. A common denominator among crisis experiences is the individual's reaction to, and attempts to cope with, them. This may encompass a large variety of behaviors and outcomes. Human response to crisis situations can lead to effective crisis resolution and potential emotional growth, or to emotional and/or physical debilitation in extreme situations.

Personality theorists have been aware of the relationship between transitional stages and personal crisis, and its implications for personality development and psychotherapeutic intervention for some time. Erikson (1950), in postulating eight stages of psychosocial development, focused attention on the concept of "identity crisis" more than a generation ago. More specifically Erikson regarded those in late adolescence as susceptible to a painful period of adaptation and potential growth as they confront the developmental crisis associated with becoming young adults. In this formulation Erikson presaged an important aspect of the concept of normal maturational crises. While personality theorists and mental health professonals have understood and dealt with the effects of life crises for many years, it is only within the past three to four decades that a body of knowledge about specific human reactions to crises has begun to develop.

The observations of Lindemann (1944) in documenting human response to disasters constituted one of the earliest studies related directly to the development of crisis theory. This work focused on bereavement reactions of survivors of those killed in the Cocoanut Grove nightclub fire in Boston, Massachusetts in 1942. Lindemann described three phases of mourning which occur in the survivor when a significant person dies: 1) shock and disbelief, 2) developing awareness, and 3) resolving the loss. Lindemann also suggested a possible link between intervention in emotional crises as exemplified by grief reactions related to sudden loss, and the prevention of emotional disorders. Subsequently Tyhurst (1951) made some significant observations about human reaction to community disasters, and described three predictable phases of an individual's reaction to crisis situations: 1) a period of impact, 2) a period of recoil, and 3) a post-traumatic period.

As a partial consequence of Eriksonian theory and the work of Lindemann (1944) and Tyhurst (1951), it was thought that other natural events in the human life cycle, e.g., marriage or childbirth, would be accompanied by some degree of emotional stress. The individual experiencing stress associated with normal life developments or maturational crises might react to this stress in either an adaptive or a maladaptive manner. Accordingly, strong interest began to develop regarding the effects of normal life crises on emotional adaptation. In line with Lindemann's early work, this interest became specifically focused on the primary prevention of serious emotional disorders (Caplan, 1959, 1961; Caplan & Grunebaum, 1967).

Gerald Caplan, who worked with Lindemann, is the individual associated with synthesizing the body of knowledge which led most directly to the concept of crisis intervention. Caplan (1961) felt that a state of crisis may occur when the individual faces a problem that appears insoluble. This causes an increase in internal tension which may result in short-term or long-term emotional upset. In developing his theory, Caplan (1964) accepted the traditional medical definition of crisis as a turning point, and postulated both long-term and short-term models of crisis. Caplan's short-term model indicates that sudden or threatened loss of physical, psychosocial and sociocultural necessities precipitates a crisis in the individual. The crisis may eventuate in an enhancement of the individual's ability to cope with stress and a higher level of functioning or it may lead to maladaptive efforts to cope with the stress and, consequently, a lower level of functioning.

When an individual is undergoing a crisis, this period can be viewed as a crisis state. Caplan (1964) described a crisis state as consisting of four predictable phases. In essence, he agreed with the formulation of

Tyhurst we have just noted. Caplan (1964) divided Tyhurst's period of recoil into two phases. In Caplan's phase two, failure of the individual's usual problem-solving methods leads to increased tension and ineffective behavior. Caplan's phase three suggested that the individual would attempt to mobilize internal and external resources and begin to utilize new approaches to the problem. Caplan agreed with Tyhurst that phase four, or the post-traumatic period, would be symptom free if the individual became stronger as a result of newly developed methods of coping with the crisis situation. Both Tyhurst and Caplan indicated that if the crisis situation is not resolved effectively, the post-traumatic period will be marked by continued tension and disorganization. Caplan further indicated that some resolution either in a positive or negative direction would occur within four to six weeks following the crisis.

Subsequent to this synthesis of human response to crisis situations, T. F. McGee (1968) suggested that crises be viewed in relation to a continuum ranging from normal developmental crises to crises with a high probability for personal disorganization. Normal developmental crises such as school entrance, emergence of adolescence, marriage or retirement, which generally have a reduced probability of requiring direct intervention, might be placed near the lower end of such a continuum. Potentially more serious crises such as job loss, disabling injury or death of a close family member might be placed near the upper end of such a continuum. More recently Baldwin (1978) has proposed that emotional crises be categorized into six major types ranging from relatively uncomplicated crises to psychiatric emergencies. He notes that "the sound practice of crisis intervention requires a paradigm for differentiation of types of crises, with implications for effective intervention strategy" (p. 539).

The elaboration of crisis intervention occurred at approximately the same time that critical attention was focused on approaches to suicide prevention (Farberow, 1974). As a result there has been a close identification between crisis intervention and suicide prevention, and some consider suicide prevention to be a special form of crisis intervention. These developments in crisis intervention and suicide prevention occurred at roughly the same time that the community mental health movements fully emerged. Community mental health programs placed great emphasis on services which were economic, readily available, goal directed, prevention oriented, and which could be understood and utilized by wide but diverse elements of the population. By their nature, crisis intervention services readily met these criteria. From a community mental health perspective, crisis intervention became known as an innovative therapeutic approach which appeared to be effective in a wide variety of settings with a broad range of clients/patients.

Crisis intervention has served as an important link between community mental health and the contemporary practice of psychotherapy.

Henisz and Johnson (1977), among others, refer to crisis intervention as having come to assume a legitimate place in the inventory of psychiatric therapies, and in many clinical situations crisis intervention is clearly the treatment of choice. Many individuals who seek some form of psychotherapeutic assistance undergo initial assessment based in part on the principles of crisis intervention. At present, crisis intervention modalities appear to be routinely considered as appropriate if not standard therapeutic approaches for a wide variety of individuals seeking help with emotional conflicts.

MODELS OF CRISIS INTERVENTION

Conceptual models

Beginning with the work of Caplan (1964), a number of conceptual models of crisis intervention have been advanced. Jacobson, Strickler, and Morley (1968) and Morley (1970) proposed four levels of crisis intervention. The first two levels consist of environmental manipulation, where the crisis intervener refers the crisis affected individual to an appropriate resource; and general support in which the behavior of the crisis intervener tends to be limited to active listening and an expression of interest. With respect to the third level, or generic approach, it is assumed that the crisis intervener possesses thorough knowledge of specific types of crises, and a variety of interventive techniques which have demonstrated effectiveness in resolving crises that follow a predictable pattern. The fourth level, or individualized crisis approach, also requires the crisis intervener to have a sound knowledge of personality theory and psychodynamics.

Schneidman (1973) has advanced a three-level categorization of emotional crises which relates to developmental concepts. He describes intratemporal crises as those which occur during a particular stage of life and which are usually specific to that stage. Intertemporal crises are those which occur as the individual moves from one developmental stage to the next. Extratemporal crises are those which occur independently of developmental stages.

A number of individuals have proposed a two-category conceptual frame of reference for emotional crises. These frames of reference consistently make a distinction between crises which can generally be anticipated and those which are not. For example, Aguilera and Messick (1974) categorize crises in two broad groups: maturational crises and situational crises; Morrice (1976) has followed this trend and refers to crises that are primarily developmental as opposed to accidental. Butcher and Maudal (1976) distinguish between dispositional crisis cases and crisis therapy cases.

In a comprehensive description of crisis events, Baldwin (1978) proposes that emotional crises be classified into six types. He describes disposition crises as related to tension resulting from a problematic situation. Crises of anticipated life transitions are associated with normative changs of life such as marriage, parenthood, and the like. Crises resulting from traumatic stress are associated with strong external stress which is usually unexpected and uncontrolled. The fourth type consists of maturational/developmental crises, which are associated with struggles for emotional maturity. Crises reflecting psychopathology are associated with that preexisting psychopathology in the individual which has significantly influenced the precipitation of the crisis. The sixth type consists of psychiatric emergencies, in which the emotional functioning of the individual has been seriously impaired as a result of the crisis event.

The models of crisis intervention proposed by Jacobson and his colleagues (1968), Butcher and Maudal (1976), and Baldwin (1978) bear some association to the concept of prevention. As used in mental health, programs of primary prevention apply specific techniques to a healthy population to prevent the occurrence of emotional disorder. Secondary prevention focuses on individuals who are already manifesting early symptoms of emotional disorder. It is oriented toward rapid intervention with such individuals to stop the development of the disorder and return the individual to healthy functioning as quickly as possible. Tertiary prevention focuses on individuals who manifest clear and persistent signs of serious emotional disorder, and is oriented toward restoring such individuals to healthier levels of emotional adaptation. The first three levels of the model proposed by Jacobson et al. (1968) would appear to be associated with primary prevention, while the individualized crisis approach would be associated with secondary prevention. Crisis intervention as described by Butcher and Maudal (1976) would be associated with primary prevention, while crisis therapy would be associated with secondary prevention. In the schema developed by Baldwin (1978), the first three classes of crises would be mainly associated with primary prevention, maturational/developmental crises would be associated with primary or secondary prevention and crises reflecting psychopathology and psychiatric emergencies would be associated with secondary and possibly tertiary prevention.

Some Currently Utilized Models of Crisis Intervention

It has been noted that crisis intervention is provided in a wide diversity of settings. For example, crisis intervention may be provided in the community as part of a "hot line" or drop-in center, it may be provided in the clinic as a specific program for a mental health outpatient service, it may be part of certain services of a general hospital, or it may be a specific program in a psychiatric hospital. The theoretical view of crisis intervention plus the setting where crisis intervention is provided will significantly influence the approach to the intervention. With these factors in mind it is proposed that models of crisis intervention be viewed in relation to the following criteria: 1) the location of the crisis intervention service, 2) the role of the telephone in the crisis intervention service and the degree of direct, face-to-face contact between crisis-affected individual and crisis intervener, and 3) the level of intervention and prevention emphasized by the crisis intervention service. These criteria provide a framework from which some of the more commonly utilized models of crisis intervention may be examined.

Telephone Crisis Intervention Telephone crisis intervention is commonly associated with suicide prevention, and it has been the subject of considerable discussion and research. This research has focused on areas such as the nature of the telephone caller (Apsler & Hoople, 1976), the process and technique of telephone crisis intervention (Lester & Brockopp, 1973), and outcomes associated with crisis intervention by telephone (Slaikeu, Tulkin & Speer, 1975). Richard McGee has provided excellent documentation of telephone crisis intervention services (McGee, Knickerbocker, Fowler, Jennings, Ansel, Zelenka, & Marcus, 1972) and has prepared a comprehensive overview and critique of telephone crisis intervention approaches (McGee, 1974). In describing crisis intervention and counseling by telephone, Brockopp (1973b) has suggested five guidelines: 1) make an initial evaluation regarding the severity of the crisis situation, 2) develop a relationship with the person in crisis, 3) assist that person to identify the specific problem or crisis event, 4) assess and mobilize the person's strengths and resources, and 5) develop a plan of action.

There are two primary types of telephone crisis intervention. The first is usually community based and relies solely on telephone contact between the crisis-affected individual and crisis intervener. Telephone crisis intervention of this type tends to emphasize referral, environmental manipulation and general support, and is oriented toward primary prevention. In his critique of telephone crisis intervention, McGee (1974) suggests that this type of telephone crisis intervention is rapidly becoming outmoded.

In the second type of telephone crisis intervention, the service tends to be linked to a mental health facility where direct, face-to-face mental health services are provided. Such a telephone crisis intervention service may constitute a central element in the 24-hour coverage of the mental health facility, or it may serve as a critical part of the facility's initial contact with potential clients/patients. Telephone crisis intervention of this type is usually community based, but it may be institutionally based. It relates primarily to the first three levels of intervention described by Jacobson et al. (1968), but it may lead to the fourth level, or individualized intervention. Similarly, its focus remains primary prevention, but it may also be associated with secondary prevention, depending on the nature and disposition of the crisis situation described over the telephone.

Crisis Intervention Associated With a Mental Health Outpatient Facility. In the past decade, crisis intervention services have become firmly established as significant programs in a large variety of mental health outpatient facilities (Wolkon, 1972; Gottschalk, Fox, & Bates, 1973). Crisis intervention in such settings appears to be especially effective when provided on a "walk-in" basis, particularly where the faciliity offers extended hours of coverage. The individual who seeks assistance at a mental health outpatient facility may not require more than immediate crisis intervention as described by Butcher and Maudal (1976) or generic crisis intervention as described by Jacobson et al. (1968). Frequently, however, such an individual requires at least crisis therapy or individualized crisis intervention.

A mental health outpatient facility may be either community based or institutionally based. To offer effective crisis intervention services, though, it must have a genuine community orientation. While the telephone in such a service is extremely important, its primacy is reduced, as greater emphasis is generally placed on face-to-face assessment of the crisis affected individual. However, telephone crisis intervention may serve as a crucial adjunct once a plan of action to deal with the crisis has been developed. Crisis intervention associated with a mental health outpatient facility would probably utilize all four levels of intervention as described by Jacobson et al. (1968), and it would employ both crisis intervention and crisis therapy as described by Butcher and Maudal (1976). It is likely that crisis-affected individuals representative of all six classes of crisis described by Baldwin (1978) would appear at such a setting over a period of time. Crisis intervention in this type of setting would be focused on either primary or secondary prevention, depending on the nature of the crisis event and the emotional status of the crisis-affected individual.

Crisis Intervention Associated with a General Hospital. Crisis intervention may be provided in a variety of locations within a general hospital. For example, crisis intervention services may be appropriate in surgical settings (Janis, 1958); they may also be appropriate in intensive care units (Lynch, 1977). In such settings the crisis event affecting the patient (and family) usually derives from the life-threatening potential of the patient's medical condition. Under such circumstances crisis intervention is based on face-to-face contact, and would employ interventive strategies associated primarily with crises resulting from traumatic stress (Baldwin, 1978). These strategies would take the form of active environmental manipulation, and include support and direct suggestions to the patient, the medical/nursing staff and patient's family. Crisis intervention in such settings is usually very brief, and mainly oriented toward the primary prevention of emotional disorder as this relates to the stabilization and/or improvement of the patient's overall medical condition.

Crisis intervention in a general hospital is most commonly associated with the emergency room. This is particularly true when the emergency room has a mental health orientation and/or readily available mental health consultation. A broad spectrum of crisis-affected individuals may seek assistance at emergency rooms and a wide range of approaches to crisis intervention can be provided in the context of hospital emergency rooms (Bartolucci and Drayer, 1973). The nature of the crisis event which has brought the individual to the emergency room along with the emotional status of the crisis-affected individual will usually determine the type and level of crisis intervention provided. For example, following assessment the individual may be released with psychosocial recommendations and no specific follow-up, he or she may be referred to a social agency or mental health facility, he or she may receive brief crisis therapy in the emergency room, or may be admitted to a psychiatric inpatient facility. If serious physical consequences have been associated with the emotional crisis, it is likely that the individual will be hospitalized medically, with mental health intervention to follow.

Crisis intervention in hospital emergency rooms is based primarily on face-to-face interaction between the crisis-affected individual and crisis intervener. Though in a minority, some crisis-affected individuals who appear at a hospital emergency room may receive generic crisis intervention following assessment with primary prevention of emotional disorder as a goal. The majority of individuals who appear at a hospital emergency room as a result of a crisis situation are usually considered for more individualized direct treatment approaches to crisis intervention. The focus of treatment with such individuals is usually oriented toward the secondary prevention of emotional disorder, and on occasion toward tertiary prevention.

Crisis Intervention Associated with a Psychiatric Inpatient Facility. It is not uncommon for an individual to experience a crisis event which is severely disorganizing, and for which brief psychiatric hospitalization constitutes a prime alternative to continued outpatient crisis intervention. A crisis intervention approach to psychiatric hospitalization has been described by Decker and Stubblebine (1972) and Smith, Kaplan, and Siker (1974). Although psychiatric hospitalization is customarily associated with 24-hour-a-day inpatient care, crisis intervention services of this type can also be provided through programs of day hospitalization or night hospitalization. Crisis intervention associated with a psychiatric inpatient facility emphasizes removing the crisis-affected individual from the stressful environment associated with the crisis.

Optimally the inpatient or partial hospitalization aspect of this type of crisis intervention is utilized for only a brief time period, and it is strongly oriented toward active follow-up, and continued crisis intervention on an outpatient basis. Treatment modalities emphasized in this approach to crisis intervention are associated with psychiatric emergencies (Baldwin, 1978) and include medication, well-structured group and individual psychotherapy, and milieu therapy. Such an approach requires face-to-face interaction between the crisis affected individual and crisis intervener. This type of intervention is usually oriented toward secondary prevention of emotional disorder, but on occasion it may be oriented toward tertiary prevention.

PRAGMATIC APPROACH TO CRISIS INTERVENTION

The following approach to crisis intervention is based on the synthesis provided by Caplan (1964), and has been influenced by the wide applicability of crisis intervention. It is oriented toward an individualized approach to crisis intervention described by Jacobson, Strickler, and Morley (1968), and it is appropriate to all classes of crises described by Baldwin (1978). This approach may be used in a variety of settings, but it has been utilized with relative effectiveness in a community-oriented, hospital-based mental health outpatient facility which operates with an open intake and without a waiting list. It is based on face-to-face contact between a crisis-affected individual (patient) and a crisis intervener (therapist), and is oriented primarily toward rapid assessment and resolution of the crisis situation on an outpatient basis. If the individual's reaction to the crisis cannot be managed adequately on an outpatient basis, the approach lends itself to consideration of brief intermediate care such as day treatment or brief inpatient care as an extension of outpatient crisis intervention.

Rapid and accurate assessment of the crisis-affected individual and the crisis event is crucial under this approach, as a clear delineation of interventive strategies can only be determined with clinical accuracy following careful assessment. When evaluating a crisis-affected individual, a number of interrelated factors contribute to accurate assessment of the crisis situation and effective crisis intervention. These factors are as follows:

1. The nature of the crisis-affected individual;
2. The nature and background of the crisis event;
3. The nature of the setting where crisis intervention is provided;

4. The nature of the crisis intervener;
5. Some strategies used in crisis intervention;
6. Anticipated outcomes for the crisis-affected individual.

The Nature of the Crisis-Affected Individual

A crisis situation may affect an individual, more than one individual simultaneously, or an entire family. Findings derived from family therapy strongly suggest that a crisis which affects an individual usually has some effect on that individual's family. An entire family may be seriously affected by the crisis reaction of one family member, and it is not uncommon to encounter an entire family in crisis (Langsley, Kaplan, & Pittman, 1968). To simplify the present discussion our primary focus will be on the crisis-affected individual, although on many occasions this individual's family will have a significant role in the crisis situation.

In responding to a crisis-affected individual, time constraints have a definite effect on the process of assessment. Yet it is criticial to formulate thorough answers about the crisis-affected individual. Accordingly it is important to develop an understanding of the individual's psychosocial background, including some evaluation of the individual's reaction to previous crisis situations. It must be clearly understood, however, that the individual's subjective experience of the crisis and its severity is one of the most important aspects of assessing that individual. It is highly important to make an early appraisal of the individual's current level of emotional integration/disintegration, with respect to 1) his or her characteristic level of emotional adaptation and 2) the intensity of his or her reaction to the crisis situation. It is equally important to elicit and carefully assess the strengths and resources the crisis-affected individual can summon in coping with the crisis.

The Nature and Background of the Crisis Event

Under the present approach the assessment of the crisis event must be as thorough and exacting as the assessment of the individual in crisis. In assessing the nature of the crisis event questions may be directed toward the following areas.

The Family Context of the Crisis Event. Attention must again be focused on whether or not the crisis is essentially an individual crisis or a multiperson crisis, which may best be described as a family crisis.

The Specific Type of Crisis Event. Under the present approach, at least three factors assist in delineating the specific type of crisis event. 1) Is the crisis related mainly to normal developmental events, or is it related to unexpected ones? 2) Does the crisis event appear to be one which will respond positively to brief intervention, or does it have a clear potential to lead to more serious personal disorganization? 3) Is the crisis event new in the experience of the affected individual, or has there been prior experience with the same type of crisis?

A Unitary Crisis Versus a Combination of Crises. It is valuable to assess whether the crisis is unitary and relatively circumscribed, or whether a series of crises is at work. Consider the potentially different implications confronting the crisis intervener in assessing the following crisis situations: divorce versus a combination of divorce and job loss versus divorce combined with job loss and the sudden death of a family member.

The Developmental Stage of the Crisis. It is urgent that the developmental stage of the crisis situation presented by the crisis-affected individual be carefully assessed. Is help being sought in the early stages of crisis development, or in the later stages? Crisis intervention may operate more parsimoniously when applied to a crisis in the early stages of development. When an individual appears who is affected by a crisis in a later stage of development, more extensive approaches to crisis intervention may be indicated.

The Intensity of the Crisis Events. Crisis events are experienced by the crisis-affected individual with differing degrees of intensity. If the intensity of the crisis event is experienced as relatively mild, the crisis-affected individual can direct attention and energy to other life events with comparative ease. If the intensity of the crisis event is experienced as relatively severe, it tends to totally preoccupy the attention and energies of the crisis-affected individual.

The Setting of the Crisis Intervention

The atmosphere of the setting where services are provided exercises a significant influence on the type and quality of crisis intervention provided. The following factors are related to the setting where crisis intervention takes place.

The Interpersonal Culture of the Setting. The initial response of a help-giving facility to a crisis-affected individual is critical in determining the individual's response to intervention. It is of great importance that the ambiance of the facility be marked by receptivity, openness and warmth. This would imply that all staff would easily communicate an appropriate sense of responsiveness, concern and warmth to the individual in crisis. These communications must occur at both verbal and nonverbal levels.

The Professionalism of the Setting. It is probable that crisis intervention is most effective when performed by well-trained, sensitive, stable individuals. All staff who come in contact with the crisis-affected individual should be expected to have unusually high levels of professional responsibility and accountability. During all stages of the crisis intervention process, strong and consistent efforts must be made to assist the crisis-affected individual in sensing that those involved in the intervention are trustworthy, purposeful and competent.

The Emotional Climate Associated with Assessment. When warmth, receptivity and sensitivity are present in the interpersonal atmosphere of the facility where crisis intervention is provided, it is likely that the staff will be characterized by a relatively high degree of availability, flexibility and openness in responding to the crisis-affected individual. Such an atmosphere leads to immediate reception of the crisis-affected individual, extended hours of operation and a willingness to expend appropriate efforts in assisting the individual in resolving the crisis. Under such conditions, rapid, well-conceived intervention can begin in close temporal proximity to assessment, if not during assessment.

The Crisis Intervener

The demeanor and personal maturity of the crisis intervener have a profound effect on the process of crisis intervention. Whether this individual is a mental health professional, a preprofessional or a paraprofessional, the approach under consideration requires certain characteristics. These may be organized around the following areas: 1) training, 2) professional demeanor and 3) personal attributes.

The Training of the Crisis Intervener. The crisis intervener should be thoroughly trained in the nature of crisis phenomena, the multiplicity of effects which crisis situations may have on human behavior, and the variety of potential resolutions of crisis situations. The crisis intervener must possess an unusually broad grasp of interventive techniques which have demonstrated their effectiveness with a wide range of individuals in crisis. It is essential that the crisis intervener have a thorough knowledge of institutional and community resources; this is frequently indispensable in crisis intervention.

The Professional Demeanor of the Crisis Intervener. The crisis intervener must be comfortable in communicating a sense of responsiveness, respect for and commitment to the crisis-affected individual. Though projecting an attitude of warmth and concern, the communications of the crisis intervener should be clear, succinct and relatively direct. An attentive and clinically uncompromising attitude on the part of the crisis intervener is frequently indicated.

The Personal Characteristics of the Crisis Intervener. Crisis intervention is a complex and demanding process which requires a high degree of sensitivity, perseverance and maturity on the part of the crisis intervener. Personal requisites for an effective crisis intervener include emotional stability and maturity accompanied by an ability to be direct and to confront the individual when indicated. A good crisis intervener should possess relatively high frustration tolerance, should function well under a variety of interpersonal pressures and demands, and should possess a high degree of personal and interpersonal adaptability and security.

Intervention Strategies

The approach under discussion emphasizes the active participation of the crisis-affected individual in the strategies of intervention. Some of the more important strategies are organized around 1) therapist posture in crisis intervention, 2) central elements in a plan of crisis intervention, and 3) specific therapeutic modalities used in the intervention.

Therapist posture in crisis intervention. In addition to being relatively available and flexible in manner, the crisis intervener must critically observe and listen to the crisis-affected individual. The crisis intervener must be attuned to both verbal and nonverbal messages, and should be prepared to respond on both levels. Though warm and supportive in overall approach, the crisis intervener frequently must be questioning and straightforward in manner, and capable of setting firm limits. Interviews with the crisis-affected individual should tend to be goal limited and comparatively well structured.

Central elements in a plan of crisis intervention. Assuming that continued participation is indicated following assessment, a clear plan of crisis intervention is developed at this point. Some of the more important elements of such a plan include the following. The *time limitations* placed on crisis intervention should be marked by at least two considerations: flexibility and individuality. As individual differences are a significant factor, it is clinically unsound to limit crisis intervention to a predetermined number such as six or eight sessions for all individuals. One individual confronted with a crisis may achieve positive resolution with two crisis intervention sessions, while another individual confronted with a similar crisis might require two or three times as many sessions to achieve positive resolution.

The *frequency and spacing of face-to-face sessions* will vary somewhat depending on the level of organization/disorganization of the crisis-affected individual and the nature of the crisis situation. Sessions immediately following assessment are frequently spaced close together, and it is not uncommon to see a crisis-affected individual two or three times during the first week following assessment. As the individual begins to use his or her own resouuces in coping with the crisis situation, sessions tend to be spaced farther apart.

Telephone contact with the crisis-affected individual can be a crucial adjunct to face-to-face contact. Under certain circumstances the crisis-affected individual may be encouraged to telephone the crisis intervener or a staff member at the crisis service. In some circumstances it may be important for the crisis intervener to initiate telephone contact. Once the process of intervention has begun, 24-hour telephone availability of a staff member at the crisis intervention service is extremely important.

Contact with family members and friends is often an important aspect of a plan of crisis intervention. In many situations the therapist may encourage the crisis-affected individual to seek out increased contact with family members or friends, as such contacts may be very helpful in working toward resolving the crisis situation. If it is a family crisis, it becomes extremely important that the crisis intervener have direct contact with family members. If the crisis-affected individual is a minor, it is mandatory that the crisis intervener initiate contact with family members.

As a special form of contact with family or friends, a *home visit* by the crisis intervener may be indicated. This is valuable in assessing the psychological atmosphere of the crisis-affected individual's place of residence, and observing directly how that person interacts with family members and/or friends. Home visiting is essential where the possibility of child abuse or neglect, other types of physical abuse or extreme social isolation may constitute active ingredients in the crisis situation.

A final aspect of the plan of intervention relates to *direct suggestions* made by the crisis intervener to the crisis-affected individual. An individual in crisis frequently has a heightened receptivity to such suggestions, and they can be quite useful in helping to restore emotional equilibrium. While quite varied in content, such direct suggestions are usually goal oriented.

Specific therapeutic modalities used in crisis intervention.

Frequently one, or at the most two, sessions of individual contact (including the assessment session) are sufficient to assist in positive resolution for an individual in crisis. *Crisis resolution during assessment* is similar to generic crisis intervention. It places heavy emphasis on clarification of the crisis situation and makes use of direct suggestions to the crisis-affected individual. Many times a second session is held to follow up the discussion of the assessment session and to solidify the process of resolution.

Two levels of individual crisis therapy may also be utilized. *Very brief crisis therapy* lasts from two to four sessions. If longer contact is indicated, *crisis therapy* might range from four to eight, or possibly ten, sessions. To the extent possible, it is important to make a tentative decision about the length of crisis therapy required immediately following, if not during, assessment. Either level of crisis therapy may be combined with participation in a *crisis group* such as that described by Allgeyer (1970), in which the process of crisis resolution will be enhanced by group participation.

Tranquilizing medication may also serve as a useful adjunctive modality if the level of disorganization of the crisis-affected individual warrants it. In crisis intervention medication may be supplied in limited amounts and for a limited period of time. It is important that tranquilizing medication be used as part of an overall plan of crisis intervention, and not as the only modality of treatment.

Crisis-oriented day treatment (or night hospitalization) may also be instituted on a brief basis if the level of disorganization of the crisis-affected individual is sufficiently severe. Crisis-oriented day treatment may be indicated when the work of crisis resolution will be enhanced by having the individual leave his or her customary interpersonal environment for a substantial period of time each day. Brief crisis-oriented psychiatric hospitalization may also be utilized if the individual in crisis presents a clear threat to himself or others. In the approach under discussion both day treatment and psychiatric hospitalization are oriented toward rapid return to outpatient status as part of crisis resolution.

Anticipated Outcomes for The Crisis-Affected Individual

The most positive outcome of crisis intervention is associated with effective resolution of the crisis situation, and improved coping mechanisms and emotional growth on the part of the affected individual. Specific outcomes depend on 1) the level of organization/disorganization of the crisis-affected individual, 2) the nature and severity of the crisis situation, 3) the measures of crisis intervention applied and 4) the degree to which the crisis situation is resolved adaptively. Assuming that some degree of adaptive crisis resolution has occurred, outcome would be associated with: crisis resolution followed by no further intervention/therapy; brief, follow-up intervention/therapy subsequent to crisis resolution; or crisis resolution followed by further intervention and, possibly, ongoing psychotherapy. Crisis situations which can be resolved during the process of assessment would probably require no further intervention. With respect to situations which require crisis therapy, the process of intervention should be oriented toward effective resolution of the crisis within the framework of crisis intervention. When serious doubt exists about the thoroughness of crisis resolution, however, brief crisis-oriented follow-up or short-term continued psychotherapy may be indicated. Where the crisis situation has involved serious personal disorganization and has required more extensive intervention, including day treatment or psychiatric hospitalization, ongoing psychotherapy is usually crucial following the period of crisis intervention.

While a primary goal of crisis intervention is rapid and adaptive crisis resolution, it is important to note that even with well-conceived, positive crisis intervention, some crisis-affected individuals may require or may choose to continue in some form of therapy following intervention. An experience with a crisis situation which requires mental health assistance continues to serve many individuals as a legitimate point of entry into a system of mental health care. These factors would suggest that crisis intervention cannot be classified as a failure, nor are contradictions necessarily inherent when crisis intervention is followed by ongoing psychotherapy when this is clinically indicated.

EVALUATION OF CRISIS INTERVENTION SERVICES

Evaluation of crisis-intervention services has not kept pace with their rapid proliferation. During the last few years, however, evaluative studies have emerged which have suggested that evaluation of crisis intervention is confounded by a number of complex issues, among which are the following:

1) What does the concept of crisis intervention mean, and how can it best be defined for evaluative purposes?

2) What are the most effective methods to define the individual in crisis?

3) Is it more appropriate to define an individual, or a family, as being in crisis?

4) What are the operations or techniques the crisis intervener actually performs when engaging in crisis intervention?

5) What factors outside of the immediate treatment setting may affect a person's reaction to crisis intervention: e.g., age, socioeconomic status, emotional resiliency, contact with family members, etc.?

6) Is the outcome of crisis intervention evaluated best from the patient's perspective, that of the crisis intervener, or some other perspective(s)?

The research literature which has emerged thus far has tended to focus on the setting where crisis intervention is practiced, as well as with the type of individual who receives crisis intervention. In an excellent critique Auerbach and Kilmann (1977) presented a comprehensive overview of outcome research on crisis intervention which focused on the following areas: programs of crisis intervention in surgical settings, suicide prevention/crisis intervention programs, and programs of crisis intervention in mental health/psychiatric settings. The following summarizes some of the elements of their critique.

Evaluation of Crisis Intervention In Surgical Settings

As noted earlier in the chapter, impending surgery constitutes an event of crisis proportions for many individuals. Evaluative studies in this area indicate that intervention should be oriented toward a specific and realistic assessment of the impending stress, although it is clear that there is an individualized reaction to stress associated with surgery. Auerbach and Kilmann (1977) indicate that studies of crisis intervention in surgical settings have demonstrated the need to develop intervention techniques which take cognizance of individual differences in reaction to stress.

Evaluation of Crisis Intervention/Suicide Prevention Services

There have been a relatively large number of evaluative studies of crisis intervention as it is practiced in relation to telephone crisis intervention/suicide prevention systems. This type of crisis intervention has been described more fully in the previous section. Some studies in crisis intervention/suicide prevention have focused on factors such as reduction of the overall suicide rate and follow-up of individual patients after utilization of suicide prevention measures. Bagley (1968) compared suicide rates in two sets of English towns following an attempt to match the towns on variables such as social class, population structure, percentage of new houses built, housing conditions, and so on. The experimental towns all had a 24-hour telephone crisis service operated either by the clergy or "intelligent layman," all of whom had received specific training in telephone crisis work. The authors stated that the average suicide rate in the towns with this service decreased 5.8 percent following the institution of the telephone crisis service. Over the same time period the average suicide rate in control towns increased 19.8 percent. Greer and Bagley (1971) studied 204 patients who presented themselves to a hospital "with deliberate self-poisoning or self-injury." These individuals were followed up after an average interval of 18 months. Forty-seven of these patients were not seen by a psychiatrist prior to hospital discharge. These 47 patients were compared with 76 patients who were treated briefly by a psychiatrist for a maximum of two sessions and another group of 88 patients who underwent longer psychiatric treatment. The authors found that subsequent suicide attempts occurred with significantly greater frequency among untreated patients than among treated patients, and that longer psychiatric treatment was associated with the best prognosis.

Crisis intervention/suicide prevention services have also been evaluated in terms of criteria which do not depend specifically on suicidal actions as outcome measures. For example, the effectiveness of telephone crisis response workers has been studied in some detail, although findings remain equivocal. Slaikeu, Tulkin, and Speer (1975), in studying outcome in relation to telephone crisis services, found no relationship between ratings of the empathy and concreteness of the telephone respondent and follow-up ratings by the telephone callers as to the performance of the telephone crisis workers.

Other studies have utilized patient follow-through for a face-to-face appointment as a measure of change. Slaikeu, Lester, and Tulkin (1973) studied whether or not the telephone caller actually showed up for a face-to-face appointment for which a referral was made during the telephone contact, and found that two factors were involved. These were the rated concreteness of the telephone crisis intervener in responding to the telephone caller, and the degree of motivation on the part of the caller for receiving assistance. In a subsequent study Slaikeu, Tulkin, and Speer (1975) evaluated the telephone callers' responses by means of a follow-up questionnaire. Results from the questionnaire suggested that many individuals who did not appear or cancelled the face-to-face appointment following an initial telephone contact apparently took some form of action to alleviate the problems which had prompted the call.

In studies of telephone crisis intervention there has been a tendency to identify an individual as being in crisis primarily on the basis of having contacted a telephone crisis intervention/suicide prevention service. In such studies data which would corroborate the nature and extent of the telephone caller's self-described crisis are frequently lacking. Questions remain about the adequacy of using such a criterion to evaluate the effectiveness of a telephone crisis response system. There appears to be a strong need to develop more concise follow-up data to assess critically what actually happens to the individual in crisis following crisis intervention via telephone. Auerbach and Kilmann (1977) also urge that research studies in this area focus greater attention on specific patient outcomes, particularly as these relate to the explicitly stated goals of the crisis service.

Evaluation of Crisis Intervention In Mental Health/Psychiatric Settings

As noted previously, a wide variety of crisis intervention services have developed in mental health/psychiatric settings. A relatively large number of evaluative studies of crisis intervention in such settings has been undertaken. In their review Auerbach and Kilmann (1977) discuss studies organized around a comparison between crisis intervention approaches and no formal psychotherapy, and a comparison between crisis intervention approaches and more traditional therapeutic approaches. They also review studies which focused on subjective factors in patients, and treatment variables which might be predictive of outcome in relation to crisis intervention. A number of these and other studies are described briefly, as they typify the present state of evaluation of crisis intervention in mental/psychiatric settings.

With respect to a comparison of crisis intervention services with no formal therapy, Gottschalk, Fox, and Bates (1973) assigned 68 patients who had come voluntarily to a crisis intervention clinic to one of two groups. The patients assigned to the first group received immediate intervention therapy, while the patients in the second group were placed on a waiting list. At the end of six weeks there was no change in the psychiatric morbidity scores of the two groups; both groups showed improvement. Polak, Egan, Vandenbergh, and Williams (1975) conducted a study in which families who had experienced the sudden death of a family member were given crisis intervention. They were compared at follow-up intervals of six months and eighteen months with two untreated control groups. The results did not support the hypothesis that such services decrease the risk of psychiatric illness, disturbed family functioning or increased social cost to the families.

With respect to a comparison of crisis intervention services with more traditional psychiatric services, Langsley, Machotka, and Flomenhaft (1971) randomly assigned three hundred patients requiring immediate hospitalization to outpatient family crisis therapy or to psychiatric hospitalization. Post-treatment follow-up indicated that the patients treated without hospital admission were less likely to be hospitalized after treatment, and that their length of hospitalization was significantly shorter. At six-month and eighteen-month follow-up periods, patients treated by family crisis therapy were doing as well as those who had been hospitalized, as indicated by two measures of social adaptation. Decker and Stubblebine (1972) followed two groups of young adults for two and half years subsequent to their first psychiatric hospitalization. The first group received traditional modes of psychiatric treatment, while the second group was hospitalized after the institution of a crisis intervention program. The researchers found that a crisis intervention approach, as compared with traditional approaches to psychiatric hospitalization tended to reduce rehospitalization over an extended time period. In a subsequent study Smith, Kaplan, and Siker (1974) found results similar to those of Decker and Stubblebine (1972), but noted that poor outcome for this type of crisis intervention tended to involve certain types of individuals.

Gottschalk, Mayerson, and Gottleib (1967) evaluated the effectiveness of short-term psychotherapy with acutely disturbed psychiatric patients. They used two groups totaling 53 patients. Treatment was directed toward crisis resolution with goals being the alleviation of symptoms and the return of the patient to premorbid levels of functioning. Therapeutic effects of this approach were evaluated at two follow-up intervals. Significant improvement was made by patients who completed therapy in terms of a psychiatric morbidity score; these gains were maintained at the time of the second follow-up. The authors found that the best predictors of a low psychiatric morbidity score at the first follow-up were low pretherapy psychiatric morbidity scores and high pretherapy scores in the areas of human relations, social alienation and personal disorganization. Subsequently, in the study by Gottschalk, Fox, and Bates (1973) noted earlier, patients were given either immediate crisis intervention or placed on a waiting list for six weeks. The authors again found that the best predictor of a patient's condition at the end of this time period was the pretreatment psychiatric morbidity score.

Treatment factors which appear to be associated with positive response to crisis intervention approaches have been evaluated in a number of studies. Rusk and Gerner (1972) studied therapist activity level as it related to outcome of crisis intervention. They administered an adjective check list related primarily to feelings of anxiety and depression to 38 patients before and after a crisis interview at a psychiatric emergency room. For patients who showed the greatest decreases in anxiety and depression from pre- to post-treatment, the authors found that the therapists talked for significantly less time in the first third of the interview and for more time in the last third. Wolkon (1972) studied time from application for psychotherapy to first appointment as a treatment variable. He reviewed 379 applicants for outpatient psychotherapy drawn from three different agencies in an effort to evaluate whether intervention is more successful when there is least amount of delay between application for psychotherapy and the first scheduled interview. He found that a greater percentage of persons with less elapsed time between initial contact and first scheduled appointment actually kept the appointment. Improvement ratings made at the termination of therapy by the therapists indicated that the shorter the period of delay between initial contact and first scheduled appointment, the greater the probability of improvement.

Maris and Connor (1973) assessed the effects of crisis therapy on 200 psychiatric emergency-room patients. They used patient reports of self-satisfaction, depression and primary complaints as outcome measures. These measures were administered at intake with a follow-up at eight to twelve months. The authors noted that participation in therapy at the time of follow-up was positively related to improvement. They also found that patients receiving larger doses of medication reflected more improvement than did those receiving smaller doses, regardless of type of medication.

In concluding their critique of outcome research in crisis intervention, Auerbach and Kilmann (1977) emphasize the need for a comprehensive model of crisis intervention which would include data from diverse sources while assisting in the structure of future research efforts. They indicate that a comprehensive model of crisis intervention should

> (a) specify operationally the criteria for classification of stressors as crises and for classification of individuals as being in a state of crisis, (b) account for the pattern of emotional arousal and development of interference behaviors for different classes of crises for different types of individuals, and (c) specify appropriate points of intervention with those techniques for given person/crisis that will maximize coping ability and minimize emotional distress.

These suggestions are consistent with those of Taplin (1971), who also has described the need to develop systematic research definitions to evaluate crisis intervention.

A number of the evaluative studies which have been discussed show promise for validating the effectiveness of crisis intervention. From a research standpoint, however, answers to a number of important questions remain unclear. A primary question concerns the manner in which crisis intervention actually operates. Crisis intervention has tended to be defined broadly and at times loosely, thus compounding the difficulties already inherent in carefully delineating the theoretical and behavioral concepts utilized as a part of it. A second question relates to the relative effectiveness of crisis intervention approaches. Some of the studies cited have made an effort to compare crisis intervention with other forms of therapy or with no formal therapy. Yet although positive claims continue to be made about the comparative effectiveness of crisis intervention, these claims are lacking clear and consistent research confirmation. Another question concerns the types of individuals for whom crisis intervention may be most appropriate. Some important beginnings have been made toward answering this question, but further research is strongly indicated. For example, clinical experience suggests that some individuals should rely primarily on their own personal and interpersonal resources when confronted with a crisis situation, other individuals may respond well to therapeutic intervention other than crisis intervention, and a large number of individuals would probably respond well to some form of crisis intervention. A fourth question relates to the type of crisis events which are most appropriate for crisis intervention. There has been a tendency to assume that crisis intervention is appropriate for individuals confronted with a broad spectrum of crisis situations. In addition to problems encountered in developing a consistent definition of what constitutes a crisis situation, there is no clear research evidence which validates this assumption.

While well-designed, carefully-controlled research efforts are most important in relation to crisis intervention, it should be recognized that almost forty years of research of varying degrees of scientific rigor on more well-established forms of therapeutic intervention have tended to result in equivocal findings about process and outcome. Nevertheless there are at least two major contributions which await more rigorous evaluative studies in the area of crisis intervention. Studies in this area utilizing careful experimental design and methodology are admittedly difficult to implement. However, such studies will undoubtedly add clarity to the concept of crisis state while adding greatly to our knowledge of human behavior during and after crisis intervention. Scientifically rigorous studies in this area would also bring greater coherence to program evaluation in crisis intervention. This in turn would lead to improvement in developing crisis intervention programs, and greater professional accountability in the delivery of crisis intervention services.

FUTURE DEVELOPMENTS IN CRISIS INTERVENTION

It is likely that crisis intervention approaches will continue to grow in acceptance, utilization and scope in the years ahead. With this growth, problems will continue to arise. If we are to expand our knowledge of crisis theory and crisis intervention, and if crisis intervention approaches are to keep fulfilling the promise they hold, these problems will require effective resolution.

Potential Problem Areas Associated With the Growth of Crisis Intervention

One of the more serious problems associated with the ongoing development of crisis intervention concerns evaluation. This problem has been the focus of a discussion in a previous section of this chapter. It is mentioned at this point to underscore its crucial importance.

Another problem area concerns the widespread utilization of crisis intervention as a therapeutic technique. Presently an extremely wide range of mental health professionals and mental health systems indicate that crisis intervention constitutes an important part of their repertoire. As a consequence crisis intervention is in danger of becoming like parenthood, with almost everyone in favor of it, but in an indiscriminate fashion. This development is suggestive of a tendency to use the term crisis intervention as a form of window dressing without having a substantive, genuine, well-planned crisis service to back it up. This approach to crisis intervention suggests a diminished understanding of the concept along with poorly developed crisis intervention services. Ultimately such a misleading use of the concept may result in active harm to the potential consumer of these services. If problems associated with this tendency are not addressed effectively, the utilization of crisis intervention may become impaired and its potential seriously diminished.

A third problem area relates to the need for careful, well-organized, systematic training for those who would be crisis interveners (Wallace & Morley, 1970). As stated by Baldwin (1977), a number of myths have confounded training in crisis intervention. One particular myth noted by Baldwin (1977) suggests that crisis intervention is a relatively simple approach to therapy requiring few special skills other than those utilized by the professional psychotherapist trained in relatively long-term therapeutic approaches. Baldwin (1977) asserts that there are special skills related to crisis intervention which must be integrated with more traditional skills before one can expect to become a well-trained crisis intervener. The present discussion has strongly supported this assertion.

A related fallacy about crisis intervention also lingers on. It implies that almost anyone can intervene in a crisis and be equally effective. While this may be true in the general sense that family and friends are usually quite helpful when one encounters a crisis situation, it is not true in a more specific sense. As noted ten years ago (T.F. McGee, 1968) more, rather than less, rigorous training in crisis intervention may be required if one is to be effective and realistic when intervening with a crisis-affected individual. It is extremely important that aspiring crisis interveners be soundly grounded in an understanding of the vicissitudes of human behavior and the multiplicity of effects of crisis events on human behavior in order to understand and help resolve conflicts associated with crises. It is equally important that the would-be intervener have a strong grasp of the feelings and fantasies that a crisis-affected individual may arouse in the intervener, be they anxious, fearful, heroic or even omnipotent. Unless training specific to the practice of crisis intervention continues to be given a high level of importance, crisis intervention may be misused, and its value is likely to be seriously questioned.

Another potential problem area for crisis intervention relates to its limitations. Due to the rapid growth and broad acceptance of crisis intervention, it may be in danger of being oversold. It is important that crisis intervention not be seen as a panacea for a wide variety of emotional disorders, and that it not be utilized with a pseudo-religious fervor to the exclusion of other therapeutic approaches. Those involved in providing crisis services should continue to make a clear assessment of when to use crisis intervention as the major form of intervention, when to use it in conjunction with other therapeutic approaches, and when it may be contra-indicated. If crisis intervention becomes oversold as a therapeutic technique or becomes utilized indiscriminately, this too will severely restrict its potential effectiveness.

The Continued Promise of Crisis Intervention

If problems associated with the continued growth of crisis intervention are clearly acknowledged and resolved, there is little doubt that crisis intervention will continue to hold great promise as modality of intervention and/or treatment.

As has been noted by Spiegel (1974) and others, a variety of life crises is encountered by everyone. In many instances these crises may be resolved solely by the individual so affected or with the assistance of family and friends. At other times, professional mental assistance may be sought. Despite improved societal acceptance of mental health care and the concomitant demystification of therapeutic techniques, many individuals remain reluctant to acknowledge emotional difficulties or to seek some form of mental health assistance directly. It is clear that many individuals still seek mental health assistance only when confronted with a life crisis or series of crises that are emotionally stressful and potentially disorganizing. There is little doubt that crisis intervention will continue to be an indispensable mental health approach in responding to such individuals. In this regard crisis intervention will continue to serve as a most important first level of assessment and intervention in providing services to individuals who are in the early stages of emotional disorganization.

Although comprehensive data are lacking, consumer acceptance of crisis intervention services appears high, particularly when such services are soundly conceived and delivered in an atmosphere of professional excellence. Consumer receptivity may relate to the emphasis placed on availability and immediacy, the here and now focus of intervention, and the clearly defined, relatively attainable goals associated with it. Despite a lack of definitive knowledge about the consequences of such intervention, results associated with crisis intervention have tended to appear rapidly, and subjective improvement is commonly noted. Crisis intervention has contributed to positive outcome in a wide variety of situations which might have led to serious emotional disorganization. As a result of crisis intervention services, many individuals have received effective assistance and have been helped through a series of situations ranging from normal developmental crises to life-threatening emergencies. There is little doubt that unnecessary hospitalization and institutionalization, if not overt tragedy, have been avoided by many individuals through the positive application of crisis intervention approaches.

One of the more significant observations associated with crisis theory suggests that at a time of crisis many individuals experience a heightened willingness to examine emotional conflicts that relate to the crisis. This observation is true for the individual who will attempt to resolve the crisis without mental health assistance, it is valid for the individual who seeks mental health assistance in connection with a crisis, and it holds for the individual who is already in some form of therapy. Rusk (1971), among others, notes that life crises present the individual with a unique opportunity, if not a challenge, to experience change and growth. This is particularly true when the crisis experience is examined carefully, understood relatively well, and resolved effectively. Mental health professionals will continue to play an important role in assisting and clarifying this process. It is likely that the prospect of positive resolution and potential emotional growth as a consequence of a crisis experience will continue to exercise a salutary effect on the future of crisis intervention.

References

Aguilera, D. C., & Messick, J. M. *Crisis intervention: Theory and methodology.* New York: Mosby, 1974.

Allgeyer, J. M. The crisis group: Its unique usefulness to the disadvantaged. *International Journal of Group Psychotherapy,* 1970, *20*, 235–240.

Apsler, R., & Hoople, H. Evaluation of crisis intervention services with anonymous clients. *American Journal of Community Psychology,* 1976, *4*, 293–302.

Auerbach, S. M., & Kilmann, P. R. Crisis intervention: A review of outcome research. *Psychological Bulletin*, 1977, *84*, 1189–1217.

Bagley, B. A. The evaluation of a suicide prevention schema by an ecological method. *Social Science and Medicine,* 1968, *2*, 1–14.

Baldwin, B. A. Crisis intervention in professional practice: Impliications for clinical training. *American Journal of Orthopsychiatry*, 1977, *47*, 659–670.

Baldwin, B. A. A paradigm for the classification of emotional crises: Implications for crisis intervention. *American Journal of Orthopsychiatry*, 1978, *48*, 538–551.

Bartolucci, G., & Drayer, C. S. An overview of crisis intervention in the emergency room of general hospitals. *The American Journal of Psychiatry*, 1973, *130*, 953–960.

Brockopp, G. W. Crisis intervention: Theory, process and practice. In D. Lester & G. W. Brockopp (Eds.), *Crisis intervention and counseling by telephone.* Springfield, Ill.: Thomas, 1973a, 89–104.

Brockopp, G. W. Training the telephone counselor. In D. Laster & G.W. Brockopp (Eds.), *Crisis intervention and counselling by telephone.* Springfield, Ill.: Thomas, 1973b, 262–272.

Butcher, J. N., & Maudal, G. R. Crisis intervention. In I. Weiner (Ed.), *Clinical methods in psychology.* New York: Wiley, 1976, 591–648.

Caplan, G. Practical steps for the family physician in the prevention of emotional disorder. *Journal of the American Medical Association*, 1959, *170*, 1497–1506.

Caplan, G. *An approach to community mental health.* New York: Grune & Stratton, 1961.

Caplan, G. *Principles of preventive psychiatry.* New York: Basic, 1964.

Caplan, G., & Grunebaum, H. Perspectives on primary prevention: A review. *Archives of General Psychiatry*, 1967, *17*, 331–346.

Decker, J. B., & Stubblebine, J. M. Crisis intervention and prevention of psychiatric disability: A follow-up study. *American Journal of Psychiatry*, 1972, *129*, 725–729.

Erikson, E. H. *Childhood and society.* New York: Norton, 1950.

Farberow, N. L. *Suicide.* Morristown, N.J.: General Learning, 1974.

Gottschalk, L. A., Fox, R. A., & Bates, D. E. A study of prediction and outcome in a mental health crisis clinic. *American Journal of Psychiatry*, 1973, *130*, 1107–1111.

Gottschalk, L.A., Mayerson, P., & Gottlieb, A. Prediction and evaluation of outcome in an emergency brief psychotherapy clinic. *Journal of Nervous and Mental Disease*, 1967, *144*, 77–96.

Greer, S., & Bagley, C. Effect of psychiatric intervention in attempted suicide: A controlled study. *British Medical Journal*, 1971, *1*, 310–312.

Henisz, J. E., & Johnson, D. A crisis model revisited. *Comprehensive Psychiatry*, 1977, *18*, 169–175.

Jacobson, G., Strickler, M., & Morley, W. Generic and individual approaches to crisis intervention. *American Journal of Public Health*, 1968, *58*, 338–343.

Janis, I.L. *Psychological stress.* New York: Wiley, 1958.

Korchin, S. *Modern clinical psychology: Principles of intervention in the clinic and community.* New York: Basic, 1976.

Langsley, D. G., Kaplan, D. M., & Pittman, F. S. *The treatment of families in crisis.* New York: Grune & Stratton, 1968.

Langsley, D. G., Machotka, P., & Flomenhaft, K. Avoiding mental hospital admissions: A follow-up study. *American Journal of Psychiatry*, 1971, *127*, 1391–1394.

Lester, D., & Brockopp, G. S. *Crisis intervention and counseling by telephone.* Springfield, Ill.: Thomas, 1973.

Lindemann, E. Symptomatology and management of acute grief. *American Journal of Psychiatry*, 1944, *101*, 141–148.

Lynch, J. L. The broken heart: The medical consequences of loneliness. New York: Basic, 1977.

Maris, R., & Connor, H. E. Do crisis services work? A follow-up of a psychiatric outpatient sample. *Journal of Health and Social Behavior*, 1973, *14*, 311–322.

McGee, R. K. *Crisis intervention in the community.* Baltimore, Md.: University Park, 1974.

McGee, R. K., Knickerbocker, D. A., Fowler, D. E., Jennings, B., Ansel, E. L., Zelenka, M. H., & Marcus, S. Evaluation of crisis intervention programs and personnel: A summary and critique. *Life Threatening Behavior*, 1972, *2*, 168–182.

McGee, T. F. Some basic considerations in crisis intervention. *Community Mental Health Journal*, 1968, *4*, 319–325.

Morley, W. E. Theory of crisis intervention. *Pastoral Psychology*, 1970, *21*, 14–20.

Morrice, J. *Crisis intervention: Studies in community care.* New York: Pergamon, 1976.

Polak, P. R., Egan, D., Vandenbergh, R., & Williams, W. V. Prevention in mental health: A controlled study. *American Journal of Psychiatry*, 1975, *132*, 146–149.

Rusk, T. N. Opportunity and technique in crisis psychiatry. *Comprehensive Psychiatry*, 1971, *12*, 249–263.

Rusk, T. N., & Gerner, R. H. A study of the process of emergency psychotherapy. *American Journal of Psychiatry*, 1972, *128*, 882–885.

Schulberg, H. C., & Sheldon, A. The probability of crisis and strategies for preventive intervention. *Archives of General Psychiatry*, 1968, *18*, 553–558.

Shneidman, E. S. Crisis intervention: Some thoughts and perspectives. In G. Specter and W. Claiborn (Eds.), *Crisis intervention*. New York: Behavioral Publications, 1973.

Slaikeu, K., Lester, D., & Tulkin, S. R. Show versus no show: A comparison of referral calls to a suicide prevention and crisis service. *Journal of Consulting and Clinical Psychology*, 1973, *40*, 481–486.

Slaikeu, K., Tulkin, S. R., & Speer, D. C. Process and outcome in the evaluation of telephone counseling referrals. *Journal of Consulting and Clinical Psychology*, 1975, *43*, 700–707.

Smith, W. G., Kaplan, J., & Siker, D. Community mental health and the seriously disturbed patient: First admission outcomes. *Archives of General Psychiatry*, 1974, *30*, 693–696.

Spiegel, R. Life's major and minor crises. In S. Arieti (Ed.), *American Handbook of Psychiatry* (Vol. I; 2nd Ed.). New York: Basic, 1974.

Taplin, J. R. Crisis theory: Critique and reformulation. *Community Mental Health Journal*, 1971, *7*, 13–23.

Tyhurst, J. S. Individual reactions to community disaster: The natural history of psychiatric phenomena. *American Journal of Psychiatry*, 1951, *107*, 764–769.

Wallace, M., & Morley, W. Teaching crisis intervention. *The American Journal Of Nursing*, 1970, *70*, 1484–1487.

Wolkon, G. H. Crisis theory, the application for treatment and dependency. *Comprehensive Psychiatry*, 1972, *13*, 459–464.

CHAPTER 10

Mental Health Consultation and Programmatic Change

Juliana Rasic Lachenmeyer, Ph.D.

Efforts at systematic change within the community will be divided into two broad topics in this chapter. The first will focus on mental health consultation: typologies of mental health consultation with an emphasis on Caplan's typology, comparison of consultation and other interpersonal processes such as education and psychotherapy, implications of the role of the mental health consultant for training individuals to be consultants, and the ways in which group consultation differs from individual consultation. Included in this section will be a lengthy discussion of indirect ways of handlng inappropriate consultee affect.

The second part of the chapter will look at programmatic efforts at social change. Two types of intervention strategies will be discussed: behavioral ones applied to community intervention, and organizational development.

Although many of the interpersonal processes of intervention are the same regardless of the orientation of the consultant, there are enough differences between behavioral interventions and mental health consultation to suggest that a separate discussion of the behavioral attempts at change would be useful. First, behavioral interventions tend to be programmatic efforts rather than individual ones. This, then, has different implications for implementation of a program. Secondly, to varying degrees, behavioral programs adhere to certain principles. Thirdly, behavioral programs emphasize constant research and evaluation. In this chapter, a brief statement of the application of behavioral principles in the community setting will be made. This will be followed by a review of the research on behavioral programs and then a discussion of the current status of these findings. Because of the topic covered, the section on behavioral intervention will include a greater discussion of research than will that section on mental health consultation.

There is a final part of this chapter that briefly focuses on the Organizational Development approach to organizational change. Although this approach has not been widely implemented within the area of community mental health, organizational development is one of the dominant organizational change strategies in industry.

MENTAL HEALTH CONSULTATION

There are two broad functions of mental health agencies: assessment of the need for services and delivery of those services. The relative emphasis on one or the other by an agency may differ. Consultation refers to the providing of technical assistance by an expert to individual(s) or to groups within an agency on aspects of their work related to mental health. The often-made distinction between product and process is difficult to maintain in any service occupation (for further discussion of this issue, see Chapter 13).

The consultant has primarily an advisory role, with no direct responsibility for the acceptance or implementation of the advice she or he gives. Even when the focus of the referral is a problem with a client, the responsibility for dealing with the client is in the hands of the consultee. The power of the consultant lies in her or his ability to influence, her or his perceived expertise and the perception of this expertise as relevant to the problem at hand. The perceptions of the consultee will be affected by the consultant's point of entry into the organization and her or his source of support within the organization.

According to MacLennan, Quinn, and Schroeder (1975), the consultation task can be one of six: a) referral or management of an individual, family or client group, or of feelings of the consultee about the client; b) concern with administration and staff organization and relationships either within an agency, between an agency and the community or between several agencies; between staff members or between administration and staff; c) assisting an individual or agency to assess the nature and genesis of mental health problems and the need for programs; d) advising on planning and development of research, training or service programs and evaluation; e) transmitting knowledge regarding general human relationships, human growth and development, social organization and mental health problems; f) transmitting skills in treatment, training, research, administration and evaluation. These six types of tasks are then collapsed into two broad categories: program consultation and human relations (consultee and case) consultation. The former refers to problems in planning, development, management, coordination and evaluation of services. These are usually done with the general administration and planning staff and may result in new services or policies. Human relations consultation deals with day-to-day functioning. The categorization scheme that has been most widely applied is Caplan's (1970): client-centered, consultee-centered and program-centered consultation.

Types of Mental Health Consultation

Client-Centered Consultation This is the most traditional form of consultation. In its early form it involved case-oriented psychiatric evaluation (Abrahamson, 1968; Aldrich, 1968; Mendel, 1966). Client-centered consultation is the most frequent point of entry for the consultant, who makes an assessment of the client's problems and suggests ways to handle them. Although the focus is on the client's problems, the goal is to improve the consultee's knowledge so that she or he can handle similar problems in the future.

Consultee-Centered Consultation In this type of consultation the problems with the client provide much of the content for the consultation. However, the focus is on the consultee's difficulty in dealing with the problems. The education of the consultee is primary. The fact that the consultation centers on the consultee may or may not be made explicit. The direct and indirect handling of inappropriate consultee affect will be discussed later in this chapter.

Program-Centered Consultation Program-centered consultation is similar to client-centered consultation except that the problems involved are those of administering programs rather than handling cases. The program itself may not directly involve mental health, and the focus is only secondarily on consultee education. According to Heller and Monahan (1977) the assumption behind this kind of consultation is that since primary care givers constantly deal with human behavior and its problems, the more they know about psychological development, behavioral dynamics and how to implement programs, the more likely that a program will reflect sound policy. They also point out that entry for this kind of consultation is not easy. Changes of this kind are usually made from within the organization. If one is called in for program-centered consultation, one should keep in mind that staff often fear change of any kind, and that administrators often realistically fear responsibility for failure.

Mental Health Consultation and Related Interpersonal Methods

Both education and consultation teach more effective handling of problems and impart general knowledge and specific skills. Bindman (1966) points out that education tends to emphasize formal, systematic approaches, with the teacher planning and presenting materials. In education the focus is on the acquisition of knowledge and skills. The teacher has evaluative and administrative authority. In mental health consultation, the content of the consultation usually comes from discussions with the consultee. The focus is on work problems, with the consultee solving current and future work problems as well as acquiring knowledge and skills. The consultant does not have administrative authority and cannot evaluate or grade the consultee (Altrocchi, 1972). While the consultant may not make her or his evaluation explicit, she or he probably does evaluate the consultee. As mentioned earlier, she or he does have the power of one whose expertise is sought as well as backing from some part of the organization, and therefore has added importance for the consultee.

Both the mental health consultant and the supervisor of a therapist in training have greater knowledge and experience than the consultee or the supervisee. They both focus on specific, related work problems and emphasize understanding general principles and technical procedures. However, the supervisor oversees the supervisee's work and is to some extend responsible for it; she or he directs and evaluates the supervisee. Both supervisor and supervisee are usually from the same profession; often the consultant and the consultee are from different disciplines. The mental health consultant is not responsible for the consultee's total work performance. The role of the consultant is usually relatively nonevaluative. A psychiatric consultant dealing with a psychiatric social worker, however, is an example of a case in which evaluation may in fact be explicit. The consultant is an outside resource person who is called in to provide what the internal staff cannot (Bindman, 1966). It should be noted that modern supervision may also make use of consultation approaches.

An administrator has responsibility for making decisions and promulgating specific policy. Although a consultant may discuss administratively related problems with a consultee or someone in the administration, a mental health consultant does not make decisions. This difference between the two roles is even more pronounced when the consultant comes from outside the organization.

Mental health consultation is similar to collaboration in that two or more people work together on a common product. They plan jointly, make decisions jointly and carry out action together. The mental health consultant is more of an adviser than a collaborator. The consultant does not participate in carrying out actions that result from a decision made by a consultee.

Altrocchi (1972) points out that the relationship between mental health consultation and psychotherapy is a source of anxiety for mental health workers as well as for consultees. For this reason the distinction is an important one. Consultation developed in part from principles of psychotherapy (Caplan, 1964, 1970). It resembles psychotherapy in that it attempts to increase the effectiveness, sensitivity and personal growth of the consultee by applying interpersonal processes to intellectual and affective learning (Altrocchi, 1972). In consultation, however, the goal is education rather than modification of a disorder. Privacy is respected (see the discussion in the next section of Caplan's "theme interference"). There is an implicit contract according to which the consultee may or may not apply what has been learned. Transference is minimal; resistance is not interpreted and is respected; defenses are supported (Altrocchi, 1972). The content of the consultation is work-related problems, not personal ones. Even consultee affective reactions to clients' problems are discussed only in relation to the consultee's current work problems with the client.

Training of the Consultant

The actual work of the consultant may differ in some respects from the ways in which she or he has been trained. First she or he must gain access to and acceptance by the consultee. This may create some anxiety (Signell & Scott, 1972). She or he must understand problems two steps removed from their actual occurrence and she or he must deal with them on multidimensional levels. She or he must work within the consultee's institution. This may mean a reduction in direct action, control and security. The consultant may also have to be more assertive and definite than many therapists are trained to be. Rogawski (1968) suggests that the consultant has to develop a "third ear" as well as understanding of psychodynamics. This understanding must be based on mutual respect. Caplan (1959) refers to the danger of treating the consultee as a patient. Since whatever action will be taken will be carried out by the consultee, the consultant must adapt the intervention for consultee use.

Group Versus Individual Consultation

Altrocchi, Spielberger, and Eisdorfer (1965) compare group consultation to group supervision, seminar teaching, sensitivity training and group psychotherapy. Contrasting group consultation to these other forms of group processes is comparable to contrasting the interpersonal processes of supervision, teaching and psychotherapy to individual consultation as discussed earlier. However, the dynamics of group influence can also be applied to group consultation. The consultant can arouse and channel peer influence. The supportive and nonjudgmental attitude of the group can lead to a sharing of problems and a reduction of consultee feelings of isolation and inadequacy. This may then lead to a more objective evaluation of problems and alternative courses of action. This is a professional group and the work requirements of such a group suggest similar attitudes and anxieties on the part of its members. Professions to some extent attract people with similar personalities (Altrocchi et al., 1965). Professions also help shape the values of their members: e.g., the profession becomes a reference group. The similarities of individuals and work situations should increase the probability that any given individual's work-oriented problems will be shared. As a consultee gains awareness of reactions common to the group as a whole, the consultee can gain insights into his or her own conflicts (Parker, 1962). If there is sufficient cohesion in the group and confidence in the consultant, nonshared but work-related problems may be introduced. Both Altrocchi and his colleagues (1965) and Parker (1958) found that inappropriate problems were rarely raised. Caplan (1964) takes a somewhat different view. He sees the discussion of inappropriate problems in groups as more likely and cautions against the use of what he calls "theme interference reduction technique" in these groups because colleagues may use defense-destroying interpretations before the consultant can stop them. Altrocchi (1972) cautions against the use of indirect method in a group for other reasons as well: not all members are likely to share the same theme; some members may move the group off the theme and towards insight. Others suggest that the consultant should not avoid discussing the consultee's feelings; however, the feelings should be work related and discussion of aspects of historical development of these feelings should be avoided.

The consultant should help the group move ahead together and try to avoid fragmentation. There may be differences between groups with respect to initial cohesion, resistance and the speed with which they will go from one phase of consultation to another (Altrocchi et al., 1965).

One advantage of group consultation is that there are more cues and hypotheses available for both consultees and the consultant than in individual consultation. There is also greater shared affect and more support for group members. Group influence can be used on individual members; for example, to influence individual members to look at cases in different ways. Intragroup and intergroup communication can be improved. It should also be easier to maintain some distance from the client (Altrocchi, 1972; Altrocchi et al., 1965).

There are some disadvantages to group consultation. Attendance takes all members away from other duties and requires greater coordination of schedules. The issue of confidentiality becomes considerably more complicated. The insecure consultee is less likely to participate. The group format is not as adaptable for individual consultee-client crises. Lastly, if there is no group cohesion, consultation will not be at all effective.

In conclusion, keeping these pros and cons in mind, the choice of group or individual consultation is affected by many factors including the training and personal preference of the consultant as well as practical considerations.

Process of Consultation

Entry. There are certain questions centering around entry into the consultation situation that have relevance for what actually occurs during the consultation period: Who asked for a consultant? Who chose this particular consultant? Why was this particular consultant chosen? (How a consultant is seen in a community may not be how she perceives herself.) Why was a consultant brought in at this particular time? What is the relationship of the consultant to those higher up in the organization? Drawing on his own experience Altrocchi (1972) points out that the consultant is entering an existing social system and as such may be tested by those in it. Clearly matters are easier for the consultant if the consultee is also the one who recommended consultation and was instrumental in, or at least did not oppose, this consultant's selection. The consultant should have some support from the administration and needs to have some understanding of the informal leadership structure within the organization.

Contract. The initial contact with the consultant is often made by phone. Goodstein (1978) suggests that the consultant should not agree to anything specific at first. The consultee may not have a complete description of the problem; she or he may see a problem but not know how to solve it; she or he may see a problem and a solution but not have the credibility or ability to carry it out. The contract between consultant and the contact person should be negotiated at a face-to-face meeting at which some mutual expectations are made explicit. Usually there is a formal and informal contract. The role of the person negotiating the contract for the consultee organization has to be specified; this may or may not be the same individual who initiated the idea of consultation, and it may or may not be the consultee. Entry into the organization by the consultant should be viewed in itself as an intervention.

Confidentiality guidelines must be drawn up with all parties concerned: what will be shared with whom under what circumstances. For example, Caplan (1970) proposed that the consultant be free to communicate with the supervisor (administration) about the client but not about the consultee; for example, the consultant should not give an opinion on the consultee's mental health to the consultee's superior. There is the question of whether a consultee should discuss a supervisor or administrator with the consultant. Confidentiality tends to be one sided; the consultee can discuss the consultant. Groups members are bound by the same rules as a single consultee. However, simply by virtue of the increase in the number of individuals, the increase in number of interactions and potential interpersonal difficulties, the issue of confidentiality becomes more complicated in group consultation.

Establishing the Consultee-Consultant Relationship. The process of establishing and maintaining a consultee-consultant relationship must go on concurrently with efforts to diagnose the problem for which the consultant was called (Beckhard, 1959). As discussed earlier, this is a relationship between two professionals. The consultant should convey that she or he expects to learn as well as to assist the consultee (Altrocchi, 1972). This includes showing respect for the consultee's competence and offering support.

In the early stages of the consultation, the group members are likely to be unsure of the consultant and to test her or him with bizarre or impossible cases (Rieman, 1963). Each member of the group has had impossible cases, so the consultant can teach them how to recognize these as well as the guilt and anxiety associated with them. After discussion with and reassurance by the consultant that the consultee is doing all that is possible, rapport with the group can be established. The consultee tends initially to present clients from minority or impoverished groups because they are different from the consultee. This can be used to help consultees examine their own attitudes towards these groups. Those who initially volunteer to present cases or to share reactions are frequently the least defensive and the most competent (Altrocchi, et al., 1965).

Defining the Problem. The boundaries of the organizational unit that is the target of the consultation must be made explicit. The consultant has to take time to define the problem. Information should be gathered, and the consultee asked to define and redefine the problem. Goodstein (1978) says that consultee definition of a problem is usually not systematic, and will include such vague complaints as: something should be done about supervisor training, or a workshop should be planned to make communication more effective. Goodstein and Boyer (1972) give an example of an initial request for a communications workshop at a municipal health department; upon closer examination it became evident that the hostility among members of the department was such that a workship would have been ineffective, and had it been attempted the consultant would have been discredited. Goodstein (1978) suggests that a consultant be presented in as neutral a way as possible and agree to as little as possible until the problems are clearly diagnosed. A consultant is often engaged for a specific task. More general, systemic problems are identified as time goes on. For example, one may be called in to evaluate a program only to find out that it has not really been implemented because of difficulties between professional and nonprofessional staff. The real problem affects the strategies one uses. How a problem is defined, of course, also largely is determined by how data are collected: observation, interview or questionnaire. The consultant should also avoid role confusion because she or he may also be a specialist in a content area.

Alternative Courses of Action. The first step in proposing alternative courses of action is to review previous action that has been taken. Discussion should facilitate communication between consultee and client, reduce anxiety among consultee(s), and lead to an understanding of the process of consultation. As mentioned earlier, the role of consultant is primarily advisory: she or he helps to clarify problems, bring in additional data, and anticipate the consequences of alternative courses of action. The consultee must arrive at his or her own solutions and carry them out.

Dealing with Consultee Problems. There are two primary ways of dealing with consultee problems, especially affective ones: indirectly and directly.

Caplan (1970), the proponent of the indirect method, suggests that the focus of consultation should switch to the consultee and away from the client when the consultee's difficulty in handling a case is due to lack of knowledge, skill, confidence or professional objectivity. Caplan's position is based on psychoanalytic assumptions. Lack of professional objectivity in an otherwise competent consultee can be the result of a sudden emergence of previously repressed impulses. The repression is caused by the expectation that severe punishment will occur if the impulse is expressed. These unconscious problems represent a "Theme Interference." The "Initial Category" is the stereotypical view of the case that the consultee maintains because it reflects his or her own unacceptable impulses. The "Inevitable Outcome" is a sense of foreboding about the case's outcome that the consultee feels because it relates to the unrecognized belief that all persons with similar impulses are doomed. The way in which one finds "Theme Interference" is by monitoring consultee interview behavior for signs of increased anxiety, overinclusion, confusion or any other unprofessional conduct. Upon finding this, the consultant should move away from the anxiety-arousing material.

Theme Interference can be reduced in two ways. The first is by "unlinking." This is an attempt to change consultee perceptions of the client so as to remove him or her from the "initial category"—to unlink him from the consultee's theme. Caplan suggests that to try this is an error; for while it may provide temporary relief from anxiety, the unconscious theme is left intact at full strength.

The "Theme Interference Reduction" technique involves agreeing with the consultee categorization of the client as part of the initial category. The consultant then demonstrates to the consultee that the case representing the prohibited theme is not necessarily doomed. This is accomplished by focusing on the client's problem. The message is that those with similar problems need not be doomed. The consultant does not make the consultee aware of the fact that the difficulty is the consultee's and is a result of an unresolved conflict. Rather, by discussing the client's case, one is discussing the case on which the conflict has been displaced. If the consultee's problem was addressed directly, the consultee would become upset; he or she would not recognize the theme or would deny its personal relevance. The intervention on the part of the consultant would be ineffective. According to Caplan, gradual awareness of the underlying conflict is also not effective. Although it would be less traumatic, it would bring the consultant-consultee relationship closer to psychotherapy.

Heller and Monahan (1977) raise some questions about Caplan's psychoanalytic assumptions. Do unconscious conflicts eixst? If so, how does one determine their presence? Can these conflicts interfere with work in such a circumscribed manner? If conflicts are strong, why do they not appear in other behavior? Why do not otherwise intact defenses provide successful resolution? Heller and Monahan also raise some questions about avoiding the consultee's awareness. If the consultee is not aware that these conflicts are the subject of consultation, the consultant does not have a full account of the conflicts and is prohibited by the indirect nature of the technique from finding out more about them. The only information about the conflicts that is available is that which can be gained by noting the topics discussed and the correlated tension produced, so that tension level and its reduction are the only information that one has. Heller and Manahan (1977) accurately point out that there are many other factors in the consultee-consultant relationship that could account for tension reduction: e.g., increased rapport and trust and a new cognitive grasp of a case. They also suggest the possiblity of ethical problems in working on another's conflicts without the person's explicit permission. There is also the practical problem of what one does if the consultee becomes aware that his or her conflicts are the focus of the consultation.

Heller and Monahan (1977) suggest that the technique without its underlying psychoanalytic assumptions may be useful. A consultee may have an "overgeneralized stereotype" due to cultural attitudes learned either early in socialization or from personal experience that has now been overgeneralized. Such stereotypes are rarely accessible through direct challenge. To exclude an individual from the stereotype can change the attitude toward the individual but leave the stereotype intact. This would correspond to Caplan's "unlinking" and is supported by Sherif, Harvey, White, Hood, and Sherif's (1961) study on prejudice. It would be better to expand the consultee's perceptual field by broadening his view of members of the stereotypical group: demonstrate that one member of that group whom the consultee knows well has unrecognized assets. In technique this is analogous to demonstrating that the doomed outcome is not inevitable. Heller & Monahan's notion of overgeneralized stereotypes might also be conceptualized as a need for cognitive restructing, as in Ellis's (1973) framework. There might be also some utility to looking at this from the viewpoint of attribution theory (Nisbett & Valins, 1971), attribution of outcomes, and perception of causality. It should be noted that while many factors can lead to tension reduction, many factors can also lead to an increase in tension or inappropriate affect. If one sees inappropriate affect on the part of a consultee in a particular case or cases which have a common element, one cannot assume that this involves an unconscious conflict. All one can say is that particular issue is important to the consultee. The "why" requires further exploration.

Some of the arguments that are made for direct methods of dealing with inappropriate consultee affect are: affect can be mobilized; discussing the problem may be useful; in a nonpunitive and noncoercive atmosphere, defenses tend to gradually disappear (Parker, 1958); ground rules and sanctions regarding discussion of affect and personal reactions can be made explicit before the intervention. Altrocchi (1972) suggests the following guidelines for the use of a direct approach. When an individual consultee behaves in ways that indicate strong affect, the consultant should check diagnostic cues for theme interference, neurotic conflict or deeply unconscious motives. If none of these is present, the direct discussion of consultee affect can proceed. When one consultee in a group shows strong affect, one can check the same personal difficulties mentioned above. One should also determine the degree to which affect is shared. If it appears to be shared, then the consultant should move ahead with direct discussion. If the affect is not shared, the consultant should not proceed. If it is shared but directed at someone in the organization who is not present or towards someone else in the group, the consultant should proceed only with the sanction of all parties concerned. When affect is shared by a significant portion of the group, does not represent deeply neurotic problems and is directly related to work at hand, then the consultant can proceed.

Those who work with groups are more likely to suggest the use of direct methods (Altrocchi et al., 1965; Parker 1958). Altrocchi (1972), suggests that groups stimulate affect; they can be guided by direct expression of affect and yet tend to control this by setting limits. Those who work with individuals sometimes suggest indirect ones (Caplan, 1964, 1970).

Termination of consultation should be agreed to by both parties.

PROGRAMMATIC CHANGE

Behavioral Approaches

Behavioral approaches to community mental health represent a change of focus on the part of behaviorists away from an emphasis on changing individual deviant behavior. The movement into the community setting was due to two factors: the societal emphasis on moving individuals from institutions back to their communities, and the rather consistent finding that although behavior modification programs are effective while the individual is in a program, there is little generalization of behaviors to other settings once the person has left the program.

The behavioral model of intervention explicitly criticizes the medical model of mental illness. To summarize this model, the physical aspects of mental illness are treated by chemical intervention, and the interpersonal aspects by psychoanalytic theory. The interpersonal aspects are considered to be analogous to medicine. One talks of "illness," "symptoms," "cure," "underlying causes." The model is that of a doctor-patient relationship. The behavioral model is that of "teacher-student." There have been societal applications of the medical model: the assumed relationship between violence and catharsis, the labeling of children, and the view of the family as a physical system. (For a more extensive discussion of these issues see Chapter 8.)

It should be noted that behavior therapy (used here as the generic term) has changed and broadened its scope. The theoretical basis is no longer only operant and respondent conditioning. It draws from social learning theory, cognitive behavior modification, self-control literature, social psychological theories such as attribution theory, experimental studies of cognitive processes and physiological processes. The underlying features are the assumption that behavior is learned and can be unlearned; there is continuity in behavior (differences are in intensity and frequency of behavior), and emphasis on research findings and ongoing assessment. Some aspects of this approach parallel a "community mental health orientation." Both are action oriented, involve problem solving and focus on the interaction of the environment and the individual, and share a commitment to applied research.

Atthowe (1973) speaks of "behavioral innovation": prevention, treatment and maintenance. He outlines the behavioral approach within community mental health. (1) The mental health professional must be a social planner who makes changes in the treatment milieu and existing social systems. (2) The knowledge and training of this social planner must be in relevant social and economic systems. The planner should be in a position to influence those who have economic and political resources. (3) There should be a comprehensive, egalitarian planning team including indigenous leaders, those with political influence and trained rehabilitation workers. (4) There should be a behavioral analysis of key behaviors, reinforcers and techniques necessary for behavioral innovation. These must be applied to people in need of rehabilitation, significant others and the community. (5) There must be built-in corrective feedback mechanisms so as to modify ineffective programs. (6) Behavioral innovation programs must be perpetuated by demonstrating effectiveness to staff and community, involving professional and community persons in planning, focusing on treatment, maintenance and prevention, providing reinforcement for all members of rehabilitation teams, basing program changes on experimental data, maintaining staff skill and enthusiasm for training and workshop. The first three points are similar to those held by most professionals in the area of community mental health. The last three reflect the application of behavioral principles to community intervention.

Ullman (1977) states that the behaviorist in community intervention should strive to prepare people for, and increase the number of, situations in which they may realistically enlarge their range of behavioral choices. She or he should also try to increase the number of activities and situations that have positive outcomes for people, and reduce the actions that are maintained by aversive stimulation. Basically Ullman is referring to an increase in ability and opportunity.

Review of Behavioral Studies in Community Settings. The conclusions based on the behavioral literature on community aftercare suggest: (a) those who receive aftercare are less prone to recidivism as long as they remain in the program; (b) if they leave the program or if the program is discontinued, the rates of recidivism are similar to control groups (Fairweather, Sanders, Cressler, & Maynard, 1969; Hudson, 1975; Hunt & Azrin, 1973; Samuels & Henderson, 1971; Shean, 1973); (c) other kinds of behavioral change are no longer maintained once an individual has left a program.

The studies on behavioral correctional programs show the same results (Cohen & Filipczak, 1971; Jesness, 1975; Martinson, 1974). A model community residential program is Achievement Place (Braukmann & Fixsen, 1975). The token system has proved effective within the program. Recidivism rates are lower than for a comparable group on probation or another who had spent two years in a state training school (Phillips, Phillips, Fixsen, & Wolf, 1973). However, some questions remain. Samples thus far have been small. Also police and court contacts are as high as for training school youth despite the drop in recidivism (Eitzen, 1975). Fewer of those arrested from the Achievement Place group were re-institutionalized (Harris, 1974). Why this should be the case is unclear (O'Donnell 1972). Further evaluation studies of residential correctional programs are currently being done.

Again, most nonresidential programs report positive results during the intervention program. Few report any data after the intervention has been terminated. Of these, one of the very few to report a maintenance of lower rate of offenses was the Alexander and Parsons (1973) study which dealt with status offenses (those which would not be considered crimes if those committing the crimes were adults).

Some of the most promising behavioral programs are those concerned with family intervention (Patterson, 1974; Wahler, 1975). In them, the methodology is relatively sophisticated. However, it should be kept in mind it is not likely that those who stay in these programs are representatives of those who were initially referred.

There has been some research on bringing about behavioral change in the community within limited and controlled settings. The availability of litter receptacles led to a decrease in littering (Burgess, Clark & Hendee, 1971; Finie, 1973; Geller, Farris & Post, 1973). Reward contingent on the use of litter baskets also led to a decrease in littering (Chapman & Risley, 1974; Clark, Burgess & Hendee, 1972; Hayes, Johnson & Cone, 1975; Kohlenberg & Phillips, 1975; Powers, Osborne & Anderson, 1973). Contingent reward led to reduced usage of electricity or natural gas (Winnett & Nietzel, 1975). The number of participants in these studies were small; they were primarily students, and there was no attempt to maintain this behavior across place and time.

More directly related to community mental health, attempts were made to help low-income groups develop self-help and problem-solving skills. Miller and Miller (1970) were able to get increased attendance at self-help meetings when specific goods, services and information were offered in return for attendance. Yet the percentage of group members who attended was low (20 percent) and participation was minimal. Briscoe, Hoffman, and Bailey (1975) taught problem-solving skills to low-income members of a community board. Following the training, the frequency of problem-solving statements during board meetings increased. Of the individual board members who had been trained, some used the skills, and some did not. There were no data to indicate whether training helped the board to accomplish its objectives. There have also been some direct attempts to help people find and keep jobs. Jones and Azrin (1973) started a job information network and Azrin, Flores and Kaplan (1975), a job-finding club. Pedalino and Gamboa (1974) reduced absenteeism on the job by setting up a lottery whose prize was $20.00 and whose tickets were contingent on a day's work. Hermann, de Montes, Dominquez, Montes, and Hopkins (1973) gave daily bonuses for prompt arrival at work to workers who had been chronically late.

The conclusions to be drawn from all these studies are first, that within institutions, in transitional programs and in community-based programs, behavioral programs have led to considerable improvement in the behavior of the target population. Secondly, generalization of behavior outside of programs has been poor. Kazdin (1975, 1977) in a review of token economy programs, reached similar conclusions.

There have been efforts to produce greater generalization. Jones (1974) trained clients to recognize stimulus-response relationships. Several studies have trained significant others as mediators of rewards (Conway & Bucher, 1976) such as parents, teachers and peers. O'Leary and Kent (1973) suggest that there is little evidence that verbal skills can be used to facilitate generalization with adults, and no evidence of this with children. Harris (1975), in a paper reviewing the research on teaching language to nonverbal children, points to the lack of support for generalization. O'Donnell (1977) states that if one trains parents, one has to then maintain *their* behavior. However, if there is no support in the environment for the new behaviors, extinction is merely being postponed. Levine and Fasnacht (1974) point out that attempts to increase resistance to extinction make the programs more complicated and less practical. Also they argue that the use of tokens may inhibit generalization by decreasing the intrinsic value of behavior.

Suggestions have been made as to how generalization across settings can be increased. Kazdin (1975) suggests greater training in self-control procedures as well as in the use of fading of the extrinsic reinforcement and of partial and delayed reinforcement. He also puts greater emphasis on the training of significant others in the environment. O'Donnell (1977) recommends specifying stimulus control and response clusters. For instance, Patterson and Cobb (1973) found that siblings rather than parents are in control of socially aggressive behavior in boys. O'Donnell also suggests that generalization and maintenance of targeted behaviors may be partially dependent on a relationship with some nontargeted behaviors: intervention with one behavior may alter another behavior in a direction that is not always understood. For example, when deviant behavior of six children with severe problems was ignored, new deviant behavior occurred (Herbert, Pinkston, Hayden, Sajwaj, Pinkston, Corau, & Jackson, 1973). Similar findings were reported by other researchers (Lovass & Simmons, 1969; Nordquist, 1971; Risley, 1968; Sajwaj, Twardosz & Burke, 1972; Wahler, 1975; Wahler, Sperling, Thomas, Teeter & Luper, 1970).

Problems in Application of Behavioral Principles. Although these problems are discussed within the behavioral setting, they are relevant in varying degrees to any programmatic effort. The behavioral approach requires active cooperation of those who control contingencies. A minimal level of consistency in the application of reinforcement consistencies is needed to make any program effective (see Lachenmeyer [1969] for a discussion of inconsistent application and control of reinforcement by target population). The consultant, although she or he may set the contingencies, does not usually administer the rewards. Also the means that the consultant has at her or his disposal to influence the mediators and thereby affect the administration of rewards is limited and does not usually include salaries and promotions. (For a lengthier discussion see Ayllon & Azrin, 1968; Paul & Lenz, 1977).

There may also be conflicts between institutional or community practices and the procedures necessary to execute the program. Consistent application and follow-through by mediators may also be limited by organizational factors such as limited manpower and finances, and by the broader organizational context within which the program operates. The implicit and explicit contingencies for staff may be quite different.

Current Limitations in the Use of Behavioral Intervention in the Community Setting. Currently there is a major emphasis in community mental health on prevention. The emphasis in behavioral approaches is on treatment. In the field as a whole we do not have enough information to make definite statements about etiology: in behavioral terms we do not know enough about the type of learning history needed for prevention. Nietzel, Winett, Macdonald, & Davidson (1977) point to a narrowness of focus on the part of some behaviorists and a mistrust of group data and group intervention as factors that also currently limit the behavioral approach to treatment. In the past there has been an abundance of demonstration projects which practitioners would then continue. The emphasis has been on applied research rather than training of paraprofessionals, parents, peers and teachers. Nietzel and his colleagues see this as a limitation from the point of view of community mental health. The behavior modifier has not been an "activist." On the positive side, she or he has emphasized objectivity and focused her or his attention on areas in which she or he has been trained. She or he is responsive to an academic reference group and attempts to separate science and politics. Nietzel and his coauthors suggest that this position should at least be reevaluated. They also maintain that some behavior modifiers are too tied to operant and respondent models and look less at the social psychological, organizational and physiological bases of behavior. This is certainly true of some of the people in the field; e.g., "behavior analysts" stick closely to an operant view. Atthowe (1973) calls for a behavioral paradigm that is equivalent to one for social change.

There currently is little data on behavioral norms for any particular group, including the rates and prevalence of problem behavior in the normal population. This could be important in any strategy for generalization and maintenance of behavior in the environment (O'Donnell, 1977). Such norms would help to determine whether in fact a problem does exist. Along the same line, we usually have a baseline on when a problem behavior occurs, but little information on when it does not.

For example, Rose, Blank, and Spalter (1975) found that preschool children had stable behavior patterns within a given setting, but that their behavior was quite different in other settings.

Improvement may also occur without intervention (Schechtman, 1970). Robins (1974) suggests that whether intervention should occur or not may depend on the nature of the problem; for example, intervention appears necessary for antisocial behavior.

Organizational Development

Although Organizational Development (OD) as an intervention strategy has not been widely used within community mental health, it is one of the major behavioral science approaches to organizational change within industry. Unlike mental health consultation and behavioral approaches to the community, OD focuses on the consultee or the deliver of services rather than the client group. According to its proponents, OD is a response to the demands of a changing organizational environment and a product of the application of behavioral science knowledge. Increasing professionalization, higher educational levels and job mobility have led to decreasing organizational loyalty and dependence (Friedlander & Brown, 1974). Because of these changes, organizational processes and structures must be more flexible and responsive than traditional bureaucratic structures (Lawrence & Lorsch, 1969). Organizational development has drawn from the following areas of study in the behavioral sciences: the relationship of social and psychological factors to work; the effects of group decision making on involvement, motivation and committment (Lewin, 1947); participation in decision making and the ownership of change resulting from the decision (Coch & French, 1948); use of groups as agents of change in organizations (Cartwright, 1951); T group and sensitivity training as educational methods (Bradford, Gibb, & Benne, 1964); the organization as a sociotechnical system (Trist, 1969); and motivation and work (Herzberg, 1966).

Research and theory lag behind the practice of OD. There are several reasons for this. First, although its practitioners share values and techniques, OD was developed through practice and therefore can vary with its users. Secondly, it is often difficult to do research within organizations. Third, in the same way that behavior modifiers emphasize the research end of the researcher/consultant role, OD specialists focus on the practitioner part of that role.

In OD, organizations are viewed as composed of people with different values, styles and skills, technologies with different characteristics, and processes and structures that reflect different kinds of relationships between people or between people and their work (Friedlander & Brown,

1974). Organizational processes and structures are the major linkage between human and technological imputs into the organization. For this reason any attempt at permanent change must involve change in technological systems, process-structural systems and individual interactions rather than in just one of these.

If one looks at organizational culture as a set of learned and shared assumptions about the norms that regulate behavior, organizational development is a broad effort to change the social norms and values rather than focusing the change effort on individuals. Hornstein, Bunker, Burke, Gindes & Lewicki (1971) say that the process of OD is the "creation of a culture which institutionalizes the use of various social technologies to regulate the diagnosis and change of interpersonal, group and intergroup behaviors, especially those behaviors related to organizational decision-making, communication and planning" (p. 343). The effort is towards permanent change, and a mechanism is established whereby continual change efforts will be planned.

Katz and Kahn (1966) say that the culture of an organization is reflected in the system of norms and values, the history of internal and external struggles, the types of people the organization attracts, the work processes and physical layout, the modes of communication and the exercise of authority. They assert that the greatest organizational conflict comes from the discrepancy between the democratic expectations of individuals and their actual part in decision making. Katz and Kahn (1966) suggest a number of changes that correspond to those recommended by other proponents of OD (Argyris, 1962; Beckhard, 1969, Bennis, 1966; Blake & Mouton, 1968, Lippitt, 1969). They are:

1. Most organizations could move toward decentralization of decision making.
2. Democratic forms could be introduced by shifting the source of authority from the officials to the members rather than by having leaders consult followers.
3. Distinctions betweeen classes of citizenship could be eliminated.
4. The Likert principle of overlapping organizational families could improve communication.
5. Feedback from organizational functioning could include systematic communication from organizational members.
6. Closed circuits of information should be opened through operational research.
7. Roles should be enlarged; this would increase members' sense of participation.
8. Group should be responsible for tasks, thereby insuring greater psychological involvement of individuals.
9. Bureaucratic structures should be treated as open systems.

OD intervention strategies can be categorized as techno-structural or human processual (Friedlander & Brenn 1974). Some techno-structural changes are socio-technical systems, job design, job enlargement and job enrichment. The sociotechnical systems approach was developed at Tavistock, England (Trist, 1969). It refers to the meshing of the technological configuration and the social structure of the work units. Job design usually involves designing a task with a view towards enhancing performance, and is derived from industrial engineering principles. The purpose behind job enlargement and job enrichment is to increase worker satisfaction. Both enrichment and enlargement are based on theories of motivation. In the former, several vertical functions are collapsed into a single more responsible function leading to a greater challenge in the job and therefore to greater motivation. However, it should be kept in mind that not everyone wants greater work challenges. In job enlargement work functions are increased horizontally: more of same level tasks are added. These should lead to greater consolidation and provide greater variety and a sense of (the task as a whole). Sociotechnical innovations involve the entire system, job design concerns sets of interrelated functions, and job enrichment is concerned primarily with a single job.

Some other specific technostructural changes involve redoing the organizational chart or introducing "flexitime" (Golembiewski, Hullet, & Kagno, 1974): a core part of the work day is set, but before and after that period an individual may come or go at his or her discretion.

Some of the human processual interventions are: survey feedback, group development and intergroup relations development. In survey feedback, data are systematically collected, analyzed in summary fashion and selectively fed back to organization members, whose input into the design, analysis and interpretation varies according to the structure of the organization. The fundamental assumption behind this technique is that the discrepancy between organizational ideals and actual responses will motivate change. There are some data to support the notion that increased participation by members leads to more positive attitudes (Alderfer & Ferriss, 1972; Baumgartel, 1959; Bowers & Franklin, 1972; Brown, 1972; Chase, 1968; Mann, 1969). Survey feedback alone, however, does not seem to lead to long-term change or to any behavioral or structural changes (Miles, Hornstein, Callahan, Calder, & Schiavo, 1969). The effectiveness of survey feedback is increased by colloboration and involvement of participants and the unit manager, and facilitated by outside consultation and specific decisions about follow-up and action steps (Friedlander & Brown, 1974).

The emphasis in OD is on group rather than individual work. Team building is based on the view of an organization as consisting of overlapping teams (Argyris, 1962). Beer (1974) categorized types of team building according to the primary issues treated: goal-setting activity, interpersonal relations development, and role analysis (clarify roles and responsibilities). Again, team building seems to affect attitudes.

Intergroup relations development in practice usually involves general problem solving. Walton (1967) lists four interventions made by a third party to manage intergroup conflict: a) reduce the potential for conflict by changing structure or personnel; b) resolve substantive issues by decision making; c) assist in managing overt conflict; d) facilitate change in relationships.

There are now several issues that remain have to be addressed: Does the change in attitudes affect performance? Does it generalize to other attitudes? What makes for successful team development? Is there any carry-over to other members of the organization?

To summarize, Organizational Development is an attempt to bring about lasting change within organizations through modifying both technostructural and human processual areas. The techniques used, especially survey feedback and team building, bring about more positive attitudes on the part of organization members. The relationship between these and lasting change is not strong. Also, many organizations currently have OD specialists as part of their organization. This leads to all the problems inherent in making any consultant a part of an organization. Greiner (1967), reviewing studies of organizational change, says that three features seem to distinguish successful interventions: strong internal and external pressures for change, a consistent pattern beginning with initial pressures and going toward gradual involvement of many levels of the organization, and shared decision making.

CONCLUSION

Mental health consultation has become a widely used method for limited intervention within the area of community mental health. Much of the work has consisted of the systematization of consultation experience. Currently there are some efforts to evaluate the effectiveness of consultation.

Behavioral interventions in the community, while still maintaining a research perspective, have a broadened theoretical base. The methodologies have become increasingly sophisticated, as have their criticisms. The most pressing issue is that of generalization. Interventions have been successful within controlled settings but generalization outside of these settings has been poor. There remains a question as to whether this is the result of poor control of contingencies in the community or of theoretical and empirical weaknesses in a behavioral approach.

Organizational development focuses on changes in staff rather than clients. It is an attempt to bring about permanent organizational change by modifying structural aspects of organizations along with individuals. The affective changes brought about by many of the Organizational Development techniques have not been found in and of themselves to lead to behavioral change.

References

Abrahamson, S. Methods of teaching. In W. Mendel & P. Solomon, (Eds.), *Psychiatric consultation.* New York: Grune & Stratton, 1968, pp. 41–48.

Alderfer, C. P., and Ferriss, R. Understanding the impact of survey feedback. In W. W. Burke & H. A. Hornstein (Eds.), *The social technology of organizational development.* Fairfax, Va.: National Training Laboratories, 1972.

Aldrich, C. K. A specialized program for residents in psychiatry. In W. Mendel & P. Solomon, (Eds.), *Psychiatric consultation.* New York: Grune & Stratton, 1968.

Alexander, J. F., and Parsons, B. V. Short-term behavioral intervention with delinquent families: Impact on family process and recidivism. *Journal of Abnormal Psychology,* 1973, *81,* 219–225.

Altrocchi, J. Mental health consultation. In S. E. Golann & C. Eisdorfer (Eds.), *Handbook of community mental health.* New York: Appleton-Century-Crofts, 1972.

Altrocchi, J., Spielberger, C. D., & Eisdorfer, C. Mental health consultation with groups. *Community Mental Health Journal,* 1965, *2(1),* 127–134.

Altrocchi, J., & Eisdorfer, C. Apprentice-collaborator field training in community psychology: The Halifax Community Program. In I. Iscoe & C. D. Spielberger (Eds.), *Community psychology: Perspectives in training and research.* New York: Appleton-Century-Crofts, 1970, pp. 191–205.

Argyris, C. Explorations in consulting client relationships. *Human Organization,* 1961, *20(3),* 121–133.

Argyris, C. *Interpersonal competence and organizational effectiveness.* Homewood, Ill.: Dorsey, 1962.

Atthowe, J. M., Jr. Behavior innovation and persistence. *American Psychologist,* 1973, *28,* 38–40.

Ayllon, T., & Azrin, N. *The token economy: A motivational system for therapy and rehabilitation.* New York: Appleton-Century-Crofts, 1968.

Azrin, N. H., Flores, T., & Kaplan, S. J. Job finding club: A group assisted program for obtaining employment. *Behavior Research & Therapy,* 1975, *43,* 683, 688.

Baumgarten, H. Using employee questionnaire results for improving organizations. *Kansas Business Review,* 1959, 2–6.

Beckhard, R. Helping a group with planning change: A case study. *Journal of Social Issues,* 1959, *15,* 13–19.

Beckhard, R. *Organizational development—strategies and models.* Cambridge, Mass.: Addison Wesley, 1969.

Beer, M. The technology of organizational development. In M. D. Dunnette (Ed.), *Handbook of industrial and organizational psychology.* Chicago: Rand McNally, 1974.

Bennis, W. G. *Changing organizations.* New York: McGraw-Hill, 1966.

Bennis, W. G., Berre, K. D., & Chin, R. *The planning of change.* New York: Holt, 1969.

Berlin, I. N. Mental health consultation in schools as a means of communicating mental health principles. *Journal of American Academy of Child Psychiatry,* 1962, *1,* 671–679.

Berlin, I. N. Learning mental health consultation: History and problems. *Mental Hygiene,* 1964, *48,* 257–266.

Bindman, A. J. Mental health consultation: Theory and practice. *Journal of Consulting Psychology*, 1959, *23*, 473–482.

Bindman, A. J. The clinical psychologist as a mental health consultant. In L. E. Abt & B. J. Reiss (Eds.), *Progress in clinical psychology*. New York: Grune & Stratton, 1966.

Blake, R. R., & Mouton, J. S. *Corporate excellence through GRID organizational development*. Houston: Gulf Publishing, 1968.

Bowers, D. G., & Franklin, J. F. Survey-guided development: Using human resources measurement in organizational change. *Journal of Contemporary Business*, 1972, *1*, 43–55.

Bradford, L. P., Gibb, J. R., & Benne, K. D. *T group theory and laboratory method*. New York: Wiley, 1964.

Braukmann, C. J., & Fixsen, D. L. Behavior modification with delinquents. In M. Hersen, R. M. Eisler, & P. M. Miller (Eds.), *Progress in behavior modification* (Vol. 1). New York: Academic, 1975, pp. 191–231.

Briscoe, R. V., Hoffman, D. B., & Bailey, J. S. Behavioral community psychology: Training a community board to problem solve. *Journal of Applied Behavior Analysis*, 1975, *8*, 157–168.

Brown, L. D. Research action: Organizational feedback, understanding and change. *Journal of Applied Behavior Science*, 1972, *7*, 569–579.

Buchanan, P. C. Crucial issues in organizational development. In H. A. Hornstein, B. B. Bunker, W. W. Burke, M. Gindes, & R. J. Lewicki (Eds.), *Social intervention: A behavioral science approach*. New York: Free Press, 1971.

Burgess, R. L., Clark, R. N., & Hendee, J. C. An experimental analysis of anti-litter procedures. *Journal of Applied Behavior Analysis*. 1971, *4*, 71–75.

Caplan, G. An approach to the education of community mental health specialists. *Mental Hygiene*, 1959, *43*, 268–280.

Caplan, G. Types of mental health consultation. *American Journal of Orthopsychiatry*, 1963, *33(3)*, 470–481.

Caplan, G. *Principles of preventive psychiatry*. New York: Basic, 1964.

Caplan, G. *The theory and practice of mental health consultation*. New York: Basic, 1970.

Cartwright, D. Achieving change in people: Some applications of group dynamics theory. *Human Relations*, 1951, *4*, 381–392.

Chapman, C., & Risley, T. R. Anti-litter procedures in an urban high density area. *Journal of Applied Behavior Analysis*, 1974, *7*, 377–383.

Chase, P. A survey feedback approach to organizational development. In *Proceedings of the executive study conference*. Princeton: Educational Testing Service, 1968.

Clark, R. N., Burgess, R. L., & Hendee, J. The development of anti-litter behavior in a forest campground. *Journal of Applied Behavior Analysis*, 1972, 5, 1–5.

Coch, L., & French, J. R. R. Overcoming resistance to change. *Human Relations*, 1948, *1*, 512–532.

Cohen, H. L., & Filipczak, J. A. *A new learning environment*. San Francisco: Jossey-Bass, 1971.

Cohen, L. D. Consultation as a method of mental health intervention. In L. E. Abt & B. J. Reiss (Eds.), *Progress in clinical psychology*. New York: Grune & Stratton, 1966.

Conway, J. B., & Bucher, B. D. Transfer and maintenance of behavior change in children: A review and suggestions. In E. J. Mash, L. A. Hamerlynck, & L. C. Handy (Eds.), *Behavior modification and families*. New York: Brunner/Mazel, 1976, pp. 119–159.

Davidson, W. S. II, & Seidman, E. Studies of behavior modification and juvenile delinquency: A review, methodological critique and social perspective. *Psychological Bulletin*, 1974, *81*, 998–1011.

Dyer, W. G., Maddock, R. F., Moffit, J. W., & Underwood, W. J. A laboratory-consultation model of organizational change. *Journal of Applied Behavioral Science*, 1970, *6*, 211–227.

Ellis, A. *Humanistic psychotherapy.* New York: McGraw-Hill, 1973.

Eitzen, D. S. The effects of behavior modification on the attitudes of delinquents. *Behaviour Research & Therapy*, 1975, *13*, 295–299.

Everett, P. B., Hayward, S. C., & Meyers, A. W. The effects of a token reinforcement procedure on business leadership. *Journal of Applied Behavior Analysis*, 1974, *7*, 1–9.

Fairweather, G. W., Sanders, D. H., Cressler, D. L., & Maynard, H. *Community life for the mentally ill: An alternative to institutional care.* Chicago: Aldine, 1969.

Ferber, H., Keeley, S. M., & Shemberg, K. M. Training parents in behavior modification: Outcome of and problems encountered in a program after Patterson's work. *Behavior Therapy*, 1974, *5*, 415–419.

Finnie, W. C. Field experiments in litter control. *Environment and Behavior*, 1973, *5*, 123–144.

Fixsen, D. L., Wolf, M. M., & Phillips, E. L. Achievement place: A teaching-family mode of community-based group homes for youth in trouble. In L. A. Hamerlynck, L. C. Handy, & E. J. Mash (Eds.), *Behavior change: Methodology, concepts and practice.* Champaign, Ill.: Research Press, 1973, pp. 241–268.

Friedlander, F., & Brown, L. D. Organizational development. *Annual Review of Psychology*, 1974, *25*, 313–341.

Geller, E. S., Farris, J. C., & Post, D. S. Prompting a consumer behavior for pollution control. *Journal of Applied Behavior Analysis*, 1973, *6*, 367–376.

Gibb, J. R. The role of the consultant. *Journal of Social Issues*, 1959, *15(2)*, 1–4.

Golann, S. E., & Eisdorfer, C. *Handbook of community mental health.* New York: Appleton-Century-Crofts, 1972.

Goldstein, S. G., & Marshall, N. R. Diagnostic consultation: An explanatory model. *American Journal of Mental Deficiency*. 1971, *76(1)*, 5–11.

Glidewell, J. C. The entry problem in consultation. *Journal of Social Issues*, 1959, *15*, 51–59.

Golembiewski, R. T. Organizational development in public agencies: Perspectives on theory and practice. *Public Administration Review*, 1969, *29*, 367–378.

Goodstein, L. D. *Consulting with human service systems.* Reading, Mass.: Addison-Wesley, 1978.

Goodstein, L. D., & Boyer, R. K. Crisis intervention in a municipal agency: A conceptual case history. *Journal of Applied Behavioral Science*, 1972, *8*, 318–340.

Greiner, L. E. Patterns of change. *Harvard Business Review*, 1967, *45*, 119–128.

Harris, S. L. Teaching language to nonverbal children—with emphasis on problems of generalization. *Psychological Bulletin*, 1975, *82*, 565–580.

Harris, V. W. *Centers for youth development and achievement: Alternative treatments for troubled youths CYDA.* Tucson, Ariz.: Centers for Youth Development and Achievement, 1974.

Hayes, S. C., Johnson, V. S., & Cone, J. D. The marked item technique: A practical procedure for litter control. *Journal of Applied Behavior Analysis*, 1975, *8*, 381–386.

Haylet, C. H., & Rapoport, L. Mental health consultation. In L. Bellak (Ed.), *Handbook of community psychiatry and community mental health.* New York: Grune & Stratton, 1964, pp. 319–339.

Heller, K., & Monahan, J. *Psychology and community change.* Homewood, Ill.: Dorsey, 1977.

Herbert, E. W., Pinkston, E. M., Hayden, M. L., Sajwaj, T. E., Pinkston, S., Cordua, G., & Jackson, C. Adverse effects of differential parental attention. *Journal of Applied Behavior Analysis*, 1973, *6*, 15–30.

Hermann, J. A., deMontes, A. I., Dominquez, B., Montes, F., & Hopkins, B. Effects of bonuses for punctuality on the tardiness of industrial workers. *Journal of Applied Behavior Analysis*. 1973, *6*, 563–570.

Herzberg, F. *Work and the nature of man.* Cleveland: World, 1966.

Hornstein, H. H., Bunker, B. B., Burke, W. W., Gindes, M., Lewicki, R. J. *Social Intervention:* A Behavioral Science Approach. New York: Free Press 1971.

Hudson, B. L. A behaviour modification project with chronic schizophrenics in the community. *Behaviour Research and Therapy,* 1975, *13,* 339–341.

Hunt, G. M., & Azrin, W. H. A community-reinforcement approach to alcoholism. *Behaviour Research and Therapy,* 1973, *11,* 91–109.

Iscoe, I., & Spielberger, C. D. (Eds.), *Community psychology:* Perspectives in training and research. New York: Appleton-Century-Crofts, 1972.

Jesness, C. F. Comparative effectiveness of behavior modification and transactional analysis programs for delinquents. *Journal of Consulting and Clinical Psychology,* 1975, *4,* 758–779.

Jones, R. J. & Arzin, N. H. An experimental application of a social reinforcement approach to the problem of job-finding. *Journal of Applied Behavior Analysis,* 1973, *6,* 345–353.

Jones, E. E., Kanouse, D. E., Kelley, H. H., Nisbett, R. E., Valins, S., & Weiner, B. *Attribution: Perceiving the causes of behavior.* Morristown, N.J.: General Learning, 1972.

Jones, R. R. Design and analysis problems in program evaluation. In P. O. Davidson, F. W. Clark, & L. A. Hamerlynck (Eds.), *Evaluation of behavioral programs in community, residential and school settings.* Champaign, Ill.: Research Press, 1974, pp. 1–31.

Katz, P., & Kahn, R. L. *The social psychology of organizations.* New York: Wiley, 1966.

Kazdin, A. E. Recent advances in token economy research. In M. Hersen, R. M. Eisler & R. M. Miller (Eds.), *Progress in Behavior Modification.* Vol. 1. New York: Academic Press, 1975, 233–274.

Kazdin, A. E. *The Token Economy.* New York: Plenum, 1977.

Klein, D. Use of the group method in consultation. In L. Parapart (Ed.), *Consultation in social work practice.* New York: National Association of Social Work, 1963.

Klein, D. C. Consultation processes as a method for improving teaching. In E. N. Bower & W. G. Hollister (Eds.), *Behavioral science frontiers in education.* New York: Wiley, 1967.

Kohlenberg, R., & Phillips, T. Reinforcement and rate of litter depositing. *Journal of Applied Behavior Analysis,* 1973, *6,* 391–396.

Kurioff, A. H., & Atkins, S. T groups for a work team. *Journal of Applied Behavioral Science,* 1966, *2,* 63–93.

Lachenmeyer, C. Systematic socialization: Observations on a programmed environment for the habilitation of antisocial retardates. *Psychological Record,* 1969, *19,* 247–257.

Lawrence, P. R., & Lorsch, J. W. *Developing organizations: Diagnosis and action.* Reading, Pa.: Addison Wesley, 1969.

Levine, F. M., & Fasnacht, G. Token rewards may lead to token learning. *American Psychologist,* 1974, *29,* 661–677.

Lewin, K. Group decision and social change. In T. Newcomb & E. Hartley (Eds.), *Readings in social psychology.* New York: Holt, 1947.

Lippitt, G. L. A study of the consultation process. *Journal of Social Issues,* 1955, *15(2),* 43–50.

Lippitt, G. L. *Organizational renewal.* New York: Appleton-Century-Crofts, 1969.

Lovaas, O. I., & Simmons, J. Q. Manipulation of self-destruction in three retarded children. *Journal of Applied Behavior Analysis,* 1969, *2,* 143–157.

MacLennan, B. W., Quinn, R. D., & Schroeder, D. The scope of community mental health consultation. In F. V. Mannino (Ed.), *The practice of mental health consultation.* New York: Gardner Press, 1975.

Mann, F. C. Studying and creating change. In W. G. Bennis, K. D. Benne, & R. Chin (Eds.), *The planning of change.* New York: Holt, 1969.

Mannino, F. V. Task accomplishment and consultation outcome. *Community Mental Health Journal,* 1972, *8(2),* 102–108.

Mannino, F. V. (Ed.), *The practice of mental health consultation.* New York: Gardner Press, 1975.

Mannino, F. V., & Shore, M. F. The effects of consultation: A review of empirical studies. *American Journal of Community Psychology*, 1975, *3*, 1–21.

Martinson, R. What works? Questions and answers about prison reform. *Public Interest*, 1974, *35*, 22–54.

Miles, M. G., Hornstein, H. A., Callahan, D. M., Calder, P., & Schiavo, R. S. The consequences of survey feedback: Theory and evaluation. In W. G. Bennis, K. D. Benne, & R. Chin (Eds.), *The planning of change.* New York: Holt, 1969.

Miller, L. K., & Miller, O. L. Reinforcing self-help group activities of welfare recipients. *Journal of Applied Behavior Analysis.* 1970, *3*, 57–64.

Nietzel, M. T., Winett, R. A., Macdonald, M. L., & Davidson, W. S. Behavioral approaches to community psychology. New York: Pergamon, 1977.

Nisbett, R. E., & Valins, S. Perceiving the causes of one's own behavior. Morristown, N.J.: General Learning Press 1971.

Norman, E. C., & Forti, T. J. Study of the process and outcome of mental health consultation. *Community Mental Health Journal*, 1972, *8(4)*, 261–270.

Nordquist, V. M. The modification of a child's enuresis: Some response-response relationships. *Journal of Applied Behavior Analysis*, 1971, *4*, 241–247.

O'Donnell, C. R. Behavior modification in community settings. In M. Herson, R. M. Eisler, & P. M. Miller (Eds.), *Progress in behavior modification* (Vol. 4). New York: Academic Press, 1977.

O'Leary, K. D., & Kent, R. Behavior modification for social action: Research tactics and problems. In L. A. Hamerlynck, L. C. Handy, & E. J. Mash (Eds.), *Behavior change: Methodology, concepts and practice.* Champaign, Ill.: Research Press, 1973, 69–96.

Parker, B. Psychiatric consultation for nonpsychiatric professional workers. *Public Health Monograph No. 53.* Washington, D.C.: Department of Health, Education and Welfare, 1958.

Parker, B. Some observations on psychiatric consultation with nursery school teachers. *Mental Hygiene,* 1962, *46*, 559–566.

Patterson, G. R. A basis for identifying stimuli which control behaviors in natural settings. *Child Development,* 1974, *45*, 900–911.

Patterson, G. R., & Cobb, J. A. Stimulus control for classes of noxious behaviors. In J. F. Knutson (Ed.), *The control of aggression.* Chicago, Ill.: Aldine, 1973, pp. 145–199.

Paul, G. L., & Lentz, R. J. *Psychosocial treatment of chronic mental patients: Milieu versus social learning programs.* Cambridge, Mass.: Harvard University Press, 1977.

Pedalino, E., & Gamboa, V. L. Behavior modification and absenteeism: Intervention in the industrial setting. *Journal of Applied Psychology*, 1974, *59*, 694–698.

Phillips, E. L., Phillips, E. A., Fixsen, D. L., & Wolf, M. M. Achievement Place: Behavior shaping works for delinquents. *Psychology Today*, 1973, *6*, 75–79.

Polk, W. J., & MacLennan, B. W. Experience in the training of mental health consultants. In F. V. Mannino (Ed.), *The practice of mental health consultation.* New York: Gardner Press, 1975.

Powers, R. B., Osborne, J. G., & Anderson, E. G. Positive reinforcement of litter removal in the natural environment. *Journal of Applied Behavior Analysis*, 1973, *6*, 579–586.

Rappaport, J. *Community psychology: Values, research and action.* San Francisco: Holt, 1977.

Rieman, D. W. Group mental health consultation with Public Health nurses. In L. Rapoport (Ed.), *Consultation in social work practice.* New York: National Association of Social Workers, 1963, pp. 85–98.

Risley, T. R. The effects and side effects of punishing the autistic behaviors of a deviant child. *Journal of Applied Behavior Analysis*, 1968, *1*, 21–34.

Robbins, P. P., Spencer, E. C., & Frank, D. A. Some factors influencing outcomes of consultation. *American Journal of Public Health*, 1970, *60(3)*, 524–539.

Robins, L. N. *Deviant children grown up*. Huntington, N.Y.: Krieger, 1974.

Rogawski, A. S. Teaching consultation techniques in a community agency. In W. M. Mendel, & P. Solomon (Eds.), *The psychiatric consultation*. New York: Grune & Stratton, 1968.

Rose, S. A., Blank, M., & Spalter, F. Situational specificity of behavior in young children. *Child Development*, 1975, *46*, 464-469.

Sajwaj, T., Twardosz, S., & Burke, M. Side effects of extinction procedures in a remedial preschool. *Journal of Applied Behavior Analysis*, 1972, *5*, 163–175.

Samuels, J. S., & Henderson, J. D. A community-based operant learning environment IV: Some outcome data. In R. D. Rubin, H. Fensterheim, A. A. Lazarus, & C. M. Franks (Eds.), *Advances in behavior therapy*. New York: Academic Press, 1971, pp. 263–271.

Schechtman, A. Age patterns in children's psychiatric symptoms. *Child Development*, 1970, *41*, 683–693.

Shaver, K. G. *An introduction to attribution processes*. Cambridge, Mass.: Winthrop, 1975.

Shean, G. A social learning approach to community living for chronic mental patients. *Proceedings of the 81st Annual Convention of the American Psychological Association*, 1973, *8*, 455–456.

Sherif, M., Harvey, O. J., White, B. J., Hood, W. E., & Sherif, C. W. *Intergroup conflict and cooperation: The robber's cave experiment*. Norman, Okla.: University of Oklahoma Book Exchange, 1961.

Signell, K. A., & Scott, P. A. Training in consultation: A crisis in role transition. *Community Mental Health Journal*, 1972, *8(2)*, 149–160.

Stoltz, S. B., Wienckowski, L. A., & Brown, B. S. Behavior modification: A perspective on critical issues. *American Psychologist*, 1975, 1027–1048.

Trist, E. L. On sociotechnical systems. In W. G. Bennis, K. D. Benne, & R. Chin (Eds.), *The planning of change*. New York: Holt, 1969.

Ullman, L. Behavioral community psychology: Implications, opportunities and responsibilities. In M. T. Nietzel, R. A. Winett, M. L. Macdonald, & W. S. Davidson (Eds.), *Behavioral approaches to community psychology*. New York: Pergamon, 1977.

Wahler, R. G. Some structural aspects of deviant child behavior. *Journal of Applied Behavior Analysis*, 1975, *8*, 27–42.

Wahler, R. G., Sperling, K. A., Thomas, M. R., Teeter, N. C., & Luper, H. L. The modification of childhood stuttering: Some response-response relationships. *Journal of Experimental Child Psychology*, 1970, *9*, 411–428.

Walton, R. E. Third party role in interdepartmental conflict. *Industrial Relations*, 1967, *7*, 29–43.

Winett, R. A., & Nietzel, M. T. Behavioral ecology: Contingency management of consumer energy use. *American Journal of Community Psychology*, 1975,*3*, 123–133.

CHAPTER 11

Advocacy and Community Psychology

Jane Knitzer, Ed. D.

The purpose of this chapter is to provide an overview of the roots, the meaning and applications of advocacy, and to examine the ways in which advocacy is consonant with and may be useful to community psychology.

The term advocacy has become an integral part of the vocabulary of social change agents. Advocacy refers to interventions designed to reduce or eliminate barriers within institutions or systems that result in the inequitable treatment of individuals or classes of individuals, the denial of needed services and resources, or the undermining of the individual's capacity for healthy development and self-determination. The target for change in advocacy is not the individual, but the policies and practices of the institutions with which individuals must daily interact—the schools, the courts, the welfare bureaucracies, the hospitals; the local, state and federal laws that shape so much of what happens in these institutions; the political and decision-making processes at all levels of government by which priorities and fiscal policies are determined; the administrative regulations that interpret laws and political mandates; and the practices and ideologies of professionals that get in the way of responsive help, particularly to those of a different cultural or ethnic background.

THE ROOTS OF ADVOCACY

The cutting edge of advocacy efforts was the activities in the 1960s of civil rights activists and anti-poverty warriors to end segregation and reduce the income and resource gap between the poor and nonpoor. Early advocacy efforts were often strident and adversarial, shocking communities into awareness of problems. Community organizers such as Alinsky experimented with strategies to empower the poor and to force local institutions to be more responsive to the otherwise disenfranchised (Alinsky, 1971). At the federal level, advocacy efforts were enhanced by the Great Society legislation which established a range of programs designed to eliminate poverty (Levitan, 1969). Citizen participation became a key goal—ensuring that minorities and the poor had access to information and formerly closed decision-making processes. Sometimes the poor and their advocates sought more than access; they sought control of the most visible or the most disliked institution in their own communities. In New York City, for example, parents in the city's poorest communities fought for community control of their local schools (Gittel & Helvesi, 1969). In some communities there were efforts to take control of local community mental health centers. Often the poor and their advocates challenged professionals, attacking them for their irrelevance and insensitivity in the face of the daily survival struggles of the poor. Indeed, the paraprofessional movement that emerged in those days reflected, in part, efforts of professionals to provide more responsive services to the poor and thus bridge the "two worlds" of the poor and the middle class.

At the same time, even as the notions of participatory democracy were spreading through communities and challenging bureaucrats and professionals in the human service industry, lawyers, spurred on by the welfare rights movement, began to explore ways to use administrative regulations and statutes to argue that the poor were legally entitled to greater benefits than they were receiving. In other words, advocates began to test the possibilities for using the law as an instrument of social change for both individuals and classes of individuals. From these early experiences the two fundamental tenets of advocacy emerged: the right of people to participate in decisions affecting their own lives, and the obligation of advocates to use, and where necessary modify, the existing statutory, regulatory and administrative framework to work for, not against, people.

Since the War on Poverty, advocacy on behalf of a wide range of constituencies has emerged. In 1970, for example, the Joint Commission on the Mental Health of Children, in recognition of the fact that vast numbers of children were underserved and sometimes ill-served, called for a national system of child advocacy. Although the national system never materialized, the report, in conjunction with the heightened awareness of the many unmet needs of children as a result of the Great Society programs, served as a catalyst for the extension of advocacy to a new constituency—children (Knitzer, 1976). Consumers too, stimulated by Ralph Nader, have used the tools of advocacy, as have the elderly, the developmentally disabled, and many other groups seeking greater responsiveness to their needs. Enriched by the experiences of these new constituents, the tools and techniques of advocacy have become more refined and codifiable.

ADVOCACY ASSUMPTIONS

While the boundaries and strategies of advocacy are fluid, there are four basic assumptions that form the ideological and methodological underpinnings of advocacy endeavors (Knitzer, 1976). Of these the most fundamental is the belief that people have, or ought to have, certain basic rights. This was initially, and continues to be, reflected in the commitment of advocates to ensuring that people have a right to participate in decisions affecting their lives and that they have access to the information and knowledge that makes such participation possible. But advocates are also concerned with rights in a more traditional sense: rights that are protected under the Constitution, rights that are protected in statute, and rights that have a moral rather than a legal basis—the right to adequate housing, for example, in contrast to the right not to be discriminated against in public housing.

The central role of rights has been reflected in two ways: first in a concern about the procedural rights afforded to individuals, and secondly about their substantive rights. In legal terminology procedural rights refer to efforts to ensure a fair hearing to individuals in a court of law. Procedural rights include the basic due rights: the right to notice of a hearing, the right to be present and cross examine witnesses, and the right to representation by counsel. Advocates, by extension, work to see that fair procedures exist within all programs or agencies, not only in court settings. So they challenge procedures resulting in the arbitrary suspension of students, or they may work to improve the grievance machinery within a welfare bureaucracy, or to ensure that if the cases of children in foster care are reviewed periodically, the parents, the children and the care givers receive notice of the review, and are guaranteed a right to participate. Another important function of advocates is to ensure that people have access to information (in understandable language) about programs, resources and services to which they are entitled.

The term substantive rights is used to refer to the content of a right—the substance of what is being protected. Not surprisingly, the concern with substantive rights has had a strong legal component. So in the past decade extensive legal attention has been paid to the substantive rights afforded to various groups of individuals and widespread efforts made to expand these rights, using the power of the courts. This is clear, for instance, in the landmark legal cases establishing the rights of institutionalized persons to treatment (Golann & Fremouw, 1976; President's Commission on Mental Health, 1978) and of handicapped children to an education (Lippman & Goldberg, 1973). But the value of attention to substantive rights is limited, unless there is equal attention to ensuring that resources are available to translate those rights into practice for all those affected. And so much of the nonlegal aspect of a concern with substantive rights has involved efforts to ensure the development of new or alternative resources and services.

The concern of advocates with defining and expanding the rights of those who are marginal or in some way "different" has also led advocates to focus attention on and to exploit the possibilities for using statutory, administrative and judicial procedures for enforcing and implementing both procedural and substantive rights. For advocates, in other words, the judicial decisions, legislation and the regulations and budgets governing the operations of programs and services are the essential vehicles through which specific change can be accomplished. Indeed the commitment to explore and exploit change possibilities within these arenas is central to effective advocacy. It provides a clear directional thrust and an organizing framework for selecting specific social change goals and the strategies necessary to realize them.

The second fundamental assumption is that advocacy is inherently political. Advocacy assumes an inequitable distribution of power, decision-making authority, economic and other resources, and access to information—and it takes as its constituency those who, in one way or another, are relatively powerless: the poor, minorities, children, the elderly, the handicapped. It represents an effort to change the status quo, to make professionals, bureaucracies and institutions more responsive and accountable. Consequently an effort to bring about change requires not only detailed analysis of the substantive issues involved, but of the political ones as well: who are the actors, who benefits from the status quo, who has the authority to effect change; what pressures can be brought to bear to persuade those with authority of the need for change.

A third underlying assumption is that advocacy efforts are focused on institutional failures that produce or aggravate individual problems, not on the individual difficulties themselves. Thus advocacy is different from the provision of direct services. This is not to say that advocates are not concerned with services. Very often the mark of successful advocacy is reflected in increased access to services, or in higher quality services. But advocacy interventions, unlike direct service interventions, focus upon problems within institutions and systems that impinge upon individuals. Thus both the strategies and the risks inherent in advocacy differ from those involved in the provision of direct service. Yet while the fundamental assumptions and strategies of advocacy may differ, the boundaries are not rigid. So professionals providing direct service in the traditional sense can and do take an advocacy stance on behalf of individual clients, and advocates can and should be sensitive to the feelings, conflicts and capacity of their clients for psychological growth.

Finally advocacy assumes an interrelationship between individuals and the social, political, economic and legal forces which determine both the public perception of a problem and the underlying structural factors that shape its boundaries. Thus methodologically and substantively advocacy relies upon an ecological perspective to trace the manifestations of a particular issue through different levels of social processes, to generate a range of remedies responsive to the problem at these different levels, and to try to anticipate the consequences of a corrective action on other parts of the system. In other words, advocates attempt to see "the whole picture" even though they may only be able to change a small piece of it.

THE MAJOR ADVOCACY PARAMETERS

Unified only by a commitment to these critical assumptions, advocacy in practice reflects many different forms, styles and organizational complexities. In the following section we will discuss the major advocacy efforts.

Type of Advocacy

The most basic distinction of all advocacy hinges on whether the advocacy is on behalf of one individual or a class of individuals. There are trade-offs in the choice of engaging in case or class advocacy; both are necessary, but each leads to different outcomes (Boggs, 1977). In case advocacy the benefits are relatively immediate and directly affect the individual with the problem. In class advocacy the benefit to the constituency is often more likely to be long range; the passage of new legislation, for example, may not affect those who suffer now, but will reduce barriers for those in need in the future. As a way of combining the strengths of both case and class advocacy, some projects link case advocacy with mechanisms for aggregating and challenging repeatedly identified abusive practices using class advocacy tools. So, for example, Riley (1971), in a discussion of case advocacy on behalf of a client faced with an interminable wait for a clinic appointment, shows how case-linked class advocacy led to a change in hospital appointments and waiting-room practices.

Constituency

The potential constitutencies for advocacy are virtually unlimited, although in general the boundaries reflect some combination of categories of need and/or status. Thus some advocacy is responsive to a limited constituency (all patients in a particular institution; all the developmentally disabled in a particular country; all adjudicated delinquents in one court); some is responsive to a broader constituency (all the elderly in a city; all children in a state).

Auspices

Who pays for and authorizes an advocacy effort clearly has a major impact on the scope of the project. There are three general patterns. In the first place, advocacy may be established under auspices that are independent, in terms of funding and authority, of those institutions and systems it seeks to challenge. The Children's Defense Fund, for example, which is a national child advocacy organization, accepts money only from foundations and private contributors. It will not accept government funds on the theory that to do so would reduce its freedom to criticize the ways in which government policies and practices result in the neglect or abuse of children. Other independent projects are citizen-based, authorized and funded through volunteer efforts.

Another set of advocacy efforts is based within, or linked to, the systems which are to be challenged. Often these are funded with public monies. In the early debates about advocacy it was frequently argued that no institutionally-based, publicly funded advocacy could be effective because the advocates would be inevitably coopted and compromised. While this remains a danger, it is also true that at least some institutional settings can be a home for effective advocacy, particularly case advocacy.

Much institutionally-based advocacy has been centered within specific agencies: a school, a hospital, a court. To a lesser extent, governmental bodies—local councils, state offices of the governor—have also provided the base for advocacy. Government-based advocacy obviously carries with it some constraints. It is least vulnerable to ineffectiveness if it is mandated by statute, but even so, the potential for engaging in meaningless rituals or being bought off by political exigencies is clear. At the same time it may provide to usually powerless constituencies access to the highest levels of decision makers.

Finally, a number of professional organizations are encouraging their members to engage in advocacy. So, for example, social workers have argued that the National Association of Social Workers Code of Ethics requires social workers to engage in advocacy (Ad Hoc Committee on Advocacy, 1969), and the American Academy of Pediatrics has produced a handbook on advocacy for pediatricians (1977). The extent to which professional organizations with an investment in maintaining and supporting professional self-interest can stimulate advocacy is questionable, although clearly individuals within these organizations can be effective. This leads, in fact, to the fourth major parameter of advocacy.

Advocate Identification

As there were early debates about the auspices of advocacy projects, so there were heated debates about who owned advocacy: professionals, paraprofessionals, lawyers, citizens or those who actually experienced the problem. Predictably such debates have lost their passion and advocates drawn from the ranks of all of these groups have been effective, working alone or in combination—as long as they share the ideology that undergirds advocacy. But it is true that some of those identified as potential advocates have found the role more comfortable than others. For both lawyers and citizens the advocacy role clearly fits into traditional patterns. For those who have actually experienced the problem, advocacy is natural extension of the self-help movement. For paraprofessionals it has been argued, although without any systematic evidence, that the advocacy role, particularly case advocacy, is a natural one, since paraprofessionals themselves are likely to have first-hand experience with the systems and procedures they are now challenging, and strong empathy for the client.

It is in fact for professionals, particularly those in the "helping" professions that advocacy has posed the greatest dilemmas. Some professionals have been concerned that advocacy resources would siphon off direct service resources. This denies the fact that a service approach to many of the problems that limit the quality of life for people is inappropriate or ineffective unless there is broader systems change. Others have been unwilling to risk jobs or status by challenging harmful practices within their own agencies or those of their colleagues. Underlying much of the resistance is also a concern that advocacy threatens the autonomy of the professional; it reduces his "helping role" and may indeed increase his sense of helplessness (Knitzer, 1978). (It is far easier, for example, to continue doing diagnostic evaluations than to try to challenge the exclusion of a severely handicapped child from a school program.) But the vision of the role of the professional as an autonomous helper, however appealing, is simply inaccurate. Like it or not, complex bureaucracies, regulations and other nets that constrain providers of service and client alike are a fact of life (McGowan, 1978b). Advocacy represents a strategy for coping with these nets. As such it can be argued that is unethical for a professional not to be trained in and sensitive to skills and concepts of advocacy.

The remaining dimensions of advocacy—target for change, strategy, geographic boundary—are all interrelated. The target to be changed determines the strategy, and, to some extent, the geographic boundaries of the effort. For purposes of discussion, however, each will be considered separately.

Target for Change

Advocates speak of the target for change in two ways: first, to refer to the particular system within which change must occur; and secondly, to identify a specific administrative regulation, statute or procedure within that particular system that is to be eliminated or modified. Thus the target for change in advocacy can be as varied as the problems that mobilize advocacy. A case advocate, for example, might take as the target for change a regulation within the welfare system resulting in the denial of public assistance to a needy family. Or the target for change may be the legislative framework which undergirds an entire system. The Children's Defense Fund, for example, based on a study of children in foster care has taken the position that eliminating federal fiscal incentives to long-term foster care is essential to any restructuring of the child welfare system at the local and state levels and has made this a major advocacy goal for the coming years. (Children's Defense Fund, 1978). In between these two extremes lie a range of targets for change, requiring varied strategies and time commitments. Budgets and administrative policies (written or unwritten) exist within every individual agency and across agencies. Ordinances and statutes at local, state and federal levels of government define programs and practices. Each of these singly or in combination may become the target for change. In fact in practice, because accomplishing either incremental or more fundamental restructuring of social processes requires change at many levels, in each substantive area in which advocates have emerged, efforts have typically been directed at all these targets.

Strategy

Case Advocacy. The most extensive systematic analysis of the strategies used by case advocates has been in relation to child advocacy. Using a critical interview technique McGowan (1978a) examined reports of advocacy interventions in a variety of agencies around the country. In her analysis three major approaches are available to advocates: collaborative strategies, in which the advocates seek to enlist the cooperation of those within the system to be changed, and which presuppose a responsive setting—a supportive administrator, or board, for example; mediating strategies, in which the advocate bargains or negotiates for the change; and the more adversarial strategies such as applying pressure, threatening exposure or even, in rare instances, initiating legal action. Whatever the approach, however, effective case advocacy is dependent upon the advocate's knowledge of how the system to be challenged works both formally and informally.

Class Advocacy. There is considerable overlap between the approaches of class advocacy and case advocacy as McGowan has identified them. Class advocates, however, are more likely to rely on four additional tools: investigative research, publicity (media, newspapers, public hearings), coalition- and constituency building and litigation, to accomplish their goals. Class advocacy also differs from case advocacy in that it is a vehicle for directly influencing the shape of public policy either at a local, state or national level. Consider, in this light, four major types of class advocacy: legislative, administrative, legal and monitoring.

Legislative advocacy refers to efforts to ensure that statutes protect the needs and rights of groups of individuals, and that appropriations are sufficient to implement such protections. Legislative advocacy involves a range of activities: identifying gaps in existing legislation, proposing alternative legislation, evaluating proposed changes in terms of their impact on a specific constituency or developing substantive evidence to support or propose changes, educating legislators and their staff about the issues and direct lobbying. Influencing the legislative process is of course not something new. What is new is its application on behalf of constituencies which in the past had little voice in the political process.

Legislative advocacy is not without pitfalls (for example, navigating the tax laws that limit how much lobbying a group can do), and most human service advocates are relative novices at it. But because governmental laws and dollars shape the context in which people get or fail to get "help," services, housing, and the like, such advocacy is increasingly central.

Administrative advocacy is the least glamorous, the most tedious and often one of the most important forms of advocacy. Administrative advocacy refers to efforts to influence the regulations or guidelines of private and particular governmental agencies. It is especially vital at the state and national levels. Administrative advocacy is dependent upon the advocate knowing what the bureaucracy has done, is doing or plans to do. Such information is not always readily available, either because it does not exist or because administrators would prefer that it not be available. And so advocates rely on relationships with the administrators, threats of exposure, the use of freedom of information laws or, most typically, some combination of all of these. Administrative advocacy assumes a tension between the bureaucracies and the decision makers within it and the advocates—but it does not assume that all those working within a system are bad, or all those on the outside are good.

Bureaucracies are a fact of life. Administrative advocacy marks one strategy for coping with them.

Legal advocacy or litigation is a tool of last resort for advocates. Class-action litigation is costly and time consuming, so that even a successful court challenge may not directly benefit the named plantiffs. But it can also be an effective way to heighten awareness of a particular pattern of abuses, and increasingly it is becoming a tool through which to try to accomplish largescale systematic change. For example, in the initial right-to-treatment suits, lawyers were particularly concerned with establishing the principle of a right to treatment. The focus now is broader and lawyers, often with the help of social workers, psychologists and planners, are seeking "remedies" which will be effective in implementing the established right. They are requesting that the court's order specify both structural changes necessary to modify the responsible system or systems, and mechanisms to ensure the continuing implementation of these structural changes.

Monitoring advocacy, or what has been called accountability advocacy, is perhaps the least developed of all the tools advocates use. Monitoring refers to the ongoing efforts of advocates to hold systems accountable, to ensure that they are doing what they are supposed to be doing and to ensure that changes become incorporated into ongoing processes and functioning. Monitoring has been particularly useful in efforts by local communities to make certain that federal programs for the poor, the elderly and children are in fact in compliance with the federal mandates. Monitoring of local and state budgets to ensure adequate resources for constituents has been less developed but is becoming increasingly important. So, for example, in one innovative effort, several advocacy groups have banded together and designed a project to train members of community planning boards in the assessment and monitoring of the city funds available for the direct service and administrative costs of serving families and children in a particular locality.

Geographic Boundaries

The geographic boundaries of advocacy exist on a continuum from "block advocacy," to advocacy within one particular community, to advocacy with a state or national focus. Attention to such boundaries is important in that it affects the targets for change and the strategies of choice. A local advocacy project, for example, with few resources would be unlikely to take as its major goal change in federal legislation, or mount a major class-action lawsuit, although it could work with other groups in support of such change.

MODELS FOR ADVOCACY

While it is not the purpose of this chapter to review systematically or in detail existing advocacy projects, it is appropriate to highlight briefly some of the different combinations of the major parameters just described that have worked their way into programs. First consider models of case advocacy. Much case advocacy is informal and ad hoc. It happens because someone is angered by what is happening to a child or a teenage parent or a non-English-speaking grandmother with a handicapped grandchild, and tries to intervene. But there have been efforts to make case advocacy available to people on a more systematic basis.

Wolfensberger (undated), for example, has developed a program of citizen advocacy for the retarded that has now been replicated in over 40 states. In his model a retarded or developmentally handicapped individual is assigned to a volunteer advocate who engages in either "expressive" or "instrumental" advocacy in the person's behalf. In Wolfensberger's terms expressive advocacy refers to efforts to provide emotional support, protection and friendship to an individual. As such it is close to traditional big brother, big sister volunteer efforts. Instrumental advocacy, on the other hand, is consistent with the view of advocacy presented here and demands knowledge of and challenge to institutional barriers.

Newberger and his colleagues have developed a model for case advocacy under institutional auspices, using paraprofessionals, in which the advocates respond to whatever environmental stresses the client seeks help with (Morse, Hyde, Newberger, & Reed, 1976). Interestingly, this project grew out of a research study conducted in a hospital setting on the relationship of environmental stress to social illnesses. The researchers decided that it was unethical to conduct detailed interviews with subjects about the stress they experienced and not do anything about it. Consequently they built an advocacy component into the study in which paraprofessionals, under the direction of a lawyer, followed up on requests for help with housing, food, legal or other problems not typically addressed by hospital personnel.

In both these approaches the advocates are available to respond to any requests for help. Other case advocacy is triggered in response to a complaint or grievance by a client. This more limited case advocacy is typically found within closed institutional settings: psychiatric hospitals, nursing homes and juvenile correctional facilities, for example (Linnae, 1975; Keating, Gilligan, McArthur, Lewis, & Singer, undated). It is designed to protect individuals against abuses within the institution. Such advocacy is most closely linked to the traditional role of the ombudsman, who hears both sides of a complaint and then attempts to resolve differences (Peel, 1968). There have also been efforts to expand the ombudsman model beyond closed institutions to bureaucratic settings. So, for example, the Office for Special Services for Children in New York City, which is part of the mammoth social services bureaucracy, has established what it calls the "Natural Parents' Rights Unit" to respond to complaints from the natural parents of the 28,000 children in foster care in New York City.

Programs that combine case and class advocacy tend to be conducted under independent auspices and are either limited by geographic category or by constituency. Thus, for instance, the Philadelphia Urban League sponsored a child advocacy project that explicitly included components of case advocacy, public education and community organization (Who Speaks for Children? 1976). That project took all children who lived in a particular Philadelphia community as its clients.

Another form of combined case and class advocacy has recently emerged in response to a federal mandate. The Developmentally Disabled Assistance and Bill of Rights Act of 1975 (P.L. 94-103) requires that each state establish an advocacy and protection system to protect the human and legal rights of each developmentally disabled person. The legislation further stipulates that such systems must be independent of any public agency that directly or indirectly provides services, and must be empowered to pursue legal, administrative and other appropriate remedies. It is too soon to evaluate its impact or the range of systems that the states have set up, but the federal law will clearly serve as a catalyst for increased case advocacy (Baucom & Bensberg, 1977).

As is true of case advocacy, much class advocacy has been informal, brought about through the ad hoc efforts of a community or volunteer organization to deal with a particular issue. Organizations established specifically for the purposes of conducting class advocacy are a relatively recent phenomenon. They have emerged as a new institutional form in response to the failures of other institutions. These new organizations vary primarily by the range of strategies they employ and by the level of intervention, with most operating within a state or national context. For example, the Children's Defense Fund (CDF) as a national children's rights, child advocacy organization has an interdisciplinary staff and uses a range of strategies, including litigation and constituency building, with primary emphasis on lobbying and monitoring federal policies. In contrast the State of California has a statewide child advocacy organization that uses only one strategy: lobbying. The Massachusetts Advocacy Center, like CDF, has an interdisciplinary staff and focuses on children's issues in a number of substantive areas, but it relies to a large extent on administrative advocacy. A similar range of approaches can be found in other substantive areas around which organized class advocacy has emerged.

ADVOCACY AND COMMUNITY PSYCHOLOGY: THE COMMON GROUND

Thus far we have examined the roots, assumptions and major dimensions of advocacy. The question to be addressed now is why such knowledge is important to community psychology. There are at least four major reasons.

Shared Values and Assumptions

The first and perhaps most compelling reason is that advocates and community psychologists share many basic assumptions and values. The language of advocates and community psychologists may differ, but the underlying stance does not. Both community psychologists and advocates, for instance, are committed to expanding opportunities for individuals to develop to their fullest capacity. Community psychology explicitly seeks to draw on and respond to the strengths of individuals and communities. It seeks to maximize the psychological sense of competence within individuals and develop, as Iscoe (1974) has said, "competent communities." To accomplish this, community psychology has been concerned with the support structures available to communities and to subgroups (for example, minorities) within communities. And it has been concerned with reducing barriers to services and resources. Advocates too seek to ensure that support structures necessary for effective participation exist— that the powers of citizen advisory or reviews boards are well defined in statute, that training funds are available to minimize ritual participation, that individual advocates are available to teach parents, the elderly, the handicapped how to navigate the bureaucracies and secure the benefits to which they are entitled.

Both community psychology and advocacy also share a similar approach to traditional definitions of social problems and apply paradigms that will lead to the generation of new solutions to old problems. Both reject the "blaming the victim" mentality that has trapped and continues to trap helpers, change agents and clients alike in a circle of ineffectiveness (Ryan, 1971).

As a case in point, consider in brief the advocacy process in response to the failure of the schools to provide appropriate programs, or sometimes any schooling at all, for handicapped children. Until fairly recently the problem was owned by the parents and children. It was their problem and their task to try to get the schools to be more responsive. But then, in a precedent-setting advocacy effort, the parents of handicapped children in Pennsylvania redefined the problem. They joined together and challenged the legality, under the Constitution, of the *schools'* excluding their children. In a landmark decision the court upheld the parents (Lippman & Goldberg, 1973). Since then, advocates have also sought legislative solutions to challenge the state and federal statutory structure that permits the noneducation of children with handicapping conditions.

This leads directly to yet another similarity in fundamental perspective. Community psychology was one of the earliest social science disciplines to see the relevance of the concept of ecology for the analysis of social problems. In the words of the Swampscott conference, held in 1966, "Community psychology is devoted to the study of general psychological processes that link social systems with individual behavior in complex interaction" (Bennett, Anderson, Cooper, Hassol, Klein, & Rosenblum, 1966, p. 7).

Community psychology, in other words, goes beyond a focus on the intrapsychic and the interpersonal. It acknowledges the power and legitimacy of specific organizational practices and policies (the exclusion of two-parent poor families from the public assistance program, for instance), as well as general institutional forces such as racism. And it seeks to trace the impact of these practices, policies and social forces upon the individual. The methodology for the analysis of human behavior in a broad context is still limited. But there is no question that the attempt by community psychologists to map the patterns and meaning of interactions between individuals and systems is ecological.

Advocates, as indicated earlier, likewise rely upon an ecological perspective. In fact advocacy may be said to be applied social ecology, for effective advocates working on a specific problem must trace the roots and ramifications of that problem throughout an ecological network, both to define the problem in all its complexity and to formulate correctives that will make a difference.

Case Advocacy: A Program Model

Shared perspectives and values are one reason for community psychologists to learn about advocacy. The second major reason for community psychologists to be knowledgeable about advocacy is that case advocacy, in all its variants, represents a model for program development that is particularly suited to the skills and interests of community psychologists. Conceptually case advocacy has the potential to fuse, in one intervention, efforts to enhance the individual's sense of psychological power (competence) with efforts to enhance power as it is more typically defined: economic or political power. Not all case advocates are aware of the psychological opportunity implicit in case advocacy. Indeed it is likely that most case advocates have focused only on the more traditional dimensions of power as they have sought to ensure food stamps for people, or to force housing agencies to find a new apartment for a family with a child hospitalized for lead paint poisoning.

Yet as Morse wrote in discussing the hospital-based advocacy project referred to earlier:

> "While it is oriented toward securing goods and services for people . . . advocacy also aims to provide families and individuals with the technical and psychological resources to solve their own problems. The steps that the advocate takes to secure a new apartment for a family, for example, really constitute a learning process for that family, a process which, once learned may be applied to seeking solutions to other problems (1976, p. 5).

Community psychologists, by virtue of their training, should be particularly effective in finding ways to encourage the learning process. And because they recognize the importance of securing goods and services and manipulating external forces on behalf of an individual, community psychologists should be more comfortable than most mental health professionals in developing programs that combine psychological and nonpsychological goals. Yet up until now, only a few community psychologists have been involved in the development of case advocacy programs (Davidson & Rapp, 1976).

New Intervention Strategies

The third major reason for community psychologists to learn about advocacy skills and processes is that advocacy, and particularly class advocacy, represents an opportunity to expand the repertoire of intervention strategies available to most community psychologists. In theory community psychologists are committed to interventions at all possible levels: individual, group, organizational, institutional and social. But in reality the skills and experiences of community psychologists tend to cluster at the first three levels. The skills and experiences of advocates, in contrast, tend to cluster at the last three levels. Like community psychologists, advocates are "participant conceptualizers," but they focus their analytic efforts primarily on systems and structures, and less on people. Advocates, for example, have developed skills in analyzing and developing regulations or legislation that should be part of the training of community psychologists, to facilitate their involvement in broad social change. More reciprocity between advocacy and community psychology will not only be useful to enrich individual community psychologists, however. It may also enrich the theoretical framework of community psychology in enabling its practitioners to have better understanding of social change processes. Participating in advocacy, particularly class advocacy efforts, gives community psychologists the opportunity to provide an empirical test of theoretical assumptions about social change.

Need for Evaluation of Advocacy

Finally, there is as yet an unaddressed need for the systematic evaluation of both case and class advocacy efforts. What, for example, is the impact of a specific case advocacy project on institutional policies? Can case advocacy alone be effective as a therapeutic strategy? What are the long-term consequences of major class-action litigation for human service systems and for individuals? What are the components of a successful advocacy project? How can the impact of advocacy be traced? Community psychologists are in a strong position to undertake such evaluation: their values overlap with those of the advocates, and their training equips them to devise useful evaluations.

THE LIMITS OF ADVOCACY

Advocacy is not a substitute for readily available high quality services, nor is it an alternative to a social policy that provides families with adequate jobs, income, housing and services. It is useful in the service of both these goals. Sometimes advocates opt for the long-term benefit, at the expense of an individual. Sometimes advocates, like others, disagree about priorities, strategies and tactics (Polier, 1977). Yet under the rubric of advocacy during the past decade, a set of generic strategies and skills has emerged that can be translated across issues and disciplines with some effectiveness. And so, even with its limitations, the status of advocacy as a catalyst for social change is assured. Perhaps in the next decade the status of community psychology as a catalyst for advocates will also be assured.

References

Ad Hoc Committee on Advocacy. The social worker as advocate: Champion of victims. *Social Work*, April 1969, *14*.

Alinsky, S. D. *Rules for radicals*. New York: Random House, 1971.

American Academy of Pediatrics. *Handbook on child advocacy*. 1977.

Baucom, L. & Bensberg, G. *Advocacy systems for persons With developmental disabilities*.

Lubbock, Tex.: Research and Training Center in Mental Retardation, Texas Tech University, 1977.

Bennett, C. C., Anderson, L. S., Cooper, S., Hassol, L., Klein, D., & Rosenblum, G. *Community psychology: A report of the Boston conference on the education of psychologists for community mental health.* Boston: Boston University Press, 1966.

Boggs, E. Collective advocacy (systems advocacy) versus individual advocacy: An issue paper. In L. Baucom and G. Bensberg (Eds.), *advocacy systems for persons with developmental disabilities.* Lubbock, Tex.: Research and Training Center in Mental Retardation, Texas Tech University, 1977.

Children's Defense Fund. *Children without homes: An examination of public responsibility to children in out-of-home care.* Children's Defense Fund of the Washington Research Project, Inc., 1978.

Davidson, W., & Rapp, C. Child advocacy in the justice system. *Social Work*, 1976, *21*, 225–232.

Gittell, M., & Helvesi, A. G. *The politics of urban education.* New York: Praeger, 1969.

Golann, S., & Fremouw, W. *The right to treatment for mental patients.* New York: Irvington, 1976.

Iscoe, I. Community psychology and the competent community. *American Psychologist*, 1974, *29*, 607–613.

Joint Commission on the Mental Health of Children. *Crisis in child mental health: Challenge for the 1970's.* New York: Harper & Row, 1970.

Keating, J., Gilligan, K. M., McArthur, V. A., Lewis, M. K., & Singer, L. R. *Seen but not heard.* Washington, D. C.: Center for Correctional Justice, undated.

Knitzer, J. Child Advocacy: A perspective. *American Journal of Orthopsychiatry*, 1976, *46*, 200–216.

Knitzer, J. Responsibility for delivery of services. In J. S. Mearig & Associates (Eds.), *Working for children.* San Francisco: Jossey-Bass, 1978.

Levitan, S. *The great society's poor law.* Baltimore: The Johns Hopkins, 1969.

Linnae, P. *Ombudsman for nursing homes: Structure and process.* Washington, D. C.: USDHEW, Administration On Aging, 1975.

Lippman, L., & Goldberg, I. *Right to education: Anatomy of the Pennsylvania Case and Its implications for exceptional children.* New York: Teachers College Press, 1973.

McGowan, B. The Case Advocacy Function in Child Welfare Practice. *Child Welfare*, 1978, *52*, 275–284. (a)

McGowan, B. Strategies In Bureaucracies. In J. S. Mearig & Associates (Eds.), *Working for Children.* San Francisco: Jossey-Bass, 1978. (b)

Morse, A., Hyde, J., Newberger, E., & Reed, R. Environmental correlates of pediatric social illness: Preventive implications of an advocacy approach. Paper presented at the Annual Meeting of the American Public Health Association, 1976.

Peel, R. *The ombudsman or citizens defender: A modern institution.* Philadelphia: American Academy of Political Science, 1968.

Polier, J. W. External and internal roadblocks to effective child advocacy. *Child Welfare*, 1977, *56*, 497–508.

President's Commission on Mental Health. *Legal and ethical issues*, Appendix IV, Washington, D. C.: Government Printing Office, 1978.

Riley, P. Family advocacy: Case to cause and back to case. *Welfare*, 1971, *50*, 374–383.

Ryan, W. *Blaming the victim.* New York: Pantheon, 1971.

Who speaks for children? Child advocacy in Philadelphia: A community development approach 1971–1976. Philadelphia: Urban League, 1976.

Wolfensberger, W. Toward citizen advocacy for the handicapped. Nebraska: Psychiatric Institute, University of Nebraska Medical Center, Undated mimeo.

CHAPTER 12

Family Therapy and the Community

Harry Aponte, M.S.W.

Family therapy has been perceived and described mostly from its position relative to individual therapy. Conceptually it has been a radical and successful departure from the individual orientation. But the comparison with individual therapy for the most part has been narrowly based on the vicissitudes of professional competition within the clinical arena and has missed the significance of family therapy as a social phenomenon reflecting a reinterpretation of society into ecological or systems terms.

Family therapists have themselves addressed the focus of their concern—the family as a social unit—but even they, while speaking to the individual in the context of the family and to the family itself, have often neglected the logical sequel to their theory, which lies in the community, the larger social context in which that individual and his or her family function.

THE FAMILY-COMMUNITY CONTINUUM

The evolving structure of the relationship of the family to the community of which individuals and families are a part is assuming greater social and political significance. This issue was dramatically raised in the United States during the late sixties when many people, particularly those representing poor minorities, protested that community mental health clinics were giving only token recognition to the family styles and values of groups other than those in the mainstream—white middle-class. They complained that clinicians were not including the sociopolitical context of the community in which minority families were developing in the formulation of the emotional problems of poor people.

The same questions in various forms are being raised internationally as a political issue as the mental health movement spreads. The thrust of the argument has been that mental health professionals are working to change people to adapt to the very social institutions and conditions that were creating their problems. Without going into the history of this controversy, certainly the following question must be raised: if one perceives human behavior as the product of the ecological context, how can one stop at the boundaries of the family when defining the dimensions of an emotional problem?

A further reason for including the community in our conceptualizations of the dynamics of the family is that institutions in our modern industrial society are so much a part of our lives that the functional boundaries of the family are becoming increasingly more interwoven with these same societal units. Take as a case in point the rearing of children. In relation to children, parents are usually seen as functioning as sources of nurturance, discipline, identification and as the advocates, providers and executive organizers of their lives. However, through social engineering societal institutions are sharing in and assuming more of the traditional parental functions. For example, how much do parents control and participate in the health care of their children? What say do they have about the distribution of publicly funded health facilities in their communities? How fully informed are parents about diagnostic questions and choices of courses of treatment? To what extent can parents participate in an active way in the treatment of their children in a hospital? The more a child's rearing is defined by society in medical terms, the more the medical establishment, the corresponding insurance agencies and health-related government bodies will assume control of the family's functions in relation to the child.

When it comes to the education of the child, the impact of society is dramatic. By law, children must go to school. For economic reasons most children go to public schools, where there is total control over the educational courses the children are inducted into. Children are taught citizenship, health care, sex, death. Discipline is in the hands of the school masters who decide the rules. Standards for education, what is taught and the level of proficiency expected are determined by the schools. The schools can enforce their standards because withholding a diploma will deny a youngster access to a higher level of education, to a career, to a job. All this power—and parents have virtually no say over any of these inputs and influences on their children's minds and characters.

The environment in which a child is raised, which impacts directly on the parent's ability to provide and care for a child, is also increasingly outside the control of the parent. Parents pick a community in which to raise children, and government and business interests decide whether highways will be built there, public housing, schools and playgrounds, whether government contracts will be granted in one area versus another, and so forth. Television, public or commercial, is programmed by people who cannot respond to communities or families. Their decisions are governed by dynamics which have little relationship to what parents are pursuing for their children.

And, of course, an increasingly more powerful competitor with parents for control of children is the mental health professional and the mental health agency. Mental health professionals are telling judges whether children are or are not criminals and whether parents are fit to raise their children. They tell schools whether a child should or should not be in regular classes, or even in school. Mental health professionals decide whether a child should be institutionalized. They are labeling children as disturbed and assuming the responsibility for "fixing" them. They separate children from parents in confidential sessions and then advise or direct parents on how to parent their own children.

Our society has surrounded families with guidance, direction, care and regulations that progressively restrict the latitude of parents to decide for and with their children. How then can we define emotional problems as belonging to the individual or even to the family alone if people's lives are increasingly dependent on community institutions? We can do so only by ignoring the reality before us. The family's and individual's community is intimately involved in shaping the family and its individual members. The community's contribution to the generation of emotional problems and to the perpetuation or solution of them is simply a fact of life. Politicians and community organizers make a living out of struggling with institutional life. Clinicians often do not recognize how relevant the community is to their office practice and when they do, they do not know what to do about it.

PROBLEMS OF CONCEPTUALIZATION AND INTERVENTION

Indeed the therapist's first concern is the individual or family before him or her. What is good for this person or persons, within the framework of social responsibility, is the primary responsibility of the therapist. This means that the clinician looks for change in the contexts of the social units before him to the extent that these changes will serve the needs of those he or she is to treat. The family therapist includes the family in any formulation of the dynamics of the problems of family members. The technical interventions may or may not be executed with all family members present but to the extent possible will be calculated to impact on the actions of the whole family. However, the family therapist who sees the community as part of the continuum with the family will also include the community in his or her understanding of a problem and in the field of intervention.

The conceptual and technical problem for the therapist is that this ecological perspective asks that he who is concerned about a discrete clinical problem take into account a very broad social context. The family as the most intimately and continuously associated context in which the individual lives represents the critical leap into the ecological perspective. By itself, with all its component systems, the family is an extremely complex social system in which the individual develops and functions. But when the family is seen as contiguous with community institutions, the complexity of the ecological context that the therapist must consider is that much greater.

In the clinical situation, the therapist's vision is funneled through the symptom, problem or issue presented by the patient or clients. A child is fearful of going to school. Another youngster has run away from his parents. A mother has severely injured her child in a moment of extreme frustration. A man has developed disabling headaches and has quit work.

Psychoanalysis focuses on the individual patient as the bearer of the emotional problem and proceeds to explore and intervene in that individual's life in the transferential relationship with the analyst. Group therapy also concentrates on the individual while circumscribing its arena of intervention to the group. The clinician in these situations serves as the entrance and exit door to the therapeutic unit. The patient or group relates to the therapist as the pivotal figure who creates the therapeutic context.

However, in the family, the individual has underlying him a complex social system which by its very nature is independent of the therapist. The family is a natural social unit that does not lend itself as easily as the individual or therapeutically created group to being sealed off by a therapist nor to centralizing the therapist in its life. There is too much going on between the family members that is critical to survival for the family to divert too much of its energy from itself out to the therapist. It is harder to deal in fantasy for long with a family in therapy. If one member begins to do so, others will draw him away because of their own concern for the consequences of such ruminations on their lives. Also the family members have common vital roots outside the family that are too much of a concern to all of them—jobs, schools, friends—for the family to cut off considerations about these realities in the therapy. The family tends to draw the world into the therapy and to pull the therapist out into its world.

But the nature of the family is not enough to force a broadening of the therapist's perspective if he or she by personal inclination or training insists on not seeing beyond the identified patient or the interviewing room. In meeting with a family the therapist can limit his or her view to a single individual and interview the individual in the group rather than try to understand the family as a whole. In the same way, the therapist can resist the family's pull to enter the world outside itself. And the family can be conditioned to relate to the therapist strictly in terms of the therapist's interests.

The vital question for the therapist with a clinical concern is how to understand the problem presented with all its supporting dynamics. If, as is being argued here, to do this the therapist needs to consider the entire ecological context in which the problem is being generated and maintained, the therapist addressing a discrete personal problem of an individual, a couple or parent and child, is confronted with a contextual field that may appear too broad, complex and indistinct for the therapist to function clinically.

RESTRUCTURING REALITY AND ITS ANALOGUE

As complicated as is this ecological context, the therapist cannot practically comprehend the entire world impinging on the problem, but may begin to touch the parts of that world that are most directly affecting the issue and that are accessible to the therapist's realm of vision and intervention. The dynamics of the ecological complex are interlocked in ways that radiate out from any single issue in patterns that can be traced.

The ecological complex out of which an action is generated is composed of interdependent systems that relate to one another in structural patterns that accord with the nature of the action taken. The components of each of these systems organize their relationship to one another in a system and towards the other systems in the ecological complex in patterns, sometimes referred to as the eco-structure, which are specific to the operation the system is to engage in. Any dysfunction of these operations which becomes characteristic of a system and among systems carries with it a structural organization of the ecological complex that accounts for the problem.

At the most abstract level, three of the key structural relationships can be conceptualized under the terms boundary, alignment and force. Boundary refers to structural relationship which convey the inclusion or exclusion of components of a system in a particular operation. Alignment speaks to the working, together or in opposition, of the components in relation to one another with respect to the operation. Force describes what combination of components has the power to determine the actual outcome of the transactions that make up the operation. These eco-structural relations are dynamic in that they take place in actions that are enacted in time and space and are always changing according to the development of the system.

Clinically we deal with symptoms, problems that are of current concern to the person and institutions involved. The history of structural patterns which were the precursors to the current problem can throw light upon the infrastructure of the issues at hand, but their understanding cannot of itself solve the problem. Only a reorganization of the structural relationships in the systems currently creating and maintaining the problem will change the outcome of the interaction among these components.

The clinician dealing with what is commonly considered a mental health problem has the technical problem of determining how to unravel the threads of the structural patterns which lead to and from the problem he or she is addressing. We believe it is technically feasible to follow these threads through their ecological context to the extent that the therapist can have access to the social systems contiguous to the circumstances surrounding a problem. The greater number of the social units creating these circumstances that one can have enact the problem or issue with the therapist, the more readily apparent will the eco-structural underpinnings be. Their accessibility to the therapist also facilitates therapeutic intervention.

Since there are practical limits on how far one can go in engaging these parties in the real circumstances of their lives in which the problems appear, the clinician conducts this living-out of an issue in the relatively artificial circumstances of the clinical interview with whomever is available, and hopes to extract from that transaction an idea not only of how the persons present in the interview deal with one another and the therapist about the problems, but how they structurally link up with those people and institutions in the ecological context outside the session which contribute most directly to the problems.

The ecological perspective is founded on the concept that patterns of behavior usually have direct links to structures in all kinds of systems, other than those represented by the person or persons acknowledged as the problem bearers. These links can be virtually absolute so that a change in one system necessarily changes another, or they can be less rightly but more complexly associated. For the therapist, exploration of the nature of this link is critical. To a large extent the family therapist interested in an individual's problems assumes these links to exist in the family. Linkages between a single individual's behavior or emotional state and other family members, while commonly found, vary in their absoluteness and complexity. The relationships of the community to the individual's problem likewise vary in their degree of connectedness to one another.

Where the link is absolute, one knows that to change a component in the eco-structure of a problem is to change another which is tightly associated with it in the problem, whether the other component is or is not in the session. If there is an absolute link between a couple's marital problems and their child's symptoms, the resolution of the marital problem will immediately result in the disappearance of the child's symptom. However, more often than not there is a looser and more intricately complex relationship between the youngster's problems and those of his parents, so that a change in one will affect the other, but only partially.

The therapist may intervene directly in the linkages among family members and community whether they are or are not all present in a session. However, the therapist may also take an indirect approach and go after analogues of the dysfunctional structural pattern. Here the therapist assumes that the circumstances of the analogue are sufficiently closely associated to the real-life situation that an intervention in the analogue will affect the targeted reality. When the family therapist intervenes directly in the reality of the problem he works with the same organization of people and circumstances as are involved in the issue. When the therapist works with the analogue, he works through a somewhat different combination of people and/or partly or totally different circumstances that still bear, for at least some of the people involved, the same systematic structures that generate or maintain their problem. Whether directly in reality or in the analogue, the therapist goes after the same dysfunctional structural pattern. However, it also needs to be noted that every well-timed intervention simultaneously affects the structural complex directly involved in a problem as well as others analogously related to it. For the therapist the question becomes whether to explicitly direct an intervention more towards the reality of the problem or its analogue.

In the therapy session the therapist has family members live out some of their conflicts. Even when they engage in a struggle over the issue that they came about, to some extent that very enactment, while providing a real situation that the therapist directly intervenes in, can also be said to provide a structural analogue to the family's struggle at home, where it takes place without the participation of the therapist.

Direct negotations of family relationships in a session will for an individual member also be analogous to a whole series of other structurally similar conflict-laden situations in other family contexts and in situations outside the family. A change in the relationship of a child to a parent in a session may alter in a similar way the child's relationship to the parent at home as well as to other parentlike figures in school. Working directly with the reality along with a party to the problem can be like seeing the parents of a troubled child without the child and attempting to help the child by intervening with the parents in the aspects of their problem that they believe are upsetting the child. To work analogously with the same issue the therapist may deal with the parents on ways their differences make it difficult for the therapist to relate to the two of them simultaneously, substituting self for the child.

There are many reasons why a therapist will choose to approach a problem through an analogue. Most commonly the therapist will do so to avoid stubborn resistance and make the most of people's potential, which may be more available in circumstances outside of those directly related to the problem. Also the therapist who does not have a person's, or a group of people's, world at hand in an interview can, through the analogue, make a bridge from the context of the family session to family and community contexts not directly accessible to the therapist.

The mother of an eight-year-old boy who refused to talk or respond to teachers thought the teacher could get her son to talk and work with her if only the teacher would follow the mother's ideas of how to deal with him. But the mother did not believe the teacher would listen to her. A therapist went behind a one-way mirror with the mother and requested the mother to instruct a cotherapist, who was on the other side of the mirror with her son, how to assign a school task to him and supervise him in carrying it out. The mother was hesitant, but after several tries and some encouragement from the therapist, began to instruct the cotherapist, through the telephone connecting the observation room to the interviewing room, on how to be firm but engaging with her son. Through repetition and persistence on the mother's part, the cotherapist learned how to execute what the mother was asking her to do and to everyone's pleasure, the boy responded. The mother walked out of the session confident she could communicate to the real teachers her expectations of a different approach to her son, which she did indeed succeed in doing.

The context in which this mother instructed the cotherapist was for her structurally analogous to her relationship with her son's teacher. A great deal of therapy is carried out through interventions in analogous contexts. Psychoanalysis epitomizes interventions in the analogue as the analyst comes to represent a whole series of other persons and contexts for the analysand. The analyst, however, is focused on the intrapsychic reorganization of the individual. The family therapist assumes a degree of responsibility not only for the individual but also for the relationships among the persons included in all the systemic contexts that impinge upon the issues relevant to the therapy. For the family therapist the structural links within and outside the family are accessible both through the analogue and directly through the system of absolute and complex linkages that connect people and organizations to one another.

There is an infinite number of ways therapists use the analogue. A direct intervention into the reality of a problem may involve only those present in a session or may be directed at the linkages between those present and those outside the session.

For examples of direct interventions with the persons included in the structured patterns supporting a problem one can look at Minuchin (1974) and Minuchin, Montalvo, Guerney, Rosman & Schumer (1967). Minuchin has had the family of an anorectic girl have a meal with her in his presence. Auerswald (1968) may have the agencies that are impacting on a family's life participate in an interview with the family. Speck (1969) brings the social network together in one room. Aponte (1976) will interview family and school personnel together in the school. In each of these situations, to the extent that the therapist addresses primarily issues that exist among the principals present and that can be enacted by them in the session, the therapist has direct accessibility to the reality of the problem.

On the other hand, Bowen (1972) may address a family member in a session about issues that exist between that person and other family members who are not present. Elkaim (1979) may have a group of families reorganize their relationships to one another so that they can go out and take joint action in relation to a particular school. While all the parties involved in these issues may not be present in the models developed by Bowen and Elkaim, to the extent that they are directly addressing the linkages between those present and those absent from the session, they are directly and not analogously dealing with the reality of the problem.

The therapist can affect family and community members who are not participating in the therapy through the analogue as well as through the immediate reality of the circumstances of a problem. The part of the community that contributes to the problems of an individual or family can be dealt with in therapy, whether that component of the community is present at those sessions or not.

A CASE IN POINT

A case example will help illustrate how an individual child's problem can be rooted in a complex of systems that include the family and the broader community context, and will show how these can be included in one's field of intervention analogously or directly.

A family came to a clinic because a fourteen-year-old boy, Arnie, who is black, was beyond his mother's control. He was skipping class and staying away from home overnight. His mother had no complaints about Arnie's brother or two sisters, who accompanied them to this interview. In her telephoned request for an appointment, Arnie's mother had so dramatized his misbehavior that when at the beginning of the session she gave the therapist an opening to explore other related problems in the family, he reached out for those first. The therapist was working from the hypothesis that the mother's stress on the boy's problem could be an indication that Arnie was being scapegoated and might well be screening out other family problems. The opportunity given the mother to talk about other difficulties not only took the focus off Arnie, but also allowed her to describe her own horrendous life experience. Let us start twenty minutes into the session, with the mother's personal story.

Mother: He [her second husband] said he wanted to take care of me and the baby. I said okay. Well, that was good for a while, then the first time he hit me it was like me and his sister was playing and he came in—and I was pregnant—he knocked me down on the floor. And I was his wife . . . We had got married . . . He said, "Don't you ever do nothing to my sister 'cause I love my sister." That kind of dawned on me—that he loved his sister and always hugging on his sister and nobody ever paid no attention and so I went on and had the child and then I moved in another house. After I moved in another house—now, I'm talking about his father [points to Arnie], then after I moved into another house, then he started constantly, constantly beating me. But I said maybe he'll stop it, you know. We went off to Georgia and got married because I was already married and didn't have my divorce. Then, after I got married, I came to Philadelphia and I was pregnant with him [points to Arnie] and didn't know it. I had him in sixty-four and I didn't know what to do—none of my family up here and nobody to talk to. So I was constantly beat and then I heard that with the girl he was with before me, that's what he did. Anyway, we moved from where we stayed. He was like very, very jealous of me. I couldn't say "Hi" to anybody. It was like constantly, constantly beat. My kids were seeing all of this. I tried to take up for myself, I tried to take up for my children the best I knew how. I never want to hurt nobody, never, not in words and not with my hands or a stick or nothing, never. I would never hit him back. He hit me with a lamp—that's how I got that right there [points to scar under her left eye]. I got this [she shows the therapist a large scar on her back].

Therapist: How did you get that?

Mother: That's where he cut me. That was before he stabbed me ten times. I didn't do nothing. So then his son came up, his older son. He came up and he was like, twenty-three. My oldest daughter just had turned twelve and he got her pregnant. I didn't do nothing about that. I was scared.

Therapist: It's almost too much for me to take—what you are describing. I don't know how you survived.

And later the mother added to her narrative:

Mother: And, see, where my kids is having it good—nobody to hit or knock on them, I used to go to school nasty, dirty because my mom worked. She didn't have time to take care of us. When I came home, the first thing I got was a . . . [the mother turns to her children] Now, you all have heard this and so, therefore, it is nothing new to you . . . [then she turns back to the therapist] down south we had wood, like a slab of wood. I would get hit with one across the back or across the head because of my father. He wanted to have a relationship with me and there was a beating every day. Every day. I would run and the neighbors would make me come back home. They would tell me it is not true until my grandmother came to stay with me and she found out that I was not lying. This went on from nine until seventeen and that's the life that I had to live and, right now, I still think about it. [She later told how she had run away from home to the man who became her first husband.]

She described her current life of deprivation and its effect on her mind and health:

Mother: You know, like right now I am having financial problems. I know that's bugging me. Still, when I'm not having financial problems, it still seems something just keeps my head hurting all the time—tension. Then I feel like I just want to burst out and just cry and cry and just don't stop crying. Now today, I broke down and I cried a little bit because I get, I guess, unemployment and it comes whenever it gets ready and that's all I have to live on and DPA don't pay me but twenty-eight dollars every two weeks and try to live off that. Easter's here and I haven't got my unemployment check and so, no Easter for the children and, see, quite naturally, that's going to get me upset. All the weight is like falling on me.

To what extent did the social conditions of this woman's circumstances contribute to her vulnerability to her father and to her husbands? As a child with limited rights she felt trapped. As a woman, poor and black, she thought herself dependent on her men. She looked to each man she married to support her and her children financially. She personally experienced herself as immature, in her words, "a little girl," which complemented her view of herself as "scared." With three youngsters around her and other grown-up children who were out of the home, she still talked as if she were all alone. When one looks over this woman's life, her victimization at the hands of her father, husbands and society, is it any wonder that she would present herself as so helpless and vulnerable? Could one conceive of trying to understand this woman without taking into account not only her family but also her social experience?

She left the therapist feeling enervated, which made him wonder whether the children themselves lived overwhelmed by the mother's burden past and present. While the mother spoke of herself as victimized and needful, the therapist could not find a way to alleviate her pain. He was disturbed by her story, and felt pain for her. But also in some impalpable way he was blocked out by her. Had the unrelenting series of disappointing relationships left her untrusting and closed to others?

The therapist had observed in the session that Arnie was more attentive to his mother's unhappy story than the other children and that, unlike his siblings, he volunteered answers and explanations that might facilitate her narrative. Considering the therapist's personal reaction to the mother, he wondered whether Arnie's emotional difficulties might not be related to some sense of frustrated responsibility for his mother, coming at a time for him when, developmentally, he needed to differentiate himself from her. The therapist wanted to test his hypothesis and so he requested the mother to ask all the children for help—support which he suspected she did not allow them to give and which possibly she had learned not to expect from anybody. If this were the case she would feel overly stressed by her situation and the children would experience anxiety for her, but also helplessness about assisting her. The therapist wanted to see whether and how she could allow herself to depend upon her children to carry their part of the family responsibilities and to see how the children individually and in combination would respond to her.

The mother was crying as she told her story. Her distress as she recounted her experience was real. In urging the mother to ask for help from all her children, the therapist was also directly intervening in the structure of the relationship that was being displayed in that session between mother and children as she communicated her despair. He was asking her to allow the children within the boundaries of some of her immediate concerns, to give them an opportunity to align themselves with her and to allow them a measure of responsibility and power in the family so that they could positively affect her situation and theirs. This was a direct intervention on the part of the therapist in the unhappiness the mother was exhibiting before her children. In the session this situation was analogous to how she appeared to be worrying her children at home from day to day without allowing them an opportunity to effectively assist her.

On the supposition that the children's taking on more responsibility for their lives in the family would facilitate Arnie's efforts at constructive differentiation (assuming there was a link between the two), the therapist continued to press for the mother to obtain help from her children. Behind this same intervention there also lay the hypothesis that this woman who had survived all that had happened and was still happening to her, had the ability to confront her current problems more effectively than she conveyed.

The mother's relationship to the therapist provided an analogue to her relationship to her community. The therapist's implied belief in her and her children's ability was meant to communicate something about what this woman and her family might expect of themselves in their relationship with community institutions. The therapist attempted neither to withdraw in despair from her situation nor to patronize her and take over for her. He urged her to ask more of her family in the session itself.

Therapist: Do they know what you are going through right now?

Mother: I tells them, but sometimes I tell them I don't have no money and they make a face or get mad. I try to explain it to them. I sit them down and try to talk to them. Sometimes they'll listen and sometimes they won't. They ask me for things that I don't have and that makes me upset and I try to tell them I don't have it to give them. They like get upset about it. Like, see, I tell them: sometime if you all make a little money, I say, bring it home, you know, to help me. It seems like I don't have no help.

Therapist: Okay, why don't you ask them now for some help. Let's talk about it now—about the help that you need from them.

Mother: [To the therapist] What would help me is like—what I have I don't mind giving, but when other children come in and they eat, it takes out of their mouths. I tell them don't give food away and they slip and do it. I try to explain it to them and they still slip and do it. Just little things like that. And, see, looks like they could tell when I come in the house if I'm upset they know something's on my mind, that ends is not meeting and I try not to take it out on them. [Therapist gestures for her to address the children directly.] Okay, when I come in and sometimes they have a houseful of children and when I'm coming in my house and seeing other children, knowing ends is not meeting, it is going to make me upset of thinking that any meal the child gives somebody else it will be taken from you all and when I be telling you all I don't have no money, I don't unless I go borrow money from somebody. You know, when I get my check—eighty-two dollars—if you pay forty dollars out of eighty-two dollars, that still don't leave me no money. It's hurting. Sometimes I come in the house and I won't feel like talking and I don't want to hear no noise because that upsets me because I can't think. I'll be trying to think of what the next move to make. That's my problem. That's my problem not having nobody else to talk to. That's a problem . . .

Therapist: You are asking them for something but they are not answering you. This conversation is just going one way.

Mother: I done told them this more than once, and so I sometimes . . .

Therapist: Get an answer. You have a young woman here [the 17-year-old Reena] and you have a young man [Arnie] over here. The others [Kenny, 11, and Cindy, 9] are listening to you also. You have people who can certainly answer you. Now get some answers.

Mother: First, do you all understand what I am saying? What I am trying to say?

Children: Yes.

Mother: You understand? Well, what do you think about what I am saying?

Arnie: I think about it a lot.

Mother: I mean do you think I could save more money if nobody else is coming in and eating? Okay? Just like I told you I was having money problems and that means no money is coming in from nowhere. You know it is hard for me to save because it is just me and trying to pay bills. I got my income tax back but what I had to do was pay the back bills that was behind. You understand? Now what I got to do is try to go find some more money, and how am I doing that cause I am not working nowhere?

Therapist: You started to get them to answer you and you need to get them to answer you more because that's the only way you are going to find out whether they understand you and whether they are going to work with you.

Subsequently, as the mother sought a response from the children, again only Arnie made an attempt to say something. His wish to help his mother was sincere and unique among the children, but inadequate. This family was underorganized. The family structure was undifferentiated, as could be seen in the way the mother addressed all the children as one, not designating and creating distinct functional roles for each child around family tasks. This kind of underorganized family structure is not unusual among poor ghetto families. It tends to leave the parent overburdened with more of the family responsibilities than one person can cope with.

To help Arnie who tried to act like the responsible child, the therapist would need to get the children to take their respective and appropriate portions of the responsibility to assist their mother, which would mean that at least Reena as the oldest would have to assume her own special role. The mother remonstrated with Reena for not helping at home, but did not make clear her expectations of her nor did she seem to support her consistently in carrying out what was being requested. The therapist asked the mother to enact her problems in soliciting Reena's cooperation in the session itself, to ask her right then about how she wanted Reena to help. The therapist was encouraging a change in the mother's relationship to her daughter to take the pressure off Arnie. The therapist was intervening in the real context of the session around the issue of the mother asking her children to help shoulder the family responsibilities. It was hoped that a change in the way the family negotiated this issue in the session would carry over into how in reality they related to one another around these household tasks at home.

Therapist: As I hear it, you are not giving her the chance to take some of the burden.

Mother: I don't know what burden—what would she take? What would she do?

Therapist: Ask her.

Mother: I don't know what to ask.

Therapist: I'll ask her for you.

Reena, I want to talk to you. Your mother is—well, you know what she is going through right now. She says, as I understand it, that you don't really understand what she is going through and that you don't want to take on some of the burden of her responsibilities at home. Is that true?

Reena: I don't understand.

Therapist: She says you don't want to help her.

Mother: Okay, like when I tell you to clean up, I can tell you to clean up, I can tell you to cook, tell you to, say, clean the bathrooms—not only you, but some of the rest of them. But, you being the oldest, you should see that Cindy do it. When I come home—okay, what happens? The radio be on, the crowd be at the house, you be dancing. And how do you think I feel when I come in the house and I am already upset? Don't you think by your being seventeen years old that you should have a responsibility for seeing that Cindy do her work and telling Arnie to do his, and if he don't do his or Kenny don't do his, that you are supposed to tell me?

Therapist: Hold on, now. Give her a chance to answer.

Reena: What do you want me to answer?

Therapist: I'll restate that. Your mother says she wants you to help her with the cleaning of the house. She wants you to get Cindy to also help clean the house. Do you?

Reena: Yeah, but they hardly don't listen. So, if they don't listen to me I don't want to be bothered with them.

Therapist: Okay, who doesn't listen?

Reena: They listen every once in a while, but none of them don't usually listen.

Therapist: You would like to do the cleaning of the house and get them to help?

Reena: Yes. Sometimes I have been in the house all by myself and go ahead and clean up everything and Mom come home and she just goes up in her room and go lay down. But, sometimes, when they make me mad, and don't listen to me, I don't do nothing.

Therapist: Who doesn't listen to you?

Reena: None of them out of these three don't listen to me.

Therapist: Okay, your mother has just talked about Cindy a minute ago. Why doesn't she listen to you?

Reena: I don't know. I don't know why she don't listen to me.

Therapist: Find out.

Reena: Cindy, why don't you listen to me? [To therapist:] I can't ask her no questions.

Therapist: Why not? Now, I don't understand why you can't ask your sister why she doesn't listen to you.

Reena: It seems funny because I have never done anything like that.

Therapist: Okay, but you are her older sister and your mother has put you in charge and said to you: Reena, I need you to help me clean the house and I want Cindy to help you. I want you to tell Cindy what to do about that. She is telling you that you can ask her the question.

Reena: I tell her, but she says "Don't tell me to do nothing. I ain't doing nothing."

Therapist: Ask her now. Your mother has said that you can ask her. Ask her why she doesn't listen to you.

Reena: Why don't you listen to me when I tell you to help clean up?

Cindy: You be hollering at me a lot.

Therapist: Talk with her about it.

Reena: How I be hollering at you, Cindy?

Cindy: Because when, before Momma gets home, you keep saying clean up the house and you keep on making me wash the dishes for you.
Reena: I keep making you wash the dishes for me or I tell you to wash the dishes?
Cindy: You tell me to wash the dishes.
Therapist: [To Reena, who is ready to discontinue the dialogue] Go ahead.
Reena: That's all.
Therapist: You haven't worked it out with her. Solve the problem. You have a problem with her. Talk with her about it.
Reena: I don't know what to ask her. I just asked her why she don't listen. She said because I always hollering at her, but I don't think I holler at her. I just say, Cindy, go on in and do such and such thing and she say, "No, you ain't watching me, you don't tell me what to do. My mother ain't even home."
Therapist: Get her to respond to what you just said.
Reena: Why when I tell you to do something you always saying "You ain't watching me" and you gonna tell Momma when she gets home that I told you to do different things?

The mother was not accustomed to asking for assistance. The therapist directed her to her oldest, Reena. Reena told how she could not help because she herself could not get the younger children to respond to her. Cindy only took direction from her mother. Reena did not know how to request cooperation from her sister, just as their mother did not know how to elicit Reena's assistance.

The mother felt burdened with the whole responsibility because she felt she could not count on Reena, who did not feel supported by her mother or respected by her sister. In the session the therapist had them live out the organizational pattern related to these household tasks, and intervened directly in the way the mother and Reena talked to one another and to Cindy.

The therapist proceeded to encourage Reena to talk about her sense of frustration about trying to carry out her responsibilities. He was attempting to attune the mother to her daughter's discouragement. As the therapist pushed this issue further, the girl told how she too suffered, and how she too did not expect others to be of any help to her.

What the girl revealed about her troubles in school was new to the mother.

Therapist: Reena, I feel bad for you. Do you want to be lonely?
Reena: No. I just don't like telling nobody nothing.

Therapist: You must be afraid of telling people things. You must feel that you can't trust them. Am I right?
Reena: I don't know. I . . .
Therapist: What were you going to say?
Reena: I just don't like school a lot now. I don't like it no more.
Therapist: Where do you go to school?
Reena: Clayton.
Therapist: What grade are you in?
Reena: Eleventh.
Therapist: In your eleventh year and you don't like it any more? Since when don't you like it?
Reena: About two months ago I started not liking it. I used to go every day and go on time every day. Now I don't even do that no more because when I was in school there used to be a lot of activities. The principal just is stopping everything.
Mother: Well, you're just about out of school now. Think about your education. That's what you think about. Don't think about that principal.
Therapist: Okay, let's understand what it is. What activities did they have before?
Reena: Well, they had a lot of contests and like I won Queen of ninth grade and I used to help raise money for a lot of people in school and in the neighborhood. I was in the student council and I was like in choir and stuff like that.
Therapist: In school? And you are not in that now?
Reena: No.
Therapist: Why not?
Reena: 'Cause it ain't like it used to be. It is all boring.
Therapist: They don't have student council anymore? They don't have choir?
Reena: Not for our grade they don't
Therapist: You would just like to be doing some other things besides going to school. Would it matter whether you were doing it in school or at some other place?
Reena: No.
Therapist: If you were doing some kind of activities like raising money or something like that, would that make you feel better?
Reena: Yes, 'cause at school the only thing we do is sit around. The teachers make jokes.
Therapist: Don't you learn?
Reena: When I first started going to school . . . when I first knew my English teacher, I went and told my counselor that I couldn't get along with her. There was something, something

that I didn't like about her. I couldn't really tell what it was, but it was just like her ways, like students would ask her something and she would look at us like we should know. She would like roll her eyes at us and stuff like that and I told him that I was uncomfortable with that teacher and they just left me in there anyway. They didn't take me out of there. I think I got an F or an E in her class. I do her work but it seems like I still don't make any effort at all.

Therapist: So, really at school even the teaching part of it is just not making you happy. [To Mother]: Did you know all this?

Mother: All I knew is that last part of last month is when they wrote me and told me that Reena had missed a lot of days out of school and that's when I went to school and that's when I heard everything.

Therapist: But you didn't hear this. That's very important, what she has just told you.

Mother: I told you she don't never talk any more.

Therapist: But she just did. She just did.

The therapist concluded the first session with an agreement between the girl and her mother that they would go to the school and meet with the girl's counselor, the vice-principal and her teachers, if possible. This would be an attempt to intervene directly in the relationship between family and school, but in a way that was consonant with the family goals of having the mother more effectively in control of her own and her children's life circumstances, of drawing the mother and daughter closer together, of assisting the mother to help her daughter act more competently at home and at school, and, through all these changes, to relieve Arnie of some of his frustration over his inability to help his mother and open the way for him to address the development of his own autonomy.

The meeting with the school officials took place a week after the family interview. In the session the counselor and vice-principal reflexively began to organize the meeting as a review of Reena's poor performance in school, putting mother and daughter on the defensive and eroding what little confidence they had about their right to challenge the school. The therapist interrupted the staff to ask that mother and daughter be given a chance to present their case. It seemed that, because of the therapist's involvement, the school officials were able to give room to the mother and daughter to take more initiative. The therapist encouraged the mother to speak up and to support Reena in talking for herself. In keeping with his structural goals for the family he wanted the mother, and not himself, to give Reena this backing, if possible.

Reena and her mother were able to demonstrate to the school the girl's genuine interest in her classwork and how she felt unsupported in school this year. The counselor and vice-principal agreed to look into their complaints and to meet with both of them to follow up the meeting. The mother walked out of the session saying she would never again allow herself to be intimidated by an institution like a school and Reena spoke energetically to her mother about the meeting and some of her other experiences in school.

DISCUSSION

In the first two sessions, which are covered here, the sweep of the eco-structural environment with which Arnie was having trouble covered the oppressive socioeconomic circumstances of the family, its underorganization, the overburdened and unsupported mother, children unable to help their mother, an oldest daughter discouraged at home and at school, and Arnie, an adolescent torn between a frustrated wish to help his mother and his need to explore a more independent life of his own.

The therapist's efforts in the session were primarily directed at the communications among the family members and himself. To the mother the therapist offered an understanding ear as she related her problems, but he basically treated her as a competent person who had resources within herself and her family that would permit her to cope with her concerns. He aligned himself with her and offered to enter within the boundaries of her family life and Reena's school, but in a way that amplified rather than detracted from the mother's power in both contexts. In that way the reality of the way in which the therapist related to the mother provided an analogy for how she could relate to the school and other societal institutions.

In the session the therapist observed Arnie responding to the distress his mother was communicating. However, his mother did not appear able to make use of his supportive gestures, just as she did not with the therapist. Paradoxically, in her great need she seemed to depend only on herself. Arnie's moves to help her reflected his immaturity and constricted life experience, which made his efforts ineffectual. One could see he was sympathetic to his mother's predicament and was failing in his attempts. What made it worse was that his older sister Reena was sitting in on the session withdrawn from her mother.

The therapist chose to pursue this structural arrangement of the family, which was working against Arnie, by intensifying the mother's and Reena's involvement in the session. If he could get Reena to support her mother in the session by offering to help more at home, this transaction would link up with Arnie's relationship to his mother by saying to Arnie that it was not all up to him. Such a reorganization of positions in the interview could carry over into the home as far as household chores and other operations involving the mother and her children were concerned.

Unfortunately Reena was herself a casualty of the family problems and of some difficulties in school. Her failure to help her mother was linked to other setbacks of her own. Like her mother, she felt alone and was distrustful. She was also losing interest in school. The therapist concluded that he had to assist Reena in these contexts before she could be successful in helping her mother. Part of the session was given over to making Reena trust the therapist enough that she could tell him of her concerns. Then the therapist could put the mother in his place to respond emotionally to Reena's plight.

The next session, which took place in Reena's school, was an example of a direct intervention in the real context of Reena's trouble in the community. It brought the mother and Reena, together with the therapist, into the school to meet with representatives of the institution. To maintain the links between this experience and those in the first session, the therapist had to conduct the school-family interview in a way that was consistent with the structural goals set in the first session. The therapist attempted to reinforce the mother's power in the session vis-à-vis himself and the school officials. Reena herself needed to feel she could assert herself, and mother and daughter had to feel emotionally closer as a result of the experience. If this were achieved in the process of righting Reena's situation in school, the structural link of these operations in the school context could reinforce a restructuring of the mother-daughter relation at home.

In the two sessions discussed here, there were interventions directed at the reality facing the therapist in the family session and in the family-school interview.

Both sessions provided opportunities to intervene in family and family-school relationships through the analogues represented by each situation and through direct structural links which exist within the family and between family and school.

SUMMARY

Any and every action is the outcome of the dynamics of its ecological context. There are no limits to this context. To the clinician the ends are only the horizon beyond which his or her vision and personal interventions cannot reach.

This world of interactive forces may appear to be too broad to be grasped. Yet it is no more impenetrable than the world within the individual psyche, whose depths can never be plumbed no matter how much it is subjected to analysis—psychoanalysis or any other. True, this ecological complex includes the dynamics of the individuals involved as well as their various relationships through a whole series of interconnecting systems. But as one picks up the threads of actions and follows them to their various sources, one thinks in terms of the aspects of the various systems that relate to the actions in question.

Technically these systems in the ecological context of the problems to be addressed are accessible through interventions in the analogue or more directly in the reality of the context in which the problems arise. The therapist can make a therapeutic intervention with an individual, a family and a community, and within the interfaces between them. Every intervention impacts on the actual relationships of the people in a session and on those outside the session who are dependent upon those in the interview. These linkages to the outside make it possible for the therapist to deal with aspects of the eco-structural underpinning of a problem which stretch beyond the people and circumstances in the session.

Underlying the thinking behind this therapeutic perspective is the assumption that there is a structural continuity between the structural patterns linking the individual, the family and the community and that an intervention in one of thse systems may have a corresponding impact on the others, depending on the strength of the linkages between the organization of one with another. A theoretical perspective that includes the family and community will call for techniques which engage the larger systems. But what will distinguish this kind of community involvement from what is generally understood as social action is that the interventions in the community are primarily for the specific therapeutic goals of the family and its members. It means intervening in the relationship between the family and the community in ways that are consistent with the life objectives of the family and its members.

Family therapy is a term that refers to a therapeutic approach which focuses on the family. However, it essentially reflects a systems view of human problems. Because of the dependence of the family on the community and in many respects the blending of its functions with community institutions, the approach logically draws the community into its perspective for the therapist who would see it. The family is as much a part of the community as the individual is part of the family, and the family therapist bears the responsibility of finding ways to understand the individual and family in the context of the community and of intervening in that whole interdependent complex of individual, family and community systems for the benefit of the family that comes for help.

References

Aponte, H. The family-school interview: An eco-structural approach. *Family Process*, 1976, *15 (3)*, 303–311.

Attneave, C. J. Therapy in tribal settings and urban network interventions. *Family Process*, 1969, *8 (2)*, 192–210.

Auerswald, E. H. Interdisciplinary versus ecological approach. *Family Process*, 1968, *7*, 202–215.

Bowen, M. Toward the differentiation of a self in one's own family. In J. Framo (Ed.), *Family interaction: A dialogue between family researchers and family therapists*. New York: Springer, 1972.

Elkaim, M. Broadening the scope of family therapy or from the family approach to the socio-political approach. [To be published in *Terapia Familiare*, 1979.]

Illich, I. *Deschooling society*. New York: Harper & Row, 1972.

Illich, I. *Medical nemesis*. New York: Bantam, 1977.

Minuchin, S. *Families and family therapy*. Cambridge, Mass.: Harvard University Press, 1974.

Minuchin, S., Montalvo, B., Guerney, B. G., Jr., Rosman, B., Schumer, F. *Families of the slums: An exploration of their structure and treatment*. New York: Basic, 1967.

Rabkin, R. *Inner and outer space*. New York: Norton, 1970.

Speck, R. V., & Rueveni, U. Network therapy—A developing concept. *Family Process*, 1969, *8 (2)*, 182.

Part IV

EVALUATION OF COMMUNITY MENTAL HEALTH PROGRAMS

The issue of program evaluation in community psychology is relevant to many of the topics discussed in the present volume, including paraprofessionals, crisis intervention centers, prevention programs, halfway houses and other alternatives to institutionalization. Evaluation has attained increasing significance not only from the natural concerns of program participants in determining a program's effectiveness but also because of "recent amendments mandating self-evaluation by each community mental health center" (Reardon, 1977, p. 350). The following chapters, therefore, hold an important position in this text on community psychology. Unfortunately, although community psychologists recognize the necessity of program evaluation, many types of programs tend to be evaluated in an inadequate manner, if at all.

In a thorough discussion, Cowen and Gesten in Chapter 14 present the myriad difficulties associated with program evaluation in community settings. After an initial delineation of the differences between community mental health and community psychology viewpoints, the authors consider methodological problems involved in evaluation research including data bias, criterion selection and control pitfalls. In addition, more subjective "process-centered" evaluation issues, such as obtaining cooperation from program participants as well as gaining acceptance as an evaluator, are included in the chapter. Cowen and Gesten's proposed methods of coping with the program evaluation difficulties discussed are particularly interesting since these suggested solutions directly arose from the authors' considerable experience in the area.

Charles Lachenmeyer argues in Chapter 13 that community mental health programs are subject to the inherent inefficiencies of public social service programs as well as to inefficiencies particular to themselves. Both sets of inefficiencies can be identified by comparing these programs to the model for estimating organizational efficiency and effectiveness that is based on the logic of the private sector. Lachenmeyer outlines this model and then suggests an evaluation design that is based on a complete description of a community mental health program.

An approach to program evaluation not considered in either of the two chapters in this section has a methodological viewpoint. Campbell and Stanley's (1963) quasi-experimental designs could be applied to evaluate programs in community settings. Recognizing that the strict control present in the laboratory is often impossible to attain in a field, or in this case, a community setting, the authors suggested various quasi-experimental designs which could be substituted for the more typically utilized "one-group pretest-posttest design" (p. 177), or the "static-group comparison" (p. 182), in which an experimental group exposed to a community program is compared on a posttest one with a group not previously shown to be similar to the experimental group. Some of the methodological sources of invalidity produced by the use of the above two designs include "history" effects or exposure to factors other than the community program; "selection" effects, or the choosing of a particular group such as volunteers for crisis therapy and comparing these individuals with nonvolunteers; and "mortality" effects, or a greater loss of individuals from the experimental community program group than from the "comparison group." To avoid some of these difficulties, various alternative quasi-experimental designs were developed. For example, Campbell and Stanley suggested the use of the "time-series" design (p. 207) consisting of several pretest and posttest observations following a program's initiation. A more commonly used design is the "nonequivalent control group design" (p. 217), in which an experimental and a "control" group are both tested but individuals are not randomly assigned to each group. For example, a primary prevention program may be instituted in one school with a second school serving as a control. A more extensive overview of the various designs described by Campbell and Stanley as well as of the manner in which these quasi-experimental designs control for methodological errors are inappropriate in this context. The point of the discussion, however, is that within a community setting more innovative evaluative approaches must be utilized because of limitations inherent in a field community setting.

As discussed in Chapter 14, ethical considerations are also important in applying evaluation procedures to community settings. If experimental approaches are used, individuals who are randomly assigned to control groups may feel deprived. If the programs instituted indeed are effective, these individuals would also have benefited from the program (Schulz & Hanusa, 1978).

References

Campbell, D. T., & Stanley, J. S. Experimental and quasi-experimental designs for research on teaching. In N. L. Gage (Ed.), *Handbook of research on teaching.* Chicago: Rand McNally, 1963, pp. 171–246.

Reardon, D. F. A model for communicating about program evaluation. *Journal of Community Psychology*, 1977, *5*, 350–358.

Schulz, R., & Hanusa, B. H. Long-term effects of control and predictability-enhancing interventions: findings and ethical issues. *Journal of Personality and Social Psychology*, 1978, *36*, 1194–1201.

CHAPTER 13

A Complete Evaluation Design for Community Mental Health Programs

Charles Lachenmeyer, Ph.D.

This chapter will attempt to fill in two perceived gaps in the evaluation research literature having to do with community mental health programs. The first part will present a simple model of the optimal functioning of such programs. On the basis of this model it will be argued that there are two sets of problems with such programs: those attributable to public social service programs generally; and those attributable to community mental health programs in particular. It will be concluded that, although these problems are intractable, the evaluation of the managerial efficiency and effectiveness of these programs (and, in fact, of all social service programs) is not at all precluded. An evaluation design for so doing will be presented.

THE MODEL

Private enterprise has provided a model of organizational design which gives precise definition to the concepts of efficiency and effectiveness. One can argue at length that big corporations do not approximate this model, but this does not negate its analytic utility.

Simply stated this is the model:

a. People have needs.
b. A number of people who share the same need can be said to create "demand."
c. There will be greater or lesser demand depending on the number of such people.
d. Organizations are designed to fill demand by selling the requisite goods or services.
e. Optimally, organizations also have units whose purpose it is to gauge demand: given such units, organizations become self-sustaining and maximally adaptive.
f. Said organizations operate within set constraints. Perhaps the two most significant are legal constraints, as with consumer protection laws, equal opportunity laws and so on, which are reflections of

the broader social context of operations; and economic constraints, as with inflation and competition.

g. The organization is also designed so that the requisite units monitor these constraints and adjust to them when necessary.

From this simple model can be deduced these definitions of efficiency and effectiveness:

a. An organization is efficiently designed, generally, to the extent that all the actions of participants are structured and interrelated to produce the necessary goods and services to meet demand.
b. An organization is effective to the extent that it meets demand and makes a profit (or otherwise satisfies some consensually determined standard of performance).

Three points are significant here. First, "effectiveness" is subject to the test of consensual determination: i.e. the majority of some preselected parties must agree with the definition of effectiveness. Since it is easiest to gain such agreement with the use of numbers (Lachenmeyer, 1973a), numerical estimates of effectiveness are emphasized: e.g., "profit" for management, "cash flow" for management, "earnings per share" or "growth in earnings per share" for real or potential stockholders. More nebulous definitions may be popular but they rarely have any significant or long-lasting impact: consider, for instance, "social responsibility" for Juanita Kreps of the United States Department of Commerce. It is important that such consensual determination itself is expressible numerically: i.e., that there is percent agreement with the definition of effectiveness among the preselected parties.

The second important point: the preselected parties must have a direct and significant relationship to the continued viability of the organization, e.g., "management" or "labor" or "the investing public." Certainly the phrase "direct and significant relationship" is ambiguous, but a simple test is possible (this is further elaborated below). The preselected parties can be said to have such a relationship to the extent that their hypothesized elimination threatens immediately the very survival of the organization. If the New York City government is conceptualized as a large, complex organization, the elimination of the investing public, as expressed by their failure to purchase New York City bonds, threatens the government's very survival in its current form; that is, threatens bankruptcy; and therefore, the investing public's definition of New York City government's effectiveness "counts"; hence investors are a significant preselected party.

The third and final important point is, as Scriven (1972) notes, process (i.e., efficiency) and outcome evaluation (i.e., effectiveness) cannot be distinguished; both are necessary and interrelated judgments. In the parlance used herein, efficiency and effectiveness have this necessary evaluative interrelationship: to be effective an organization must be efficient. Actually it is possible to precisely answer the obvious deduced question: what levels of efficiency guarantee what levels of effectiveness? To an extent this will be answered in the second part of this chapter. But to do so completely would require elaboration of the model well beyond our limited objectives (see, however, Lachenmeyer 1973b, 1977a, 1977b). Suffice it to say here that there will always be some inefficiency and that this inefficiency will be more or less tolerable depending on the desired and attainable levels of effectiveness. Desirable and attainable levels of effectiveness can be determined by all manner of constraints: for instance, the state of the competition, government regulatory efforts, inflation, and so forth. And this suggests a final important deduction from the simple model.

Every effective and efficient organization must have built into it a knowledge acquisition mechanism to attempt to track demand levels, market conditions, prevailing and shifting definitions of effectiveness, constraints on operations and any other external contingencies that have an effect on its efficiency or effectiveness. Now this mechanism may be formal and structured as with market research departments, personnel departments, product development departments and the like in large corporations, or it may be informal and unstructured as with the entrepreneur running his own business who trusts his own intelligence-gathering and -generating capacity. Whatever form it takes, if an organization is to survive in a constantly shifting environment, it must acquire such knowledge and anticipate future contingencies. Admittedly such attempts may be faulty, and at the extreme they may be *ex post facto* adjustments to unanticipated occurrences, as with the "sudden" oil crisis of 1973 to present; but nonetheless they must be present. All of this can be codified into this very important evaluative standard: organizations in private enterprise may approximate the model presented above in varying degrees, but they must incorporate knowledge about it within their structure in order to approximate it at all. And, of course, they must approximate it in order to survive.

With the groundwork thus laid, it is now appropriate to inquire about the optimal functioning of public service programs.

Public Service Programs

All that has been said about optimally designed organizations is equally true about optimally designed "programs." This word substitution entails no inherent analytic discontinuities. However—and this is critical—when one tries to apply this model to public service programs there are important analytic disruptions.

With *all* public service programs government intervenes as a mediating party between the public, which underwrites the cost of program creation and program implementation, and program workers and clients. Thus, rather than demand directly determining program design and functioning, public service programs are subject to this more complex relationship: legislators (at various governmental levels) must determine the degree to which the public has certain needs, and in response the legislators must draw up the necessary legislation to create programs to satisfy those needs.

There is this initial and profound ambiguity: in representative government, should legislators use their own best judgment in assessing the needs of their constituencies or should such assessments be left to the members of their constituencies?

If legislators are to use their best judgment, then the dilemma is clear: how do they know what the needs of their constituencies are? To say that there will be an inevitable problem in data acquisition is to trivialize the dilemma. Legislators, as human beings, even when honestly seeking such data, will be subject to personal prejudice, self-interest, whim, idiosyncratic interpretative processes and the like. And of course there is no guarantee that the seeking of such data will occur at all.

On the other hand, if need assessments are left to the members of constituencies, how are individual judgments to be aggregated and distilled so that the programs that are designed serve the "common good"? This is at once a problem of data acquisition *and* decision making even where the data are available, which, it is clear, many times they are not.

Simply, every legislator faces the problem of competing constituencies, and has the fundamental need himself to survive in office by carefully weighing, balancing, selecting and often times tactfully ignoring the competing solicitations of these various constituencies. And more often than not, in so doing rational need assessment falls prey to crude power differentials between constituencies as they try to best one another: some lobbying efforts are more efficient and effective than others irrespective of the data-based superiority of one need assessment and solicitation over another.

Assuming legislators somehow resolve these dilemmas, which they do, and proceed to construct public service programs, which they do, they are faced with another intractible set of problems. They must obtain the support and cooperation of their colleagues. Political compromise and logrolling *are* the legislative norm, so that even if the optimally designed program is possible, even if the most critical needs of the greatest number are accurately determined and the legislator draws up the best possible program to satisfy these needs, he must "sell" his colleagues on the desirability of his program. Obviously his colleagues themselves will have their own personal prejudices and idiosyncracies and will be faced with competing constituencies coalesced into lobbying efforts of varying degrees of efficiency and effectiveness. So even the best intentioned legislator with the greatest desire to create truly efficient and effective public service programs must appeal to the self-interest of his colleagues and invariably trade off bits and pieces of his lofty aspirations in the process of compromise and logrolling.

In addition to these distortions in the optimal model, there are other deep-seated problems in the legislative process that deserve note. By and large, legislation is created by lawyers and thereby shaped by the processes of legal reasoning. Generally it is inherent in legal reasoning that decisions be made on the basis of advocacy argument rather than on data-based argument: i.e., lawyers are trained that it is legitimate to win arguments by persuading some significant third party (judge, legislative body, jury) as to the superiority of those arguments, irrespective of their ultimate truth value. This contrasts sharply with the behavioral science notion of hypothesis construction and testing in which only "true arguments" are supposed to emerge as superior. The ultimate consequence for public service program construction is the formulation and implementation of those programs as advocated by the most persuasive legislators and constituents. Significantly, data acquisition as the basis for program design and implementation is considered to be of legitimate, secondary importance. Note: it is not that such priorities are explicit; rather, even more sinister in terms of taking possible corrective action, it is that this is the way of things with legal reasoning. Programs may be agreed to be superior or inferior while factually it is not assured that they are one or the other.

By their very nature legislative decisions are more immune to changes in the social context than economic decisions. To an extent, the time horizons of the legislative process are the arbitrary products of consensus: even where legislation self-destructs after a fixed period of time, that period of time is fixed by legislative fiat with only secondary attention paid to exogenous variables which may affect the efficacy of the legislation in question. On the other hand, the economic forces of the marketplace must be carefully monitored if an entity, be it the family unit or a large corporation, is to prosper in the economic sphere. In fact, forecasting these economic forces in five- to ten- to twenty-year periods is "big business" for big business.

With respect to public service programs there is this consequence: such programs, once mandated into law, tend to persist through time irrespective of their marketplace merits—irrespective of their real or projected demand levels. No business, large or small—in fact no private organizational effort—would survive for very long in the face of contrary demand levels. Yet public service programs can and do persist and grow under such conditions because they are often legislated into existence independently of such concerns, or, at the least, once created, exist separately from them.

Perhaps this point belabors the obvious. Yet what is not so obvious is that attempts at legislative reform, including emphasis on "program evaluation," tend to overlook the fundamental nature of the problem. Demand level over time is not only of secondary importance in public service program design and implementation, but once a program is in place, it is often advantageous to have little or no demand for its services. The fewer the clients, the lower the visibility; the lower the visibility, the less the likelihood of being monitored: or, even more simply stated, the fewer the clients, the fewer the complaints about problematic service. Thus the vicious cycle is completed: programs are legislated into existence with changes in levels of demand being of secondary concern; thus programs can persist even with diminished demand; and diminished demand is itself advantageous because it lowers visibility; therefore truly vacuous programs can persist generation after generation.

And even where the legislative process somehow factors in corrective action as with an emphasis on "program evaluation," demand itself can be manipulated in the public sector. This is simply a matter of "legislating" demand by altering the eligibility criteria of program clients. It is important to note that the process may not be that explicit. We once evaluated a major court referral program in New York City (Lachenmeyer, 1974) whose charter mandated that it service sixteen- to twenty-year-olds. Most of its clients had been young adults who had been arrested for marijuana usage as a first offense. With the shift in police priorities (but not the law) from making such arrests in the early 1970s came a decline in demand for this program's services. Faced with an obvious dilemma, *program administrative personnel* took it upon themselves to change the eligibility criteria and thereby to "create" demand. In going through their records we discovered a significant number of fifty- to sixty-year-old vagrants!

Finally, just as demand can be manipulated in the public sector, so too can competition. The above-mentioned program had no competition for many years. And this is the norm: public service programs are legislated monopolies in their given jurisdictions. It is interesting to speculate whether the creation of programmatic competitors would result in the greater efficiencies one sees in the private sector under such circumstances. The drug program's monopoly ended abruptly with the creation of a similar program for young offenders by the Vera Institute of Justice. The effects were dramatic as the staff of both programs scrambled to enroll and service clients. It could well be that more competition could be a better solution for the inefficiencies of such programs than program evaluation.

If all the foregoing were to be summarized in one sentence, this would be it: public social service programs are a species apart from private programs or organizations; they differ in their method of creation and sustenance, and in their very rationale for existence. To attempt to deal with any problems of design by "evaluating" their efficiency and effectiveness without thoroughly understanding these fundamental differences is to begin the evaluative process in total naïveté, to say the least.

Community Mental Health Programs

Certainly community mental health programs are but a genus of this species, and therefore are subject to all of the same problems. However, no attention has been paid in the literature to them. Rather, a familiar additional problem set has been given much attention.

It is well recognized that community mental health programs suffer the problem of need definition. What is mental health? What is mental illness? When is third-party (public or private) intervention required? Should this intervention be coercive or voluntary? If coercive, should it be based on existing criminal statutes or on other forms of legislation? Or, in fact, should legislation be required at all as an initiation point of intervention? Where legislation is deemed appropriate, what form and scope should it have? How can this form and scope be made consistent with the demands of a "free society"? (For discussions of these problems, see Chu & Trotter, 1974; Kelly, 1971; Kittrie, 1971; Lin & Stanley, 1962; Rosenhan, 1973; Sanford, 1972; Steadman, 1973; Szasz, 1970; World Health Organization, 1973.)

In assessing public mental health "needs," one is in the domain of defining mental illness. Even presupposing an adequate definitional base, which is far from certain, significant questions remain about the assessment of demand. The basic problem involves the assessment of levels of psychopathology in a chosen population and sample independently of levels of treatment with respect to that population and sample: that is, demand has traditionally been assessed by counting rates of treatment as garnered from the records of the appropriate programs (Dohrenwend & Dohrenwend, 1969.) This is obviously problematic since admission to treatment can depend on many other factors than "true" demand, particularly where legalistic coercion is involved. Moreover, even where epidemiological studies have been conducted, wide variation in prevalence rates have been reported, indicating severe validity and reliability problems (World Health Organization, 1973.) If one bears in mind the question, how is need to be defined? and notes as well its presuppositional status to demand assessment, such problems are not at all surprising. Yet one's attention must not be diverted from the fundamental dilemma here: in the optimal model when I "need" a product, I am willing to pay for it and (within limits) I define this need; if many others do the same, then there is ascertainable demand to which some organization or program can respond appropriately. With psychiatric disorders no such clear-cut relationship exists: "patients" and "significant others" such as family, teachers, friends, strangers, police officers, program personnel, legislators, judges, lobbyists—the list goes on and on—all of these parties can and do effect psychiatric need definition and demand level in direct or circuitous ways. Further, although the public's role is a direct one with regard to financing, the public's role in defining need and fixing demand is not. The sum result of these complications is the measurement problems in assessing demand as noted above, perhaps best expressed by the familiar question: how can the prevalence of psychiatric disorders be measured reliably and validly?

And it should not be overlooked that the foregoing discussion itself presupposes at least a first approximation of community mental health programs to the optimal program model on the dimension of gathering need/demand data. Aside from externally sponsored efforts in this area, efforts that themselves are conceived as being short-term and programmatic, the author knows of no community mental health program in existence that internally assesses community psychiatric needs or demand for its services and adjusts the scope and nature of its services accordingly. This is a major departure from the optimal model, with far-ranging implications. And it should be emphasized.

Certainly all of the preceding questions and problems, severally and jointly, pose grievous dilemmas for community mental health programs. If need definition is problematic, it follows directly that demand assessment is also, and that service definition to satisfy that demand is equally problematic as well. What is treatment as opposed to custody? What is therapy? Is therapy treatment, or custody, or both? Are different therapies appropriate for different mental health problems? If so (and it is difficult to conjure up any other than an affirmative answer), which therapies are best for which mental health problems, for what reasons? (See Anthony, Buell, Sharratt, & Althoff, 1972; Chu & Trotter, 1974; Erickson, 1975; Kiesler, 1966; Mannino & Shore, 1975; Mechanic, 1969; Meltzoff & Kornreich, 1970; Rosenhan, 1973; Sanford, 1972; Schofield, 1964; Stone, 1975; Szasz, 1970).

Finally, and this is also well known, if the service definition is problematic, so too is the evaluation of service delivery. Is therapy more "successful" than no therapy at all? Can therapy be said to be successful at all, and is the evidence sufficient to make this judgment? How can it be known whether therapy (or any other form of mental health services) is being delivered in the most efficient and effective manner? And this last question implies a set of derivatives: how can it be known whether community mental health programs are cost effective? What training is necessary for program employees? How is expertise in service delivery best certified? What is the best possible compensation structure for employees of community mental health programs? (In addition to the sources cited in the previous paragraph, see Campbell, 1969; Ennis & Siegel, 1973; Moos, 1975; Scriven, 1972; Struening & Guttentag, 1975; Weiss, 1972).

Obviously these lists of problems and implied questions could be greatly extended. For example, if need definition and service definition in this area are problematic, then the optimal geographic location of these programs must also be. And so on.

Given the expressed mission of this chapter to avoid unnecessary redundancy in this area the foregoing discussion will terminate with two obviously critical points. First, it is not enough to underscore problems in need definition, demand assessment, service definition and the evaluation of service delivery in community mental health programs *and then proceed* to design them, implement them, theorize about or discuss them. For to undertake or to advocate any of these things as all of the writings in this area do, presupposes the solution of these problems and the answering of these and other momentous questions. At the least, such problems and questions raise the issue of the very "legitimacy" of such programs. And this issue can be resolved only by asking, should community mental health programs exist at all?

The second critical point adds weight to the first. Community mental health programs are subject to their own special problems and generally to the problems of all public service programs by way of the previously noted deviation of such programs from the model of optimal program design. Although this chapter could dally over the relationship between these superordinate and subordinate sets of problems, the conclusion is obvious enough: community mental health programs are in a very real sense doubly problematic. And the force of this conclusion cannot be dismissed lightly. In fact, any effort at evaluating or constructing a rationale (theory, model, etc.) in order to evaluate community mental health programs must face these problems foursquare and must account for them by building them into the proposed evaluative design. To do less is to court failure from the very beginning.

The second part of this chapter will propose an evaluative design which fully accounts for these problems and thereby approximates (and elaborates) the model of optimal program design mentioned at the beginning of the chapter.

A SUGGESTED EVALUATION DESIGN FOR COMMUNITY MENTAL HEALTH PROGRAMS (AND ALL PUBLIC SERVICE PROGRAMS)

Explaining the Evaluation Design

First, several comments are necessary in explanation of the "evaluation design." To the author's knowledge, all previous theorizing in this area has defined the process of evaluating programs as that of certification of the qualitative worth of a program. That is, to put it most simply, the purpose of evaluation has been viewed ultimately as the ascription of qualitative judgments to said program (organization, activity, etc.), whether these judgments be crudely expressed as "goodness" or "badness," or, in more sophisticated form, as "cost/benefit ratios," "effectiveness/efficiency indices," and the like. Some corrective action is presupposed to occur once such judgments have been rendered, but typically any such action is seen to be outside of the evaluator's jurisdiction, even where recommendations do result.

That there is an ontic hiatus between quantitative evaluative estimates and the ascription of evaluative judgments is well known. How can "effectiveness" or "efficiency" be measured? What is the best fit between numerical estimates, once derived, and the final evaluative judgment rendered? These questions have fueled much of the research and theorizing efforts in this area (Scriven, 1972; Struening & Guttentag, 1975; Weiss, 1972).

The evaluation design to be elaborated below deals with these dilemmas and their implications by recasting the meaning and scope of program evaluation. In effect, this is done by highlighting the "enlightened constituency" concept so fundamental to optimal program design, as mentioned previously. Even though there are many parties who should be involved in such judgments, as Erickson (1975) notes, with public service programs the "enlightened constituency" is the public whose taxes underwrite the cost of such programs. True, legislators, employees and clients are involved in the evaluative process, but that process is *about* them—they provide the data base—and it is conducted *for* the public, to enlighten and inform it.

This conceptualization is by no means restricted to the public sector, and in that sense is totally apolitical. For example, nonprofit private enterprise exists for the benefit of its clients (consumers) and its employees, so that evaluation consists of enlightening and informing consumers and employees as constituents. Profit-oriented private enterprise exists for the benefit of its consumers, its employees and, perhaps most critically, its investors: when a company is publicly owned the latter group consists of its stockholders. All of these form the constituency to be informed by the evaluative process.

As in the case of private enterprise, there may be multiple constituencies. And there may well be conflicts of interest expressed as differences in the definition of effectiveness, as Erickson (1975) notes. But these conflicts of interest are not endemic to the evaluative process. There is no instance of programmatic (organizational) activity in which a "most important" or "base constituency" cannot be identified *for* whom evaluation is ultimately conducted.

The criteria for identification are straightforward enough. What consitutency is underwriting the cost of the program or organization? For public service programs, this is the public. For public companies, it is the stockholders and consumers. For privately held companies, it is the original investors and consumers.

This is certainly not to deny the evaluative interest of other identifiable constituencies. Their need to know is important indeed. All that is being asserted is that there is in all cases a constituency whose need to know is superordinate and, in fact, all inclusive.

For those who would balk at the dollars-and-cents criterion offered, a more palatable and consistent translation is possible: of all the likely constituencies of the target program, if only one were to conclude that the program was no longer viable (effective) and that program was ultimately eliminated as a result, which constituency would that be? The answer would identify the base constituency.

Legislators did pursue the Vietnam War over a tragic decade, but the public's judgment won out. The New York City government may continuously reassert its financial health, but the investing public's judgment will win out. Management of large corporations may smile in the face of bankruptcy but the consumers' and investors' judgments will cause bankruptcy sooner or later.

In brief, the base constituency's judgment may be superceded or manipulated or suspended for the moment, but ultimately that judgment will determine the longevity of the programmatic activity.

Certainly that judgment may be ill informed or unjust. But it is the very purpose of evalution research to provide the information base to guard against these possibilities.

Evaluation, then, is recast herein as an information-gathering process to make the base constituency of an organization or program fully knowledgeable about the organization or program it is underwriting. It is up to these people to make the ultimate evaluative judgment. All the evaluator can do is structure, derive and provide the requisiste information. The optimal evaluation design is that one which permits the derivation of the most complete information available and that one which is structured to do so. The evaluator can fight life-and-death struggles over the dissemination of this information but these considerations are extraneous to the evaluation design itself.

The specific design proposed is based then, on a simple but powerful premise: if evaluation is to provide complete information, then it must be based on a complete series of possible questions about the target program. It follows that if one structures the questions as well as their extensivity and intensivity and their ordering so as to approximate informational completeness, then program evaluation will be accomplished upon application of the questions to the target program.

Simply, it follows that the optimal evaluation design is one which consists of the most complete set of questions.

Since deviations from the best possible program play such a large part in subsequent distortions in public service programs as noted in the first part of this chapter, the optimal evaluation design will ask questions about these distortions. It is in this sense that such distortions are accounted for by this evaluation design: an appropriate subset of questions is asked in order to tap them.

As any good lawyer knows, questions presuppose their answers. Recently my small European car had a collision with a large American sedan. The damage to my car was $20; the damage to the American sedan was estimated at $600. The lawyer for my insurance company, upon learning this fact while planning for a court date, asserted, "The question is, 'How could so much damage be done to the American sedan?' " The best legal defense is one where all the answers have been framed and all the possible eliciting questions have been deduced and therefore anticipated prior to their use by either party to the legal proceedings.

The implications for this evaluation design are straightforward. The sequence of questions must presuppose the total informational picture desired which, in turn, is represented by the total array of answers. Thus if the first subset of questions inquires about the people responsible for the creation of the program, the presupposed answers imply that the identification of these people will give insight into any "hidden agendas" that may contribute to the inefficiency or ineffectiveness of that program.

Elsewhere (Lachenmeyer, 1973b, 1977a, 1977b) this author has presented a first and second approximation of the presupposed model of informational completeness. Here the author will list the total series of questions, assuming that the first part of this chapter gives a sense of the key analytic model entailed. It is important that the ordered list of questions as presented can be used as a "mockup" for the construction of the requisite information-gathering tools, be they questionnaires, interviews, observation checklist or combinations of all three.

Even more important, the ordered series of questions can be asked by any party and therefore the information gathering can be done by program personnel themselves. Thus the key requirement of the optimal program design, that that program "monitor its environment," can be approximated by the use of the evaluation design.

Inquiring about Program Start-Up

The first set of questions inquires about the reasons for and context of the program start-up. If in answering these questions it is determined that the program exists because of the political clout of a special interest group, then the evaluator should emphasize the budgetary questions which follow. The rationale is simple: since the program may be maintained even if it does not serve a base constituency, in the interests of at least this base constituency the necessary information can be provided to minimize program or organization costs.

Reasons for establishment of the program:

A. How did the program get started?
   1. Who established it?
   2. In what forum were the original start-up decisions made?
   3. On the basis of what information, derived from what sources, shared with whom, for what purposes, were these decisions made?
   4. Who shared in the decision making and what were their role?
   5. How was the initial budget compiled?
   6. How was it articulated with the initial program structure; i.e., how were initial staff recruited and paid, and how were their jobs defined and interrelated?

B, Why was the program started?
   1. To what extent do the answers to all the above questions provide the answer to this one?
      a. To what extent does the program exist because of funding patterns or legislative or administrative fiat alone?
   2. What are the intended effects of the program?
      a. What is its exact mission, and what needs is it to fill for which constituency with what estimates of demand?
      b. Was this unambigously stated at the time of start-up?
      c. Was consensus reached about the statement of mission? If so, by whom, and to what levels of agreement?

Inquiring about Program Effectiveness

If the answers to these questions suggest that the program exists to satisfy real needs and extensive demand, then questions as to effectiveness and efficiency should be asked. Two sets of questions are involved. Each of these sets of questions in turn implies a standard of comparison. One cannot know whether a program is more or less effective or efficient in the absolute. One can know, however, whether a program is *more or less effective or efficient than another program or some more abstract standard of comparison* such as "more of less effective or efficient than its originators intended it to be." With respect to effectiveness, it is wise to ask questions about the standard of comparison at the beginning of the evaluative process. Effectiveness questions will be listed first, to be followed by efficiency questions:

Effectiveness Questions:

A. Does the program have a mission to deliver services to satisfy a significant demand level?
   1. Are the needs to be filled clearly defined?
   2. Is the demand level accurately estimated?
   3. Are the services to be delivered clearly defined?
      a. Are there any problems in defining the services to be delivered?
      b. Can alternative definitions be stated in response to these problems?
      c. Is there a limited range of such definitions?
      d. From this limited range of definitions can a coherent service delivery plant be articulated? (Note: if the range of definition is unlimited, a "coherent" plan is impossible to formulate.)

B. If the program has a mission to satisfy a significant demand level, is it achievable?
   1. Are there or have there been any programs similar to this one?
      a. If so, who established them, etc. (i.e., continue with questions A 1–6 and B 1–2 in order to establish the "reality" of the reasons for the existence of these comparative programs).
   2. Have any of these programs accomplished or achieved this mission?
   3. Does the mission sound reasonable; i.e., does it appear on the face of it to be achievable?
      a. Does consensus exist as to this reasonableness?
      b. Among whom does consensus exist and on what grounds have they reached such consensus?

C. When is the program considered to have successfully completed its activities with a client (i.e., when can service delivery be said to have been successfully completed)?

D. When does the program stop doing that which it does for its clients; e.g., if it processes cases, what is the final stage in the processing?

At best the answers to B, C and D should be related as follows: the last action of the program with respect to a client should approximate "success," and success should be identical with filling the client's needs (and, in the aggregate, identical with meeting a significant demand level). Actually, it is rare that these correspondences occur; i.e., it can be expected that public service programs have an array of actions which terminate the relationship with the client, and that among these will be some that do not have to do with a judgment of success of the program (e.g., all the paperwork entailed), and it is equally likely that judgments of success will be contingent on activities that have little to do with the program's mission (e.g., getting a pension rather than delivering a stipulated service may be deemed successful by personnel). Given the optimality of convergence but the reality of divergence among the anticipated answers to these questions, this set of questions is suggested:

E. Do the final activities with respect to a client achieve success, and does success equal the mission of the program (convergence)?

F. To what extent do the final activities with respect to a client inhibit a judgment of success, and to what extent does the program, even though judged to be successful, fail to satisfy its mission (divergence)?

G. Are there any similar programs?
   1. What is the relationship between the final activity, success and mission of any similar programs; i.e., to what degree is there convergence or divergence?

That completes the list of effectiveness questions. Now let us ask efficiency questions.

Inquiring about Program Efficiency

Efficiency questions have to do with the structure of the program in achieving effectiveness. Two general types of questions are involved: how does the program operate, and how should it operate? The first question type entails separate, specific questions about the program, its personnel, lines of authority, budget and so forth. The second question type entails standards of comparison for each of these specific questions.

Efficiency Questions:

A. What is the organizational chart of the program?
   1. Who are its members and what are their qualifications?
   2. How do their qualifications relate to the tasks they are to perform?
   3. What should their qualifications be and how should they relate to the tasks to be performed?
      a. Given similar programs, who are their members, what are their

qualifications, and how are these related to the tasks to be performed?

b. What performance criteria would best serve in the assessment of who should be placed in what position with which responsibilities? (General criteria for comparison purposes can be stated but are beyond the scope of the present chapter.)

Different levels in the chart will imply different tasks to be performed. Generally, there will be several types of tasks: doing (i.e., action); getting somebody else to do (management); gathering information about what has been or should be done (evaluation and planning). These categories are not the only ones available and are crude, but they are useful nonetheless (see Lachenmeyer, 1973a, 1977a, 1977b). Specific efficiency questions can be asked about each type of task.

B. Action: program member to client.
   1. How are clients selected?
   2. How are clients "sorted"; how are they categorized for subsequent processing?
   3. In what numbers are they selected and sorted?
   4. How are they subsequently processed?
      a. Are the ways in which they are processed contingent upon how they are sorted?
      b. What is done to, for, or with them?
         (1) When, where, with what frequency and duration?
   5. Are the records that are kept meaningful; i.e., if one were to gather information to see how people are processed, could the records be used to do this accurately and completely?
   6. How *should* they be selected, sorted and processed?
      a. Are there any similar programs, etc., etc.?
      b. What other standards of comparison are available, etc., etc.? (Again, these exist, but are beyond the scope of the present discussion; see Lachenmeyer, 1977a, 1977b).

C. Action: program member to program member.
   1. Who says or does what to whom (when, where, how often, for how long) with what intended or unintended effects on the categorizing, sorting or processing of clients?
   2. Who *should* say or do what . . .
      a. Are there any similar programs . . . etc.?
      b. Are there other standards . . . etc.? (Again, these are available, but beyond the present discussion; Lachenmeyer, 1977a, 1977b.)

D. Planning: program member to program member.

1. How are workers made aware of policy?
2. Are there planning sessions?
   a. How frequently, for how long, and who is involved?
   b. What is discussed, for what reasons?
   c. Do all members participate?
   d. Is there free discussion of ideas including due note taken of any exceptions and questions raised?
   e. Are meaningful records kept? (Meaningful in that they refer to some aspect of patient or client flow).
3. What provision is made for implementation of the plans?
4. What provision is made for follow-up to assure implementation?
5. How do members react to a plan once consensus has been reached?
   a. Do they resist implementation? If so, what strategies do they use?
   b. Do they react rapidly and responsively?
   c. Do they initiate implementation attempts spontaneously?
6. How *should* planning occur?
   a. Are there any comparable programs?
   b. Are there other standards? Here these other standards can be stated simply:
      (1) Planning sessions are usually required to fully inform workers of policy. Written memoranda require face-to-face contact and follow-up as supplements.
      (2) The sessions should involve those members directly affected by a policy and should be as frequent and long as necessary to arrive at consensus and create understanding.
      (3) The discussion should have no punitive aspects. Relevant material should be discussed by as many in the group of members as possible, and meaningful records should be kept of all aspects of the discussion.
      (4) Both implementation and follow-up should be guaranteed procedurally.
      (5) Resistance to implementation should be low and responsiveness and initiation high. (The rationale for these standards and their full statement cannot be elaborated here; see Lachenmeyer, 1977a, 1977b.)

E. Evaluation: program member to program member; program member to client.
   1. Who has the responsibility for evaluating the performance of other members or clients?
   2. How is this done?
      a. When, where, how often?

b. What criteria are used?
c. What evidence is gathered and what records are kept?

3. Who *should* have the responsibility for evaluating the performance of other members or clients?
   a. Are there comparable programs . . .?
   b. Are there other standards of comparison?
      (1) Assuming that evaluations should be made by those with most complete knowledge and that these people will be in the most direct contact with the member or client to be evaluated, then it is reasonable to ask: do those in most direct and prolonged contact with the member or client to be evaluated have primary responsibility for evaluating him or her?
      (2) Assuming that the person to be evaluated has the most complete knowledge, it is reasonable to ask whether there is provision for meaningful self-evaluation.
4. How *should* evaluations be done
   a. Are there comparable programs . . . ?
   b. Are there other standards of comparison?
      (1) Is the evaluation (as knowledge acquisition) continuous?
      (2) Is it based on the most complete description available of the activities of the person to be evaluated?
      (3) Have the standards of evaluation been clearly stated and consensually validated as important and meaningful?
   a. Is opinion unsubstantiated by fact?
   b. Are judgments based on incomplete information?
   c. Are uninterpretable labels ascribed to members or clients and then used as the basis for reaching evaluative determinations: e.g., "he is disloyal (or untrustworthy or abrasive)"?
5. What actions are contingent on the evaluative process?
   a. To whom and how does the evaluator report the results of the evaluation?
      (1) Is this report formal (written) or informal (oral)?
   b. What action is taken toward the person evaluated on the basis of the evaluation results?
   c. To whom and how *should* the evaluator report the results of the evaluation?
   d. What action should be taken toward the person evaluated on the basis of the evaluation?
      (1) Are there comparable programs . . . ?
      (2) Are there other standards of comparison
         (a) Where a client has been evaluated, is service delivery expedited on the basis of the evaluation?
         (b) Where a program member has been evaluated, is he or she rewarded for good performance? How?

(c) Where a member has been evaluated negatively, is he or she encouraged to do a better job, or fired? Why one or the other?

Further, if there are found to be efficiency problems on the basis of the above comparisons, then one would want to explore the reasons for these. Hence the next series of questions.

Inquiring about Efficiency Problems

Reasons for Efficiency Problems:

A. What factors have impeded efficiency?
  1. Internal
    a. The foregoing questions should identify sufficiently such things as poor management, poor planning, and low productivity.
  2. External
    a. Does the program address competing constituencies?
    b. Is there political conflict over the existence of the program?
      (1) Of what nature? Who is involved?
      (2) Is this conflict of a "selfish," personal nature or is it over questions about levels of effectiveness (in which case, refer back to the preceding effectiveness questions)?
    c. Budgetary levels
      (1) Assuming a standard that dollars should be contingent on levels of performance in order to assure maximum efficiency, is the budget so geared?
        (a) Where specific tasks are to be performed, are those workers who do the best job compensated equitably?
        (b) Where compensation is essentially based on time spent at a job, are those workers who spend the most time compensated equitably?
        (c) Where compensation is based on amount of responsibility, are workers compensated equitably according to differences in levels of responsibility?
        (d) Are task-versus-time-versus-responsibility jobs compensated according to their inherent differences?
      (2) How are the budgetary levels determined?
        (a) Are requisite comparisons of budgetary levels made with similar, efficient programs?
        (b) Do people report not doing the job or is there high turnover because of budgetary levels?
        (c) Are there recruitment problems because of budgetary levels?

B. What aspects of the program can be changed so as to achieve efficiency or effectiveness?
   1. If this program were eliminated, what impact would this have on the ultimate satisfaction of the demand levels it supposedly services or on any judgments that the services delivered are done so successfully?
      a. Are there any comparable programs to take up the slack if this is deemed necessary?
   2. Given a subunit (including possible individual members), if this subunit of the Program were eliminated, what impact . . . ?
      a. Are there any existing subunits to take up the slack . . . ?

The answers to questions P 1 and 2 should yield a crude estimate of how critical is the program or its designated subunits. Thus if a program is inefficient, and if it can be eliminated without any impact on demand satisfaction, *or* if a competitor can be found that can substitute for the inefficient program, this program should be eliminated. Likewise if inefficient subunits (including inefficient individuals) are identified and these "safely" can be eliminated or substituted by other, more efficient subunits, then this should be done.

   3. Is it worth the cost of changing selected aspects of the program (including personnel) to note the impact of such changes on levels of efficiency or effectiveness, and using this experimental strategy, to derive the optimal mix of program changes to achieve optimal levels of efficiency or effectiveness?
      a. If the answer is yes, then refer back to the efficiency and effectiveness questions to identify which aspects to change; e.g., structure, budget, etc.

Clearly this is a value judgment. The only solution to the obvious dilemma of "who says it is so" seems to be the referral of the judgment back to the base constituency.

   4. Is the program equipped for self-change contingent on self-evaluation in order to achieve acceptable levels of efficiency or effectiveness?
   5. Is there sufficient evidence, including ample prior attempts at change, to suggest that no matter what is done to, for, or with this program to achieve efficiency and effectiveness, it is impossible for it to do either? That is, the service delivery reasons for existence or judgments of success may not be capable of being satisfied by any such program.

Here the evaluator is confronted with the ultimate dilemma of the limits to public-sector program intervention, a dilemma that the public, reasonably or unreasonably, now seems to understand all too well.

Throughout this evaluation design it has been assumed that the questions were being asked of program members or other relevant "experts." Truth and accuracy of response obviously are important. A final set of questions is suggested.

Inquiring about Truth

Truth Questions

A. Are the answers to the questions true and accurate?

B. How would one ascertain this?
   1. Can sufficient follow-up (e.g., on-site inspection or other data-acquisition procedures) be undertaken to verify answers?
   2. Can one refer to sufficient follow-up done by others in the past; e.g., previous evaluation studies of the program concerned?
   3. Has the consistency test of truthful answering been employed?
      a. If the same individual is asked the same question but in varying form repetitively, does he or she respond in consistent ways?
      b. If two or more individuals sharing the same positions and performing the same general tasks are asked independently the same questions, are their answers equivalent?
      c. If two or more individuals in different but related positions (e.g., superior-subordinate) are asked the same question, are their answers equivalent?

Herein we are in the domain of the rules of data acquisition and validation, and well-known methodological principles are involved. Thus no more need be said on this subject.

SUMMARY AND CONCLUSIONS

If the presuppositional basis for this chapter were presented in one paragraph it would be that the inherent logic of public service program construction is fundamentally different from that of program construction in the private sector. Yet the only model for estimating organizational efficiency and effectiveness that we have is based on the logic of the private sector. With respect to community mental health programs the logical disjuncture is compounded: these public service programs have severe problems in need assessment, demand estimation and service delivery definition. To try to correct for this set of problems by program evaluation, without recognizing root causes, is to put the band-aid on the dying (or dead) patient.

Rather a full appreciation of the optimal program model is necessary. Once this has been accomplished, there is no great conceptual leap involved in deducing efficiency and effectiveness estimates even for such dually problematic public service programs as community mental health programs. Evaluation is transformed into information acquisition for the base constituencies of those programs—for those people who are asked to underwrite their cost. Therefore a complete evaluation design is one which goes about collecting this information. One may choose to present such a design in other than the question set/subset form used herein, which was intended to permit maximum transferability to data collection format; nonetheless any such design must incorporate the information these question lists will yield upon application. To do anything less is to provide incomplete information to the base constituency and thereby to provide faulty estimates of efficiency and effectiveness.

References

Anthony, W. A., Buell, G. J., Sharratt, S. & Althoff, M. E. Efficacy of psychiatric rehabiliation. *Psychological Bulletin*, 1972 *78*, 447–456.

Campbell, D. T., Factors relevant to the validity of experiments in social settings. In H. C. Schulberg, A. Sheldon, & F. Baker (Eds.), *Program evaluations in the mental health fields*. New York: Behavioral Publications, 1969.

Chu, F. D., & Trotter, S. *The madness establishment. Ralph Nader's study group report on the national institute of mental health*. New York: Grossman, 1974.

Dohrenwend, B., & Dohrenwend, B. *Social status and psychological disorder*. New York: Wiley, 1969.

Ennis, B., & Siegel, L. *The rights of mental patients*. New York: Avon, 1973.

Erickson, R. C. Outcome studies in mental hospitals: A review. *Psychological Bulletin*, 1975, *82*, 519–540.

Huessy, H. Tactics and targets in the rural setting. In S. E. Golann & C. Eisdorfer (Eds.), *Handbook of community mental health*. New York: Appleton-Century-Crofts, 1972.

Kelly, J. G. The quest for valid preventive interventions. In G. Rosenblum (Ed.), *Issues in community psychology and preventive mental health*. New York: Behavioral Publications, 1971.

Kiesler, D. J. Some myths of psychotherapy and the search for a paradigm. *Psychological Bulletin*, 1966, *65*, 110–136.

Kittrie, M. *The right to be different: Deviance and enforced therapy*. Baltimore: Johns Hopkins, 1971.

Lachenmeyer, C. *The essence of social research*. New York: Free Press, 1973a.

Lachenmeyer, C. Foreword; introduction; chapter five. *The final report of the juvenile justice research project* (Vol. 1–5), The New York Bar Association: Council, unpublished, 1973.

Lachenmeyer, C. *Final report in evaluation of the youth counsel bureau*. New York Criminal Justice Coordinating Council, unpublished, 1974.

Lachenmeyer, C. A universal theory and technique of evaluation research. *Improving Human Performance Quarterly*, 1977a, *6*, 9–20.

Lachenmeyer, C. *A system for the analysis, evaluation, and design of organizations, work, and jobs: Second generation social science*. United States Department of Commerce, 1977b.

Lin, T. & Stanley, C. *The scope of epidemiology in psychiatry*. Geneva: World Health Organization, 1962.

Mannino, F. V., & Shore, M. F. The effects of consultation: A review of empirical studies. *American Journal of Community Psychology*, 1975, *3*, 1–21.

Mechanic, D. *Mental health and social policy*. Englewood Cliffs, NJ: Prentice-Hall, 1969.

Meehl, P. E. Psychology and the criminal law. *University of Richmond Law Review*, 1970, *5*, 1–30.

Meltzoff, J., & Kornreich, N. *Research in psychotherapy*. New York: Atherton, 1970.

Moos, R. *Evaluating treatment settings*. New York: Wiley, 1975.

Peck, H. S., Kaplan, S. R., & Roman, M. Prevention, treatment and social action: A strategy of intervention in a disadvantaged urban area. *American Journal of Orthopsychiatry*, 1966, *36*, 57–69.

Rappaport, J., & Chinsky, J. M. Models for delivery of service from a historical and conceptual perspective. *Professional Psychology*, 1974, *5*, 42–50.

Rosenhan, D. On being sane in insane places. *Science*, 1973, *179*, 250–258.

Sanford, H. Is the concept of prevention necessary or useful? In S. E. Golann & C. Eisdorfer (Eds.), *Handbook of community mental health*. New York: Appleton-Century-Crofts, 1972.

Schiff, S. K. Community accountability and mental health services. *Mental Hygiene*, 1970, *54*, 205–214.

Schofield, W. *Psychotherapy: The purchase of friendship*. Englewood Cliffs, N.J.: Prentice-Hall, 1964.

Scriven, M. The methodology of evaluation. In C. H. Weiss (Ed.), *Evaluating action programs*. Boston: Allyn and Bacon, 1972.

Sobey, F. *The nonprofessional revolution in mental health*. New York: Columbia University Press, 1970.

Steadman, H. Some evidence on the inadequacy of the concept and determination of dangerousness in law and psychiatry. *The Journal of Psychiatry and Law*, Winter 1973, 409–426.

Stone, A. A. *Mental health and law: A system in transition*. Washington, D. C.: Department of Health, Education and Welfare, 1975.

Struening, E. L., & Guttentag, M. (Eds.). *Handbook of evaluation research*. Beverly Hills: Sage, 1975.

Szasz, T. S. *The manufacture of madness: A comparative study of the inquisition and the mental health movement*. New York: Harper & Row, 1970.

Weiss, C. H. *Evaluation research: Methods of assessing program effectiveness*. Englewood Cliffs, N.J.: Prentice-Hall, 1972.

World Health Organization. *Report of the international pilot study of schizorphrenia*. Geneva: World Health Organization, 1973.

CHAPTER 14

Evaluating Community Programs

Tough and Tender Perspectives[1]

Emory L. Cowen, Ph.D.
and
Ellis L. Gesten, Ph.D.

INTRODUCTION

The word community has of late become modish in the mental health fields. Used to modify simple or complex nouns such as psychiatry, psychology and mental health, the resulting formulae designate orientations, indeed entire fields, not recognized as entities a brief two decades ago. Those new terms, or fields, came into being as a result of felt discontent with mental health's past failings and the resulting panorama of irrepressible problems we now face (Cowen, 1973; Zax & Cowen, 1976). For many, the word community represents a way out—a hope for a better tomorrow in mental health.

It may be too strong to say that terms such as community psychology, psychiatry and mental health are not well understood. But similar, if less provocative, statements *can* surely be made: different people perceive and use those terms quite differently, and those terms have had clearer connotative, than specific denotative, meaning. That is an understandable—not yet necessarily grievous—reality. The fields, after all, are young; they lack a solid data base and are, quite frankly, still groping to identify promising new approaches; i.e., to separate the wheat from the chaff. However understandable that lack of clarity, it is difficult to write about evaluating community programs without an approximate working definition of their nature and scope. That is our first order of business.

Traditional clinical psychology approaches and the new ways of community mental health and community psychology are both alike and different (Cowen, 1978). Their most important shared similarity is the

[1] Work on this chapter was done in part under the support of a grant from the NIMH Experimental and Special Training Branch MH 11420-02, for which the authors express their appreciation.

prime goal of optimizing people's psychological well-being—i.e., their adaptation, adjustment, happiness and effectiveness. They differ considerably, however, in the situations they address, their timing, locations and "gut" defining-practices. Thus clinical psychology and its sister professions of psychiatry and social work have been singularly oriented to the assessment and repair of psychological casualty—i.e., deficits in the state of well-being. Over long time periods the fields have done what they could to develop diagnostic tools that richly and informatively portray the nature of dysfunctional psychological conditions and thus provide cues to preferred ways of intervening. The field's best and most highly tested repair technologies, as for example psychotherapy and its many variants, are then applied to those who come within the system's purview. Most mental health interventions are addressed to current, pressing conditions with long-standing, serious roots.

Whatever the virtues of that model, however understandable its gradual ascendance as mental health's dominant way, the stern test of time has revealed more and more of its deficiencies as a comprehensive solution to society's complex mental health problems. Since those problems are reviewed in detail elsewhere (Cowen, 1973, 1979; Zax & Cowen, 1976) we need here only to represent enough of their essence to set the stage for understanding the thrust of recent community developments: 1) the resources of the mental health system are both inadequate to meet need as defined, and inequitably distributed to more affluent, better educated people (President's Commission on Mental Health 1978), and 2) the mental health system has focused much too heavily on psychological casualty ("end states") and its repair (Primary Prevention Task Panel Report, 1978).

Although both community mental health (CMH) and community psychology approaches take as their point of departure deep concerns about the limited reach and effectiveness of mental health's classic repair system, they differ in the strategies used to address those concerns. Without abandoning a casualty-repair orientation, CMH strives to develop alternative approaches and settings for dealing more effectively with society's chronic unresolved mental health problems. Thus it seeks to identify problems: a) sooner, b) in less crystallized, debilitating forms, and c) at times when interventions can be more useful. The CMH Center is one structure designed to further those goals. A logical outgrowth of CMH's aims is to expand mental health's sphere of operation to include settings other than the traditional clinic, hospital or private consulting suite, such as neighborhood store-fronts, clubs, unions, schools, churches, which provide earlier access to psychological dysfunction. Another way to describe that shift is to say that CMH uses active outreaching approaches rather than the past "passive-receptive" (Cowen,

1967) stance of the mental health fields, which meant waiting for problems to find sources of help. CMH also seeks to develop more flexible approaches, which better fit the needs and styles of those in society who cannot or do not avail themselves of traditional mental health services. In that vein, the recent report of the President's Commission on Mental Health (1978) strongly emphasizes the need to bring effective mental health services to populations described as "unserved and underserved": i.e., disadvantaged inner-city minorities, children, retired people and rural dwellers. The CMH development, sensitive both to the need to expand the reach of services and to the realities of how people seek help for interpersonal problems—that is, from primary caregivers in other fields, such as clergymen or physicians, known to and trusted by them from other contexts, as well as informal caregivers and neighborhood helpers (Gottlieb, 1976; Caplan & Killilea, 1976; Collins & Pancoast, 1976; Cowen, Gesten, Boike, Norton, Wilson, & DeStefano, in press)—has also sought to develop indirect service approaches such as consultation (Caplan, 1970; Mannino, MacLennan, & Shore, 1975), that promise needed geometrical expansions of interpersonal helpgiving. And, finally, CMH has been actively and realistically involved in training new types of personnel, often atraditional nonprofessional agents, to expand mental health's resource pool and to provide flexible, realistic helping sources within a generally underresourced system (Sobey, 1970; Gartner, 1971).

The preceding helps to operationalize the community mental health movement and to provide a rough framework within which program evaluation issues can be considered. Bloom (1977) documents, in richer detail, how CMH approaches differ from past traditional mental health practices. The key common denominattor cutting through all such differences, of course, is that CMH activities are based on practice in the community. The true significance of the word community in CMH is that communities contain the settings and contexts which make it possible to develop the foregoing family of new approaches to historically difficult mental health problems.

Community psychology approaches, in contrast to those thus far considered, are predicated on different premises and strategies, particularly those of primary prevention (Cowen, 1977; Primary Prevention Task Panel Report, 1978). Such approaches a) are proactive or health-building rather than reactive or casualty-containing, b) are mass-oriented to people in general—not targeted to already disturbed individuals, and c) stress that equipping people with resources to cope effectively is the best of all ways to forestall dysfunction. Given that "set," the following approaches are central to community psychology's purposes and *modus operandi*: education, the analysis and constructive modification of social environments, reducing sources of life stress and/or developing effective methods for coping with stress, and building competencies in individuals, groups and communities (Primary Prevention Task Panel Report, 1978).

The preceding definitional foray is simply to identify the approximate turfs of community mental health and community psychology. Program evaluation and research issues considered in the rest of the chapter relate primarily to those areas. Two types of issues will be covered: a) classic research problems as they apply to community program evaluation studies, and b) less formal observations about research issues and frustrations we have personally experienced in the community arena—the latter particularly in the context of our own major, preventively-oriented, community-based intervention program for systematic early detection and intervention with young maladapting school children (Cowen, Trost, Lorion, Dorr, Izzo, & Isaacson, 1975).

SOME HAZARDS OF RESEARCH IN THE COMMUNITY

To say that community-based research is a breed apart from other psychological or program evaluation research is misleading. Unquestionably there are important communalities in the methods used, and the problems faced, by community researchers and those in other fields; e.g., evaluating the effectiveness of new educational approaches or therapeutic interventions. Even so, realistic consideration of some special qualities of communities and of doing research in community settings may provide a helpful context for specific discussion of the problems involved in evaluating community programs.

One bedrock source of difficulty derives from the intrinsic nature of community programs. Many (most) community programs develop because of an awareness on the part of those who run them of serious, unresolved human problems and service gaps. Their first goal is to bring effective help to troubled people (Cowen, 1978). In other words, such programs are service- and person-oriented. They win brownie points for the numbers of people seen and the effectiveness of the services provided.

Service is thus the prevailing ethos, and delivering good service is the push. Evaluators worship different gods and have different Excedrin headaches. Their concerns are with proper instrumentation, appropriate methodology and sound experimental design—necessary preconditions for drawing defensible conclusions from program evaluation studies. What is ideal for service is not necessarily so for research, and vice-versa. The two perspectives can, and often do clash. Providers may see a study's design as straightjacketing services—as for example, when a prospective control group means delaying, or even withholding, services for people who need them. By contrast, evaluators often justifiably feel that program pressures, such as the obligation to provide services to *all* people in need, will undermine, if not destroy, a study's interpretability.

Related conflicts arise. Although most people pay lip service to the caveat that programs (community, or any other) must be effective, the term effectiveness is itself a wispy notion. If, as often happens, a setting lacks the resources, skills or will needed to undertake outcome studies, the opinions of the program's service providers may become an exclusive metric for its evaluation. Although such views are not irrelevant to comprehensive program evaluation, taken alone they can yield a distorted picture. Granted that program personnel may "see with their eyes" and "know in their hearts" that a program is working well, such judgments, even when sincerely felt, are vulnerable to serious bias. Because a program (and the jobs it spawns) survives on the basis of demonstrated success, people closely associated with it are often motivated to search for signposts that can reasonably be interpreted to suggest program effectiveness. They may be less than vigilant about identifying opposing signs. Evaluators, by contrast, pay greater heed to so-called hard facts—e.g., behavioral indicants of relevant change and objective test or performance data—not just the opinions of potentially biased service providers and/or consumers.

Because evaluators are often foreign bodies to the service-delivery system, they may be less than *persona grata*, especially when their findings could mean life or death for a program. Evaluators thus pose potential threats both to program survival and to staff members, who may see their personal performances as being evaluated. In caricatured form, the danger exists that program workers may see evaluators as heartless "hatchets," while evaluators may see program personnel as mystics, faith-healers or simply defensive people.

Other realities add salt to that basic wound. Service people are often harassed individuals who put in a full day's work. Additional research demands in what is already seen as a back-breaking schedule are resented. Such demands come up in various forms; for instance, as time requested to complete research devices or evaluation scales, or disrupting a patient's or program's routines by observation and/or testing. The additional burdens of such requests are sometimes more apparent to service providers than are the ultimate benefits they can anticipate for them. Indeed, if woe is one high-probability consequence, line resistance to the evaluation process shouldn't be surprising.

The foregoing means that it is more likely to be the exception than the rule, in community settings, when service and research needs beam on exactly the same wavelength. Their coexistence, in some cases, represents little more than a wary "entente cordiale." More typically, providers and evaluators are cut from different cheesecloths in their orientations, trainiing, goals and ways of thinking and operating. Those responsible for service programs have little trouble identifying many new things they'd like to be doing "if only they had sufficient resources and personnel" (Sarason, Carroll, Maton, Cohen, & Lorentz, 1977). Service programs are often run with a "phenomenological sense of marginality" (the attitude being, "We need every last penny and 110 per cent of everyone's effort just to keep the program's head above water"). If evaluation is seen as taxing an already frayed resource system, it can convert mere indifference to research into active opposition. Hence one should not be surprised to find active polarities in some community settings between service and research; that is if you're for one you're "agin' t'other." Where that is so, it may be difficult for evaluators even to gain entré into a system.

The preceding is less to depict a universal reality and more to identify a real set of tugs and pulls—sometimes overt, sometimes subtle—that militate against "Mr. Clean" evaluations of community programs. Such pulls have been so real and important, in our experience, that we have chosen to devote an entire major (later) section of this chapter to documenting them in a more personal, detailed and first-hand way. For the moment, however, they should be seen as a significant contextual element to keep in mind as we consider more specific research problems in evaluating community programs.

Although the intrinsic service-research strains we have noted may top the list of significant deterrents to good community program evaluation research, several other limiting factors should also be described. Research conditions in community settings and programs are, in the main, much less antiseptic than those of the laboratory. Thus a program being evaluated may be but one of a family of programs (several with overlapping objectives) going on simultaneously in a given setting, a circumstance that makes it difficult to disentangle its *specific* effects. Too, community programs often have a longitudinal quality, and may thus be contaminated by in-process changes in agency policies or programs, funding losses or personnel relocations. Hence real-world strains and pressures not under the researcher's control are significant realities with which he must cope. Decisions made by community review bodies and growing concerns about privacy are other factors which, more and more these days, influence both whether program evaluation will take place at all, and, if it does, its specific form.

Clearly, then, doing program evaluation research is hardly a piece of cake. On the other hand, keeping in mind that the current community movement rests heavily on a combination of a) protest against a mental health delivery system that many feel hasn't worked and b) faith that the new alternatives are better, the need to identify and document effective new ways is both incontravertible and paramount.

BASIC PROBLEMS IN COMMUNITY PROGRAM EVALUATION RESEARCH

The background picture thus far painted, though not rosy, is a necessary aspect of any informed consideration of the specific problems that community program evaluators face. At the risk of oversimplifying, the latter can be grouped into several major clusters: 1) data bias, 2) problems in the choice and use of criteria, and 3) the use and misuse of "control." Although we hold no brief for the inviolability of that grouping, it is the one that will be followed in the next section of the chapter.

Data Bias

Two highly pertinent sources of data in evaluating community programs are the views of providers and recipients about the effectiveness of its services. As direct participants in the helping dyad, recipients and providers should, in principle, be able to make relevant judgments about its effects. Few people, therefore, dispute the belongingness of those "sensible," accessible data in the overall evaluation process. At the same time, they harbor sufficiently severe problems of bias that their use as a *sole* source of evidence in evaluating programs is, indeed, questionable much as their *exclusive* use in evaluating the effectiveness of psychotherapy should be questioned.

The main approaches used to obtain participants' views about a program's (procedure's) effectiveness are variants of the interview and rating scales. Those approaches have in common the fact that respondents can color or censor responses to conform to their needs and perceptions of the situation. Indeed, there may be important reasons for them to do so. Pressures on recipients include social amenities (e.g., in our society we are taught to thank people who try to help us) and the demand-qualities of the moment (i.e., sensing that a program is looking to be "stroked," or the concern that negative reactions might hurt someone's feelings or make one seem like an ingrate). Hence there are real tugs on service recipients to produce positive program evaluations. Moreover, even if a recipient does genuinely feel better after having had the program's services, it doesn't assure that the services per se, as opposed, for example, to concurrent salutary life changes (i.e., a good new job, a gratifying romantic attachment), are the critical determinant of the good new feelings. And if the program did genuinely help the recipient to feel better, the question remains as to whether the new positive feelings generalize beyond the program's situational confines in palpable behavioral ways (Bloom, 1977; Cowen, 1978).

A recipient's diminished "objectivity," through overinvolvement, can theoretically also work in the opposite direction. Thus a person who may genuinely have been helped by a program to feel better and to behave more appropriately may still downgrade it because he a) was unhappy about its fee schedule, b) resented a crowded, noisy waiting room, c) was frequently kept waiting for an appointment, or d) was turned off by some aspect of the help agent's approach or style. The point to be emphasized is that personal stakes and situational pressures on clients detract from their objectivity in evaluating the "true" effectiveness of program services.

For different reasons, the objectivity of evaluation data that providers can furnish must also be questioned. Providers, actualized mental health professionals though they may be, are first and foremost people. Like others in the species, it gratifies them to know that they are doing worthwhile, important things in life. If one measure of that is their ability to bring help to distressed people, it creates a force in them to see positive change in those they serve. Even if that set does not grossly distort their outcome judgments, since many judgments are "marginal calls," they may be influenced by an (unintended) inclination to shade -borderline judgments positively.

Rater judgments are widely used in evaluating community programs. But for many reasons—some having little to do with a program's effectiveness—they aren't always objective judgments. It is easier to identify that source of bias than to overcome it. Apart from mechanical precautions such as framing questions that reduce the potential for socially desirable responses and provide internal consistency checks, the best way to minimize (or at least identify) the distortive effects of participants' biases is *not* to rely on them exclusively in evaluating programs—in other words, to broaden the evaluation base. That can be done in several ways. One is to increase the number of outcome raters and, in so doing, to transcend perspectives. If observers with different data bases and "investments" agree about change, it increases the likelihood that the change is real. Using actual behavioral data and life performance anchor points that are relevant to the intervention's objectives is even more helpful (Zax & Klein, 1960). Concordance between improvement on such 'gut' criteria and rater judgments, inspires greater confidence in the latter as convergent affirmations of program effectiveness.

Service versus research polarities in many community settings lead to other types of data bias. Thus a service person who fails to appreciate research and/or considers its work and time demands to be excessive may not submit materials needed to evaluate the program, or may complete forms late, or carelessly. Such responses (or nonresponses) can either undermine or distort a program's overall evaluation. Experiences with our own school mental health project illustrate the point. In that program, carefully selected, trained nonprofessional child-aides provide direct helping services for primary grade children identified through screening and teacher-report procedures as experiencing various types of school maladaption (Cowen et al., 1975). The service-oriented program is located in a number of local area schools. Evaluating it, which most people agree intellectually is an important aspect of accountability, is done by a central research staff not part of the program's day-to-day service operations. Although much effort was invested in explaining the nature and purposes of the research evaluation to program personnel, it was apparent that many were not tuned in on that wavelength and perceived the request as one more burden in an overhassled, underpaid existence.

One evaluation study designed to assess program effects was based on a total sample of 555 experimental (program) and control (nonprogram) children (Cowen, Lorion, & Dorr, 1974). Theoretically classroom teachers should have submitted preprogram behavioral ratings for all children in the study. About 100 such ratings were never completed. Many others were submitted so late (when the child had already had 10, 12, or 15 program contacts) that they couldn't be used as referral (preprogram) data. Another significant fraction of the data (perhaps because some teachers didn't read the instructions carefully or care about them) fell to such mechanical failures as using checks or crosses instead of the five-point rating scales called for; omitting many items; and uniformly rating all items as 1 or 5—that is, disregarding item content and simply going through the motions of getting an unpleasant task off their backs. Such problems did not fall evenly across districts, schools or classes. Considering other natural hazards of community studies (such as having data missing because children move or teachers change during the year), one can see that sheer loss of relevant data can be enormous and can detract appreciably from the purposes of program evaluation.

The thrust of this discussion is hardly to identify good guys versus bad guys. Rather it is to reaffirm that service providers and program evaluators have different needs, objectives, stakes and procedures and that without concerted steps to bridge those gaps, serious biases develop in evaluating community programs. In the evaluation study involving over 500 children, later steps that helped to narrow the gap included 1) streamlining instruments to make them as brief and clear as possible, with content that could be seen as relevant to respondents' immediate goals and concerns, 2) advising respondents, early on, of the project's main data collection points to avoid springing unwelcome surprises on them at impropitious moments, 3) personalizing the distribution and collection of data, 4) clarifying and explaining instruments which might have been unclear, 5) building in data-feedback mechanisms that provide useful job-relevant information for respondents. Such procedures have led both to higher absolute return rates and, more important, to a reduction in the sources of data bias.

Interventions, community-based or other, seek to promote changes that transcend their own situational boundaries and endure over time. If a study's design and/or data collection mechanisms are too narrow to meet those objectives, limited or biased conclusions may be reached. Follow-up is a good case in point. Its purpose is to determine whether effects at a program's termination point accurately and stably reflect the program's impact. Data collected when a program ends can be misleading in several respects (Cowen, 1978). Ostensible improvement may evaporate because it wasn't a) real in the first place (i.e., it was a figment of the momentary demand-qualities of the situation, people's response-styles, inappropriate criteria); b) sufficiently solid to permit the person to cope successfully with later real-world demands; or c) supported by the person's post-program environmental circumstances. Conversely, without follow-up, significant program effects which take time to gestate and mature may be overlooked.

The key point, however, is that evaluations done when a program ends do not necessarily provide an accurate, permanent record of program effects, especially not in community settings. Without taking the tests of time and place into account the evaluator may form hasty or incorrect conclusions that lead either to the perpetuation of questionably useful programs or the premature dismissal of potentially useful ones.

Data bias issues post formidable problems in many areas of psychological research. Special qualities of community programs and settings, however, mean that such problems are often more serious in evaluating community programs than they are in other areas (Sarason et al., 1977). Because community psychology and community mental health are young fields still lacking a strong credibility base, overcoming their special data bias problems is an important precondition for the fields' advancement.

Criterion Measures

Problems in the choice and use of program evaluation criteria have long plagued psychological research. Criterion measures establish operationally the metric by which a program's efficacy is assessed. If inappropriate choices are made, the program will either not be evaluated at all or will be evaluated on dimensions orthogonal to its goals. Thus proper program evaluation requires a clear statement of program objectives (overall, and for groups of clients or individual clients), and the use of criterion measures that reliably and validly reflect those dimensions (Bloom 1977). Since core psychometric issues of reliability and validity have been extensively reviewed many times, they are not featured in the ensuing discussion. The latter point emphasizes criterion problems favored by the special circumstances involved in community program evaluation research.

Criterion Appropriateness. Many community programs are based on indirect, rather than direct, services. Thus we conduct parent education programs hoping that they will improve the adjustment and well-being of about-to-be-born, and/or young children. Similarly, mental health consultation with clergymen or physicians rests on the fact that people in such positions are often called on to help psychologically troubled individuals. By providing relevant knowledge and skills to such primary care-givers—i.e., by strengthening their resources for dealing with such problems—we hope that they will better be able to relieve personal distresses that their clientele thrust upon them.

Mental health education and consultation programs are often based on the assumption that if they positively change participants' knowledge, feelings and attitudes, improved adjustment in the program's ultimate intended targets (i.e., the children or clients with whom indirect service recipients interact) will follow automatically. However logical that view seems, it remains an assumption (Kelly, 1971a; Cowen, 1978). Because such programs' direct (often only) contacts are with intermediaries, even if criterion measures used with them are well-chosen, and confirm the facts that the program was enjoyed and found to be useful and led to important new "learnings," and to improved, more positive attitudes, such changes do not per se insure improved behavior or adjustment in the program's ultimate target persons. The latter, of course, is the acid test of the program's effectiveness. Thus evaluations of indirect service programs based *exclusively* on changes in immediate service recipients are victimized by criterion networks that fail to correspond to the program's goals. Because many community programs are based on an indirect service model, there is serious danger of discordance between a program's goals and assessment criteria. Some (a small minority of) community programs based on the indirect service model *have* successfully demonstrated positive behavioral and adjustive effects in ultimate targets—i.e., children—rather than in intermediaries such as adults involved in parent education (Hereford, 1963; Glidewell, Gildea, Kaufman, 1973).

Misfires in the Choice of Criteria. The background realities of doing research in the community noted earlier in this chapter, sharply affect the selection and use of criteria for evaluating community programs.

Two such characteristics—resentments about research and time pressures on service personnel—hit especially hard. Though it is all well and good for an evaluator to think of ideal measures for program evaluation, formidable reality hurdles must be negotiated before they become operational. Thus an evaluator may with good reason believe that direct observation of a client's behavior and/or formal testing, are the assessment procedures of choice for a given program. But not everyone (i.e., program staff and clients), is willing to be observed. Staff may find such observations to be intrusive, threatening or simply an unnecessary pain in the neck. Clients may see it as an invasion of privacy, or as being "used" in a process that produces no tangible benefit for them. Thus keenly felt concerns, at multiple levels, can thwart the use of observational or testing procedures in evaluating community programs. Because observational frameworks (e.g., teacher-pupil and pupil-pupil interactions in the classroom) are complex and time-consuming to develop, involve serious reliability and validity issues, and call for major investments of energy in training judges and the like, the possibility that they might not be usable (even if perfectly well developed) turns some investigators off to that potentially important cluster of criterion measures for evaluating community programs, before the fact.

Testing presents related problems and elicits similar resistances. Tests often pose issues well beyond the obvious ones of an instrument's appropriateness to the assessment task at hand, or its reliability and validity. A test or test battery may compete for time with the program's ongoing activities and thus be seen as disruptive or annoying. We have had the experience, for example, of having a classroom teacher blow the whistle on program evaluation testing because he or she saw it as eating up class time excessively. If there is a basic climate of antipathy to being evaluated, such negative reactions can be triggered by relatively minor incidents (e.g., the evaluator's car breaks down and he or she misses a scheduled testing). Whatever the reason, the net result may be to put an end to formal test evaluation.

Another deterrent to the use of tests in program evaluation, one of recent, growing concern, is the mounting social specter of invasion of privacy. Current concepts of what *might* invade a person's privacy are becoming ever more elastic and increasingly restrict the content of test instruments. Thus those working in community settings (such as neighborhood groups, schools, health centers) have become more wary about the basic use of tests in the first place, and also about what they should or should not properly include. Some content areas that may have face-valid relevance in assessing how well a program has met its stated goals (for instance, improving disturbed parent-child relationships or sexual adjustment) may, under some conditions, be too sensitive or threatening to assess.

The perennial specter of time also seriously limits program evaluation testing. Typically, community programs have multiple and complex goals. To determine whether those goals have been well met may in the ideal call for time-consuming assessment procedures which people are unable or unwilling to go through. To the extent that that is so, the evaluation will be killed off completely or seriously restricted. The practical task for the evaluator may *not* be to assess the program's overall efficacy, but to come as close as possible to that goal, given 20 minutes of available testing time. Such a circumstance sharply limits the criteria that can be used, and "pulls" both for "quick-and-dirty" global judgments which lack operational specificity and, because of their transparency, for generalized response sets (Cowen, 1978).

As is true in many areas, evaluating community programs is also limited by the state of the art with respect to criterion measures. If there are no good measures of variables X, Y and Z, and those happen to be important in assessing how well a program has met its goals, evaluation is restricted accordingly. That is more than just a theoretical problem for many variables of prime concern to community programs (health/pathology, adjustment/maladjustment, effective versus ineffective coping styles). For example, a school-based intervention program may have the legitimate goals of improving young children's self-concepts and sense of security, and internalizing their locus of control. But if we lack satisfactory measures of such variables for six-year-old children, the practical choices for the evaluator are to develop them *de novo* (rarely done because it is a demanding, unrewarding, time-consuming task), use psychometrically unproven devices, or use existing, psychometrically sounder measures that come as close as possible—to approximate, it is hoped—the variables in question.

Other, more specialized criterion problems also confront the community program evaluator. More and more these days we recognize that an instrument that is valid and appropriate for one group may be worthless for another. Intellectual assessment devices that are just fine for white middle-class children are often ill-suited to other ethnic, cultural and racial subgroups (Mercer, 1973). Although the preceding is a widely cited example of criterion bias, it is not the only one. A measure's language, format and style, not to mention the very trappings of the test situation, can be natural and normal for some but alien to others. The point is that many community program evaluation studies seek to compare program outcomes (intellective, adjustive or whatever) across groups. Even bypassing the prior question of whether the program's services are equally appropriate for the groups being compared if the criterion measures are not, there is the real danger that "irrelevant" factors such as linguistic style, lack of item clarity, inappropriateness of content, will be confounded with differential program outcomes for the two groups.

An even narrower instance of the preceding general case can be cited.

Community studies not only compare diverse cultural groups but also, frequently, study program effects across multiple settings exemplifying larger classes (for example, neighborhood store-fronts, schools, community mental health centers). Unfortunately, frameworks (criteria) used internally by such settings to assess performance and/or program effects can vary sharply—a situation that poses serious problems for evaluators. The evaluation of the Primary Mental Health Project (PMHP)—our own school mental health program, currently in more than 25 schools in several local area school districts— has been plagued by exactly that problem (Cowen et al., 1974). PMHP's core aims are to improve children's behavior, adjustment and educational performance. Because the project is school based, educational performance is *one* reasonable way to evaluate its effectiveness. In early PMHP evaluations, the ancient A, B, C, D, E report-card metric was a convenient objective index of educational standing—precisely because it transcended settings and districts. That formerly straightforward, interpretable criterion measure has yielded to an array of imaginative, highly varied new grading practices, often individualized by school district. Grading systems involving checks, stars or coded stamp marks and so on, are a dime a dozen. Some districts, eschewing all objective signposts, use free prose reports (the record-holder, in our experience, being one that sent children home with a 23-page prose report). For the researcher the latter are difficult, if not impossible, to quantify; moreover, they encompass areas of functioning that are eons removed from the classic three—for example, comments about a child's identify, self-image, social skills, which may require a psychological lexicon to be properly decoded.

This is not to cast stones at well-intended efforts to find less accusatory, less competitive, richer, more informative ways to describe a child's school performance. Indeed, as parents or citizens we may applaud such efforts. But for a program evaluator in search of a simple, standard, cross-district estimate of educational performance, the situation can be chaotic. Much the same is true for educational achievement indices. Districts are highly individualized about the tests they use, for whom they are used, and when they are given. In fact, some districts exclude sizeable numbers of youngsters from formerly standard testing procedures. The evaluator thus may either be left without an appropriate performance or achievement measure, or obliged to make hazardous transformations of organs to apples in seeking to do cross-district or cross-setting comparisons on such measures.

Community realities guarantee that the complexities of selecting and using appropriate criteria in program evaluation studies, will continue to pose thorny problems for some time to come. The following are guidelines we have found useful in reducing (without entirely resolving) such problems: 1) taking prior steps to promote understanding, accepting attitudes about research help to create a climate that allows greater latitide in selecting criterion measures; 2) selecting criteria in the light of a program's goals; if programs have multiple, complex goals, critieria should reflect that complexity; 3) using criterion measures that are as brief, clear and relevant to respondents' program roles and concerns as possible; 4) developing criterion networks that avoid exclusive reliance on the impressions of involved, fallible observers; that is, using, wherever possible, multiple outcome criteria including relevant behavioral and performance criteria; 5)using unobtrusive measures more widely; the latter are both relevant to the objectives of a community program and relatively easy to obtain. In a delinquency prevention program, for example, it seems more important to know that a juvenile has or has not been incarcerated than to know how his Rorschach F+% has changed. In a school prevention program, if less than significant changes are found on a teacher's problem behavior checklist of marginal validity, it may be reassuring to know that a principal had only twenty five percent of the disciplinary referrals that a control principal had had during the school year.

Control Problems

Controls are needed in research to assure that observed changes in key dependent measures (outcomes) are due to aspects of program rather than to potential contaminants that could produce similar findings. The generality of that statement implies, as it should, that good control is essential in many types of psychological research. Again, however, qualities of community contexts predispose special control problems in community evaluation research.

Because the control role is thankless, entailing, as it does, the multifaceted intrusions and disruptions of research studies and their extensive time commitments, without palpable "benefit" (usually defined as needed program services), few people or settings relish it. That fact of life restricts the size of the theoretical pool of control settings before studies ever start. Another before-the-fact restriction is that proper control groups must approximate the experimental groups in several key respects. Although the specific correspondence points vary depending on a program's goals and the attributes of experimental samples, they often include age, sex, race, intelligence, SES and, in community mental health programs, preprogram adjustment status. Both because being a control group is no fun and because control groups must have specific features, the task of locating satisfactory control groups can be a major, time-consuming hassle.

Understandably then, many community program evaluation studies are either concluded without control groups or with less than ideal controls—conditions which can sharply restrict the researcher's conclusions. Without a control group; the experimenter may have to depend heavily on within-group pre-post comparisons. Although such data can be helpful, they are subject to hazards: a) they do not take into account spontaneous change or remission or the salutary effects of concurrent life change; b) if the main criteria used are judgments (self or other) about change they are susceptible to response biases and social desirability effects; c) if the program involves young children, without a control group, it is difficult to account for normal development during the program period; d) if the evaluation net includes test data, post-program findings may reflect statistical regression effects in test readministration.

Another reality factor that works against sound control is that some community programs are bound by fixed starting and termination dates. Take, for example, a school program which must be conducted within the school year. Funding and/or public relations pressures call for the program to start promptly, whether or not an adequate control group has been located. Even the most conscientious efforts to find such a group may founder for several months. By then a class's adjustment and sociometric patterns may have changed so much that it can no longer be assumed that E-C similarity on the relevant criterion measures has the same meaning for the two groups.

The snares involved in finding good control groups in community evaluations have led to alternatives designed to "end-run" complex matching problems. One is the so-called "own-control" approach in which a group goes through an inert waiting period before a program starts or, alternatively, serves as an inert matched control group for an experimental group for the program's duration, after which it moves into its own (delayed) program period. Even though that can be a helpful procedure, it is subject to certain problems (for instance, subjects with less obviously pressing needs may be assigned selectively to the delay group; flak involved in withholding a promising service from those with evident need). Again the specter of service-research conflict rears its head.

One seemingly attractive approach to control is to split a given setting (e.g., a school) or sample within the setting (e.g., children referred for mental health services) down the middle, offering the program's services to half the sample and using the other, matched half as controls. That approach, as we have learned from hard experience, can sound better in principle than it works out in practice. For one thing, personnel in the setting who live intimately with the problems posed by the target group don't necessarily go for the idea—however noble its purpose—of withholding service from individuals in obvious, perhaps desperate, need.

To push the matter against such a *vox populi* may win a battle (setting up a pristine design) and lose a war (being able to conduct and evaluate the program). Thus community program evaluation studies must be done in a way that respects a setting's everyday realities and ways of operating. They simply cannot be muscled through.

Another factor that limits within-setting control designs is that people, understandably, communicate with each other. If, for example, consultation with teachers is an active program component, it's difficult to be sure, and perhaps unreasonable to expect, that useful new learnings teachers acquire will *not* be shared with their fellows *or* will be applied uniquely to the program, but not the control, children in their classes. The program evaluator thus needs to be concerned with unintended seepages between E and C groups, and with the consequent dilution of the control condition.

It should not be assumed that control, even if initially well-established, is a permanent state of bliss. Particularly in community settings, careful, well-planned matches can succumb to many adventitious factors beyond an experimenter's control. We have had painful first-hand experience with several such misadventures and still bear the scars to prove it (Cowen, et al., 1974). The need to start a program by a certain date often means that the experimenter can, at best, establish only an approximate before-the-fact control. Thus, he or she may intend ultimately to match Es and Cs on six or eight variables, but can only do that for sure on obvious, countable, demographic ones (such as age, sex, SES) when the program starts. Other data (for instance, adjustment, personality or sociometic measures) requiring individual or small-group testing take more time to collect and score. Necessity thus forces E to proceed on the basis of the reasonable assumption that if he or she is virtuous in matching Ss on the obvious variables, God will be merciful with less accessible ones. But things don't always work out so neatly. And when the final returns are in, the group may prove to be seriously mismatched on one or more variables, thus completely upsetting the control applecart.

Even seemingly idyllic initial matches often yield to in-process community realities. Thus, people move—hardly a minor problem, given that some schools, particularly in the inner city, report pupil turnover rates of 150 percent during a single school year. Program personnel, who furnished essential predata, change jobs and cannot be used for post-program evaluations. Some settings (e.g., individual schools), whether E or C, systematically resist the evaluation and either fail to submit data at all or submit them in unusable form. Additional, more concrete examples of such problems as we experienced in evaluations of our own school mental health program are presented elsewhere (Cowen et al., 1974).

Given the lengthy list of potential booby traps menacing control in community program evaluation research, one can understand why so many studies are done without controls. Although certain techniques can be used to compensate in part for initial, or inadvertent later, E-C mismatches, they are less than ideal. For example, a statistical technique analysis of covariance, is designed specifically to partial out initial mismatches between groups. Another approach—that is, dropping Ss from one or both groups so as to align their preprogram profiles—entails several serious risks such as: 1) Ss may have to be dropped disproportionately from one group, distorting its basic character; 2) so many Ss may be lost that the solidity of the comparison is undermined. The serious dilemma that the researcher must often resolve is between maintaining robust, representative samples and having a tight match. A frequent trade-off solution is to accept some matching noise to preserve reasonably robust, representative samples. The point to be stressed, however, is that control in community program evaluation studies rarely works according to theoretical ideals taught in graduate courses in research methodology.

The obvious challenges of achieving proper demographic/statistical control in program evaluation research are, alas, not the only ones that the researcher faces. There are more subtle questions of psychological control. Take as an example our own school mental health program (Cowen et al., 1975) which has, over the years, depended heavily on teacher judgments of children's classroom behavior as one basic source of evaluation data. Is that "objective" task the same for E and C teachers? Probably not! Teachers in experimental schools have the cognitive set of evaluating a *program*. Their judgment about individual children may be colored by how much they like and respect the program and/or its personnel. In other words they can distance their ratings of children from themselves and their own performance. A control teacher faces a psychologically difficult task. She has no program metric. Her job is merely to rate children's behavior at two time points during the year: relatively early and relatively late. Under such circumstances she may adopt as her implicit rating set the question: "How good a job have I personally done with this child this year?" Such a set pulls for more favorable end-of-year ratings.

Another situation in which mere statistical control may be insufficient is if a new intervention coincidentally involves a significant change in the (boring) everyday routine of the target Ss, as in a program in which nonprofessional aides work with institutionalized retarded children. Such a program involves two things: its planned, presumably "active" ingredients and establishing a meaningful relationship, in a fun-and-games context, with youngsters who otherwise live a relatively dull daily routine. It is difficult, if not impossible, to separate the effects of those potentially confounded elements without another (more psychological, than statistical) control group; that is one which involves a new personal relationship and break in routine but does not include the presumably active (therapeutic) elements of the planned intervention. That might be achieved by a program based on recreational activities and movies in the context of a generally warm relationship.

Two characteristics of community settings—their complexity, and the fact that they are often active laboratories for exploring new programs—also undermine the adequacy of demographic/statistical criteria as the sole basis for matching program and nonprogram control groups. A theoretically ideal situation for an evaluator is when the program under study is the only one in either the experimental or control settings. Indeed some evaluators tend to see the world that way even when it isn't. In most community settings (e.g., CMH centers, schools), however, it is a rule rather than an exception that many, varied, everchanging programs-formal or informal, enduring or ephemeral, targeted to the same, or closely related, variables—coexist simultaneously. An example of such a situation can be cited from our school mental health project (Cowen et al., 1974). Theoretically the PMHP program was the study's sole, or at least prime, independent variable. But the program was housed in the real educational world, not in a vacuum tube or an antiseptic animal lab. Alongside it, to varying extents in different schools, were other progams (such as reading improvement; circle discussions), some constant others in and out, intended as PMHP, to upgrade interpersonal and academic skills or to minimize problems in those areas. When such programs come together in the school's melting pot, it is difficult to disentangle their separate effects. What E may see as a "pure" experimental program, is more often that program plus unknown or ignored others. Such a constellation is compared to a control setting which, though it does not contain the program E hopes to evaluate, has several others targeted to similar objectives. Indeed, the matter is often more complex in that the very decision to assign a new program to a setting may be based on the fact that, compared to other similar ones, it is deficient in the kinds of services that the program provides. The other side of that coin is the fact that a control setting may be given additional services to help compensate or balance out for the experimental setting's new-found bonanza. The intrinsic control problems posed by such instances are often exacerabated by the fact that some of the multiple programs in E or C settings may be short-lived, change in process, or be joined by new programs, while they are still active. However many headaches those problems create for an evaluator, they are an immutable part of of the community's reality and a further reason why it is so difficult to achieve proper control in community program evaluation research.

FIELD ISSUES IN COMMUNITY EVALUATION RESEARCH

Students often graduate from clinical/community training programs unprepared for the special challenges and hazards of community research. Research difficulties they later experience may be due to either inadequate research preparation or an inability to adapt what they have learned to the special features and constraints of community settings. Often the novitiate's struggle is tied less to the technical aspects of evaluation research and more to a failure to conceptualize adequately, and relate to, the community being studied. Although consultation is usually available for operational research issues such as "How does one do goal-attainment scaling?", with whom does one discuss a perplexing, nonclosure-producing, initial meeting with a CMHC staff whose new crisis-intervention program is to be evaluated? Trained for the most part to assess and treat problems at the level of individuals in distress, new Ph.D's often find it difficult to shift focus to the group, organization or systems level (Goodstein & Sandler, 1978). Community researchers tend to acquire requisite skills for the latter through front-line experience rather than formal training.

In contrast to the methodological issues in community research, the material to follow focuses on relational or process-centered aspects of community evaluation (Kelly, 1979). Although observations at that level may seem to be less focused than the earlier ones, the issues they raise are at least as important to doing good community evaluation research. Areas to be covered include: 1) securing permission and negotiating cooperation for evaluation studies, 2) quid pro quos in community research, and 3) the relation of evaluator to the client system. The impressions to be shared again come primarily from our (at times painful, but never dull) experiences with PMHP (Cowen et al., 1975). Although some of our struggles over the twenty-two-year history of researching PMHP doubtless reflect both our own ineptitude and the specific demands of school contexts, many are generic to community evaluation (Cowen et al., 1974). Our goals in sharing them are to help others who face similar concerns, and to begin to formalize a theory of systems intervention.

It is important for the ensuing discussion to keep in mind that researchers/evaluators and a community can come together in two distinctly different ways: a setting or its representative may seek out the evaluator with a specific program concern in mind or researchers may for their own reasons seek entry to the setting. Although subsequent relations may develop differently depending upon who is courting whom, invited and uninvited researchers sometimes face similar problems. Indeed, occasionally surprising reversals occur as when a researcher whose study was commissioned by an agency's director is stymied by an uncooperative staff, or a researcher who barely secured administrative approval for his evaluation encounters a surprisingly supportive and cooperative program staff. Be that as it may, our experience suggests that the nitty-gritty issues described below must be faced by community researchers regardless of who initiates the first contact.

SECURING PERMISSION AND NEGOTIATING COOPERATION: COMMUNITY PSYCHOLOGIST AS SALESPERSON AND POLITICIAN

Securing Permission

Securing permission and negotiating cooperation for an evaluation study are separate processes which may easily be confused. Permission to do the study typically comes from a program director or administrator who functions at some distance from the staff level at which the actual evaluation is to be done. The processes involved may be routine and proforma, or complex and time-consuming, depending on such factors as the nature of the proposal, the competence and interactive style of the researcher, characteristics of the administrator and his accountability systems, and whether the administrator or evaluator initiated plans for the study. Although securing the ncessary permission(s) can be time consuming and frustrating, doing so is no more than a precondition for the research. It is a mistake to assume that cooperation of key program people will follow automatically. The evaluator must be prepared to commit time and energy both to securing permission *and* winning the cooperation of key program personnel. For the most part, he or she must consider those to be separate processes.

Without formal approval from someone in authority, the most brilliantly conceived study cannot be moved off the drawing board. A simple question follows logically. From whom should one seek permission? Using the school system as an example, is it necessary to go directly to a superintendent or his designated representative for a study which will take place in a single school? The rules are surely different in different systems, and when in doubt, one can always ask. Even so, experience has taught us several things. First, it is important to know about a system's formal structure for screening research proposals. Faced with increasing requests from researchers, many community agencies including school systems have assigned responsibility for reviewing proposals to individuals or committees. The latter operate within fairly specific guidelines; approving proposals is far from automatic for them. Because the review process often takes weeks or months, it is important that proposals be prepared well in advance of the project's planned starting date.

If the system does not have a formal review body, a good strategy is to seek initial approval from a highly placed administrator such as the superintendent or his designate rather than at the individual school or principal's level. Rigidity in applying such a rule should, properly, vary as a function of such project variables as size, potential "risk" to participants, and sensitivity of the information being gathered, as well as such person variables as the superintendent's administrative style and the status and power of principals within the system. We have learned that it is prudent to start at higher levels and to work one's way down through the hierarchy, particularly when entering a new system. If those first steps prove to be casual or unnecessary, little will have been lost. But to overlook them is to take the risk that someone "upstairs" might bring the study to a premature end on grounds that have little to do with its merits—concern, or even anger, at being bypassed, for example. "End-running" responsible administrators can create an adversary relationship between investigator and key community members rather than the desired sense of colleagueship and collaboration.

An informed, involved superintendent can be a powerful ally. For example, in one system the superintendent helped to select target schools for a major evaluation of classroom environments. He even suggested ways to deal with a "resistant" principal whose reservations about mental health services were well known in the district. In that case, knowing the superintendent's leadership style and communication preferences was a key to the success of an evaluation program conducted over several years. In time it became less essential to check with him on each specific proposal, and approvals were increasingly obtained at the individual school level.

Getting Cooperation

Administrative approval does not assure staff cooperation. Indeed, in some cases, such as those involving ongoing administrative-staff conflict, too close an identification with an administrator can be a genuine liability to the researcher. It is, therefore, important to know the relationship of administrator to his staff, and whether or not the proposed study has been discussed and accepted by staff. Failing that, an unsuspecting evaluator might find himself in the unenviable position of having to be the first one to explain to a staff why its favorite program was being considered for cutback. Being cast in such a role does little to strengthen the evaluator's position.

Under certain circumstances it is preferable that the community researcher be present when a new study is being introduced. This may be especially important when the idea for the study comes from outside of the system. In principle the investigator best understands the purposes, design and mechanics of the research. More than one well-meaning, highly supportive school administrator has unwittingly confused, or worse, subverted a study by trying to brief a staff about it during the last five minutes of a long faculty meeting. That can easily happen when "alien" research concepts are introduced to a suspicious or resistant group by someone, however well intentioned, who doesn't clearly understand them. The presence at an initial meeting of a researcher who happens incidentally to be trained to understand and facilitate group processes can also provide useful insights into how the organization functions, and fine opportunities to correct misimpressions and to build rapport.

The community researcher's clinical skill is an important—perhaps the *most* important—asset in seeking to win staff cooperation in research. For instance early, but highly critical, judgments must often be made about how best to structure an initial meeting about a research project with the staff. Consider briefly the pros and cons of group versus individual formats for meeting with prospective teacher participants. Obviously a group format makes for the most efficient use of an evaluator's limited time. Efficiency is highly correlated with effectiveness, at least when the group climate is favorable. On the other hand, the presence of one or more vocal skeptics or a general attitude of confusion or suspiciousness can create a highly unfavorable, negatively-charged group dynamic which may be difficult, if not impossible, to overcome. Notwithstanding the powerful support of a very respected principal, one of our studies was set back a full year by just such a miscalculation. Although individual meetings may be incredibly inconvenient and time consuming, they provide a better format than the group for dealing with resistance or for explaining a complicated program or research design. Most important of all, meeting individually with teachers often communicates persuasively to them that they are important people whose feelings are valued.

One obvious and thoroughly sensible strategy for winning staff cooperation is to involve participants in planning a study. That approach is not, however, without danger. For example, in a classroom observation study it may be very important for the teacher *not* to know which of her behaviors are being recorded, which students are targets and why, or even whether teacher or student is the focus of a given observational unit. If such details are known to teachers, potentially biasing information is either released or can be deduced, making it more difficult to interpret the study's findings. Another frequent (ticklish) problem occurs when a participant not familiar with the fine points of research suggests a modification in design that would significantly compromise a study's validity. Child-aides in PMHP, for example, often express the need to discuss their contacts with children before completing research evaluation forms. Although doing so might well help them to feel more comfortable about the ratings, their usefulness would be seriously diminished.

When it comes to communicating with community members about a prospective study, evaluators tend to err more by omission than by commission. Put otherwise, we get into more trouble because we undercommunicate than because we talk too much or give away the family secrets. Given some basic trust on the part of the community and a sense of humor on the part of the evaluator—a quality omitted in Kelly's profile of the good community psychologist (1971b)—most staff can accept the need to restrict certain facts. That sense of trust helps to make clear that all information will be shared at the conclusion of the study. (It helps even more to be sure that that *happens.*)

Active collaboration with teachers has improved cooperation and thus significantly strengthened our project's service/research base. School personnel, rather than program staff, for example, were primarily responsible for identifying typical interpersonal problems of children in class, used to frame both a program to train children in interpersonal cognitive problem-solving (ICPS) skills and measures used to evaluate it (Gesten, Flores de Apodaca, Rains, Weissberg, & Cowen, 1979). Similarly, classroom teachers contributed significantly to the identification of key behavioral items included in a recently developed competence rating scale (Gesten, 1976). Asking staff members about the questions *they* would like to have answered adds a useful perspective and helps to establish a community's investment in a study. Collaboration can be further fostered, formally or informally, by including someone from the host system as a member of the core research evaluation team. As an insider with special knowledge of the organization and its people, such a person can be far more effective than the evaluator in negotiating cooperation.

Two other precepts which help to create a cooperative research climate can be identified. First, in the preventive sense, it is, if possible, important for evaluation to be built into a new program from its inception. When evaluation is seen as an unnecessary add-on, it detracts from its perceived importance to the staff. Moreover, most people (understandably) like to know their program-related responsibilities from the start rather than hearing about them after the fact. Since evaluations typically require staff time (to complete forms, juggle schedules, and so on), letting people know their obligations in advance is a simple but important courtesy. Participating in evaluation studies is not intrinsically rewarding for a staff; hence it is important that contracts be laid out carefully in advance, inconveniences minimized and surprises avoided. The second, related precept concerns meeting schedules. It is easier for teachers to cooperate when meetings are held at *their* convenience rather than the researcher's. In our case that has meant being available for training sessions in the schools as early as 7:30 A.M., and/or for periods as brief as five to ten minutes during lunch breaks. That seemingly small point can have great significance for teaching staffs besieged by classroom problems and paperwork demands.

THE RELATION OF RESEARCHER TO CLIENT SYSTEM: ON BEING A STRANGER IN A STRANGE LAND

Typically program evaluators are to some extent outsiders to the host system. That may be changing a bit in some areas today in that mental health agencies, pressed to account and given outside dollars, hire their own research staff in greater numbers than before. Even so, many agencies still prefer to contract for evaluation services because of the healthy impetus for change that can result from unbiased examination, as well as the credibility that a relatively independent evaluator can give the service agency (Specter, 1977). But being a foreigner to the community along with the service-research strains noted earlier may mean that the evaluator's relationship to participants in the study will be polarized from the start. If such inherent barriers are not recognized and broken down, the evaluation will suffer and perhaps fail.

The outside evaluator's relationship to agency staff can be significantly affected during an initial contact. Consider, for example, the matter of introduction. Service versus research tensions (and with them, future problems that the researcher will face) can be shaped by the actual form of the initial introduction. It may make a real difference to teachers, for example, if the person is introduced as "Dr. Robert Jones, a researcher from the State University" or "Robert Jones, a community psychologist, who, incidentally, used to teach third grade." Although both descriptions are "correct," they leave different impressions. The former may evoke the stereotype of an ivory-tower rat runner; it also emphasizes the newcomer's status (power). The latter, by contrast, provides more information, is less threatening, and suggests a common area of interest and experience. Although even the most benign introduction need not necessarily deflect anxiety about a truly controversial site or research-planning, visit (such as one that might shut an agency down), most evaluation studies do not have so dramatic a potential. Thus any time that can be spent planning for the initial meeting, which should include matters such as the form of the introduction, an overall agenda and its sequencing, may facilitate the entry process with staff. That same objective may also be furthered by a post-conference processing meeting to identify concerns and clarify procedures in light of staff reactions.

To establish credibility and build rapport, the community researcher must first learn (about) the system. Two bodies of information, each framed by an orienting question, are especially critical in that regard. First, what are the de facto and de jure roles and procedures that govern an agency's operation? Without such knowledge effective communication with staff is very difficult and one's status as an outsider may be continually underlined by comments such as: "That's not how we do things here!" or "Dr. Smith would never allow us to release that type of information!"

Related to the need to clarify agency procedures is the second question. Who is really in charge? The task here is to identify the "Charlie(s)" or "Charlene(s)" in the system who *really* know what's going on, and most important, can make things happen. It is often a mistake to assume that the person formally charged with a particular responsiblity is in fact the person in charge. That point was made clear to us during recent efforts to establish an Infant Stimulation Program in a neighborhood health center. Notwithstanding strong and seemingly sincere support of high-level professionals and administrative staff, problems and delays developed every step along the way. Needed forms were not prepared on time, materials went unordered and necessary appointments and logistics were difficult to arrange. All of that changed the day we discovered the secretary who was running the center. No one had explained to us how critical it was to the success of *any* center program for her to be kept fully informed and involved. Angered (or at least feeling rejected) by our oversight, she had done little to help and had, in fact, contributed to bogging down process. Ultimately the secretary became a key member of our team—indeed the only person who was able consistently to cut through the setting's "organizational craziness" and get things done on time.

Many strategies can be used both to learn about a community or agency being studied and, in the process, to become less of a stranger to the system and its people. One simple but critical way to achieve that goal is to spend time, formally and informally, with staff, getting to know their roles and perceptions. Along with that, it is often a good idea to attend certain community functions, especially those that relate to the phenomena to be studied or evaluated. Doing so communicates an active interest in the community. In addition such visits can furnish insights into the system's strengths and weaknesses, not to mention patterns of relationships among key staff. An example of that strategy is found in our current work in the area of social problem-solving training for primary grade teachers. Our goal has been to develop and evaluate a teaching model for use by kindergarten teachers with their classes. Rather than imposing a ready-made program on volunteer teachers, we spent several weeks observing teachers, children, and overall class environments. By so doing we hoped, first, to build cordial relationships with teachers, and second, to gather information that could contribute meaningfully to a final, ecologically valid curriculum.

Just as researchers become more familiar with communities through observation and active inquiry, communities come to know them better through the same processes. The reduction of distance is often accompanied by increased trust and sharing, factors which can greatly facilitate the research process. To be sure, there is a risk in such collegiality. Thus the community researcher may overidentify with the system and lose some objectivity in the process. A researcher who, for example, oversympathizes with the plight of overworked, underpaid service providers may unintentionally influence the outcome of evaluation studies by his or her choice of criterion measures, the rigor of the statistical tests and confidence intervals selected and, most important, the way in which results are packaged and interpreted. Although such dangers do indeed exist, we believe that they are, for the most part, less frequent and/or serious than those resulting from the researcher's underinvolvement with, or lack of knowledge about, the community settings and programs she or he seeks to evaluate.

QUID PRO QUO AND THE NATURE OF COLLABORATIVE COMMUNITY RESEARCH

Sometimes a researcher's entry into a new system or community is stymied, or at least made difficult, because of the setting's history of contacts with previous investigators. The most common complaint of school personnel in this regard concerns the lack of feedback they have gotten from all the time and cooperation invested in prior studies. Often the researcher is not heard from again after the data have been collected. Equally upsetting is the fact that some of the research reports school personnel do receive are either too technical or esoteric to address the real concerns of participants or so general and vague as to say nothing. As a result schools (justifiably so) often feel "ripped off" by their past experiences, and therefore seriously question the motives of the newly arrived researcher. Because of such experience many systems have shut their doors, permanently, to researchers from academic settings.

Entry is much easier for the individual who takes a community's needs and reinforcement systems into account from the start. A helpful orienting question for the researcher is: Which concrete measurable benefits might this study or set of studies have *for the host system?* Put otherwise, what will the community derive from its cooperation and the inconveniences it will suffer? What the *researchers* stand to benefit is clear: they obtain material that can facilitate their own visibility and professional growth, develop publications, and, they hope, give them tangible forms of recognition from their own host systems. But rarely, for example, are school personnel included as coauthors on publications. Although that step might in many cases be appropriate, given the extensive inputs of community personnel to many research studies, it may not always have palpable meaning to those listed as coauthors.

But if publications generally lack relevance for community service personnel, there are nonetheless other benefits that such participation can theoretically provide. First, research can be designed, at least in part, to address questions that are relevant and important for the target group. Whereas teachers, for example, are eager to find out about teaching techniques that might foster learning and minimize acting-out in hyperactive youngsters, they are disinterested in studies of self-reinforcement patterns if abstract results are presented to them in probabilistic statistical language. It is indeed possible to design studies that provide useful information both for agency personnel *and* researchers; the problem is that not enough effort has been invested in so doing.

Another benefit of participation is a direct outgrowth of the preceding point: the need to present research findings in formats that maximize learning. To that end we have, for example, found that workshops to discuss research findings are much more helpful to consumers than one-page written summaries. Teachers who participated in a major evaluation study of classroom environments and their impact were invited to a workshop during which the main research findings were shared in a variety of concrete, straightforward, practical ways in order to maximize their participation. The response was so positive that a follow-up was requested; indeed a program of direct teacher consultation may emerge from that effort.

Sometimes unique tradeoffs can be arranged to encourage the participation of service personnel in research programs. Thus, through a special arrangement with a university, teachers joining a social-problem-solving training program received tuition-free graduate credit—credit that ultimately translates into pay raises. In turn each teacher had to: a) attend two and a half hours of intensive training per week for four full months; b) master a complicated curriculum which they taught to their class three times per week, in thirty-minute units; and c) participate in various aspects of the evaluation process. Although that package requires more work than an average graduate course, it also provides more tangible benefits in terms of direct impact on teaching. We believe that course credit is legitimate partial compensation for the unusual amount of time and effort teachers put into the development and conduct of the program. Although many teachers also found the excitement of the new approach and the possible end product of improved child adjustment to be prospectively significant benefits, formal course credit has certainly helped to solidify their commitment.

SUMMARY

Community settings are not experimentally ideal places for conducting program evaluation research. Some of their marker-characteristics such as an action-service orientation, program flux, complexity and vulnerability to community pressures can and do limit the design of program evaluation studies, the types of criteria that can be used and the nature and amount of control that can be exercised. Those problems, individually and collectively, pose major barriers to sound program evaluation research. They are forces which are strong, or stronger, in the community area than in other areas of psychological research. Although steps can be taken to reduce their impact, they are not likely to be overcome entirely in all cases.

One practical consequence of that reality is that a much needed research (effectiveness) base for conceptually exciting, new community mental health and community psychology approaches has been slow to develop. To date the *élan vital* for those fields has been rational rather than empirical; that is, there has been a conviction that past prevalent mental health ways have not and will not provide a comprehensive answer to society's existing mental health problems. That faith can carry a field only for so long; beyond that, tougher facts are needed.

Conceivably, in its efforts to portray a complex community reality, the present chapter has come across more pessimistically than intended. We do not, for example, mean to imply that the many research problems cited are pemanently 'etched in bronze.' Unquestionably, constructive steps can be taken to strengthen community program evaluations in design, choice of criteria and manner of control. Indeed we have tried throughout to provide concrete examples of just such steps and have, in addition, devoted a major section of the chapter to softer, less-often attended-to, practical issues of how best to engage and interact with community settings to facilitate a more receptive research climate.

But even so, community realities will continue to militate against ideal evaluation research. The potential vulnerability of data from single community program outcome studies highlights the need for replication and a tolerance for the gradual cumulation of fragmented bits of program effectiveness data that point toward more coherent wholes. Although neither of those constraints is alien to science's basic way, they may be more formidable in the community area than in other spheres of psychological research. Our choices, however, are limited. To arrive at socially useful knowledge about effective new ways in community mental health and community psychology calls for persistent efforts, under trying field conditions, to solidify the fields' empirical footings.

References

Bloom, B. L. Evaluating achievable objectives for primary prevention. In D. C. Klein & S. E. Goldston (Eds.), *Primary prevention: An idea whose time has come,* Department of Health, Education and Welfare Publication No. (ADM) 77–447. Washington, D.C.: U.S. Government Printing Office, 1977.

Caplan, G. *Theories of mental health consultation.* New York: Basic, 1970.

Caplan, G., & Killilea, M. (Eds.), *Support systems and mutual help: Multidisciplinary explorations.* New York: Grune & Stratton, 1976.

Collins, A. H., & Pancoast, D. L. *Natural helping networks: A strategy for prevention.* Washington, D.C.: National Association of Social Workers, 1976.

Cowen, E. L. Emergent approaches to mental health problems: An overview and directions for future work. In E.L. Cowen, E. A. Gardner, & M. Zax (Eds.), *Emergent approaches to mental health problems.* New York: Appleton-Century Crofts, 1967.

Cowen, E. L. Social and community interventions. In P. Mussen & M. Rosenzweig (Eds.), *Annual Review of Psychology,* 1973 *24,* 423–472.

Cowen, E. L. Baby-steps toward primary prevention. *American Journal of Community Psychology,* 1977, *5,* 1–22,

Cowen, E. L. Some problems in community program evaluation research. *Journal of Consulting and Clinical Psychology,* 1978, *46,* 792–805.

Cowen, E. L. The community as context. In M. P. Feldman & J. Orford (Eds.), *The social psychology of psychological problems.* Chichester, England: Wiley, 1979.

Cowen, E. L., Gesten, E. L., Boike, M., Norton, P., Wilson, A. B., & DeStefano, M.A. Hairdressers as caregivers: I: A descriptive profile of Interpersonal help-giving involvements. *American Journal of Community Psychology,* 1980, *8,* in press.

Cowen, E. L., Lorion, R. P., & Dorr, D. Research in the community cauldron: A case report. *Canadian Psychologist,* 1974, *15,* 161–166.

Cowen, E. L., Trost, M.A., Lorion, R. P., Dorr, D., Izzo, L. D., & Isaacson, R. V. *New ways in school mental health: Early detection and prevention of school maladaptation.* New York: Human Sciences, 1975.

Gartner, A. *Paraprofessionals and their performance.* New York: Praeger, 1971.

Gesten, E. L., Flores de Apodaca, R., Rains, M. H., Weissberg, R. P., & Cowen, E. L. Promoting peer related social competence in young children. In M. W. Kent & J. E. Rolf (Eds.), *Primary prevention of psychopathology, Vol. 3: Promoting social competence and coping in children.* Hanover, N.H.: University Press of New England, 1979.

Glidewell, J.C., Gildea, M. C-L., & Kaufman, M. K. The preventive and therapeutic effects of two school mental health programs. *American Journal of Community Psychology,* 1973, *1,* 295–329.

Goodstein, L. D., & Sandler, I. Using psychology to promote human welfare: A conceptual analysis of the role of community psychology. *American Psychologist,* 1978, *33,* 882–892.

Gottlieb, B. H. Lay influences on the utilization and provision of health services: A review. *Canadian Psychological Review,* 1976, *17,* 126–236.

Hereford, C. F. *Changing parental attitudes through group discussion.* Austin: University of Texas Press, 1963.

Kelly, J. G. The quest for valid preventive interventions. In G. Rosenblum (Ed.), *Issues in community psychology and preventive mental health.* New York: Behavioral Publications, 1971a.

Kelly, J. G. Qualities for the community psychologist. *American Psychologist,* 1971b, *26,* 897–903.

Kelly, J. G. Tain't what you do, it's the way that you do it. *American Journal of Community Psychology,* 1979, *7,* in press.

Mannino, F. V., Lennan, B. W., & Shore, M. F. *The practice of mental health consultation.* New York: Gardner Press, 1975.

Mercer, J. R. *Labeling the mentally retarded: Clinical and social system perspectives on mental retardation.* Berkeley: University of California Press, 1973.

President's Commission on Mental Health, *Report to the President (Vol. I.)* Washington, D.C.: U.S. Government Printing Office, Stock No. 040-000-00390-8, 1978.

Primary prevention Task Panel Report, *Task Panel reports submitted to the President's Commission on Mental Health (Vol. 4).* Washington D.C.: U.S. Government Printing Office, Stock No. 040-000-00393-2, 1978, pp. 1822–1863.

Sarason, S. B., Carroll, C., Maton, K., Cohen, S., & Lorentz, E. *Human services and resource networks.* San Francisco: Jossey-Bass, 1977.

Sobey, F. *The nonprofessional revolution in mental health.* New York: Columbia University Press, 1970

Specter, G.A. The uses and abuses of the outside evaluator. In R. D. Coursey (Ed.), *Program evaluation for mental health: Methods, strategies, participants.* New York: Grune & Stratton , 1977.

Zax, M., & Cowen, E. L. *Abnormal psychology: Changing conceptions* (2nd Ed.). New York: Holt, 1976.

Zax, M., & Klein, A. Measurement of personality and behavior changes following psychotherapy. *Psychological Bulletin,* 1960, *57,* 435–448.

Author Index

C

D

E

M

S

T

U

Subject Index

GIBBS & others: Community psychology